TRADITION AND CHANGE
A History of Reform Judaism in Britain, 1840–1995

Anne J. Kershen is Barnet Shine Senior Research Fellow and Director of the Centre for the Study of Migration at Queen Mary and Westfield College, University of London and a member of the Faculty of Leo Baeck College. She has appeared on radio and television and is the author of *Uniting the Tailors* (1995), *150 Years of Progressive Judaism* (1990), *Off the Peg* (1988) as well as chapters in G. Alderman and C. Holmes (eds), *Outsiders and Outcasts* (1990) and D. Cesarani (ed.), *Making of Modern Anglo-Jewry* (1990). She is married with a grown-up family.

Jonathan A. Romain was born in 1954. He graduated in Jewish history and Hebrew literature from University College, London, and then studied for the rabbinate at Leo Baeck College. Since 1980 he has been the Rabbi of Maidenhead Synagogue and has also gained his Ph.D in Anglo-Jewish History. Previous publications have included *Signs and Wonders* (a Hebrew primer), *The Jews of England* and *Faith and Practice: A Guide to Reform Judaism Today*. Together with Bernard Kops he produced *In a Strange Land* and he is currently working on a book on mixed-faith marriages. He contributes articles to a variety of journals and broadcasts regularly on the radio. He is married to Sybil Sheridan and they have four sons.

TRADITION AND CHANGE
A History of Reform Judaism in Britain, 1840–1995

Anne J. Kershen and Jonathan A. Romain

VALLENTINE MITCHELL
LONDON

Published in Great Britain by
VALLENTINE MITCHELL
Newbury House, 900 Eastern Avenue,
London IG2 7HH

and in the United States of America by
VALLENTINE MITCHELL
c/o ISBS, 5804 N.E. Hassalo Street,
Portland, Oregon 97213-3644

British Library Cataloguing in Publication Data
Kershen, Anne J.
Tradition and Change: History of Reform
Judaism in Britain, 1840–1995
I. Title II. Romain, Jonathan A.
296.83460941

ISBN 0 85303 316 1 (hardback)
ISBN 0 85303 298 X (paperback)

Library of Congress Cataloging-in-Publication Data
Kershen, Anne J.
Tradition and change : a history of Reform Judaism in Britain,
1840–1995 / Anne J. Kershen and Jonathan A. Romain.
p. cm.
Includes bibliographical references and index.
ISBN 0-85303-316-1 (hc : alk. paper). – ISBN 0-85303-298-X (pbk.
: alk. paper)
1. Reform Judaism–Great Britain–History. I. Romain, Jonathan
A. II. Title.
BM197.K47 1995
296.8'346'0941–dc20 95–15877
CIP

Printed in Great Britain by
Bookcraft (Bath) Ltd, Midsomer Norton, Avon

This book is for
Martin, Deborah and Paul, and James

AJK

and for
Daniel and Gabriel
and their story

JAR

Contents

Illustrations

Acknowledgements

This book could not have been completed without the help of a number of people. Special thanks are due to Raymond Goldman who supported the project from its inception through to its completion. Many thanks also to Rabbi Tony Bayfield, Ena Black, Philip Braham, Jon Epstein, David Jacobs and Harold Langdon for reading the manuscript and making helpful comments. Particularly appreciated has been the long-distance contribution of Professor Todd Endelman who, from the other side of the Atlantic, read the work in manuscript form and made invaluable comments.

Rabbis Curtis Cassell, Douglas Charing and Hugo Gryn gave helpful advice, as did Professor Geoffrey Alderman, Professor Philip Alexander, Dr Gerry Black, Dr David Feldman, Professor Bill Fishman, Dr Tony Kushner, the late Joseph Munk, Professor Aubrey Newman, Harold Pollins, Charles Tucker and Bill Williams. Thanks are also due to Maurice Ross of the West London Synagogue for providing access to the archives, Rickie Burman and Ian Lillicrapp of the London Museum of Jewish Life, Rosita Rosenberg of the ULPS, Hyam Maccoby and Roy Segal of the Leo Baeck College Library, the Librarians of the Mocatta and Queen Mary and Westfield College Libraries, the archivist at the Parkes Library, University of Southampton, the Curator of the Manchester Jewish Museum and the staff at the British Museum, Newspaper Library.

A special thank you to Rudi Leavor of the Bradford Reform Synagogue for his help, advice and loan of the synagogue's Registers.

Anne wishes to thank her colleagues in the Department of Political Studies at QMW, her children Deborah and James and son-in-law Paul for their patience and her husband Martin for his understanding and love, and conversion to easy-to-cook food while this book was being completed. Jonathan is equally grateful to his wife Sybil and their four sons, both for time left alone and time when he was dragged off to play football or have sword-fights. He also wishes to express his appreciation to Doris Angel whose cups of coffee and supply of cards kept him going as he travelled through over a century's worth of committee minutes.

Finally, Anne and Jonathan wish to pay tribute to each other's good humour and each other's expertise in different fields, which have made working together for the last five years such an enjoyable experience.

Preface

Tradition and Change traces the remarkable growth of what began as a small, independent, London synagogue established as a result of schism, which grew into a nation-wide movement. The foundation of the West London Synagogue of British Jews in 1840, by nineteen Sephardim and five Ashkenazim no longer satisfied by the traditional religious observance, heralded the birth of Reform Judaism in Britain.

It is a powerful story which addresses broad themes in British Jewish history while at the same time charting the progress of a movement built by dedicated voluntary effort into a highly professionalised body which has never lost sight of its founders' original aims and ambitions. *Tradition and Change* clearly identifies the divisions that existed demographically and geographically within an established mid-Victorian Anglo-Jewish community which was coming to terms with the demands of the modern, industrialising world and its religious questionings. It traces the pattern of Reform in London and the provinces, the impact of the arrival of eastern European immigrants towards the end of the nineteenth century and the implications of Political Zionism and the Bolshevik Revolution. The growth of Reform did not take place in a vacuum, the events surrounding its formative years have to be seen within the broader communal and national socio-political framework.

At the same time the book reflects events which lie at the heart of the religious character of British Jewry. The arrival of refugees from Nazism in the 1930s and the contribution of Continental refugee rabbis to the United Synagogue and Reform synagogues proved to be central to the post-war direction of Jewish religious observance in Britain. A Britain at war saw the six Reform synagogues forming an association, which with the peace developed into the second-largest synagogue movement in Britain, one which was sufficiently confident to embrace the ancient traditions it valued and to introduce the radical innovations it deemed necessary. Today it is a movement prepared to confront contemporary issues which challenge established norms. The title of the book reflects the twin elements that are at the heart of Reform Judaism.

A movement such as RSGB could not succeed without the countless unpaid activists who spent innumerable hours attending committee meetings, organising fund-raising events, leading membership campaigns and many other activities. Some of those individuals are referred to in the book, but the vast majority could not be mentioned for lack of space. Their omission is not intended as a slight to any one of them. As a general rule only those people are named who were involved in particular developments or who were the first to chair a new committee. A full list of the Chairmen and Presidents is provided in Appendix 4.

This book is divided into two clearly defined halves. The first, Part One: The Formative Years, 1840–1929, is largely the work of Anne Kershen and has the autograph of the social historian. Part Two: Reform as a Movement, 1929–95, is primarily the work of Jonathan Romain. This concentrates more specifically on institutional developments within the Reform Movement. Only passing reference has been made to current theology and religious observances, as these have been covered fully in Jonathan's earlier book, *Faith and Practice: A Guide to Reform Judaism Today*. *Tradition and Change* is therefore clearly the collaborative work of two authors, with two very different styles and two different emphases. No excuses are made for this. It is the authors' hope that the book will be of interest to both the general reader keen to discover how Reform in Britain has grown, and historians for whom this is the first time British Reform has been documented fully. We do not expect it to be the final word, but hope it will add to greater understanding of some of the dynamics that have been at work in British Jewry over the last century and a half.

Anne J. Kershen and Jonathan A. Romain
London and Maidenhead, 1995

Abbreviations

ABS	Associated British Synagogues
AJA	Anglo-Jewish Association
AJET	Advancement of Jewish Education Trust
AJEX	Association of Jewish Ex-Servicemen
ARZA	Association of Reform Zionists of America
ARZENU	International Federation of Reform and Progressive Religious Zionists
ASGB	Association of Synagogues in Great Britain
CCJ	Council of Christians and Jews
CJE	Centre for Jewish Education
ECAPS	Eastern Counties Association of Progressive Synagogues
FLPJYG	Federation of Liberal and Progressive Jewish Youth Groups
JEDT	Jewish Educational Development Trust
JIA	Joint Israel Appeal
JJBS	Jewish Joint Burial Society
JRU	Jewish Religious Union
JTO	Jewish Territorial Organisation
JYTF	Jewish Youth and Tercentenary Fund
PJS	Progressive Jewish Students
RSGB	Reform Synagogues of Great Britain
RSY	Reform Synagogue Youth
SATMAH	Students at the Manor House
ULPS	Union of Liberal and Progressive Synagogues
US	United Synagogue
WUPJ	World Union for Progressive Judaism
WUPJYS	World Union for Progressive Judaism, Youth Section
YASGB	Youth Association of Synagogues in Great Britain
ZF	Zionist Federation of Great Britain

Notes on the text

Hebrew terms are explained in the Glossary.

For the sake of brevity, 'Reform' has been used as a noun and refers to the Reform Movement.

Synagogues have often been referred to by a shortened version of their full name: for example, 'West London' for 'West London Synagogue of British Jews', or 'North Western' for 'North Western Reform Synagogue'.

The term 'Progressive' is used as a generic term to refer to the modern approach shared by both Reform and Liberal synagogues.

PART ONE

The Formative Years, 1840–1929

1 Schism, 1840

On 15 April 1840, at a meeting held at the Bedford Hotel in Russell Square, London, West Central, 19 Sephardim[1] and five Ashkenazim[2] signed the following Declaration. It heralded the arrival of Reform Judaism in Britain.

> We the Undersigned, regarding Public Worship as highly conducive to the interests of religion, consider it a matter of deep regret that it is not more frequently attended by members of our Religious Persuasion. We are perfectly sure that this circumstance is not owing to any want of a general conviction of the fundamental Truths of our Religion, but we ascribe it to the distance of the existing Synagogues from the places of our Residence; to the length and imperfections of the order of service, to the inconvenient hours at which it is appointed; to the unimpressive manner in which it is performed and to the absence of religious instruction in our Synagogues. To these evils, we think that a remedy may be applied by the establishment of a Synagogue in the Western part of the Metropolis, where a Revised Service may be performed at hours more suited to our habits, and in a manner more calculated to inspire feelings of Devotion, where Religious Instruction may be afforded by competent persons, and where to effect these purposes, Jews generally may form an United Congregation under the denomination of British Jews.[3]

In the sermon he gave at the ceremony to mark the consecration of the first West London Synagogue of British Jews, on 27 January 1842, David Woolf Marks concluded with the following message to the assembled congregants and guests, 'let it not be supposed that this house is intended as a synagogue of ease or convenience'.[4] It was a clear warning both to those who might have thought that Reform Judaism would be an easy option and to those who castigated it for the same reason. As will be illustrated in the pages that follow, the events surrounding the emergence of Reform Judaism clearly demonstrate that convenience, that is, the choice of a less demanding form of religious practice, was not the motive behind the schism of 1840. So what persuaded those 24 middle-aged, middle and upper-class members of Anglo-Jewry to turn their backs on the Orthodox Jewish community of London and begin their search for a satisfying form of public worship that would fulfil the fundamental Truths of their religion? Was it the influence of a new vision and innovative thought or were there other forces at play? To find the answer we must examine a variety of factors which include the structure of Anglo-Jewry, attitudes towards religious observance during the first decades of the nineteenth century, the Founders' socio-economic background, the Anglo-Jewish female's religious role, the seminal stages of German Reform and its influence, if any, on the origins of Reform Judiasm in London.

Following the expulsion of the Jews from England by Edward I in 1290, the practice of Judaism was forbidden for almost 400 years. The Readmission of the Jews to England or, more accurately, the legitimisation of their presence,[5] took place in 1656 under the rule of Oliver Cromwell who, at that time, was keen to acquire the commercial and financial expertise a Jewish presence would bring. There are no records of a written proclamation announcing the 'Readmission'[6] but by July 1656, 356 years after their expulsion, Jews were once again free to live, work and worship in England. The resettlement of Jews in England without specific legal restraints was a central factor in the genesis of Reform Judaism in Britain.

The earliest Jewish community of the Readmission was composed of affluent and cultured Sephardim. By 1660 the community, which numbered between 30 and 40 families, had acquired a house in Creechurch Lane, at the eastern edge of the City of London, in which to hold services and the lease of a parcel of land in Mile End, slightly further to the east, for use as a cemetery.[7] The government and the Crown of England imposed no controls on the practice of Judaism or on its practitioners; the Sephardim were self-governing and answerable to no-one in their communal organisation. In order not to antagonise Charles II, the newly restored monarch, or disturb the fragile nature of the Readmission, the governing body of the Sephardi synagogue, the

Mahamad, drew up a series of laws – *Ascamot* – by which it would govern the newly established community. The *Ascamot* drawn up clearly demonstrate the concern of the Sephardi Elders to reassure the host society that there was no intention to seek converts or to encroach upon Gentile territory. *Ascama* One, the law which would create such problems in the 1830s, forbade, under threat of *cherem* (excommunication) the establishment of another house of prayer within six miles of the existing synagogue, except for the purposes of wedding or mourning.[8] Another *Ascama* forbade the publication of works in Hebrew or Ladino (the Hebraic/Spanish language) while another forbade public debates on religious topics and prohibited attempts at conversion. An established community perhaps, but one clearly not at ease.

The Sephardi community of London burgeoned and increased its wealth. However, not all of its number were rich and self-supporting and what was to become a network of charitable institutions was set in motion by the more fortunate. Among their number were the families of Mocatta and Henriques, ancestors of the future founders of Reform Judaism in Britain, who contributed funds for a purpose-built synagogue to be located close by the first house of prayer. A synagogue which would accommodate 400 men and 160 women, a synagogue in which the liturgy was, and would remain, that brought from Spain and Portugal. A synagogue which would be known in the centuries to come simply as Bevis Marks.

Swiftly on the heels of the Sephardi arrivals came Ashkenazim from central and eastern Europe who settled in London during the last quarter of the seventeenth century. They were poorer and less cultured than the Jews of western Europe with little or no experience of the ways of western society, having spent a ghettoised existence in the towns and villages of Germany and Poland. Some came to England to escape the massacres which followed the Chmielnicki Revolt of 1648–49, others in the hope of finding economic opportunity. They brought with them the trades and ways of the ghetto and the more traditional religious practices of central and eastern Europe. Steeped in tradition, ultra-Orthodox in their religious observance, they followed a liturgy that differed from that of the Sephardim and their vernacular was Yiddish (the Hebraic/Germanic language). By the end of the seventeenth century the Ashkenazi community of London had acquired a cemetery in east London and had established a synagogue, to become known as the Great, in Dukes Place, on the borders of the City.[9]

For Anglo-Jewry the eighteenth century was a combination of wealth and poverty, of country gentleman and town beggar, of banker and hawker, of restrictions and liberties, of anti-Semitism and tolerance, of a decline in synagogue decorum and an increase in religious apathy. In socio-economic terms the Jews of England were horizontally stratified: the lower orders consisted of artisans, pedlars, hawkers and second-hand clothes dealers, the middle orders were shopkeepers, silversmiths and watchmakers while at the upper level were bankers, bullion brokers and merchants.[10] For all but the latest arrivals it was a century of transition, assimilation and Anglicisation. The absence of government restrictions on business and social intercourse meant that where interaction took place the tensions of the period were transmitted. In church and synagogue the role of religion was placed increasingly under examination. Dissent and reform were in the air. Interaction with the host community left its mark in both secular and religious terms. Though some conformed with the enlightened philosophy of Moses Mendelssohn which advised Jews to 'Adapt yourselves to the customs and constitution of the land in which you live yet, at the same time, adhere firmly to the religion of your ancestors',[11] others grew lax in their attitude to religious observance; some even became apostates.

Demands for religious change and the increase in religious apathy were manifest in synagogue and church. Writing on the state of the English church in 1795, the Reverend Watson commented, 'There never was an age...in which atheism and infidelity have been more generally professed'.[12] At the same time a pamphlet designed to alert the Ashkenazi hierarchy to the indecorous behaviour of members of the Great Synagogue was published. It criticised the inattentiveness of worshippers, the vulgar sale of *misheberach* (special prayers for personal blessing) and congregational behaviour more suited to the 'coffee house or stock exchange'.[13]

In the Anglican church demands for reform were largely directed towards the abuses of privilege and the inadequacies of administration. In the established synagogues of London demands were directed towards ritual reform and a West End location. In 1803 Jacob Mocatta urged the Sephardi synagogue to confront the changing structure of the Anglo-Jewish community and their corresponding spiritual needs. He requested the replacement of the Portuguese vernacular with English and an examination of the educational role of the synagogue. A committee was set up and a spiritual leader appointed. But though the Haham, Raphael Meldola, reportedly took an 'energetic interest' in the affairs of the community, little changed.[14]

In the decades that followed, further criticism and appeals for reforms were largely ignored by the lay elders and clergy of Bevis Marks. The plea for the opening of a branch synagogue to the west of the City, where a number of affluent Sephardim had made their homes, remained constant.[15] The socio-economic effects of the industrial revolution were notable within the Jewish community. Their assimilation and *embourgeoisement* encouraged a movement westward, away from the eastern edges of the capital, to its more salubrious west end. Eminent Jews who had established a position at the higher levels of society and commerce were to be found living in Mayfair and Bloomsbury, having migrated westward via Tottenham and Stamford Hill; locations which, at the beginning of the nineteenth century were considered of a rural nature.[16] And while Sir Moses Montefiore and others were content to make the four and one half mile trek on foot from the luxurious elegance of Park Lane to Bevis Marks or to the Great Synagogue, a minority, including his brother Horatio, resented the walk. Some stayed away from synagogue, gradually withdrawing from community and religion. Others, wary of the threat of *cherem* or unwilling to offend their religious beliefs by taking a dubious or secretive option, declined to ride. They argued that there was no reason to retain *Ascama* One which, one hundred and sixty years on, was anachronistic. But the Sephardi Elders remained resolute and when, in the 1820s, an attempt was made to hold a service elsewhere, those involved were placed under threat of *cherem*. Having no desire to be excommunicated the offenders recanted. The discontent festered on.[17]

The autocratic attitude of the Elders of Bevis Marks was another source of annoyance. It was the catalyst that finally drove Isaac d'Israeli, father of Benjamin and an advocate of Reform, from the synagogue and from Judaism. In 1813 d'Israeli was appointed a member of the *Mahamad* by the Sephardi Elders. He declined the position and, as a matter of principle, refused to pay the fine imposed as a result of his so-called defiance. Four years later he withdrew from the Jewish community and subsequently had his children baptised. At the consecration of the first Reform synagogue, in 1842, Isaac d'Israeli is said to have remarked that had the synagogue existed at the time of his disagreement, 'I, and all my family would have continued to profess Judaism to this Day'.[18] No doubt a public denial of the Oral Law appealed to his anti-rabbinism. For, in the early years of the nineteenth century, certain members of the Anglo-Jewish establishment were not only beginning to re-evaluate their religious position but, in addition, were questioning the relevance of the rabbinic tradition in the modern world. Was it really for all time?[19] The debate was not restricted to Jewish circles. In the 1830s, as the differences between the traditionalists and the reformers were heightening, the Protestant Church, most particularly the evangelicals, was articulating both its belief in the authority of the Bible and its criticisms of the rabbinic laws. The influence of Protestant bibliocentricity cannot be ignored in the origins of Reform Judaism in Britain.

Discontent and unrest were not solely the province of the members of Bevis Marks. The Minute Book of the Great Synagogue in Dukes Place, the cathedral of the Ashkenazi community, records the dissatisfaction of certain of its members. Complaints related to undignified behaviour and the somewhat chaotic nature of services. An entry in the Vestry Minute Book for 1825 reveals that the lay leadership believed it 'Important that some immediate steps be taken to generally improve the harmony of the devotional service'.[20] There were those too who, in common with some of their Sephardi brothers, pressed for a branch synagogue. Their appeals were refused.

The decade of the 1830s was one of growing tensions. The Elders of Bevis Marks combined concessions, such as agreeing to the occasional English sermon and to the opening of a branch synagogue 'if it is absolutely necessary',[21] with the imposition of accompanying restrictions. English sermons had to be submitted three days in advance in order to ensure they did not contain 'anything inimical to our religious doctrines or any matter hostile to the established institutions of the country'.[22] Any branch synagogue would have to be under the supervision of Bevis Marks, with 'any changes in the ritual to be approved by all the community'.[23] When it seemed as though these provisions might prove to be acceptable the Elders withdrew their offer.

Clearly dissension and discontent were rife throughout the

established communities. What is also clear is the determination of the Orthodox laity and clergy not to consent to any but the most insignificant requests for reform. There was strong opposition to, and fear of, change. Fear, not so much of the response of the host society – though the desire to censor English sermons suggests a degree of unease – but fear of losing communal control to newcomers who would weaken their hold, fear that the loss of affluent members might result in the State being called upon to support members of the Jewish poor; fear that giving a little might lead to sacrificing a lot. The abbreviated title of the committee established by the Elders of Bevis Marks in 1838 in response to a request for changes in line with those intended in the Reform synagogue in Hamburg is indicative of the static nature of the Jewish Orthodoxy in early Victorian England. It was called 'the Preservers of Sacred Institutions'.[24] In both the Ashkenazi and Sephardi camps matters were coming to a head.

Of primary importance in any history of the foundation of the first Reform community in Britain is the composition of the group which produced the Declaration of 1840, that which became known as the 'Society' of Dissenters or Founders – depending on individual point of view. A knowledge of this enables us to understand the origins of Reform Judaism in London and to comprehend the subsequent direction and development of the West London Synagogue of British Jews. Almost all of our Founders were members of the 'Cousinhood', the élite of Anglo-Jewry.[25] The Cousinhood was composed of Montefiores, Goldsmids, Mocattas, Henriques, Cohens and Rothschilds. The obvious omissions from the list of Reform Founders are the names of Cohen and Rothschild. The latter was a family which remained true to the high church of Anglo-Jewry throughout the years in question. There were 24 signatories to the Declaration of April 1840.[26] Of those, 19 were Sephardim. One, Solomon Lazarus, of Ashkenazic origin, had transferred to the Sephardi synagogue in 1837, either through marriage or, perhaps, in the hope that it would introduce reforms more rapidly. The remaining founders were Ashkenazim.

Of the 24 signatories, nine were Mocattas, members of one of the oldest Anglo-Jewish families. Mocatta roots in England date back to the period of the Protectorate when Moses and Emanuel, of Marrano origin, arrived in London from Italy via Amsterdam.[27] Brokers, bankers, philanthropists and scholars, the Mocattas were among the most eminent of Anglo-Jewish families. Even before the schism of 1840 the two senior Mocattas, Moses and Daniel, had expressed their discontents. While *Parnas Presidente* (presiding warden) of Bevis Marks, Daniel Mocatta attempted, unsuccessfully, to mediate between the Orthodoxy and the would-be Reformers.[28] Moses was a scholarly man, a patron of the progressive writer Grace Aquilar whose novels projected the liberal view of the English Jew.[29] He was very much the Englishman who was a Jew by religion. Moses Mocatta and his fellow Founder, Horatio Montefiore, both believed that the practice of Judaism should be understood as well as followed. It was for this reason that they encouraged the translation of the *Mishnah* into English by Revd M. Raphall and David de Sola.[30] David Mocatta, Moses's son, was a successful architect and his appointment as a Fellow of the Royal Society and his vice-presidency of the Royal Institute of Architects was an example of the way in which the Anglicised Jew had become part of English life. His involvement with the early years of Reform Judaism was not restricted to synagogue attendance: David Mocatta was responsible for the design of the second synagogue, consecrated in Margaret Street in 1849, and was also the guiding light behind the 'ultimate' Reform synagogue in Upper Berkeley Street, consecrated in 1870 and considered by the *Jewish Chronicle* to be a 'magnificent monument of architectural ability'.[31]

In addition to a multiplicity of Mocattas there were three Montefiores. The most renowned and respected member of that family was Sir Moses. Six feet three inches in height he has been likened to a colossus, a giant amongst his fellow men, Jews and non-Jews. It must therefore have been very hard to support a movement which was so alien to a brother. But this Horatio Montefiore did, perhaps spurred on by a degree of sibling rivalry. Horatio, married to a Mocatta, 'was one of the principal founders of the London Reform Community'.[32] His obituary in the *Jewish Chronicle* remembered him as a charitable, affable man, always eager to promote the cause of knowledge.[33] Horatio's two cousins, Jacob and Moses Junior were also founders. However, in 1844 Jacob resigned from the Council of Founders of West London as 'he could not withstand the pressure of his parents-in-law' who were members of the Orthodox New Synagogue.[34]

Isaac Israel Henriques was a warden of Bevis Marks Synagogue when it was consecrated in 1701, he and his family having settled in London in the 1680s. Three of Isaac's descendants signed that April 1840 Declaration, two of them Jamaican born. Trade with the West Indies had encouraged a number of Jewish merchants and bankers to establish links with the colonies and Reform family connections can be traced to the Caribbean, Australasia and South Africa. The remaining Sephardi signatories were Hannael de Castro, Joseph Samuda, Jacob Melhado and Solomon Lazarus. With the exception of the last, all were members of old-established Sephardi families with broad economic and secular interests covering the spectrum of law, commerce and banking.

Of the five Ashkenazi signatories, three were members of the Goldsmid family, descendants of Aaron Goldsmid who arrived in London from Amsterdam in 1725.[35] By the close of the eighteenth century Benjamin and Abraham Goldsmid, Aaron's sons, had reached the very highest levels of English society, acting as hosts to luminaries such as Lord Nelson and even George III.[36] In spite of their affluence and success their lives ended in tragedy. Both brothers committed suicide, Benjamin in 1808 and Abraham in 1810. Aaron's grandson, Isaac Lyon, though not a Founder, became a member of the West London Synagogue in 1843.[37] His preoccupation was the political emancipation of Anglo-Jewry. It was Isaac Lyon's son Francis who was in the forefront of the movement for synagogue reform. At the time of his death in 1878,[38] the Revd David Woolf Marks wrote of Francis Henry Goldsmid that 'to him more than anyone else we owe...that our congregation was brought...into being'.[39] Francis was Liberal Member of Parliament for Reading from 1860 until his death. A barrister by profession, he was in fact the first Jew to be called to the Bar and sufficiently concerned about his Jewish beliefs not to appear in court on the Sabbath.

Nine years before the 1840 Declaration the Goldsmid family had publicly expressed its sympathy for the style of worship practised in the Hamburg Temple. In 1831, apparently in a fit of pique at the willingness of the Board of Deputies, Anglo-Jewry's representative body,[40] to accept less than total Jewish emancipation, Isaac told the then Mr Moses Montefiore that he 'did not care about that measure and would establish a new synagogue with the assistance of young men'. He would 'adapt the present form of prayer to that in use in the synagogue in Hamburg'.[41] 'Young men' such as the graduate intellectuals who acted as lay preachers in the early Reform synagogues of Seesen, Berlin and

Hamburg? Sir Isaac never followed up his threat, was not a signatory to the 1840 Declaration and appears to have had little direct involvement with the early organisation of the West London Synagogue of British Jews.

Francis Goldsmid was one of the most hardworking of the Founders, a fact recorded in an address presented to him three months after the consecration of the synagogue in 1842. It read as follows:

> Deeply impressed with the value of the services rendered by you in the formation and establishment of the West London Synagogue of British Jews: we the undersigned Founders are desirous of recording our unanimous sense of obligation to you for the energetic and cheerful manner in which on all occasions you have devoted your time and abilities to the arduous duties of Honorary Secretary of our Institution.[42]

Even in the early years the Goldsmid family's Reform connections were not restricted to its male members. In 1841 the Founders resolved to 'procure some lectures delivered in German synagogues to be translated into English'.[43] This task was carried out by Isaac's daughter, Anna Maria, though there is no evidence that the sermons were ever given in public, either in the lecture hall close to University College, which was used in the latter months of 1841, or in the Burton Street Synagogue. Did the Founders disagree with the ideology or did their newly appointed Reader and Lecturer, David Woolf Marks, wish to deliver original rather than imported work? The role of the female in the foundation of British Reform Judaism appears, on the surface, to have been negligible. Were the wives and daughters of the Founders in any way influential in the creation of West London? After all it was not considered essential for a Jewish woman to attend religious services, her traditional place was in the home if she were middle or upper class, ensuring that all ran smoothly for her spouse. Judith Montefiore, wife of Sir Moses, challenged this convention by regular synagogue attendance when 'her health and the weather permitted'. If this was the attitude of a member of the Orthodoxy, how much more likely that women such as Louisa Goldsmid, wife of Francis, member of the Langham Place Feminists in the 1850s and champion of the movement to establish a women's college at Cambridge, would have supported, even encouraged, their husbands' attempts to establish an independent synagogue, located closer to home – a synagogue which might well have reduced the Jewish female's hidden and 'other' role. A West End branch would facilitate more regular synagogue attendance, even in inclement weather, and would provide greater incentive for involvement in charitable activities. The West London Synagogue certainly found favour with its female membership. A contemporary account reveals that, in the months following the consecration of Burton Street,[44] 'No more than half-a-dozen ladies' seats were ever left unoccupied during services'.[45] This is in contrast to the Orthodox synagogue where female attendance was markedly poor.

It has been suggested that the Goldsmid family's support for the creation of a synagogue of British Jews was directly linked to the issue of Jewish emancipation. In his article 'The Origins of the Jewish Reform Movement in England',[46] written in 1976, Robert Liberles suggests that the family played a major, indeed the major, role in the creation of the West London Synagogue of British Jews. He postulates the belief that they saw it as an independent vehicle through which they could advance their ambitions for the total removal of Jewish civil disabilities. Until 1838, the constitution of the Goldsmid's family synagogue, the Great in Dukes Place, decreed that the Board of Deputies was to be the sole communicant with the British government on political issues. Thus the Great's representatives would articulate the opinions of the majority. These were less ambitious than those of the Goldsmids. Under pressure, in December 1838, the elders of the Great conceded that 'no individuals...are precluded from exerting their influence with the government'. But the voice of an individual, or indeed individuals, without the backing of a communal body and its membership, for example a synagogue, may have seemed of little consequence to the government and its Prime Minister. So was West London seen as the alternative route to the ear of Sir Robert Peel? In February 1845 Isaac Goldsmid made a direct appeal to the Prime Minister for the removal of civil disabilities. As he explained, the Jews were the 'only class among her Majesty's subjects still exposed to their degrading influence'. Goldsmid may have been encouraged in his approach by the knowledge that, as a Tory Minister in the late 1820s, Peel had taken a benevolent view of the removal of disabilities from the Catholic and Protestant Dissenters. But the letter was sent from Isaac Goldsmid's home address – not from the Burton Street

Synagogue – and was signed by an 'Independent Group', not by members of the West London Synagogue of British Jews.[47] In reality that 'Group' was composed entirely of members of West London, but this was not a stated fact. Under separate cover, on the same day, Isaac Goldsmid wrote a second letter to the Prime Minister, also dispatched from his home. This acquainted Peel with the divisions that existed within the Jewish community. The letter's main thrust was an appeal against the Marriage and Registration Acts of 1836. These, though enabling Acts for other dissenters, in the terms of the Jewish reformers, forced the Burton Street congregation into dependence on the Board of Deputies for certification of its synagogue secretary. The Board, under the presidency of Sir Moses Montefiore, was opposed to the Reform congregation and refused to recognise it as a synagogue or David Woolf Marks as its marriage secretary. Thus, though before the Act of 1836 marriages within a Reform synagogue would have been considered legitimate by the State – which recognised 'marriages amongst persons professing the Jewish religion, where both parties to the marriage profess that religion'[48] – after the Act's passage, the Reformers were denied that legitimacy by their co-religionists. In his letter to Peel, Goldsmid pointed out that the Board of Deputies was recognised by a 'portion of Jews only' and that by its attitude towards the Reformers it had 'excluded a body of Jews comprising amongst its members fifty or sixty of the most respectable Jewish families'.[49]

Goldsmid's statement is not one to be expected from a family that was solely involved with West London in order to further the cause of emancipation. His correspondence with Peel clearly identifies division and dissension – something he would not have stressed if his sole concern was the fight for the removal of civil disabilities – unity rather than disunity seemingly being the image to be promoted. It seems more likely that frustration with the procrastinations of the Board of Deputies and disagreements with the established synagogue over its refusal to introduce ritual reform or to open a West London branch encouraged Goldsmid, who lived in Regents Park (Central London) and would not work on the Sabbath, to join forces with a group of gentlemen who were experiencing similar disagreements and had the same reforming ambitions.

The increasing divisions of the 1830s made it inevitable that the differences between the Reformers and the Orthodox establishment would result in schism. Conciliation seemed hopeless and the Founders set out to reinterpret their Jewishness in response to the demands of modernity. In the months that followed the Declaration of 1840 they began to structure the ritual and liturgy of their synagogue. A priority was the form of prayer to be followed. Discussion centred around pragmatic matters such as discourses in the English language, length of service and the use of Portuguese pronunciation,[50] issues which had been at the very heart of the schism. In July of that year the Founders' most radical proposal is recorded in the Minutes, the abolition of the Second Day of the Festivals,[51] a reform not mentioned in the original Declaration and one which had not yet been introduced in the Reform Temples in Germany, but one advocated by David Woolf Marks, the future minister of West London.

London-born David Woolf Marks (1811–1909) was taught Hebrew at a very early age, having begun by studying the *Mishnah* when he was only eight years old. In his late teens he became *Ba'al koreh* (*Torah* reader) at the Western Synagogue[52] and in 1833 was appointed Assistant Reader and Secretary to the Liverpool Congregation, one of the largest outside London.[53] Established in the late eighteenth century the synagogue was Orthodox but progressive. English sermons were given as early as 1806. The congregation's tolerance and respect for David Woolf Marks was such that when he refused to read the Law on the Second Days of the Festivals his anti-rabbinist stance was tolerated and the synagogue provided a substitute reader. The Liverpool community was not without divisions, but although a Reform breakaway was rumoured, it was an Orthodox group, frustrated by the dictatorial attitude of the old hierarchy in Seel Street, that seceded in August 1842.[54] While at Liverpool, Marks taught the young John Simon (1818–1897), later Sir John, Serjeant-at-Law. John Simon, who took up law after his father opposed his becoming a religious minister, was born in Jamaica and educated in England. His experience as the only Jew at his English public school[55] may well have led him to consider his religion in the context of a non-Jewish world and have been influential in his becoming a staunch advocate of the denial of the Oral Law. In 1842 John Simon wrote a pamphlet in which he argued that the perfection of the Written Law negated any need for the Oral Law; the latter could not be divine as it often contradicted the word of the Scriptures. In fact

David Woolf Marks attributed his introduction to Reform Judaism and his initial doubts as to the immutability of the Oral Law to his discussions with the young John Simon.

David Woolf Marks was brought to the notice of the London Reformers by Dr Joshua Van Oven,[56] who introduced the young man to 'some Hebrews who espoused the new cause'. Records do not reveal when the first meeting took place but Marks was formally interviewed in July 1840 by a committee of five. His appointment as Reader and Secretary was confirmed that September. According to their Minutes, the Founders considered him to be a 'person extremely eligible for the situation'.[57] Marks, who we must remember was not an ordained rabbi – in common with many English ministers of the time he had not obtained *semichah* – viewed his new position with optimism, it was one which he believed would enable him to 'cast off the abuses which have too long veiled our Holy Religion and to render its practices and observances more in accordance with its pristine purity'.[58]

It is appropriate at this point to consider how much influence David Woolf Marks had in determining the ritual and liturgy of the West London Synagogue of British Jews. By May 1840 the Committee of Founders had determined both the source and length of prayers. They were to be short, in order 'to engage as far as possible the unwearied devotion and attention of the congregation', to combine the Ashkenazic and Sephardic liturgies and to favour the Sephardic pronunciation.[59] However, it was only after the Founders' meeting with Marks that the abolition of the Second Day of the Festivals appears to have been openly considered. The Council of Founders' Minute Book reveals that in July 1840 a decision was taken that the 'services which may be appointed for THE SACRED DAY OF THE FESTIVALS be...One day New Year, 1st and 7th day Passover, One day Pentecost, 1st and 8th day Tabernacles only'.[60] Significantly the final decision on the abolition of the Second Day was delayed until Marks's appointment was confirmed. Was he the driving force behind this reform? Without his insistence would London have delayed making such a radical move? Sixteen years later the Manchester Reformers, swayed by the more conservative elements, delayed abolishing the Second Day until four years after their break with the Orthodoxy. It was a procrastination which, in 1858, found disfavour with what was, by that time, the established West London Synagogue of British Jews.

That first Reform Prayer Book was drawn up by David Woolf Marks in consultation with Professor H. Hurwitz, holder of the first chair of Hebrew Studies at University College, London and the Reverend Dr Morris Jacob Raphall, the distinguished Orthodox rabbi from Birmingham. The trio followed the guidelines and directives of the Founders.[61] The Prayer Book provides clear evidence that the Reformers and Marks, who surely would have been conversant with the central European liturgies, were determined to create a Prayer Book for a congregation of 'British' Jews. Marks believed that 'Jews should adapt the ritual to the wants of its members'; the Prayer Book of the West London Synagogue of British Jews was to reflect this belief. Even so, services remained in Hebrew though the Prayer Book carried a full English translation.[62] David Woolf Marks later revealed that he had 'taken council with the Elders' and had agreed to have the service *all* in Hebrew on condition that the Elders undertook to 'have the children carefully taught the sacred tongue' – a clear indication of his concern that the service be understood as well as followed. Initially the Elders kept their promise faithfully, but the next generation was less mindful of its duties and grew lax in the Hebrew education of their children. A formal religion school for the children was not opened until 1886, but even after that date the practice of private Hebrew tuition from rabbis or learned Jews, particularly for the more affluent, was maintained.

The Prayer Book opened in the traditional Orthodox fashion, from right to left, and provided for Sabbath and Festival services which never exceeded the desired two and a half hours, a positive reform of the lengthier traditional practice. Doctrinal changes were manifestly anti-rabbinic, restricted to the omission of non-scriptural passages, including the *piyutim*, and the avoidance of the phrase 'who has sanctified us by His commandments', where such commandments were not derived from the Scripture. Areas of controversy such as the doctrine of the personal Messiah, the doctrine of the Resurrection of the dead and the restoration of the sacrificial cult were, as was the *yigdal*, all retained until 1881 when some minor changes were made. Michael Goulston has suggested that Marks's theology revealed certain inconsistencies and ambiguities which demonstrate an eclecticism. While pronouncing his Mosaic-centredness there are hints of an allegiance to traditional practice. In the words of Goulston, 'the ethical, behavioural, and attitudinal elements of *Torah* received his rational assent, because they are universal. The particularist and dogmatic facets of revelations were accepted in an act of piety and theological affirmation, reinforced by a partly critical acceptance of the biblical text.'[63]

Between 1841 and 1843 five volumes of prayers were produced. These were: (1) Daily Prayers, *Chanukah*, Sabbath, *Purim* etc., (2) Evening Service for Three Festivals, Morning Service for Festivals, *Torah* Readings, Additional Service, Prayers for Feast of Tabernacles and an original prayer for seasons, (3) Prayers for New Year, (4) Prayers for *Yom Kippur* and (5) Original prayers for the naming of a girl child, burial and mourning. With only minor changes these prayer books were used by West London and its affiliated synagogues until the 1930s.

The other major departure the London Reformers made from Orthodox tradition was the formal denial of the Oral Law, a more accurate description being the formal denial of the divinity of the Oral Law. The issue was touched upon covertly in the Introduction to the Prayer Book published in August 1841. However, a formal, public denial did not take place until the consecration of the Burton Street Synagogue. The sanctity of the Oral Law was a question which had been occupying the thoughts of the more progressive members of Anglo-Jewry – and the Church – for some years. In his Introduction to the Prayer Book, Marks described how Hebrew ritual and prayer had undergone many changes and how some items previously considered 'genuine remnants of our ancient temple worship' were in fact the outcome of later persecutions and suffering 'now fast disappearing'. The Sacred Prayer Book (Oral Law) was not 'as final and immutable a character as the Sacred Code itself'. In the sermon he gave at the consecration of the first Reform synagogue in Britain, Marks put forward the view that while the Written Law, 'that sacred volume of the Scriptures, commanded by God to be written down for the unerring guidance of his people until the end of time', was immutable, the Oral Law, which was created by the rabbis, was not of divine origin. It was to be respected but it could, in common with other rabbinic writings, be subject to debate and, when appropriate, change.[64] As Rabbi Curtis Cassell has said, 'incorrectly the Founders were attributed with the wholesale denial of the Oral Law'. In reality they were 'questioning its divinity'.[65]

The appointment of a minister, or as the Founders specified, a 'reader and lecturer', the conversion of an Owenite chapel for a synagogue in Burton Crescent, Burton Street,[66] in the West Central district of London, and the preparation of a prayer book occasioned the first warning from the Orthodoxy. The Ashkenazi Chief Rabbi Hirschell and the Sephardi Reverend David Meldola wrote jointly to the Board of Deputies. In their letter they stressed that 'schism has introduced its baneful influence amongst us...should these reports unfortunately prove true...then let us reflect and consider what it behoves us to do'.[67] Leading Reformer, Moses Mocatta, rejected the offer of a meeting with the Sephardi Elders. He doubted that they would, in reality, make any concessions. His response stated that, though not seeking schism, the Reformers desired 'substantial improvements in the public worship' in order that their descendants would be handed down 'our holy faith in all its purity and integrity'.[68] Two months later, with no concessions forthcoming on either side, the Elders of Bevis Marks threatened the imposition of a *cherem*:

> 'Any...member of our congregation combining to erect a synagogue westward and its carrying into effect the principles they advocate...will be considered as a violation of the *Ascama* of Kaal, and render such and every member of our congregation so acting virtually excluded from Yahid and liable to all penalties of that *Ascama*.[69]

On 10 September 1841, two weeks after the Sephardi community's Caution was issued, the Chief Rabbi and Reverend Meldola, together with members of the Board of Deputies, prepared the following Declaration: 'Any person or persons publically declaring that he, or they, reject or do not believe in the authority of the Oral Law, cannot be permitted to have any communion with us Israelites in any religious rites or sacred act.'

In the hope that the Reformers could still be persuaded to return to the fold, publication of the Declaration was withheld. The Chief Rabbi argued that its immediate publication and circulation would 'convert a temporary difference into a irreconcilable enmity'.[70] Resolve, however, did not weaken and on the Saturday preceding the scheduled consecration of Burton Street, the Declaration, or *cherem*, was finally issued, to be read in synagogues all over the country on 22 January 1842. The exact number of communities that complied with the request is not recorded but it is clear that some did not. The Orthodox

Liverpool Synagogue refused, combining respect for its former reader with their progressive bias; the Western Synagogue also ignored the demand. Plymouth, supposedly,[71] burnt the Declaration, while the Manchester Synagogue, itself in the process of nascent reform, debated the issue and (though no records exist) appears to have had the formal Declaration read from its Orthodox pulpit. The authenticity of such a *cherem* was unclear. It formed the subject of a public discourse given by one of the protagonists of the Manchester Reform Community of British Jews, Professor Tobias Theodores, in 1854. In his lecture Theodores questioned the right of those mid-nineteenth-century ecclesiastics to declare a *cherem*. They had not received classic *semichah* (rabbinic ordination) and therefore, he contended, the 'law of one congregation is not obligatory on any other'. According to Theodores, while a 'Declaration' may have been proclaimed, no classic *cherem*, which required the 'Flourish of a multitude of horns or trumpets' had been issued.[72] The debate was sufficiently contentious to persuade Nathan Adler, following his appointment as Chief Rabbi in 1845, to abolish the right of all future incumbents to impose a *cherem*.

Whether the Reformers were excommunicated remains a topic for debate. However it is clear that in those early years they were distanced from the Orthodox communities. The Sephardi Founders were not permitted to occupy their usual synagogue seats or to participate in the charitable or administrative activities of Bevis Marks. In the years that followed, a number of appeals were made for the revocation of the *cherem*. In 1845 the Elders of Bevis Marks went so far as to articulate doubts as to the existence of a state of *cherem*. The clergy remained firm. On an individual level there was a gradual relaxation, but the West London Synagogue of British Jews as an institution remained beyond the pale. With the passing of time the sympathies of the Jewish and national press moved towards the Reformers. By 1845 the *Jewish Chronicle*, once opposed, was under the editorship of the progressive Marcus Bresslau. By contrast to his predecessor, he posited the belief that the dissenters were the victims of a 'system of petty persecution'.[73] In 1846 the *Voice of Jacob*, possibly influenced by the views of Theodores, by that time a regular contributor to its pages, questioned whether the Declaration and Caution constituted an actual *cherem*.[74] The stalemate was blamed on the influence of a 'few wealthy immigrants from the uncivilised and barbarous states of Africa',[75] the reference being to Sephardi Jews who had migrated to England from the North African states of Morocco, Algeria and Tunisia. The division within the Anglo-Jewish establishment was reported in the national press, the Liberal *Morning Advertiser* considering the ban a 'severe and unrelenting persecution'.[76] It must be remembered that these events were taking place when the issue of Jewish emancipation, and its place within the debate on the role of Church and State, was in the forefront of the political arena. The *cherem* on the individual Founders, if it had existed at all, was formally lifted at the beginning of 1849 following a number of appeals to the Elders by, among others, Hannael de Castro who, though a signatory to the Declaration, had retained his association with Bevis Marks. In 1849 Moses Mocatta made the concession and formally admitted that the Sephardi dissenters had transgressed *Ascama* One and asked that the penalties imposed upon them should be lifted. Thus legally, although the *cherem* on the West London Synagogue of British Jews remained, the Dissenters had been brought in from the cold.

Let us now look at the Founders' Declaration in terms of their needs and ambitions. Location was of primary concern. The majority of the founders resided in the Hyde Park, Regents Park or Bloomsbury areas of London.[77] To ride to synagogue on the Sabbath and Holy Days would have been unacceptable, walking in inclement weather, particularly for wives and children, made synagogue attendance unattractive. There was also an expressed concern at the 'absence of religious instruction' and a desire for the introduction of sermons which not only would be in English but would be 'inspiring and instructive'. The latter was also a point of contention in the established Christian Church where sermons, when given, were frequently inaudible and so lacking in physical expression that a contemporary account suggests that they might have been given by a corpse. It was hardly surprising that the evangelicals enjoyed a resurgence of support in the years leading to 1850.

We know that our Founders were also concerned to 'rediscover and excite feelings of devotion', not easy when the service was over-long and carried on amidst constant chatter. But what was their intent in entitling their new synagogue one for *British* Jews? Was it, as was suggested by the *Morning Chronicle*, to 'eradicate past national differences and indicate unity amongst the native Jews of Great Britain'?[78] 'Britain' was used as a means of camouflaging the cultural and territorial differences of western, central and eastern Europe, just as it did those of England, Ireland, Scotland and Wales and, in addition, as proof that communal and religious differences and divisions were not insurmountable.

The Reverend Morris Joseph, David Woolf Marks's successor as Senior Minister at West London, believed that the successful conclusion to the emancipation struggle was directly related to 'the spiritual awakening among the Jews which itself constituted a plea for civic freedom'.[79] But it took another 18 years for civil disabilities to be removed and the first Jewish incumbent of a seat in Parliament was a member of the Orthodoxy. In fact the Minute Book of the West London Synagogue reveals that by 1853 the members, rather than initiating moves, had become somewhat apathetic and were only following the lead 'of the London Congregations' when a petition for the removal of Jewish disabilities was presented to the House of Lords in the name of the reform congregation.[80] This fact provides us with further evidence that the fight for emancipation was not the prime motivating force behind the creation of the West London Synagogue of British Jews.

What we do not find in the Declaration or indeed elsewhere in the Founders' statements or appeals, is any hint of *wissenschaft des Judentums*, the scholarly and scientific study of the Jewish religion and the history of its people. There was no public airing of intellectual ideas, though the European precedents were there. In Germany as early as 1806, the journal *Sulamith* was published as a vehicle through which to promote Reform philosophy and the process of integrating Judaism and society.[81] In the 1830s the *Allgemeine Zeitung des Judentums* was founded by the progressive reformer Ludwig Philippson as a medium through which Jewish matters, and particularly religious debates, could be brought to its readers' attention. At the very time when Reform Judaism was sprouting in London the *Archives Israelites* appeared in Paris even though at that time there was no independent 'Reform' community in France. But the reformers did not have to look overseas for models. Religious unrest in England was propagated by the Tractarians through the *British Magazine* and the *British Journal* in the 1830s and Protestant non-conformity through the journal *Nonconformist*.[82] Indeed, it must be argued that the bibliocentricity we find in the origins of Reform Judaism in London owes more to English Protestantism, mediated through upper-class Anglo-Jewry, than to any religious thoughts from abroad. However, the Reformers remained silent, even after 1841, when the *Jewish Chronicle* and the *Voice of Jacob* made their first appearances. Though at that time both journals were opposed to the Dissenters and their house of prayer the Reformers made no attempt to publish an independent journalistic response. This cannot be put down to shortage of funds. Was it rather a reluctance to advertise communal divisions during the struggle for emancipation – unlikely – or torpor with regard to the ideological dimensions of Reform Judaism in its nascent state? There is a distinct absence of the form of intellectual debate, carried on in journals, that emerged from Berlin and other parts of Germany during the second and third decades of the nineteenth century.[83]

The pattern of Reform that developed in early nineteenth-century central Europe bore little similarity to that which developed in Britain. However, the assumption is frequently made by those who are not acquainted with the early periods of both central European and London-based Reform Judaism that the latter 'began life as a German import'.[84] The origins of Reform in London are not to be confused with events in Manchester and Bradford, cities which, as Chapter 3 will illustrate, had much stronger ties with central Europe. The beginnings of London Reform were remote from those of Germany, but did the West London Synagogue of British Jews owe anything to the birth of Reform in central Europe in the first four decades of the nineteenth century? In those early years there was little, if any, cohesion among European reform thinkers and it was not until 1845, when the first Rabbinical Assembly, for preachers and rabbis, was held in Brunswick, that any collective identity or 'movement' is discernible. The first decades of the nineteenth century were marked philosophically, by the emergence of humanist thinking in the form of the Enlightenment and *Haskalah*, and politically, by the march of Napoleon through Europe. Jews were subsequently hurled into citizenship, often forced to give up their self-governing ghetto communities. The result was that many found a need to reinterpret the meaning of 'Jewishness' in a modern secular society. The reimposition of civil disabilities after the fall of Napoleon only served to accentuate the dilemma. Some Jews made a total break and defected. Others had to choose between Orthodoxy, steeped in the traditional observance and beliefs of the past, and the socio-economic benefits which would result from a form of practice which incorporated the demands of modernity. Early nineteenth-century reformers urged Jews to 'keep pace with the spirit of the times'.[85]

The response was the creation of a number of Reform 'temples', the use of the word temple signifying that it was not solely the domain of the Jews and also, according to Israel Jacobson, that it was a 'small weak imitation of Solomon's Temple'.[86] Israel Jacobson was a layman and advocate of Jewish emancipation and the corresponding modernisation of Judaism who, in 1810, opened the first of those temples in Seesen, Westphalia. The Seesen Temple, the chapel of a school run by Jacobson, was radical in construction; it even had a bell tower. The service incorporated Hebrew and German prayers, organ music and choral song. An important element was inter-faith worship and there was a marked attendance by Christian laity and clergy. In 1813 the Kingdom of Westphalia collapsed, the Temple was closed and Jacobson left for Berlin where the Jewish community was manifesting dissatisfaction, drift and defection.

Berlin Jewry reflected polarised religious practice, from strict Orthodoxy through to radical Reform. Following his arrival there in 1814 Jacobson organised a series of Reform services in his house. Such was the volume of support from Jews and Gentiles that services were transferred to the larger house of Jacob Beer where a temple was constructed out of three rooms. The opportunity to practise a modern form of Judaism attracted a number of young progressive intellectuals who became actively involved as lay preachers and organisers – the young men to whom Isaac Goldsmid referred in 1831. Radical though it may have been, there was no mixed seating, even if there was no formal partition! The rapid success of the Beer Temple was ultimately its downfall. Reforms were haphazard and in some cases controversial: for example, the use of Sephardic pronunciation for what was essentially an Ashkenazic community – once again linguistic snobbery taking precedent. A largely traditional prayer book was produced and gradually the services began to assume the chaotic nature of the Orthodoxy. Young intellectuals such as Isaac Marcus Jost and Leopold Zunz withdrew their support. The final nail in the coffin was the Temple's popularity with the Christian laity and clergy. In 1823 the State, concerned over the possibility of apostasy and supported by members of the Orthodox Jewish community opposed to the emergence and survival of Reform, announced that the Temple's continued existence made Jews 'even more dangerous to civil society than they were before'.[87]

While the early experiments in Seesen and Berlin failed as a result of State control and intervention, the third attempt, in Hamburg, proved successful. Following the Napoleonic occupation a section of the increasingly secularised, wealthy and acculturated Jewish community of Hamburg sought a form of denationalised religious observance which was reflective of their emancipationist ambitions. With the arrival of Eduard Kley, formerly a preacher at the Berlin Temple, the project took a positive direction. In 1817, the Israelite Temple Association was founded with the intention of 'reviving dignity and meaning to Jewish worship'. Sermons were to be in German and choral song would be accompanied by an organ. There was a strong emphasis on youth, with confirmation and youth education of primary importance. They were indeed looking to the 'citizens' of tomorrow. The Hamburg Temple was opened in 1818 and attracted the support of a largely middle-aged, middle-class membership. A prayer book was commissioned from two laymen, S. I. Frankel and M. I. Bresselau. A contentious issue was the Messianic return to Zion. How was this to be interpreted in a society where religion and citizenship went hand in hand? The solution was reached by a combination of substitution and omission. The return to Zion was to be considered a universal, not particularist, issue which would benefit all and be brought about by God's will, in God's time. The dilemma over citizenship and Messianism was one acknowledged by David Woolf Marks in England. Though he had a preference for the concept of a personal Messiah his eventual solution was to remove the political dimension.[88] Marks preached that Messianic belief need not conflict with the Jew's role as an Englishman; the return to Zion would take place when political constraints were lifted and peace reigned supreme.

In spite of opposition from the German Orthodoxy, support for the Hamburg Temple grew to the point at which, in 1841, it was enlarged and its original prayer book revised. But aside from Isaac Goldsmid's remark some ten years before and the appeal to the Elders of Bevis Marks in 1836, the influence of the Hamburg Temple is barely discernible in the origins of the West London Synagogue of British Jews. In both England and Germany certain

Jews were reconsidering their Jewishness. But whereas in central Europe it was a forced reappraisal, in England it was a slower, more relaxed process which resulted from economic change and expansion, not political pressure and limitation. There was choice. Sir Moses Montefiore felt no need to alter his traditional observance in order to improve his social and civic standing, and in truth he does not appear to have suffered as a result. The Goldsmids were frustrated but do not appear to have benefited by their independent approach to Peel, but nor did they put into practice any of their earlier references to the Hamburg Temple.

There appear to have been few if any direct links between the beginnings of West London and European Reform, though Goulston has suggested a similarity between Marks's introduction to the 1841 Prayer Book and that of the one published in Hamburg in 1819.[89] It was later suggested that, before the appointment of David Woolf Marks in 1841, Isaac Marcus Jost was asked to secure a suitable candidate in Germany for the position of reader and lecturer at West London. He approached Dr Zacharias Frankel, Chief Rabbi of Dresden, who refused, stating that 'no sufficient principle of reform was put forward and that, in order to do battle, they [West London] must have a standard to raise'.[90] On closer examination, the choice of a foreign minister appears out of keeping with the Founders' ambitions and certainly was not recorded in the Minute Book. It contradicts the nationalist bias of Founders who chose the denomination British, resolved that their sermons be in English – surely something of a problem for a central European appointment – adopted the description 'synagogue' as opposed to the central European Reform epithet 'temple' and showed no inclination to use the Hamburg prayer book. If an early approach was made overseas it was more than likely due to an anxiety that an English-born minister might not be found. The appointment of David Woolf Marks appears the natural choice and confirms that while the English Reformers were conscious of the events taking place in central Europe they were not influenced by them, though there may have been a subconscious acknowledgement of their effect. The foundation of a West London Synagogue of British Jews therefore appears not only as a pronouncement of nationality, citizenship and unity as a means of overcoming the Sephardi–Ashkenazi divide, but also as a statement of independence in relation to Reform congregations overseas.

So how do we assess the origins of Britain's first Reform congregation? It clearly was not born of convenience – of the Reformers' desire to avoid 'difficulty or trouble'[91] which would have saved time spent appealing and debating with the Orthodox clergy and laity and would have avoided painful family differences. If 'ease of action' were the object then might not the Reformers have ridden, albeit unseen, to the synagogue, entering the service late and leaving early? Convenience would have determined which days of the festivals should be observed, maybe even *which* festivals, in order to avoid loss of work. This might have saved time, money and aggravation but would it have satisfied wives and daughters who wished to attend services on a regular basis at a synagogue that was accessible at all times of the year?

Nor was the consecration of the Burton Street Synagogue the result of its Founders' deep and searching philosophical and ideological debates. There are no records of these. The authors of the pamphlets in support of the Denial of the Oral Law, Benjamin Elkin and John Simon,[92] though early members of West London, were not signatories to the Declaration nor did they serve on any of the Founders' committees before 1842. There was no advertised attempt to recruit young intellectuals nor any published journals which strove to analyse the role of the Jew in contemporary society.

The 24 Reformers were modern, conscientious Jews who wanted to relate their modernity to religious observance in an honest, decorous manner. They doubtless considered the criticisms of 'rabbinism' that were directed at Judaism, most specifically from evangelical sources,[93] and were very much aware of the current debates about the powers of Church and State and thus about citizenship.[94] They were clearly concerned at the growth of apathy and apostasy, drift and defection, in an increasingly assimilated society and wanted to ensure a Jewish future for themselves and their heirs, a future that would be fulfilling and in keeping with the Founders' Anglicised and assimilated lifestyle. They were neither revolutionaries nor proselytisers. They did not seek to overthrow the Orthodoxy, if the established synagogues were not prepared to change or innovate then they would follow their own paths, however stony. They were certainly not conversionists or missionaries. Proselytisation was not encouraged and membership charges were kept deliberately high in order to maintain exclusivity. The Founders were essentially conservative reformers who, having achieved their ambition, worked hard to ensure that their synagogue travelled along the lines they had laid down. Following its controversial beginning, the West London Synagogue took a far less confrontational course. There were hurdles to overcome and a need to establish a foothold both within and beyond the Jewish community. Having achieved these goals the Founders seemed content to remain as they were. Having laid important foundations the governing laity then seemed content to become, as Israel Zangwill stated in 1892, 'a body which had stood still for fifty years admiring its past self'. How much truth there was in his words the next chapters will show.

NOTES

1. Jews who followed the ritual, liturgy and tradition of the Sephardim from the Iberian Peninsula, the Netherlands, Italy and North Africa.
2. Jews who followed the ritual, liturgy and tradition of the Ashkenazim from central and eastern Europe.
3. Minute Book of the West London Synagogue of British Jews, 15 April 1840, archives of the West London Synagogue, Upper Berkeley Street, London.
4. D.W. Marks, *Sermons* (1851), p. 23.
5. There were undoubtedly a small number of Jews in England throughout the period of the expulsion and by the sixteenth and early seventeenth centuries a number of marranos – Crypto-Jews who privately carried out the tenets of the religion while outwardly appearing to observe the rites of Christianity. See C. Roth, *A History of the Jews in England* (1978 edn), pp. 132–48.
6 T. Endelman, *The Jews of Georgian England 1714–1830* (1979), p. 16.
7. A. Hyamson, *The Sephardim of England* (1951), p. 14.
8. Hyamson, op. cit., pp. 28–32.
9. Roth, op. cit., pp. 197–203.
10. See Endelman, op. cit., for a detailed account.
11. W. Gunther Plaut, *The Rise of Reform Judaism* (1963), p. 7.
12. The late-eighteenth-century Reverend Watson, writing in his 'Defence of Revealed Religion', quoted in E.R. Norman, *Church and Society in England 1770–1970* (1976), p. 22.
13. H. Simons, *Forty Years a Chief Rabbi* (1980), p. 93.
14. Hyamson, op. cit., pp. 224–5.
15. Hyamson, op. cit., pp. 270–3.
16. Endelman, op. cit., pp. 258–71.
17. Hyamson, op. cit., pp. 270–3.
18. C. Cassell, 'The First Nine Years of the West London Synagogue of British Jews' (unpublished manuscript, undated), p. 306. For the details of Isaac d'Israeli's dispute, see A.L. Shane, 'Isaac d'Israeli's Quarrel with the Synagogue', *Transactions of the Jewish Historical Society of England*, Vol. XXIX (1988), pp. 165–75.
19. S. Singer, 'Jewish Religious Thought in Early Victorian London', *Association of Jewish Studies Review*, Vol. X, No. 2 (1985), pp. 181–211.
20. Minute Book of the Great Synagogue, 5 Jan. 1825, Acc. 2712/1/A/6, Greater London Record Office.
21. Hyamson, op. cit., p. 284.

22. Endelman, op. cit., p. 162.
23. Hyamson, op. cit., p. 274.
24. Roth, op. cit., p. 257.
25. C. Bermant, *The Cousinhood* (1971).
26. Minute Book of the West London Synagogue of British Jews, 15 April 1840, loc. cit.
27. *Encyclopaedia Judaica* (1971), Vol. 12, p. 138.
28. Cassell, op. cit., p. 21.
29. D. Cesarani (ed.), *The Making of Modern Anglo-Jewry* (1990), pp. 98–100.
30. Hyamson, op. cit., p. 258.
31. *Jewish Chronicle*, 23 Sept. 1870.
32. *Encyclopaedia Judaica* (1971), Vol. 8, p. 687.
33. *Jewish Chronicle*, 23 Aug. 1867.
34. Hyamson, op. cit., p. 391.
35. *Encyclopaedia Judaica* (1971), Vol. 7, p. 734.
36. Endelman, op. cit., p. 251.
37. Membership Book of the West London Synagogue of British Jews 1840–1849, p. 5, archives of the West London Synagogue, loc. cit.
38. Sir Francis died from injuries received when he alighted from a train approaching Waterloo station before it reached the platform.
39. Cassell, op. cit., p. 10.
40. For background to the Board of Deputies see below.
41. L. Loewe (ed.), *Diaries of Sir Moses and Lady Montefiore* (1983 edn), Vol. 1, p. 83.
42. Cassell, op. cit., p. 10.
43. Minute Book of the West London Synagogue of British Jews, 2 March 1841, archive of the West London Synagogue, loc. cit.
44. The location of the first West London Synagogue, see below.
45. Letter from H. Behrends, dated 18 March 1842, A/J Archives, MS 140, Hartley Library, University of Southampton.
46. Robert Liberles, 'The Origins of the Jewish Reform Movement in England', *Association of Jewish Studies Review* (1976), pp. 121–51.
47. Peel Papers, British Library, MS 40612, Folios 163–4.
48. I. Finestein, 'Jewish Marriages and the English Law', *The Jewish Journal of Sociology*, Vol. VII, No. 1 (1965), p. 12.
49. Peel Papers, British Library, MS 40560, Folios 126, 128 and 130.
50. Unlike Yiddish, the vernacular of many of the Ashkenazim, the Portuguese pronunciation did not reflect a lower-class, unacculturated image.
51. Minute Book of the West London Synagogue of British Jews, 15 July 1840, loc. cit.
52. Also known as the Westminster congregation, see V. D. Lipman, *Social History of the Jews in England 1850–1950* (1954), p. 14.
53. C. Cassell, 'David Woolf Marks', in A.J. Kershen (ed.), *150 Years of Progressive Judaism* (1990), pp. 19–21.
54. Henry Behrends letter, loc. cit. For divisions within the Liverpool community see G. Alderman, *Modern British Jewry* (1992), pp. 20–21 and 31.
55. A. Tropp, *Jews in the Professions 1881–1991* (1991), p. 21.
56. Joshua Van Oven was one of the founders of the Jews' Free School. He died in 1838 and thus did not live to see the Reform Community established.
57. Minute Book of West London Synagogue of British Jews, 10 Aug. 1840, loc. cit.
58. Quoted in B. Williams, *The Making of Manchester Jewry* (1985 edn), p. 104.
59. Minute Book of the West London Synagogue of British Jews, 18 May 1840, loc. cit.
60. Minute Book of the West London Synagogue of British Jews, 28 July 1840, loc. cit.
61. Minute Book of the West London Synagogue of British Jews, 8 May 1840, 14 Oct. 1840, 2 March 1841 and Cassell, op. cit., pp. 46–8.
62. Prayer Book of the West London Synagogue of British Jews (1841).
63. D. Marmur (ed.), *Reform Judaism* (1973), p. 61.
64. Marks, op. cit., pp. 6–7.
65. C. Cassell, 'The Founders of the West London Synagogue of British Jews and their Approach to the Oral Law' (unpublished paper, undated), p. 14.

66. The first West London Synagogue was known as the Burton Street Synagogue though its correct postal address was Burton Crescent, Burton Street.
67. Minute Book of the Board of Deputies of British Jews, letter dated 20 May 1841, p. 5601.
68. Minute Book of the West London Synagogue of British Jews, 24 June 1841, loc. cit.
69. Minute Book of the West London Synagogue of British Jews, 21 Aug. 1841, loc. cit.
70. J. Piccioto, *Sketches of Anglo-Jewish History* (1956 edn), p. 374.
71. According to Rabbi Curtis Cassell, in a letter to the West London Synagogue Review in August 1953, the story of the burning of the *Cherem* is a myth. In fact the story originated from a report in the *Morning Chronicle* dated 4 February 1842 which said that the President of the synagogue at Portsmouth had committed the Bull of Excommunication to the flames. In the retelling Portsmouth became Plymouth but, according to a letter which appeared in the *Jewish Chronicle* of 11 Feb. 1842, 'most distinctly, ...nothing of the kind as described, took place...'.
72. T. Theodores, *The Rabbinical Law of Excommunication* (1854).
73. *Jewish Chronicle*, 1845, issue No. 13.
74. The *Voice of Jacob*, 13 March 1846.
75. The *Voice of Jacob*, 16 June 1847.
76. *Morning Advertiser*, 22 Feb. 1846.
77. Peel Papers, British Library, MS 40612, Folio 164.
78. *Morning Chronicle*, 28 Jan. 1842.
79. 'Jubilee of Political Emancipation', *Transactions of the Jewish Historical Society of England* (1908), Vol. VI, p. 102.
80. Minute Book of the West London Synagogue of British Jews, 10 May 1853.
81. M. Meyer, *Response to Modernity* (1988), pp. 28–30.
82. See D. Chadwick, *The Victorian Church*, Vol. 1 (1966).
83. See Meyer, op. cit., Ch. 2.
84. S. Brook, *The Club* (1989), p. 116.
85. Meyer, op. cit., p. 29.
86. Meyer, op. cit., p. 42.
87. Meyer, op. cit., p. 52.
88. Marmur, op. cit., p. 61.
89. Marmur, op. cit., p. 57.
90. *Jewish Chronicle*, 11 Dec. 1863.
91. The *Oxford English Dictionary*'s definition of the noun convenience being 'freedom from difficulty or trouble'.
92. See Chapter 2.
93. In his excellent new book David Feldman argues that the evangelicals' charge of rabbinism was a major factor in the birth of Reform Judaism. While a desire to 'cleanse the synagogue' was no doubt a force in the nascence of Reform in England, the other issues mentioned in the present chapter cannot be ignored or marginalised. See D. Feldman, *Englishmen and Jews* (1994), pp. 36–65.
94. Ibid.

2 Founding Fathers, 1842–1870

Israel Zangwill's comment, made in 1892, that the West London Synagogue had 'stood still for fifty years admiring its past self' was well founded. As late as 1896, heated exchanges accompanied proposals to introduce some English prayers into the service. A bitter debate, which nearly resulted in another schism, followed the proposed introduction of psalms in English into the service. Sir Philip Magnus, previously third minister of West London, opposed the move, believing it would presage an all-English service.[1] Acting Senior Minister Morris Joseph and the now 85-year-old David Woolf Marks both thought the service too ministerial and lacking in congregational participation. They favoured increased usage of English. Marks was aware that in spite of his earlier insistence on the teaching of Hebrew the practice was not enforced by the majority of parents. On the side of progress, Alfred Henriques also argued that the Manchester Reform community had incorporated English in their services for some time, suggesting that Philip Magnus's speech was 'more suited to 1840 than 1896'. However, no drastic changes were made to the liturgy and it can be argued that the conservatism of the Berkeleystreeters was a prime force in the emergence of Liberal Judaism during the early years of the twentieth century. But that is moving half a century ahead. We must look first at the form and direction of the West London Synagogue of British Jews during its nascent years. The agenda laid down between 1840 and 1870 was to shape Reform Judaism in Britain for almost a century.

Having established their synagogue our Founders had a number of hurdles to clear before they could settle down to mere self-congratulation. Forms of service and of prayer, congregational responsibility, charitable activity and interaction with national and international Jewry were issues which were debated and decided. In 1870, for the second time in its brief history, the Synagogue relocated westward, this time to one of the most affluent and salubrious parts of the capital, an area that appeared on the London Map of Poverty devised by the late-nineteenth-century social scientist, Charles Booth, as predominantly gold, the colour of upper-class affluence.[2] It was a relocation which befitted a membership that remained exclusive and dominated by the Cousinhood until well into the twentieth century.

The first item on the agenda of the Council of Founders was the creation of a religious format which would satisfy their aims and ambitions, a ritual and liturgy which would combine modernity and religious observance. While the Prayer Book, published in 1841, had provided a written guide to the future, the consecration of the Burton Street Synagogue, which took place at 3 p.m. on Thursday 27 January 1842, was the setting for the first public articulation of Reform Judaism in Britain. The Founders and their minister were conscious of the difficulties that lay ahead for those who had initiated such a bold move. In a private meeting that preceded the formal proceedings Moses Mocatta invested the young David Woolf Marks with his minister's cloak. (This ceremony itself was a radical movement away from Orthodox tradition, towards that common in the English Church.) In his private address Mocatta stressed the controversial and delicate position David Woolf Marks and the founding Reformers now held. He warned that: 'for any least deviation, unqualified censure will be heaped upon us, and the self-styled orthodox of our co-religionists will gladly seize on the minutest point to vilify our MINISTER [sic] and cast obloquy on our congregation.'[3]

For his first formal sermon Reverend Marks took as his theme Joshua Chapter 22. This was a direct response to Hirschell and Meldola who earlier had used the same biblical source to attack the Dissenters. Marks explained that the Orthodoxy had taken the quotation 'you have built you an altar to rebel this day against the Lord' out of context. Quoted in its entirety the chapter illustrated how those Old Testament defectors, in common with the seceders fifteen hundred years later, had attempted to strengthen the Jewish religion. Marks insisted that tradition and ceremony were no substitutes for duty to God: 'We must not confound the form with the substance', he said. He then proceeded to indict the Orthodoxy for allowing conditions to develop which encouraged infidelity and apostasy: over-long services, infrequent sermons, no religious instruction for the young, indecorum and degradation of women. He followed his attack with a defence of the two 'reforms' which had caused the greatest furore, the abolition of the Second Day of the Festivals and the Denial of the Oral Law. It was the element of flexibility and freedom to respond to change, not to be bound by ages-old rabbinical decisions, that was central to the birth of Reform. Marks justified the abolition of the Second Day on the grounds that science had developed to a point at which the days of the festivals could be calculated 'to a fraction of a minute'. He explained that, in the future, holy festivals would be celebrated only on those days commanded by 'God through our legislator Moses'.[4] The Reformers would no longer continue to celebrate festivals on 'the days when He commanded it not'. In his defence of the Denial of the Oral Law Marks stated that the *Mishnah* and the *Talmud* were 'human compositions' and therefore not to be accepted unconditionally as was the *Torah*; 'for Israelites there is but one immutable Law, the second volume of the Scriptures'.

Marks then proceeded to describe the form that future services would take. They would begin at a time that would enable 'the entire congregation, men, women and children to assemble prior to the commencement of prayers',[5] these to be read aloud by the minister. The congregation would respond to the psalms and hymns chanted by the choir. To avoid distraction, offerings would be announced at the end of the service on the three major festivals and other suitable occasions. Girls and boys would be confirmed at the age of thirteen and, in keeping with tradition, services would be 'in Hebrew only'.

For a congregation which had been condemned as radical it was a mixed order, conservatism intermingled with elements of progress. There was no hint of mixed seating, an innovation which, even when proposed as late as 1910, was not found acceptable. It is not until 1910 that a suggestion for mixed seating is recorded in the Minute Book of the West London Synagogue.[6] Even at that time the suggestion met with strong opposition, in spite of the fact that the move 'involved no infraction of the Mosaic Law', was accompanied by the belief that as a result synagogue attendance would increase and had been accepted as part of Reform ritual in both central Europe and North America.[7] Mixed seating was not introduced in the West London and Manchester Reform synagogues until the inter-war years. Nor, in those earliest years of London's Reform congregation, was there even a hint that the inconvenience of walking to synagogue in inclement weather, in ill health or in old age, could be overcome by riding. The radical Gustav Gottheil, minister of the Manchester Synagogue of British Jews from 1860 to 1873, was obliged to walk to the Reform Park Place Synagogue from one side of the city to the other for, as he later explained, 'It would not do for us to have ridden'.[8] The use of transport to enable synagogue attendance on the Sabbath and Holy Days was a gradual and unheralded phenomenon. In Germany the issue was debated in the 1830s, but nothing was resolved until 1871 when, at the Synod in Augsburg, it was publicly ordained that: 'If the distance from the residence to the house of worship, age or delicate health prevented attendance at divine service, then it was deemed permissible to remove this obstacle by riding to the place of communal worship...either on the railroad or in a vehicle.'[9] There are no records of West London or either of the two provincial communities following the central European lead in the nineteenth century. Thus, while location, decorum and modernisation of practice, in terms of liturgy and ritual, featured at the top of the Founders' list, convenience evidently did not.

Neither of the two Anglo-Jewish newspapers sent representatives to the consecration of the Burton Street Synagogue though both took the opportunity to criticise the event. The *Jewish Chronicle*, recently founded and under the joint editorship of two staunch members of the Orthodoxy, David Meldola and Moses Angel, declared that a representative of the paper was 'prevented by the prohibiting proclamation of the ecclesiastical authorities of the community as well as our own feelings' from attending. The *Chronicle* attacked the new congregation and its minister, stressing that David Woolf Marks had not, as he had suggested in his sermon, narrowed or totally eradicated the divisions that existed between the German and Portuguese synagogues by the creation of a synagogue of British Jews. On the contrary the congregation had added 'a new distinction...greater than ever existed amongst Jews prior to its formation'.[10]

The other Jewish journal, the *Voice of Jacob*, was edited by Jacob Franklin who, though born in Portsmouth, had grown up in Liverpool. Franklin had recently arrived in London from Manchester where he had been founder and director of the

Mechanics' Institute.[11] Though an enlightened thinker, as evidenced by his publication of articles by Professor Tobias Theodores, an individual who later became a leading Reformer in Manchester,[12] Franklin was an upholder of traditional Orthodoxy. Initially, though he later changed his view, he supported the excommunication of the Dissenters. In the journal's report of the consecration it was suggested that officers of the Converting Society, attracted by the Dissenters' bibliocentricity which could be likened to contemporary Christian non-conformity, had been present. It is unlikely that any converts would have been won amidst such a glittering and affluent gathering. Two missionary societies were active in London during the nineteenth century, their main objective being to encourage Jews to convert. The London Society for Promoting Christianity amongst Jews was founded in 1809, and the British Society for Propagating the Gospel amongst Jews in 1842. The success rate is difficult to gauge, one estimate putting the number of baptisms in the six years 1843–49 as 180.[13] A study carried out in 1989 shows that 'most Jews converted in England by missionaries were...drawn from the poorest and least respectable strata of the community'.[14]

The consecration of the West London Synagogue of British Jews drew the attention of the national press. *The Times* paid little attention to the communal divisions which the event highlighted or to the content and structure of the service, save to say there was a 'small but well trained [all male] choir'. Emphasis was on social content, on the 'leading members of the new congregation' which constituted the 'most respectable among the Jews'.[15] The *Morning Chronicle*'s report debated the designation 'British Jews' and suggested that the title manifested an intention to eradicate past national differences and was thus indicative of a desired unity among the native Jews of Great Britain – a plus for the removal of civil disabilities. The overseas Jewish press was divided in its opinion. *Der Orient* considered that Marks's first sermon could have been a model for the Frankfurt Reform Association whilst the *Allgemeine Zeitung*, more cautious, suggested that the 'new spirit' would have to prove itself.

The events in London were being noted and, to an extent, emulated far beyond Europe. In the Caribbean, the Jewish community of St. Thomas, Jamaica, was split over the introduction of reforms in the ritual and liturgy of their synagogue. The wealthier members of the congregation were in favour of change, the less affluent opposed.[16] In 1842, the would-be reformers appealed to David Woolf Marks at West London for help. Although the North American continent was far closer, its Jewish community was small, having not yet expanded to the proportions it was to assume before the First World War. Until 1840 there was no ordained rabbi and the few Jewish communities that did exist had only made tentative attempts at Reform. The total Jewish population of America was less than 10,000 and did not exceed that figure until central European refugees and immigrants, seeking economic opportunity in the New World, made their way across the Atlantic. In Charleston, South Carolina, America's largest Jewish community, which numbered some 600, had seen the Reformed Society of Israelites, founded in 1825, subsequently collapse in 1833. Reform re-emerged some ten years later but it was not until the end of the 1840s, in the person of Isaac Mayer Wise, that Reform Judaism in America found a leader.[17] Thus it was to London that Jews – Orthodox as well as Reform – in North America, the Caribbean and indeed Australasia and South Africa, turned for guidance. The St. Thomas reformers asked Marks to send out some West London Prayer Books and, on their behalf, to engage a minister who was anti-rabbinic and who, in addition, in order to provide sermons in the vernacular, spoke good English. Though he was able to comply with the request for prayer books Marks could not find a suitable candidate for minister.[18] There was no alternative but to reappoint the Revd Carillon, the previous, Orthodox, minister of the community. Carillon did not approve of the West London Prayer Book, which denied the Oral Law and omitted certain favoured Portuguese hymns. After a short while he resigned and subsequently took a post in Montego Bay. Fifteen years later the matter remained unresolved. Reform, which its adherents believed 'ennobles the mind',[19] had still not been accepted in St. Thomas, though a few months earlier, in the neighbouring island of Curaçao, the foundation stone of a Reform synagogue was laid.[20]

That earliest West London congregation was small. The Membership Book for the period records some 54 male and female subscribers, almost all members of the Cousinhood.[21] Even so it was thought necessary to employ an assistant minister and in November 1842 the Revd Dr A. Lowy was appointed to the position he was to hold until his retirement in 1893. Albert Lowy was born and educated in central Europe, the only non-English minister to be appointed to the congregation until the 1920s. Lowy assisted with the running of the synagogue and contributed to the composition of prayers. The *Jewish Chronicle* considered his work for the Day of Atonement to be the 'gem of the congregation's liturgy'.[22] In 1866 Marks and Lowy were joined by a third minister, Philip Magnus, whose training had been partially funded by money from a newly established Ministers' Training Fund.[23]

The issue of training young men for the ministry does not appear to have been of consequence in the early days of West London's history but, as the years passed, concern grew over the recruitment of future ministers, men who would fulfil the theological and pastoral role Reform Judaism demanded. The question of suitably trained clergy was one also debated by the Jewish Orthodoxy and by the English Church. The latter, aware of the need for specialised colleges which would produce men suited for the cloth, opened eight theological seminaries between 1836 and 1876.[24] As Anglo-Jewry became increasingly assimilated and Anglicised it became apparent that Jewish ministers would be required to preach in English, play a more pastoral role and interact with their counterparts of the Christian faith. Foreign cantors and readers were not suited to the needs of an increasingly Anglicised community. In the early 1850s Chief Rabbi Adler proposed the establishment of a Jews' College where boys could receive a combined secular and Hebrew education, before they entered University College London. In 1837 Jews, who at that time were excluded from entering the older universities such as Oxford and Cambridge, became eligible to proceed to a degree at the secular University College.[25] Chief Rabbi Adler did not advocate specific training for *semichah*. It could be argued that this was because of his desire to maintain control over the London and provincial communities by ruling out competition from other ordained ministers. West London, though not invited to participate in the setting-up of the Jews' College, was asked for a list of members in order that they could be circulated about the proposed college.[26] Evidently, the Reformers' money would have been acceptable even though they themselves were not. The request was refused.

The demands of the expanding membership of West London as well as that of the Manchester Reform community,[27] which was established in 1856 and which until 1873 employed ministers of

European origin, highlighted the need for English-born ministers to be trained specifically for Reform communities. In 1861 a fund to provide an annual £50 to 'defray the expenses of maintenance and education of Mr Philip Magnus' was established.[28] One beneficiary of the fund was Laurence Simmons who, in 1881, became the first English-born minister to be appointed to the Manchester Congregation of British Jews.

It was not until 1880 that a training plan for Reform ministers was formally laid down. The stipulations were as follows: Candidates had to be 17 plus, to have matriculated from a British university and to be morally and religiously fit for the ministry. They should then proceed to a British university (University College) to study Hebrew and religion to graduate level. To facilitate their training for the ministry they would receive a stipend of £100 for three years or longer. On obtaining their degree they should then advance to a Jewish theological seminary in Germany or elsewhere for two or more years. Following completion of studies, the intended minister was to be examined by the Chief Minister of West London, or one of the Emeritus ministers. He would then be inducted as a 'Jewish Minister' with the ministry of West London as the preferred position. In case of misconduct the Council of West London was at liberty to discontinue the stipend.[29]

Having established a formula, produced a set of prayer books and engaged two ministers, the Reformers had to address the issues of birth, marriage and death – the very essence of communal life. Death had to be accommodated. The Reformers realised that they would no longer be permitted use of the Orthodox cemeteries and in March 1841 a sub-committee was established to look for a suitable site for a burial ground.[30] The following year, three-quarters of an acre of ground in Balls Pond Road, Islington, north London, was purchased for the sum of £540.[31] The ground was consecrated in July 1843. During the interim period an arrangement was made with the independent Maiden Lane Synagogue (the breakaway from the Western), for members to be buried in its cemetery, and it was there that the young wife of Founder Horatio Montefiore, who had died in childbirth, was laid to rest.

It was the attitude of the Orthodoxy over the burial of an advocate of Reform, who had retained his membership of an Ashkenazi synagogue, that demonstrated yet again the intransigence of Chief Rabbi Nathan Adler. Although not a signatory to the dissenters' declaration of 1840, Benjamin Elkin was a supporter and benefactor of Reform. At the time of the schism, in 1842, he wrote a pamphlet in defence of the denial of the Oral Law entitled, *Is the Oral Law of Divine Origin and Binding on the Jews?*, which drew him into the circle of English anti-rabbinists. Elkin's wife died before the establishment of West London and was buried in the Ashkenazi cemetery. In order that he could be buried beside his deceased spouse Elkin maintained his membership of the Great Synagogue. After his death in 1848 the Chief Rabbi declared that as Benjamin Elkin had been a member of the Reform community only the undertaker or the beadle of the Orthodox cemetery could officiate at his burial service. Benjamin Elkin had anticipated just such a move and had decreed in his Will that 'if the bigotted party who excommunicated us should put any obstacles... that I desire that I should be buried in the Cemetery of the West London Synagogue'.[32] His wishes were carried out and he was laid to rest apart from his wife. Adler's stance may well have been the catalyst for some, who might not otherwise have done so, to take the path of Reform Judaism.

If death created divisions within Anglo-Jewry, that which should have united proved even more divisive. The issue of the legality of a Jewish marriage in its civil, as opposed to religious, form once again highlighted the polarity of the schism. This was manifest in a number of ways: in the formal appointment of a marriage secretary for West London; in the problems surrounding the marriage arrangements of the daughter of a Reformer to the son of a member of the Orthodoxy; and in the inflexibility of the newly appointed Chief Rabbi.

Following the passing of the 1836 Registration Act, which took marriage out of clerical and into secular control, in order for a Jewish marriage to be regarded as legal by the State, a synagogue marriage secretary had to be certified by the Board of Deputies. Supposedly an 'enabling' Act,[33] it had the reverse effect for the newly established Reform synagogue, which as a result became dependent on the President of the Board of Deputies, from 1840 until 1874 Sir Moses Montefiore, for sanction. Immediately after the consecration of Burton Street, Francis Goldsmid wrote to Sir Moses at the Board requesting certification of David Woolf Marks as marriage secretary of the West London Synagogue of British

Jews. The ammunition was handed to the opponents of Reform on a plate. It was customary for the President of the Board of Deputies to appeal to the ecclesiastical authorities of Anglo-Jewry, the Chief Rabbi and the *Haham*, for his opinion.[34] Montefiore wrote to the Chief Rabbi explaining that, in the light of the Reformers' stated views, he was precluded from giving the certificate but, 'not withstanding it is the Duty of the President of the London Committee of Board of Deputies of British Jews to give such a certificate...if you sanction such a view...give me such in writing'.[35] Following the despatch of the letter Montefiore recorded in his diary that he 'entertained most liberal principles in matters of religion but as President he had to give his opinion, he invariably referred to the spiritual leader of the community'.[36] The Chief Rabbi's response was incontrovertible: 'Earnestly request that you do not grant certificate as we do not consider it [Burton Street] a synagogue.'[37] Sir Moses Montefiore informed Francis Goldsmid accordingly, repeating in his letter Chief Rabbi Hirschell's earlier statement that he did 'not consider the place of worship in Burton Street to be a synagogue'. The Registrar General was then officially notified that the Board of Deputies had refused to certify Burton Street and its minister.

Goldsmid, to say the least, was vexed. In his reply to Montefiore he pointed out that, before the 1836 Act, the Board's consent had not been necessary. A marriage carried out in a synagogue according to Jewish tradition had been considered legal according to the Parliamentary Act of 1753.[38] The 1836 Act required formal registration through the Registrar General, therefore, as members of West London observed the basic Jewish principles (this being one of the fundamental issues of the schism), they should satisfy a Counsel of Justice that such a marriage was legal in the eyes of the law. The request for certification was repeated. Again it was refused. Montefiore then consulted the Solicitor-General, William Follett, and Counsel. Both found in favour of the Board. Goldsmid realised that bringing the matter out into the open, by contesting the Board in the civil law courts, would, in his words, 'exhibit to the Christian public the spectacle of Jew contesting Jew in a court of Justice'.[39] At this point Goldsmid had no desire to expose further communal divisions. He thus noted that to his mind the decision of the Board was illegal and that he could 'reserve the right to appeal to parliament'. Stalemate. However, Burton Street was determined to provide its members and their children with the opportunity to marry within the Reform synagogue. For that purpose a special Marriage Authorisation Certificate was drawn up, the text of which was as follows:

> Reverend Sirs,
> We the undersigned wardens of this Synagogue authorise you, or one of you to perform the ceremony of marriage, according to the usages of persons professing the Jewish religion, on the..........[date], between........[name, address and marital status] provided that before so doing, a Certificate be delivered to you of the marriage of the same parties on the morning of the same day, at the Office of the Superintendent Registrar.
> ....[signed by two wardens]

The issue of marriage registration and the status of West London was finally settled, not by reconciliation between the Board of Deputies and West London – their differences continued until the 1880s – but by government legislation in response to the growth of dissent within the Christian community in the first half of the nineteenth century.[40] The 1856 Marriage Act (Religious Opinions Relief Bill) authorised dissenting chapels and West London to register marriages. The Act also empowered West London to 'Certify Secretaries of other synagogues which would adopt the same ritual', provided the other synagogue had a membership of over 20 families. This gave West London the role of parent synagogue, one which in the years ahead it did not always appear to welcome. As it would need an Act of Parliament to amend that role West London is still responsible for authorising the marriage secretaries of newly established Reform congregations in Britain.[41]

When, in 1845, Nathan Marcus Adler was elected Chief Rabbi, even though his opposition to German Reform Judaism was well-known, the London Reformers hoped that he might be 'the man who would wipe out every remaining blot of strife and restore peace and harmony'. The new Chief Rabbi took office with the intention of bringing order and centralisation to early Victorian Anglo-Jewry. Sadly, Adler's response to the application by a member of the Orthodoxy for a licence to marry Jane Angel, the daughter of the keeper of the Reform Congregation's Balls Pond Road Burial Ground, demonstrated 'his intention not to walk in the path of toleration' and 'to give to the excommunication a force with which even its framers never sought to invest it'.[42] Jane Angel and her fiancé, Morris Hyman, had applied for permission to marry in an Orthodox metropolitan synagogue on 10 December 1845. There should have been no problems. But as the bride-to-be was the daughter of a Reformer this was not the case. The couple were called before Dr Adler who immediately reprimanded the groom for 'doing very wrong in becoming engaged to Jane Angel'. The couple were reminded that the Reform community was in *cherem* and unless Jane's father returned to the Orthodoxy, the Chief Rabbi could not perform the marriage ceremony. An alternative was offered. If Jane signed a paper, 'Promising never again to attend the West London synagogue and to conduct herself henceforth as a good Jewish woman', the minister of the Westminster Synagogue would be permitted to perform the ceremony. The young girl must have been disturbed by such a harsh attack on her father and herself. No doubt more in shock than sorrow she said that she had always believed herself to be a good Jewish woman and pleaded with the Chief Rabbi to meet her father. Adler refused. Jane was then given a prepared document for signature. It stated that she promised 'to conform to Orthodox laws and customs', and further, that she would 'never visit the Burton Street Synagogue again'. Hyman's behaviour left something to be desired. He threatened that if Jane did not sign he would call the wedding off and have nothing more to do with her. Jane signed and agreed to appear with Hyman the next day, before one of the *dayanim*, and attest to what she had signed. Once that was done, Adler's authorisation would be forthcoming.

Details of the events were relayed by Jane's father to Francis Goldsmid who, initially disbelieving, agreed to meet Jane straight away. Following the meeting he wrote to the Chief Rabbi asking for verification and requesting a copy of the document. The request was refused. A series of unsatisfactory exchanges followed. On 8 January 1846 Goldsmid wrote to Adler saying that, as the statements made by Jane Angel had not been contradicted, the members of West London could only assume them to have been 'substantially correct'. He added that the course adopted by the Chief Rabbi had done little to promote the desired union between the Reformers and the Orthodoxy. In spite of all that had gone before Jane married Hyman in the Orthodox synagogue.

The incident is a sad illustration of the intolerant and hardened attitude of the Orthodoxy towards an innocent caught up in the controversy over Reform. This harshness was further underlined by double standards. Before Adler's appointment four marriages had taken place, under Orthodox conditions, between a member of West London and a member of the Orthodox community[43] and, just months after Jane's cruel treatment, Nathan Marcus Adler personally solemnised the marriage of Reformer H.G. Henriques's sister to a member of the Great Synagogue, in the house of her brother.[44]

The Reformers' early relationship with London's Anglo-Jewish community was punctuated by sectarian differences. These might have been soothed had the organisation which was established to represent Anglo-Jewry as a whole taken an objective and unifying stance. The London Committee of Deputies of British Jews, as the Board of Deputies was named on its establishment in 1760, was an informal body which until 1836 had no written constitution. In that year a constitution was drawn up and 22 deputies were formally elected from the four main London synagogues. However, the increasing power of the industrial north could not be ignored and in 1838 the Jewish communities of Manchester and Liverpool were invited to elect representatives. The fact that those elected resided in London proved no barrier. What was unacceptable was the election of a deputy who was 'any member of a place of worship which shall not conform on religious matters to the ecclesiastical Authorities'[45] and while Sir Moses Montefiore remained President of the Board no relaxation of this ruling could be expected.

As assimilation and Anglicisation accelerated there were those, including David Salomons and Lionel de Rothschild, who questioned the archaic attitude towards the Reformers. By the mid-nineteenth century the Board was coming under fire for a variety of reasons: for its autocratic administration, for meetings held in camera, for its iniquitous elective system and for its restricted franchise.[46] In 1853 it was announced that, as a first step towards modernisation, the Board would hold open elections. For a while it seemed as though Reform might gain a foothold. As it was not possible for members of West London overtly to apply for election, four prospective candidates put themselves forward as would-be representatives of provincial communities. They were Elias Davis, who lived in Tavistock Square and was a member of both the Great Synagogue and West London; Jacob Levi Elkin (son of Benjamin), President of West London; Samuel Ellis, a resident of Euston Square and a member of West London since 1842; and David Jonassohn, a coal-mine owner from Sunderland who, though a member of the Israelite Congregation of Sunderland,[47] had joined West London in 1848 as a protest against the Chief Rabbi's unyielding and insensitive behaviour following the death of his friend Benjamin Elkin. The provincial communities that supported the four Reform candidates were Norwich, Portsmouth, Chatham and Sunderland. It is not clear whether the out-of-London synagogues supported their proposed deputies as a display of opposition to the power of the metropolitan Chief Rabbi or out of loyalty to individuals such as David Jonassohn who had been a member and benefactor of the Sunderland congregation for 40 years.

The events surrounding the election of the four Reform deputies, and their subsequent exclusion from the Board, have been covered in great detail by Israel Finestein,[48] so only a brief outline of the shameful proceedings will be provided here. The protagonists were, on one side, the exclusionists, Sir Moses Montefiore, his nephew Louis Cohen and Henry Harris, President of the Maiden Lane Synagogue, and on the other side, the elected Reform deputies. A state of tension had followed the election of the 'outsiders' and in an attempt to resolve the situation the Board held a series of meetings. On 18 August Louis Cohen put down a motion which defined the anti-Reformist position. It stipulated that 'if a member or seat holder does not conform to the ecclesiastical authorities then he is not eligible to be a Board member'. This stance was opposed by Baron de Rothschild, Anthony Rothschild and others,[49] and at an Extraordinary Meeting of the Board, extraordinary in more ways than one, the four newly elected members took their seats. Sir Moses Montefiore enraged at their presence asked the 'strangers' to withdraw. If they would not do so voluntarily he threatened to send for the police and have them forcibly ejected. This announcement resulted in uproar, Montefiore left the chair and the meeting.[50] Three of the newly elected members followed suit, the fourth, David Jonassohn, refused and, in an act reminiscent of David Salomons' removal from the House of Commons by the Serjeant-at-Arms, stayed put until he was touched on the shoulder and thus 'physically ejected'. The meeting ended in chaos.

Attempts were made to find a compromise. One suggestion put forward was that the Board operate two separate bodies, one secular and one religious. The Reformers were acceptable only to the former. Henry Harris opposed this, saying that the 'Board should only be composed of those professing Orthodox principles'.[51] The final vote on the issue of the Reform deputies was taken on 8 December 1853. The liberal wing of the Board, supported by the provincial communities which took a non-conformist approach to the problems of Orthodoxy, faced Henry Harris and Louis Cohen, the latter adopting a Shakespearian tone, stating that 'I will eat, drink and trade with them [the Reformers] but take no part with them in any religious ceremony'.[52] There was an echo of the excommunication of 1840 – which had operated on a religious but not a social level. When the votes were finally cast there were 23 for admission of the Reformers and 23 against. Sir Moses Montefiore was left holding the casting vote. Reluctant to make the final decision, he turned to Sir Frederick Thesiger, later to become Lord Chancellor, for advice. Thesiger found that as the Reformers were not qualified to act as *yehidim* and were not members of Orthodox synagogues, under the terms of the Board's constitution, they were ineligible for the position of deputies. As a result of the dispute a number of provincial communities withdrew their representatives from the Board, while others reduced their representative number. The episode did little to enhance the reputation of the Board, which appeared increasingly to be out of touch with the realities of a modern industrialised society.

The differences between the West London Synagogue of British Jews and the Board of Deputies were not settled until 1886. After the retirement of Sir Moses Montefiore in March 1874, the Board, finally free to admit Reformers, amended its constitution and invited West London to send two delegates.[53] West London refused, explaining that certain clauses in the Board's revised constitution were inconsistent with the principles of a Reform congregation. The specific clauses referred to were numbers 1, 6 and 24. These required that: under Clause 1, synagogues were to be certified by ecclesiastical authorities, namely the Chief Rabbi and the leader of the Sephardi community; under Clause 6, the guidance of the Board on religious matters was to remain as heretofore; and under Clause 24, a certificate of the Board of Deputies confirming that the applicant constituted a Jewish synagogue had to be presented.[54] In other words the Reformers were required to conform to Orthodox practice. Impasse yet again. In an article published in the *Jewish Chronicle* in March 1874 Julian Goldsmid defended his synagogue's refusal to send delegates to the Board. He explained that had West London done so the Board's authority 'would have been tacitly accepted'.[55]

The issue was then shelved until 1883, when the invitation was renewed. West London responded by saying that there had been no change in the Board's constitution since the discussions of 1874. However, attitudes had changed and a committee was set up to consider amending the Board's constitution. The result was the following clause: 'Nothing in this clause shall abridge or affect the individual right or actions to its own internal affairs of any congregation whose security is certified under the provisions of the Act 19 and 20 Vic. c. 119.'[56] It was a victory for the Reformers, who elected Sir Julian Goldsmid MP and Sir Philip Magnus as their deputies. In its annual report a seemingly relieved Board of Deputies reported this as a 'A gratifying circumstance'. [57]

After such a long battle, how worthy was victory? True, there was an element of communal prestige, but the significance and impact was measurably reduced as a result of the setting-up, 12 years earlier, of the Anglo-Jewish Association (AJA). This provided Reform Jews in London and the provinces with a secular communal platform. The defeat of the French by the Prussians in 1871 had left the Paris-based Alliance Universelle Israëlite in chaos and the Association was established in London with the intention of continuing the work of the Alliance. The Anglo-Jewish Association's published objective was to 'raise the status of the Jew and enable Jews in England to interact with their co-religionists overseas so that they were no longer wrapped up in insular self-sufficiency'.[58] The inaugural meeting of the AJA 'combined ministers of nearly every congregation in London', including all three from the West London Synagogue of British Jews as well as Francis Goldsmid, Serjeant John Simon, Elias Davis, F.D. Mocatta and Ellis Franklin. However it would be wrong to assume that the Association was a Reform stronghold. Membership was almost equally divided between the Orthodoxy and the Reformers. Jacob Waley, a founder of the United Synagogue, was elected founder president, Francis Goldsmid, vice-president and Albert Lowy secretary. Though the Association's *raison d'être* was the promotion of understanding and support for Jews overseas, there is no doubt that dissatisfaction with the lukewarm and rigid attitude of the Board which, according to Dr Benish, was 'tied down by red tape', prompted the search for an alternative.[59] Seven years later, in 1878, the Conjoint Foreign Committee, an amalgamation of the AJA and Board of Deputies, was created to act as Anglo-Jewry's foreign policy arm. The necessity for, and attraction of, Board membership was subsequently diminished.

While communal and national issues such as emancipation and the ongoing dispute with the Board of Deputies continued in the broader arena, congregational matters demanded attention. The issuing of the Bull of Excommunication (*cherem*) initially restricted the Founders' charitable activities. The ethos of Victorian philanthropy was the provision of help for the deserving poor and immediate approval was given to a continuation of this practice under the auspices of the West London Synagogue of British Jews. The sum of £375 was collected in the Poor Box on the day of the consecration of the Burton Street Synagogue.[60] The Council of Founders agreed that regular donations be sent to Jewish communal organisations and to individual applicants in London, the provinces and overseas. Paralleling the activities of Lady Rothschild who, in the 1840s, was involved with the foundation of a number of Jewish ladies' philanthropic societies, Miriam Mocatta established a committee of Reform ladies to distribute relief among the poor. In true mid-Victorian tradition the undeserving poor were treated less charitably. West London asked for a police presence outside the synagogue on the Sabbath so that its members would not be pestered by beggars. The local constabulary was requested to provide the same constable each week in order that the more important worshippers could be respectfully recognised!

Music played an important part in Reform ritual. Thought and time were expended on the constitution of the all-male choir and the choice of music to be played at the consecration of Burton Street.[61] For 16 years the choir remained a male preserve. The inclusion of female voices was consistently opposed. The arrival of the female voice coincided with the installation of an organ in the Margaret Street Synagogue, the successor to the Burton Street Synagogue. In 1858, in order to 'increase the impressiveness of the service' it was decided to install an organ,[62] a decision in keeping with the general 'movement for better music' manifest in non-conformist and Church of England churches throughout mid-Victorian Britain. It was also an innovation totally at odds with Orthodox practice which would not tolerate instrumental music in the synagogue on the Sabbath or Holy Days. This dogmatic view was later to have an important bearing on the choice of a successor to David Woolf Marks at the end of the century.[63] West London's decision to incorporate organ music in the service demonstrates the more powerful influence of Anglican Protestant non-conformity as opposed to German Reform Judaism where organ music had been incorporated in the services in Seesen and Hamburg in the second decade of the nineteenth century. Not all houses of worship could afford the luxury of organ and organist. Some churches were forced to settle for a barrel organ instead.[64] But the affluent membership of West London could well afford to purchase a 'superior instrument' such as the one installed in 1858 which cost £750 and remained in place until the congregation moved to Upper Berkeley Street in 1870.

It was because of the youthful nature of the choir that the Reformers' attention was drawn to the inadequacy of secular education among the children of the poor. Until 1870, and the passing of the Education Act, primary school education for the poor was in the hands of voluntary organisations, the church and Lord Shaftesbury's Ragged Schools. It is not surprising that West London's young choristers, and children from other, Orthodox, synagogues, were deficient in the matter of education. Influenced by the example of the church and the more Orthodox Jews' Free School, founded in the East End in 1817 (a Westminster Jews' Free School was established in 1820), the Reform synagogue opened the West London Metropolitan School in 1845 with an initial intake of 61 boys. The school's prospectus highlights extant communal divisions, and West London's tolerance, as it stated clearly that pupils would be admitted 'without reference to locality or to the particular synagogue of which their parents may be members'.[65] This broad-based approach attracted the support of David Salomons – a more liberal-minded traditionalist member of the Cousinhood – and may well have furthered the Reformers' cause in his eyes. Few children entering the school could read or write but within a short while they learnt basic grammar and arithmetic. In 1846 a school for girls was opened. It is perhaps significant that in that same year, clearly concerned by the Reformers' move, the Chief Rabbi encouraged the opening of a

A Meeting was held at the
Bedford Hotel Southampton
Row on the 15th of April 1840
(A.M 5600) In pursuance of
the following declaration.

"We the Undersigned, regarding
Public Worship as highly conducive
to the interests of Religion, consider
it a matter of deep regret that it
is not more frequently attended
by the Members of our Religious
Persuasion. We are perfectly sure
that this circumstance is not
owing to any want of a general
conviction of the fundamental
Truths of our Religion, but we
ascribe it to the distance of the
existing Synagogues from the
places of our residence; to the
length and imperfections of the
Order of Service; to the inconvenien

1 The Declaration of 1840 *(courtesy The London Museum of Jewish Life)*

& hours at which it is appointed; to the unimpressive manner in which it is performed, and to the absence of religious Instruction in our Synagogues. To these evils, we think that a remedy may be applied by the establishment of a Synagogue in the Western part of the metropolis, where a revised Service may be performed at hours more suited to our habits, and in a manner more calculated to inspire feelings of devotion, where Religious instruction may be afforded by competent persons, and where to effect these purposes, Jews generally may form an United Congregation under the denomination of British Jews.

Anxious for the accomplishment of these objects, it is our wish that a meeting may be called for the purpose of considering the best means of carrying them into effect."

Horatio J Montefiore
Aaron Asher Goldsmid
Abm Mocatta
Jacob Montefiore
M Mocatta
David Mocatta
Benjamin Mocatta
Albert Cohen
Francis H Goldsmid
Frederick D Goldsmid
Montague Levyson
H $ De Castro
Daniel Mocatta
Abm Lindo Mocatta
J G Henriques
A Mocatta
E Mocatta Jr
David Q Henriques
J Q Henriques
H A Melhado

Solomon Lazarus
Isaac Mocatta
M Montefiore Junr.
Joseph D'Aguilar Samuda

At the above mentioned meeting held on the 15th of April 1840 (AM 5600) Present — Messrs. Daniel Mocatta Aaron Mocatta, Moses Mocatta, Aaron A Goldsmid, Abraham Mocatta Jr, David Mocatta, Jacob Montefiore, Horatio Montefiore, Frederick D Goldsmid, Montague Levyson, Emanuel Mocatta, Benjamin Mocatta, Abraham Lindo Mocatta, Abraham Mocatta, Joseph G. Henriques, Joseph D'Aguilar Samuda, Isaac Mocatta, Solomon Lazarus, and Francis H Goldsmid.

Mr. Daniel Mocatta having been appointed Chairman; and Mr. Francis H. Goldsmid Honorary Secretary;

It was resolved,

1st That it is expedient to establish a Synagogue in the Western part of the Metropolis, and that it be established under the denomination of "Synagogue of British Jews"

2ndly That a revised Service be there performed in the Hebrew Language, in conformity with the principles of the Jewish Religion, and in the manner which may appear best calculated to excite feelings of devotion.

3rdly That religious Discourses be periodically delivered in the Synagogue in the English Language.

4thly That a subscription be forthwith entered into in order to carry these objects into effect.

The following subscriptions

2 Jacob Henriques (above left), Horatio Montefiore (above right), Abraham Mocatta (centre), F.D. Mocatta (bottom left) and David Mocatta (bottom right) *(courtesy The London Museum of Jewish Life)*

3 Francis Goldsmid

4 The interior of Upper Berkeley Street

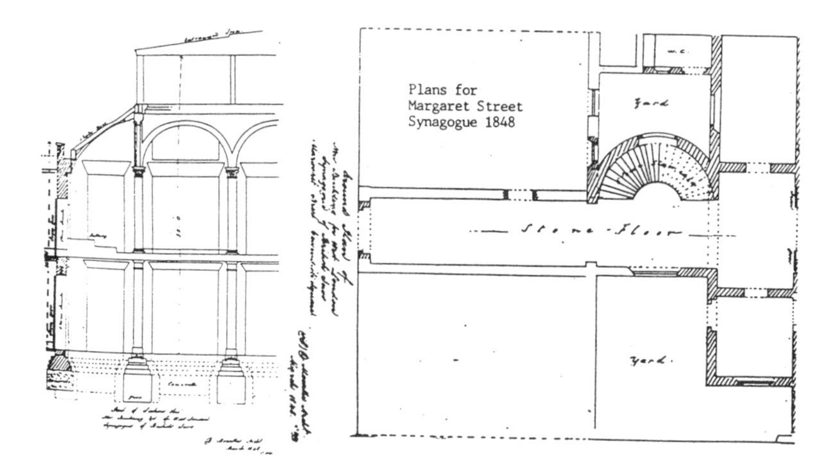

5 The plans for the Margaret Street Synagogue *(courtesy The London Museum of Jewish Life)*

6 The exterior of Manchester's first Reform Synagogue in Park Place

7 The interior of the Bradford Reform Synagogue *(courtesy The London Museum of Jewish Life)*

West End girls' school under the auspices of the Orthodoxy.[66] In 1854 sufficient funds became available for the Reformers to purchase a site in Red Lion Square which could accommodate both boys and girls under one roof. The school's history is told by its changing name. In 1870 it became the Jewish Middle Class School. Support gradually dwindled as the effects of both the Education Acts of 1870, 1880 and 1891 and the availability of boys' public schools such as University College, Hampstead, took their toll on the number and gender of pupils. In 1897, by this time known simply as the Jewish High School for Girls, the school was closed down.

It is quite clear that in those early years the Council of Founders was kept busy laying foundations for the future. But those foundations had to be real as well as abstract. The Burton Street Chapel had satisfied the earliest needs but it was generally agreed that a 'permanent synagogue' was desirable.[67] A fund was set up to raise sufficient money for the purchase of a plot of land and the construction of a synagogue building. When the decision was taken in 1846 the anticipated cost was £5,000. The completion of a custom-built Reform synagogue did not take place in London until 1870 – in Manchester it happened 12 years earlier. However, Burton Street had become too small and a move had to be made, even if on a temporary basis. The Council of Founders determined the boundaries within which their second synagogue should be located. The area chosen clearly delineates upward social mobility, the parameters being: 'Oxford Street to the south, Portland Place to the west, Tottenham Court Road to the east and the south side of Fitzroy Square to form the north boundary'. The eventual choice was 50 Margaret Street where a new synagogue, which would seat 250 men and 150 women, was fashioned out of the existing building, to a design, by David Mocatta, which reflected 'the Oriental origin of the people for whose peculiar religious observances it has been set apart'.[68] The cost was £5,500.

The Margaret Street Synagogue was consecrated on 25 June 1849. This time the *Jewish Chronicle* was represented though the report which appeared was not without criticism. This was directed at the absence of congregational participation and at Reverend Marks's sermon which had referred to the differences still extant between the Orthodoxy and Reform. The major issue remained the Denial of the Oral Law. The *Chronicle* considered Marks's words 'not befitting a consecration ceremony'.[69] All the newspapers, Anglo-Jewish and national, were unanimous in their praise for the 'elegance of the synagogue fittings, the decorum that prevailed throughout the service, in a synagogue which achieved harmony of proportion and colour and good acoustics'. If we cast our minds back to the original Declaration of 1840 it would seem that the Reformers had made considerable progress towards achieving their ambitions.

For the next 21 years Margaret Street was the focal point of Reform Judaism in England. One of the Founders' earliest aims had been to 'have a view of current affairs and to operate as a synagogue of British Jews'. The Marriage Act of 1856 had ensured that subsequent Reform congregations would have to be approved by West London in order to perform legally acceptable marriages. This and the erudition and status of David Woolf Marks made it the natural point of reference for religious issues which required a congregational statement or response. David Woolf Marks was at the height of his career and was respected far beyond the Anglo-Jewish community. In 1855 he was appointed to the Chair of Professor of Hebrew at University College London, a post he held until 1898. His reputation as a preacher was renowned and grew as he travelled and lectured throughout the country. The two major Jewish abduction cases, which took place in the 1850s and 1860s, one in Italy and one in Wales, both elicited a 'Reform' spiritual viewpoint. In 1858 a seven-year-old Jewish boy, Edgar Mortara, was abducted from the home of his parents in Bologna, Italy, 'under the pretext of his having been secretly baptised' by his nurse when he was one year old. He was kept in the care of the Catholic Church in a convent in Rome while the fight for his return was carried out on the international stage. In spite of the personal intervention of Sir Moses Montefiore it took some years before the situation was resolved. The second case involved one Esther Lyons, an 18-year-old Jewess who, in 1868, ran away from her parental home in Wales and spent a night in the home of a Baptist minister. Esther's father accused, and subsequently sued, the minister, Mr Thomas, for abduction. The case, which continued for almost two years, was finally closed in 1870, having gone to the Court of Appeal where the defendants were found innocent. In both instances, as the theological voice of Reform Judaism, David Woolf Marks upheld the view of the Orthodoxy. Following the Lyons case, Dr Adler could not help but acknowledge 'the graceful manner in which the head of the West

London Synagogue of British Jews supported the cause of traditional Judaism in a recent judicial ordeal'.[70]

The Senior Minister of West London was also called upon as a prime witness in a case brought against the Chief Rabbi by a *shochet* [overseer of *kashrut*] whose overseas licence Adler refused to acknowledge. The Reform minister had earlier been noted as attaching little or no importance to the issue of *kosher* meat and thus was not expected to attest in favour of the Chief Rabbi. In the event, David Woolf Marks came down on the side of Orthodoxy and tradition and supported Dr Adler. This surprised everyone, including the journalist from *The Times* who had reported the case as it was considered of 'considerable importance to the Jewish population'.[71] It was no doubt due to the conservative attitude adopted by Marks over certain tendentious issues that the divide between Orthodoxy and Reform was gradually narrowing.

During the 1850s and 1860s as the wealthier members of Anglo-Jewry moved westward to Mayfair, a middle-class Jewish suburb was developing slightly further west in Maida Vale. As a consequence the membership of West London expanded. But though this was reflected in good attendance on Saturday mornings other services were suffering a distinct reduction in numbers. The religious census of 1851, which only included Orthodox synagogues, confirmed that Jewish synagogue attendance was poor, only 24 per cent of the Jewish population of London was recorded as having attended services, as compared to the Church of England which registered at 33 per cent and the Catholic Church which was registered at 34 per cent.[72] In fact it was said of the Christian church that there were 'a large number of professors whose only outward sign of religious character is an attendance at the Sunday morning service... week evening services have almost passed into disuse'.[73] By 1865 attendance at West London had deteriorated to a level at which the discontinuation of the minor evening services came under discussion. Two years later a number of those services, including *Shabbat minchah*, were suspended.[74] In spite of this, in 1865, David Mocatta and Jacob Elkin were instructed to 'Look for a new site'. The Margaret Street lease was due to expire and it was decided to build the 'ultimate synagogue'. A site in Upper Berkeley Street, closer to Mayfair than ever, was chosen and plans were drawn up for the construction of a synagogue which would accommodate almost

1,000 souls in the 'most impressive surroundings'. The cost of building and fitting out the new synagogue was estimated at approximately £30,000, a sum far in excess of the anticipated £5,000 of 1846 and the cause of some unease, as evidenced by the response to a suggestion made by some of the more traditionalist members of the council that work be suspended during the Sabbath and the festivals. The possibility of an extra 10–15 per cent on building costs resulted in the majority agreeing to the suggested Saturday building programme.[75]

The consecration of Upper Berkeley Street took place on 23 September 1870. Three months earlier, in a private ceremony, the memorial stone was laid. Within a cavity was placed 'a glass bottle containing newly minted coins, the latest edition of *The Times*, *Jewish Chronicle*, *Jewish Record*, a fragment of the ancient walls of the temple and a commemorative parchment'.[76] The consecration service could have been the occasion for a public reconciliation between the Orthodox and the Reform. The *Jewish Chronicle* even went so far as to suggest that the Chief Rabbi should officiate. The council of the West London Synagogue sent invitations to the ministers and wardens of all the London synagogues. By that time the independent Ashkenazi synagogues had been drawn together under an Act of Parliament into the United Synagogue, which had an elected governing body and 'a' as opposed to 'the' Chief Rabbi.[77] In his report on the constitution of the new union Lionel Louis Cohen stated his belief that its establishment would 'increase the harmony and stability of the whole community'.[78] Even with such a well-structured and legally established body the ecclesiastical leaders of the Orthodoxy, the Chief Rabbi and the *Haham*, refused the invitation to the consecration, lacking the confidence – or desire – to thus sanction the West London Synagogue of British Jews. Admittedly Adler and Marks now acknowledged one another and exchanged pleasantries in a social setting but crossing the religious threshold of Reform was something that did not happen until the next century when Nathan Adler's son Hermann, as the incumbent Chief Rabbi, attended memorial services for F. D. Mocatta in 1905 and David Woolf Marks in 1909. On receipt of his invitation to the consecration Sir Moses Montefiore expressed a wish to see 'unity happily restored before the day of the consecration'[79] though quite how is not made clear. Once again, as so often before, Montefiore was saved from having to make an overt pronouncement of his views, as he was drawn overseas, this time on behalf of the Jews of Damascus.

The members of the Orthodox community turned out in full force for the consecration of the new Reform synagogue which was described as a 'magnificent monument of architectural ability and artistic taste'. The design of the synagogue reflected the popular Moorish style. Its portal, elaborately triple arched, led to a prayer hall which was 70 feet square. A central feature was the Ark which had open grille work, thus ensuring that the scrolls were visible throughout the service. Located directly behind the Ark was the organ which, in 1870, cost £1,000 to build. There was a centrally positioned reading desk reflecting the importance placed upon the sermon. In later years this, together with the Ark and the *bimah*, was moved to the east to provide further seating. The intricately patterned ceiling – damaged in the Second World War – was enhanced by the ornate window in the dome. The new synagogue building was, justifiably, favourably compared to Margaret Street which had been likened to a 'private residence'.[80]

The consecration service was performed by the Reverends Marks, Lowy and Magnus. Marks used the occasion to compare the state of Jewish observance at the beginning of the 1840s with that of 1870. He noted the improvement in devotion and numbers, emphasising the large attendance enjoyed by the synagogue, the reference being to Sabbath not weekday attendance! Even the Orthodox synagogues had problems in providing the *minyan* required for weekday services and at times had to hire '*minyan* men' as the services were normally attended only by mourners saying prayers for the departed.

What then characterised the first thirty years of a synagogue whose membership remained largely that of the intellectual and mercantile élite of Anglo-Jewry? Even in the late 1860s there were few German names to be found among the members. The West London Synagogue of British Jews does not appear to have attracted many Jews who left central Europe in the 1850s and 1860s. If those refugees and immigrants retained any religiosity, in the main they turned to the Anglo-Jewish Orthodoxy. A small minority, eschewing Judaism but not religion, converted to Christianity through the Unitarian Church.

The removal of Jewish disabilities was achieved in 1858 – legally and all embracingly in 1866[81] – but credit was due to the liberal Orthodoxy not to the Reformers who, at least as a co-ordinated group, appear to have dropped out of the battle by the 1850s.

During its first three decades the West London Founders made no radical alterations to their liturgy or ritual. Changes that were proposed, such as the emendation of Volume 4 of the Prayer Book in 1865, were decided by the laity and subsequently put to the ministers. The West London Synagogue of British Jews was run by its Council of Founders and their committees, not by the clergy. The ministers had to refer to the governing laity on nearly all synagogue matters, taking instructions as to when and where to preach.

There was little evidence of the influence of central European Reform Judaism. The German synods of the mid-1840s were handicapped by the revolutions of 1848 and were followed by little collective action. Jews in Germany, on the threshold of emancipation, no longer saw religion as a political issue. The result was a decline in religious activity.[82] During the 1860s there was a revitalisation and Ludwig Philippson called for a new synod. After a preliminary meeting in Cassel in 1868 a larger conference was called the following year in Leipzig. Eighty-three scholars and rabbis from Germany and overseas attended. But though Gustav Gottheil, the German-born Manchester Reform rabbi was present, there are no records of the attendance of any of the London Reform clergy nor any reference to the event in the archives of the West London Synagogue. It chose to maintain its independence and conservatism.

This chapter begins with the consecration of the Burton Street Chapel, Britain's first Reform synagogue. It closes with the consecration of the 'Ultimate Synagogue' in Upper Berkeley Street. The intervening years set the pattern for a century to come. But though West London appears to have played the major role, the history of the birth and development, during the second half of the nineteenth century, of the two provincial communities, Manchester and Bradford, and the failure of certain others to achieve recognition, or to become firmly established, is central to an understanding of the development and growth of Reform Judaism in Britain in the twentieth century. As the next chapter illustrates, the lay leadership of the West London Synagogue maintained an élitist stance, reluctant to become involved in the formation and development of nascent Reform congregations and unwilling to be responsible for the creation of others. As a result those congregations that did emerge in the nineteenth century followed an autonomous route. Had this not been so, had West

London become more closely involved in the form and direction of provincial and suburban Reform Judaism in those early years, then the structure of the Reform synagogues of Great Britain and the part played by its constituent members might well have been very different.

NOTES

1. *Jewish Chronicle*, 22 May 1896.
2. At the end of the nineteenth century Charles Booth produced a 'map of poverty' which showed at a glance levels of poverty in the capital in gradations of colour ranging from black for the poorest and 'vicious' members of society through to gold for the upper classes and most affluent. See A.J. Kershen, 'Henry Mayhew and Charles Booth, Men of Their Time', in G. Alderman and C. Holmes (eds), *Outsiders and Outcasts* (1993), Ch. VI.
3. Minute Book of the West London Synagogue of British Jews, 27 Jan. 1842.
4. D.W. Marks, *Sermons* (1851), pp. 20–l.
5. That is, at 10.30 a.m. as opposed to the Orthodox tradition which was to begin at 9 a.m. or 9.30 a.m.
6. Minute Book of the West London Synagogue of British Jews, Vol. 2, 21 Jan. 1910.
7. Minute Book of the West London Synagogue of British Jews, Vol. 2, 13 Feb. 1910.
8. R. Gottheil, *The Life of Gustav Gottheil* (1936), p. 17.
9. W. Gunther Plaut, *The Rise of Reform Judaism* (1963), p. 110.
10. *Jewish Chronicle*, 4 Feb. 1842.
11. D. Cesarani, *The Jewish Chronicle and Anglo-Jewry 1841–1991* (1994), pp. 8–9.
12. See below.
13. D. Feldman, *Englishmen and Jews* (1994), p. 54.
14. T. Endelman, *Radical Assimilation in Anglo-Jewish History* (1990), Ch. 5, pp. 144–71.
15. *The Times*, l Feb. 1842.
16. C. Cassell, 'The First Nine Years of the West London Synagogue of British Jews' (unpublished manuscript, undated), pp. 203–17.
17. Wise was born in Bohemia in 1819; he studied in a *Yeshivah* near Prague but it is doubtful if he received *semichah*. In 1846 he arrived in New York. According to Michael Meyer, 'It was Wise who, more than anyone else, succeeded in stimulating, unifying and giving direction to American Reform'. See M. Meyer, *Response to Modernity* (1988), pp. 238–44.
18. See below for the training of ministers for Reform synagogues.
19. *Jewish Chronicle*, 9 Feb. 1866.
20. *Jewish Chronicle*, 7 Dec. 1865.
21. Membership Book, West London Synagogue of British Jews, 1842–1849, Archives of the West London Synagogue.
22. *Jewish Chronicle*, 5 June 1908.
23. Minute Book of the West London Synagogue of British Jews, Vol. 2, 19 June 1861.
24. G. Kitson Clark, *The Making of Victorian England* (1962), p. 170.
25. For the processes which made university graduation and fellowships open to Jews see G. Alderman, *Modern British Jewry* (1992), p. 24n.
26. Minute Book of the West London Synagogue of British Jews, 8 Feb. 1852.
27. See below, Chapter 3.
28. Minute Book of the West London Synagogue of British Jews, 19 Sept. 1861.
29. Minute Book of the West London Synagogue of British Jews, 8 Feb. 1880.
30. Minute Book of the West London Synagogue of British Jews, 23 March 1841.

31. Minute Book of West London Synagogue of British Jews, 23 March 1842. In 1897 land for a burial ground was purchased in Golders Green, north London, and in 1968 in Edgware, Middlesex.
32. C. Cassell, unpublished biography of David Woolf Marks, pp. 31–2.
33. H. Henriques, *Jewish Marriage and the English Law* (1909), p. 27.
34. In accordance with the constitution of the Board of Deputies the Chief Rabbi and the *Haham* of the Spanish and Portuguese congregation are the Board's ecclesiastical authorities.
35. Minute Book of the Board of Deputies of British Jews, 7 Feb. 1842.
36. L. Loewe (ed.), *Diaries of Sir Moses and Lady Montefiore* (1983), Vol. l, pp. 301–2.
37. Cassell, unpublished history of West London, op. cit., p. 130.
38. I. Finestein, 'An Aspect of the Jews and English Marriage Law during the Emancipation', *Transactions of the Jewish Historical Society*, Vol. III, No. l, 1965, pp. 3–22.
39. Minute Book of the Board of Deputies of British Jews, 22 Feb. 1842.
40. See Kitson Clark, op. cit., p. 187.
41. In the case of new Reform synagogues it has become customary for the President of the West London Synagogue only to exercise his authority in consultation with the Chairman of the West London Synagogue of British Jews.
42. *The Appeal of the Congregation of the West London Synagogue of British Jews to their Brother Israelites throughout the United Kingdom* (1846), p. 10.
43. Letter Boxes of the West London Synagogue of British Jews, 1841–64, Archives of the West London Synagogue of British Jews.
44. *Jewish Chronicle*, 21 Aug. 1846.
45. Minute Book of the Board of Deputies of British Jews, 5 May 1841.
46. I. Finestein, 'The Anglo-Jewish Revolt of 1853', *Jewish Quarterly* (Winter 1978), p. 106.
47. For the history of the Sunderland Jewish community, see A. Levy, *History of the Sunderland Jewish Community 1755–1955* (London, 1956). For further details of David Jonassohn see ibid., pp. 42–51.
48. See Finestein, 'Anglo-Jewish Revolt of 1853', op. cit.
49. *Jewish Chronicle*, 26 Aug. 1853.
50. *Jewish Chronicle*, 31 Aug. 1853.
51. *Jewish Chronicle*, 8 Sept. 1853.
52. *Jewish Chronicle*, 16 Dec. 1853.
53. Minute Book of the West London Synagogue of British Jews, l March 1873.
54. Minute Book of the Board of Deputies of British Jews, 6 March 1874.
55. *Jewish Chronicle*, 13 March 1874.
56. The 1856 Marriage Act, Vic. c. 119.
57. Annual Report of the Board of Deputies of British Jews 1887, p. 12.
58. *Jewish Chronicle*, 7 July 1871.
59. Ibid.
60. Minute Book of the West London Synagogue of British Jews, 31 Jan. 1842.
61. Minute Book of the West London Synagogue of British Jews, 19 Dec. 1841.
62. Minute Book of the West London Synagogue of British Jews, 24 Nov. 1858.
63. See below.
64. D. Chadwick, *The Victorian Church*, Vol. I (1966), p. 519.
65. *Voice of Jacob*, 11 April 1845.
66. In 1853 the school became jointly one for boys and girls. The authors are grateful to Dr Gerry Black for the information on the Westminster Jews' Free School.
67. Minute Book of the West London Synagogue of British Jews, 26 May 1846.
68. The report of the consecration of the Margaret Street Synagogue, which appeared in *The Times* of 26 June 1849, goes on to describe the 'graceful and airy' design, the elegant women's gallery and the harmonium and reading desk at one end next to the door and the 'altar, ark and pulpit at the other extremity...highly embellished'.
69. *Jewish Chronicle*, 29 June 1849.
70. *Jewish Chronicle*, 1 July 1870. For details of the Lyons case in Cardiff see U. Henriques, 'Lyons versus Thomas: the Jewish Abduction Case', *Transactions of the*

Jewish Historical Society of England, Vol. XXIX (1982–86), pp. 287–321, and for the Mortara case see Loewe (ed.), op. cit., Vol. II, pp. 82–99 and 127.

71. *The Times*, 15 Dec. 1868.
72. *1851 Religious Census*, pp. 1852–53, Vol. LXXXIX.
73. Chadwick, op. cit., p. 538.
74. Minute Book of the West London Synagogue of British Jews, 26 March 1865 and 24 Dec. 1867.
75. Minute Book of the Building Committee of the West London Synagogue of British Jews, 17 Jan. 1866.
76. *Jewish Chronicle*, 23 June 1870.
77. The private Act of Parliament which created the United Synagogue was passed in 1870 and united the Ashkenazi metropolitan synagogues. It was as a result of the suggestion of the Home Secretary that references to 'a Chief Rabbi' were substituted for the original 'the Chief Rabbi' as it was felt that it was not within the realm of the State to bestow such a singular title – and power – on a representative of an independent religious body. For the history of the United Synagogue, see A. Newman, *The United Synagogue 1870–1970* (1977) and G. Alderman, *Modern British Jewry* (1992), pp. 85–9.
78. Newman, op. cit., p. 4.
79. Loewe (ed.), op. cit., p. 232.
80. *Jewish Chronicle*, 23 Sept. 1870.
81. Lionel de Rothschild was able to take his seat in Parliament in 1858 as a result of a special resolution passed in the House of Commons. The Parliamentary Oaths Act of 1866 introduced a new oath which subsequently enabled any elected Jewish member to take up a seat in the House.
82. Meyer, op. cit., pp. 185–91.

3 Beyond the Capital, 1856–1914

The origins of the West London Synagogue of British Jews, Britain's first Reform synagogue, lay in the desire of its founders to practise Judaism in a decorous manner which would reflect both the fundamental truths of religion and the needs of modernity. The London founders hailed from a common socio-economic background. They were wealthy, well-educated, cultured and Anglicised, interacting socially and commercially with non-Jews from similar backgrounds. They lived and worked in a metropolis which was at the centre of the Empire, at the heart of government, finance, the court and the Anglican church. It was a different environment to that of their co-religionists in the major provincial cities where industrial expansion and religious non-conformity were the order of the day, the former creating, and the latter attracting, many of the leading citizens of Manchester, Bradford and Leeds. In 'Cottonopolis' – among the 'dark satanic Mills' – in 'Worstedopolis' and in the commercial centre of the West Riding, Reform Judaism emerged between 1850 and 1880. As we shall see, not all attempts to establish Reform communities succeeded. This chapter looks at the origins and development of provincial, and in one instance suburban, Reform Judaism in nineteenth-century Britain, the reasons behind its successes and failures and the reaction of the Berkeleystreeters to the new arrivals.

Manchester

The beginnings of Reform Judaism in Manchester lay in the drawing together of a diversity of threads that ran through the second-largest provincial Jewish community of the nineteenth century, Liverpool being the largest. These were the emergence of a Manchester Jewish bourgeoisie in the 1820s and 1830s, the arrival of German Jewish textile merchants after 1834, the intellectual and theological influence of an immigrant scholar and, finally, the controversial role of Dr Schiller-Szinessy, Manchester Jewry's 'local rabbi' in the early 1850s.[1]

Parallel with Manchester's industrial expansion during the late eighteenth century was the growth of its Jewish community of Ashkenazi pedlars, tailors, old clothes dealers and storekeepers.[2] In the early nineteenth century they were joined by a sprinkling of German merchants, drawn by the city's steady industrial growth. The most famous immigrant arrival was Nathan Myer Rothschild who ran an office in the city from 1800 to 1810, after which time he departed for London.[3] By 1825 Manchester's Jewish community was a 'large and respectable body of well-to-do shopkeepers, export merchants and professional men, an integral part of the Manchester bourgeoisie' who in 1825 constructed a 'neat new synagogue' in Halliwell Street which became known as the Manchester Old Congregation.[4]

The 'old' congregation contained a number of affluent and Anglicised Jewish members who, in common with their counterparts in London, were engaged in the broader issues of mid-nineteenth-century city life, interacting on a communal and social basis with their Gentile neighbours. As increasing numbers of impoverished and poorly educated eastern Europeans settled in the city, the established Jewish community, concerned by the image their poorer co-religionists were projecting, laid the foundations for secular and religious education – an attitude very much in keeping with mid-Victorian *laissez-faire* philosophy which identified education and self-help as the solution to the problems of urban overcrowding and poverty. The established Jews were anxious that the foreigners become Anglicised, acceptable citizens, to be kept within the religious fold and out of the grasp of missionaries. At the secular level, the emancipation issue was uppermost. In 1834 a communal petition was presented to Parliament.[5] Unlike London's Jewish community which, as we have seen, made separate representations to government, the Manchester Jewish community, at that time, spoke with one voice.

Between 1834 and 1843, as the city's industrial status grew, there was an influx of German Jewish textile merchants. Among their number were men who would play major roles in the foundations of Manchester Reform Judaism. Twenty-nine of the 44 founder members of the Manchester Congregation of British Jews were German born, 16 originating from urban centres which included Hamburg and Berlin.[6] Amongst those arrivals were

Cologne-born David Hesse, a rabbi's son and a man destined to play a major part in the Orthodox, and subsequently Reform, communities,[7] the brothers Micholls and John Isaac. The historian of Manchester Jewry, Bill Williams, suggests that it was the social and national solidarity expressed by the German expatriates that acted as the catalyst for unity in the quest for a Jewish Reform congregation. Was it perhaps seen as another German-Jewish society?

The man who, together with Hesse, propelled the Manchester Reform idea into reality, settled in the city in the late 1820s. It was Tobias Theodores (1808–1886) who provided the ideological leadership that drew forth a following in the early 1850s. Professor Theodores, originally named Theodores Tobias,[8] was a language teacher and linguist who, from 1851, taught at Owens College which later became Manchester University. He came to general notice in 1841 when *The Times* published his letter denouncing the Damascus Blood Accusation. The *Voice of Jacob* provided Theodores with a regular journalistic vehicle through which to express his radical opinions. In 1842 he nailed his Reform flag to the mast when he produced his pamphlet in support of the Denial of the Oral Law. Though a member of the Halliwell Street Synagogue, Theodores was by this time gravitating towards Reform. In the early 1840s, as demands for improved decorum grew, he advocated pulpit instruction as a means of revitalising Judaism. However, British Reform Judaism does not appear to have satisfied the intellectual Theodores as, in later years, he was outspokenly frustrated by the conservatism of Manchester Reform Jewry and highly critical of the senior minister of British Reform, David Woolf Marks. In his diary Theodores records having received requests for 'a revision of the ritual' (which followed that of West London) in Park Place.[9] He reflected, 'But what is to be expected of the ecclesiastical authorities [West London]?' and then launched into a critique of David Woolf Marks whom he called 'Our Vatican [Pope] in Berkeley', 'who slumbers in Holy Peace, happy about the healthy state of the finances and believing in the goodness of the Almighty'.[10] According to Theodores, David Woolf Marks was not prepared to 'progress' any further. He thus concluded, as did Zangwill a decade later, that Reform Judaism in England was stagnating. On learning that Marks had accepted an invitation to preach at the independent Western Synagogue in Alban Place,

Theodores commented that 'it is as though the differences between the Catholics and the Protestants had been overcome',[11] a somewhat extreme analogy bearing in mind the independent nature of the Western. Though Marks was subject to criticism from fellow Reform Jews, according to Theodores, West London's Senior Minister found favour with the Jewish Orthodoxy because 'he despises the missionaries' and with the Unitarians because 'they too dispute the truth of the evangelical history of Christ'.[12]

When Professor Theodores died the Council of the Manchester Synagogue of British Jews paid tribute to him as one of the chief mainstays of the city's Reform community:[13] 'His wide erudition, his scholarly attainments and his enthusiastic attachment to his race and religion, gained for him the love of all the Jewish congregations of the city and the respect of all his fellow citizens.'[14] Theodores's most influential contribution to the birth of Manchester Reform was his public lecture, *The Rabbinical Law of Excommunication*, given on 29 January 1854. The question of the *cherem* imposed on the Founders and their synagogue had festered on since its imposition in 1842. The lifting of the 'Bull of Excommunication' on individuals in 1849 did not ease the situation as the Chief Rabbi together with the Sephardi community and the Board of Deputies still insisted that the Margaret Street Synagogue remain under *cherem*. The issue resurfaced in Manchester in 1853 during the dispute over the admission of Reform deputies to the Board of Deputies. The Manchester Jewish community was split over the *cherem* issue. There were two main questions at the heart of the debate, first, did the Chief Rabbi have the authority to excommunicate and exclude the Margaret Street congregation in the modern world of the 1850s and, second, was Manchester Jewry prepared to accept the Chief Rabbi's authority? David Hesse supported and led those who were opposed to the autocratic attitude of the Chief Rabbi. They were not prepared to accept that the London ecclesiastical authorities were 'competent to pronounce a decision of such importance'.[15] In his public lecture Tobias Theodores, an opponent of the Chief Rabbi and his policies, gave the issue a philosophical dimension. He lucidly explained why a *cherem* could not, in reality, have been imposed. He then proceeded to challenge Adler's bid to control and direct the Manchester Jewish community: 'Nowhere but within the boundaries of the Holy Land could the *semichah* be conferred.'[16] Following Theodores's thesis, Adler had no right to impose his authority over Dr Schiller-Szinessy, the man who arrived in Manchester in 1850 and who, in terms of qualifications and local support, set out to challenge the London-based Chief Rabbi.

Dr Solomon Mayer Schiller-Szinessy was born in Hungary in 1820. After taking part in the 1848 uprising he escaped to England via Ireland. His arrival in Manchester provided an opportunity to revitalise the Jewish community. Schiller-Szinessy's oratorial flair and scholarship, his authenticated *semichah* and Orthodox practice made him seem eminently suited to the position of minister of Halliwell Street. He was seen as the person who could reunify the Manchester Jewish community, which had been divided since 1844. Dr Schiller-Szinessy no doubt saw in his appointment an opportunity to further his career and to become the 'Chief Rabbi' of the Provinces. Schiller-Szinessy's ambitions were not based on idle speculation, he was aware that the wealthy and Anglicised members of Halliwell Street resented the superiority of London Jewry in religious affairs.[17] Having achieved communal and civic prominence Manchester Jewry saw in the appointment of Schiller-Szinessy a chance for autonomy. However, autonomy was not automatically a prelude to Reform.

By 1855 the battle lines were being drawn. The battleground would be the power of Chief Rabbi Adler and the demands for changes in the Halliwell Street ritual. Fifteen members (all but one of whom had arrived from Germany after 1834) had petitioned for changes. The reforms were intended to be 'beneficial and essential'. According to Williams, as Theodores was the spokesman they were doubtless also progressive.[18] Before 1842, the only concession the Halliwell Orthodox congregation had made to progress was the introduction of regular English sermons. These were given by David Myer Isaacs, reader at the Liverpool Synagogue. Although not altogether successful, they may have gone some way towards arresting the drift and defection manifest among the Anglicised Jews of the city who were dissatisfied with the static and indecorous state of Jewish worship. The consecration of Burton Street in 1842, and perhaps the fear that such a schism might occur in Manchester, accelerated the introduction of minor reforms in Halliwell Street. These related to the financial organisation of offerings, seat rentals and fines. An end to the auctioning of honours was also seen as an attempt to improve decorum. Not so much reform, more rationalisation. The

Manchester Jewish community was not yet ready for Reform and the split that took place in 1844 was not theological or ideological, but political, the result of a jostling for communal position and authority. It was originally a separation of the young *petit bourgeoisie* from the older established wealthy families, but the support of David Hesse for the former gave the temporary New Congregation a radical image and the man a taste for communal leadership.

By 1855 the main issues confronting and dividing Manchester's Jewish community numbered four. They were: the authority of the London Chief Rabbi and the legitimacy of the *cherem*, ritual reform, the status of Dr Schiller-Szinessy and the building of a new synagogue following the expiry of the lease on Halliwell Street. A year later the issues had been confronted and the differences had fractured into schism. On 17 February 1856 a Reform Association was established in Manchester. Among those chosen to form a 'provisional committee' were David Hesse, Horatio Micholls and Tobias Theodores.[19] The threads were being woven together: German immigrants, early settlers and intellectual leadership. The resolutions adopted by the Association, later put forward as a basis for debate with the established community, were in reality a pronouncement of support for the Margaret Street style of Reform Judaism. Briefly they consisted of the adoption of the Margaret Street Prayer Book, liturgy and ritual; the introduction of a choir; and a resolution that the Association 'combine with the general body of the Jews of Manchester with a view to carry out the purposes of this Association'.[20] The alternatives were schism or unity through Reform. The resolutions were then put to the representatives of the Halliwell Street Select Committee for consideration. Neither they nor Chief Rabbi Adler were prepared to make more than minor concessions. These might improve decorum but they would not satisfy the demands of the Manchester Reformers. For their part the Manchester Reformers offered a single concession, the retention of the 'Second Day'.

One newly built house of worship could not satisfy the now divided Manchester Jewish community and the search began for separate sites upon which to build two new synagogues. A site for the Manchester Reform synagogue was acquired at the junction of Cheetham Hill Road and Park Place, only a few hundred yards from the intended location of the new Orthodox synagogue: both were in the heart of middle-class Jewry. Unlike the events surrounding the emergence of Reform in London, there was no geographic dimension to its nascence in Manchester. The foundation stone of what was originally designated the 'Park Place Synagogue of British Jews of Manchester',[21] was laid in March 1857 at a ceremony attended by the Manchester Reformers and representatives of the West London Synagogue of British Jews.

By 1856 differences between Dr Schiller-Szinessy and the Halliwell Street congregation had reached a point at which the Doctor had no alternative but to resign. In addition to discontent over his financial status, Schiller-Szinessy's authority was gradually being eroded by the local Orthodox laity who, though concerned that he might join the Reform camp, refused to give him the authority he desired to enable him to perform marriages without the approval of the Chief Rabbi in London.[22] Schiller-Szinessy was looking round for an alternative base, though it is unclear whether, in the final analysis, he voluntarily resigned or was asked to leave. While all this was taking place within the Orthodox community the Reformers were looking for a reader and lecturer. Dr Schiller-Szinessy proved to be the sole applicant for the post. Initially he asked to be designated 'Chief Rabbi' in return for adopting the West London Prayer Book. The request was refused but he took the job all the same. It was a compromise for both parties. Schiller-Szinessy was not the Reformers' ideal choice and the Reverend Doctor did not succeed in elevating his status. Following his appointment David Woolf Marks set out to develop a working relationship with his provincial counterpart. In a letter written from West London dated 28 September 1856, he stressed the need for a 'close understanding with respect to the essential principle on which we are mutually to act'. Marks went on to emphasise the reasoning behind his denial of the Oral Law to a man who until recently had ministered from the Orthodox pulpit and, even if grudgingly, had bowed to the superiority of Chief Rabbi Adler. Marks explained that 'The principle that has guided my congregation is that whilst the Rabbinical dicta are to be regarded with great consideration they are not to be placed on a level with the Divine Code of the Bible'.[23] He then requested that Schiller-Szinessy consider Marks's views as put forward in the 1842 inaugural discourse and state how far they coincided with Schiller-Szinessy's own. Further, Marks asked whether the Manchester Reform minister-elect would be prepared to adopt

Marks's beliefs as the 'basis of your synagogue practices'.[24] Schiller-Szinessy's response illustrates his readiness to change direction in order to further his career and maintain communal authority. He assured Marks that 'your doctrine is nothing more than I have invariably taught in public and private'. Having confirmed acceptance of the Denial of the Oral Law Schiller-Szinessy then informed Marks that:

> In the congregation over which I am appointed to preside, the Second Days of Festivals will be kept, but such observances in no manner contravene the principle already admitted inasmuch as they will be observed, not as Mosaic and Biblical ordinance but purely and professedly as ancient institutions [upon] which many of our members look with a feeling of reverence.[25]

It was their difference over the Second Day that resulted in the Park Place Reform Synagogue not becoming a 'branch' of West London – although the *Jewish Chronicle* continued to refer to it as such – and the reason why the Manchester Congregation of British Jews retained an autonomy that was to set the pattern for all future Reform congregations. If Manchester would not conform with West London's requisites then it would only be deemed an associate, not a branch. In the sermon he gave at the consecration of Park Place, Schiller-Szinessy defended his congregation's retention of the Second Day. As he explained, 'the [Manchester] Reformers did not abolish any festivals, they even kept some because of tradition, as opposed to the requirements of Mosaic Law'.[26] There is to be found an explanation of the division between capital and provincial Reform Judaism in the late 1850s: in London David Woolf Marks and the Reformers, having taken the Reform path, upheld their interpretation of a biblically based theology. In Manchester, tradition still had a role to play, even if it was at odds with the purity of Reform.

The first purpose-built British Reform synagogue was as simple in design as its nearby Orthodox counterpart was elaborate. Designed by Edward Salomons and based on the Byzantine model,[27] it stood 100 feet long by 50 feet wide. There was seating for 400 men and 250 women, but only 25 sets of prayer books were ordered before the consecration. The sexes were segregated, and remained so until 1938. Even after that time the first four rows were reserved for 'men with scruples'. The Ark was positioned behind the Reader's desk at the east end of the synagogue, in an 'octagonal apse'. The architecture was in keeping with the essence of Reform, 'to blend...the antique gravity of the faith with...modern beauty of form'.[28]

The consecration took place on 25 March 1858 – two weeks after the Orthodox synagogue's ceremony had been conducted by Chief Rabbi Adler. Though Park Place followed the Margaret Street ritual and liturgy there were certain innovations. Instrumental music by means of an organ was to be a permanent feature of the new synagogue, and, in advance of London which was still debating the issue, a mixed choir of 40 synagogue members performed.[29] As David Woolf Marks had in 1842, so Schiller-Szinessy in 1858, used the consecration ceremony to defend and justify the establishment of a Reform community and its synagogue, the latter referred to as 'an edifice built by a Jew, for Jews, after designs peculiar to Jewish architects'. Dr Schiller-Szinessy made comparison with the erection of the Second Temple in Jerusalem, 'by part of Jews only...amidst and in spite of strong opposition', and the schism in Manchester, which he announced he deplored. He defended Reform ritual and liturgy by underlining the urgent need to ensure decorum and dignity and to return to biblical truth. In his view the Manchester Congregation of British Jews was the 'truly Orthodox Manchester Congregation'. Leaving the spiritual world aside he turned to the temporal, to an England that was, as he described it, 'the refuge of the oppressed'. Accordingly, it was necessary to demonstrate peace within the community and to support total Jewish emancipation. The latter goal was one which, Schiller-Szinessy appears to have believed, necessitated at least the appearance of the former. The Manchester Reform minister then proceeded to outline the form Reform Judaism would take in his synagogue. It would:

> avoid all that is detrimental to the dignity and decorum of the divine service...to cause the whole congregation to participate in the hymns sung to the Glory of God; to cause these hymns to be accompanied by instrumental music...to reintroduce those psalms of David...to introduce a Prayer Book which has, during sixteen years, given evidence of its capabilities to edify a congregation of Israel – a Prayer Book ...which possesses the positive merit of containing the best

> prayers of the two principal rituals; and to preach...in the vernacular...so that all who come hither may sing of the Glory of God and feel and understand it and take it to heart.[30]

The sermon can be criticised for its lack of the passion and conviction which was to be found in those made by Marks. But then it was given by one who only recently had eschewed Orthodoxy for Reform.

The religious ceremony was followed by a 'function' at which a number of eminent citizens explained and justified the emergence of Reform Judaism in Manchester. Horatio Micholls, president of the congregation, dwelt on the concern the Manchester Reformers felt at the increasing tendency towards drift, defection and apostasy. The Orthodox form of service contained 'so little of devotional spirit' that he was concerned for the children: without, as he explained, 'a pure, simple and convincing' service they would be lost to Judaism. Park Place provided a 'safety net' for those who might otherwise have taken a Unitarian path.[31] And indeed, as the *Jewish Chronicle* confirmed a year later, though some Jews had been 'recaptured' others had been irretrievably lost.[32] The third part of the inaugural celebration was a Sabbath service held at the newly consecrated Reform synagogue. David Woolf Marks gave the sermon. The occasion provided Britain's senior Reform minister with an opportunity to reaffirm his allegiance to the Mosaic Laws which were 'universal' and the 'Keystone of Judaism'. David Woolf Marks also took the opportunity to reassert his belief in the abolition of the Second Day, thus wagging a critical finger at the Manchester Reformers.

Without the example of West London, which path would the Manchester Reformers have followed? Would the mainly German-born congregation have adopted the Hamburg Prayer Book and Ritual, and by so doing jeopardised the support of the more conservative English families who had insisted on the retention of the Second Day? Or, conversely, if Park Place had abandoned the Second Day, would it then have become a branch of West London, thus denying it, and future Reform congregations, the autonomy enjoyed today?

Conservatism held sway for two years but then, in 1860, those in favour of the abolition of the Second Day got their way. Dr Schiller-Szinessy, unwilling to concede to the pressures for that most radical departure from tradition, resigned in protest. Three years later he took up the position of Reader in Talmudic and Rabbinic Literature at the University of Cambridge. He died in 1890.

Following Schiller-Szinessy's departure, the radical laity of Manchester Reform Jewry took control and exhibited their bias with the appointment of Gustav Gottheil as the city's second Reform minister. Gustav Gottheil was a controlled radical, a man renowned for his Reformist beliefs, though certainly not his Anglicised image, as, when he arrived in Manchester, he 'did not know a word of English'.[33] The Reverend Dr Gustav Gottheil was born in Pinne, Posen in 1827 and educated at the universities of Berlin and Halle. He acquired his religious training at the *Reform Gemeinde* in Berlin where he was third minister to the radical non-conformist Samuel Holdheim.[34] In his biography of his father, Gottheil's son recalls that, while in Manchester, 'my father was endeavouring to have his congregation advance on the path of reform'.[35] But Gottheil's new congregation was composed of Anglicised traditionalists who, though they may have given up the Second Day, still wore *tallit*,[36] held evening services and observed all the festivals.[37] Through choice or, perhaps, necessity the newly incumbent minister combined progressive thinking with elements of tradition. This moderacy resulted in his being asked to deliver a sermon and read the West London version of the Prayer for the Royal Family at the Orthodox Manchester Hebrew Congregation Synagogue. However, this apparently conciliatory gesture was opposed by the Chief Rabbi in London, who refused to allow Gottheil to occupy the Orthodox pulpit, saying that he would not tolerate Reform Jews being given 'official recognition'.[38] This hostile attitude was again manifest when Adler prevented the Orthodox *mohel* of Cardiff from circumcising the child of a woman converted to Judaism through the Manchester Reform Synagogue. In noting this event the Council of West London recorded in its Minutes that this action was 'further proof of his [Adler's] determination to persist in a line of conduct [which] the wisdom of the experience of the past might well have induced him to question'.[39]

Gustav Gottheil was concerned about moral issues on both sides of the Atlantic. He preached several sermons on the issue of black slavery in North America as, in spite of the biblical toleration of slavery, he was personally opposed to a practice which could treat a section of mankind so inhumanely. The issue was one which divided the Jewish clergy in America; Orthodox Rabbi Morris Raphall of New York (originally from Birmingham, England) defended slavery while David Einhorn was violently opposed; a stance which almost cost him his life.[40] Gottheil's overt condemnation of the pre-Civil War practice initiated a relationship between himself and members of the local Christian clergy, including Dissenters such as the Quakers and the Bible Christian Church of Salford.[41] Gottheil combined his Reform beliefs with certain traditional practices, convinced that uniformity enhanced religious practice. He proposed that 'the services and ritual should be the same in all synagogues, Orthodox ...or Reform', though he did not indicate which prayer book was to be followed. And in order that his congregants should appreciate the truths of the religion he encouraged the use of an English Bible so that 'those who did not understand Hebrew would understand what the reader was reciting'.[42]

During his 13-year ministry at Park Place, Gottheil initiated few radical changes, possibly inhibited by the conservatism of the lay leadership. The changes he did make included the introduction of confirmation services for boys and girls, a special memorial prayer for the dead on the Day of Atonement, the seven-year cycle of the reading of the law on the Sabbath and the increased usage of English.[43] He worked hard to temper the effects of the 1856 schism and to further the civic role of Manchester Jewry. It was with reluctance and regret that the Manchester Congregation of British Jews acceded to his request to be permitted to leave the congregation in order to take up the position as minister of the Emanu-El Synagogue in New York in September 1873. The move was one which suited Gottheil well. Emanu-El had been founded by a group of young German intellectual immigrants who were no longer content with the traditional ritual and liturgy. By 1855 the congregation numbered over 1,000 and prided itself on employing ministers with 'knowledge and ability'. It attracted the most 'successful and well established Jews in New York' and, as one of its spiritual leaders, Gustav Gottheil became prominent among the Reform rabbis of America.[44]

In his history of the Manchester Congregation of British Jews, Rabbi P. Selvin Goldberg, minister of that synagogue from 1940 until 1975, wrote that 'No minister in the whole history of the Manchester Congregation of British Jews exerted greater influence over his community and over the general Jewish community of Manchester than did the Reverend Laurence Mark Simmons'.[45] Simmons put the Manchester Reform congregation back on an even keel after it had suffered a decline in support and loss of direction during the four-year ministry of Gottheil's successor, Reverend I. Weiner, who was forced to resign his position in 1877 due to the 'increasing seriousness of a mental disorder'.

The Reverend Laurence Simmons was the first English-born minister to serve the Manchester Reform community. As a beneficiary of the West London Synagogue's Ministers' Training Fund he was trained at the seminary at Breslau. Simmons was characteristic of English Reform Judaism in its first century. He was Orthodox, conservative, tolerant and liberal-minded. During his ministry, which ended abruptly with his tragically early death in 1900, he earned the particular respect of the Manchester Christian community as well as that of all of Anglo-Jewry, both Orthodox and Reform. He was not afraid to exhibit his support for the Chief Rabbi if he felt the issue or occasion warranted it, and his middle path of Judaism enabled him to narrow the divide between the two Manchester Jewish communities.[46] On Simmons's death Chief Rabbi Herman Adler stated that not only Reform Judaism had suffered a loss but 'entire Anglo-Jewry' had 'reason to mourn his removal from our midst'. Simmons was a fine orator who frequently officiated at Orthodox synagogues on the Second Day of the Festivals, which he always observed. He was responsible for the reinstatement of religious classes, which were attended by children of Orthodox as well as Reform families, and of services on the Fast of Ab.[47] Simmons was deeply concerned about youth and their welfare and became chaplain of the region's Jewish Lads' Brigade shortly after its national foundation in 1895. He was also honorary secretary of the local branch of the Anglo-Jewish Association and involved with nearly every local communal and philanthropic organisation. The sole voice of criticism to be heard was that of Tobias Theodores who considered Simmons to be 'too orthodox'.[48]

By the end of the century the membership of the Manchester Congregation of British Jews was 500 souls, representing a fusion of the Anglo-Jewish establishment and later German arrivals. The synagogue's wealthy membership was the driving force of the city's cotton trade and involved with all the major Manchester charities. Members did not give collectively as 'Reformers', but individually and independently. They could always be called upon to help impoverished arrivals from eastern Europe who sought patronage in the setting-up of businesses and homes. The Manchester Reformers played a crucial role in the city's community life, controlling and directing education and philanthropy together with their Christian peers who, in some instances, were also business partners. The members of the Manchester Reform synagogue were far more involved in the social and philanthropic life of the city than their Orthodox counterparts. By the century's close, many had achieved top civic and community positions. No longer outcasts, they had become 'pillars of society'. In 1890 Nathan Laski, a member of the Manchester Orthodox community summed up Reform in the city when he said that 'the Orthodox party had a deal to learn from Reform, not only in synagogue matters, but in the part they took, locally, in the administration of charitable and educational organisations'.[49]

Bradford

Reform Judaism in Manchester owed its origins to the confluence of diverse factors. By contrast, its birth and survival on the other side of the Pennines, in 'Worstedopolis', was the result of a single phenomenon, the presence in Bradford of German-Jewish textile merchants. During the first half of the nineteenth century the worsted trade was transformed. Between 1815 and 1851 the textile industry of Bradford, most particularly the manufacture of worsted cloth, grew impressively, transforming what had been, at the end of the eighteenth century, a small rough town into a city of 'colossal greatness'.[50] The dominant role of Bradford attracted a large number of migrant worsted merchants. By 1851 less than 50 per cent of the city's population of 103,778 was local born,[51] the largest foreign contingent originating from Germany.[52] As a consequence the area in which the merchants established their businesses became known as 'little Germany'. The rate of growth can be assessed by the fact that in 1827 there were no foreign merchants in the city; 34 years later, in 1861, there were 65.[53] Not surprisingly, a number of those immigrant merchants were Jewish – virtually all the founders of the Bradford Congregation of British and Foreign Jews were either textile merchants or manufacturers, the earliest having settled in the city in the late

1820s.[54] Those early arrivals would appear to have had little interest in, or respect for, the religion of their fathers. Sir Jacob Behrens, originally from Hamburg, found his way to Bradford via Leeds and opened his factory in 1838 in a city without a practising Jewish community. However, this does not appear to have worried a man who found traditional synagogue life uninspiring. As he explained, 'All forms of service conducted on lines strictly laid down and according to dogma find no response in me'.[55]

Fortunately for the future of Judaism in Bradford not all the German Jewish textile merchants took the same view as Behrens, though it took a number of years for the founders of what became the Bradford Congregation of British and Foreign Jews to come together. One of the city's earliest Jewish arrivals was Jacob Unna,[56] who settled in Bradford in 1844 after having made his way from Hamburg via Leeds. Another early settler was Charles Semon from Danzig, who in 1864 scored a double first by becoming the city's first foreign, and Jewish, Lord Mayor. Jacob Moser, who was Lord Mayor in 1910, arrived in the city from Schleswig in 1863. By 1865, according to the *Jewish Chronicle*, Bradford boasted 'very many German Jews who are well off'. Well off they may have been but the report, based on a letter published in the *Allgemeine Zeitung de Israelites*, went on to state that 'They have no congregation, no synagogue, give no religious instruction to their children, do not have a burial ground...but inter their dead in the Christian cemetery...in general they do not wish to pass as Jews'. The letter also noted that Chief Rabbi Adler had visited the city and while there had called a meeting 'to exercise influence to form a congregation', but only six people attended and they manifested no desire to establish a community.[57] Indeed, it would have been surprising had those German Jews deferred to the Orthodox ecclesiastical authority. In fact some of those, supposedly, irreligious Jews were concerned about the future of Judaism, for the anonymous correspondent to the *Allgemeine Zeitung* refers to Bradford as 'our city', while in October 1870 the *Jewish Chronicle* reported that 15 of the city's 200 to 300 Jews had assembled for a *sukkot* service.[58] It was a start.

In the early part of the 1870s there was a positive move to establish a Reform congregation in the West Riding. The choice centred on the cities of Leeds, Bradford and Huddersfield.[59] At that time the Leeds Jewish community was the only one of the three which had established (Orthodox) synagogues and its own burial ground. The emergence of Reform in Yorkshire has to be allied to the increasing presence of central European immigrants. A small number had left Germany due to the re-emergence of anti-Semitism following the failed 1848 revolution, while others sought to take advantage of the burgeoning textile trade.[60] They brought with them the 'ecclesiastical principles which are only too characteristic of teuton enlightenment'.[61] Was it this or their concern over increasing drift and defection manifested by some of the Jews of the county that led to the convening of a meeting by Charles Semon and Charles Calman on 1 April 1873? A Jewish Association of Bradford was founded with the stated intention of 'upholding and advancing the cause of Judaism and providing for the religious teaching of the Jewish children'.[62] Youth and the future of Judaism were again the prime factors.

Traditionally, the needs of a newly established Jewish community are the acquisition of a burial ground and the holding of religious services. Shortly after the Jewish Association was founded the search began for a director of the Association. At around the same time land was acquired in Bradford's Scholemore cemetery at a cost of £800. In November 1873 Dr Joseph Strauss of Germany was appointed to the post of director. 'His task', as he described it some seven years later, was 'to cultivate a knowledge of Judaism and its literature'.[63] According to Strauss's biographer, his son Sir Oswald Stroud, a 'newly formed congregation of an advanced type in Bradford wanted a young Rabbi'.[64] Having applied for the job and been deemed suitable by a delegation sent to Germany, one of the delegates being Strauss's future father-in-law, the 28-year-old graduate rabbi journeyed to Bradford, to a Reform community that he would serve as religious leader for 49 years.

The evidence available – no records of the Hebrew Association or of the early years of the Bradford Congregation of British and Foreign Jews have been found as yet – provides little indication of the long-term intentions of the Bradford Founders. Were they just testing the water by employing Strauss as an educational director rather than as minister in order to see whether their small group would develop to a size sufficient to justify the building of a synagogue? Following his arrival in Bradford, Strauss began the task of bringing Judaism to the Jews of the city. He gave lectures every second Sunday and taught the children Jewish religious history and Hebrew. His first Sunday sermon attracted 50 people.[65] This should have been encouraging, but Strauss records his disappointment at the 'indifference of the older and wealthier Jewish residents of the city' and his dislike of the dismal Freemasons Hall, in Salem Street, where lectures and subsequently Sabbath and Festival services were held. Neither was he happy with his salary, which he considered 'very low to cover expenses'.[66] Shortage of money was to remain a thorn in his side throughout his ministry. The writer Humbert Wolfe recollects in his autobiography that, in the early 1890s, 24 years on, Strauss 'was paid less than a clerk in a warehouse'.[67] By that time the rabbi had a large family and, according to Wolfe, who provides the reader with a disenchanted view of the Jewish Bradford of his childhood, was 'aware of the exacerbating detail of his poverty... the whole house had that queer nameless smell of poverty which settles upon the spirit like soot'.[68] The rabbi constantly had to devise ways in which to supplement his meagre income. In 1880, a year before the newly built Bradford Synagogue was consecrated, obviously in financial need, following the announcement of the intended retirement of Philip Magnus, Strauss applied to West London for the position of Assistant Minister. The correspondence between Strauss and West London indicates quite clearly that level of salary was a major concern.[69] Strauss, who knew no English on his arrival in Bradford, was turned down for the post because of the manner in which he delivered his sermons. His erudition and scholarship were unquestioned and respected but David Woolf Marks, in his report to the wardens of West London, recorded that the Bradford minister's reading 'grates horribly on the ear and his English accent is so strikingly foreign'.[70] So Anglicised a congregation as West London would never have entertained a vocal discordance which Wolfe describes as a 'guttural voice with a thick German accent'.[71]

Joseph Strauss worked tirelessly for the furtherance of Judaism in what had previously been an irreligious community. On a visit to London in 1874 he met the spiritual representatives of Reform Judaism in the capital, the Reverends Marks, Lowy and Magnus. Interestingly, he also had an audience with the Chief Rabbi, Dr Nathan Adler. In his autobiography Strauss recounts how Adler had called him a 'missionary for the Jewish faith'.[72] Was Adler's hope that he might subsequently wean the Bradford community off Reform and onto Orthodox Judaism – this before the establishment of an Orthodox community in Bradford? On his return to Bradford, Strauss decided that, in future, Sabbath services would be held on Friday evenings and on Saturdays at 1.30 p.m. But though there was some increase in religious observance it was insufficient to sustain the Friday evening services, which were soon dropped due to poor attendance. Shortly afterwards Sabbath services were rescheduled to begin at 10.30 a.m.

Bradford Jewry took its religion step by step. German Reform predominated, the Bradford community initially adopting the Hamburg Temple Prayer Book. However, in 1878 pragmatism demanded a change to the ritual and liturgy of West London. Strauss had approached West London with a request to associate in the same manner as the Manchester Reform congregation in order that the Bradford Synagogue's secretary might be certified for the registration of marriages. The Council of West London refused, explaining that 'the advanced views of the majority of the Bradford community offered an impediment'.[73] The only route was the adoption of the ritual and liturgy of English Reform. Even when this stipulation was accepted West London displayed a reluctance to draw up the rules and regulations necessary for the formal association of other Reform synagogues. It was only as a result of the persistence of the Bradford Reform community and of one which was emerging in Leeds[74] that a sub-committee was set up by West London for the purpose.

Having been formally recognised by the cathedral synagogue of British Reform Jewry, the Bradford community went ahead with their plans to build a synagogue. A plot of land, formerly a timber yard, in Bowland Street was purchased for £700, the money donated by a Mr Bernard Cohen, and a programme of fund raising was initiated. In 1880, in a ceremony attended by David Woolf Marks and Horatio Montefiore from London plus a number of local dignitaries, the foundation stone of the synagogue was laid by Jacob Unna.[75] Less than a year later, on 29 March 1881, in a snowstorm, the Bradford Reform Synagogue was consecrated. Sadly, three of those most actively involved with the creation of the community and the engaging of its minister, Charles Semon, Charles Calman and Jacob Unna, died before they could enjoy the fruits of their labour.[76] It should be noted that among the Jewish communities of Britain in the nineteenth century, Bradford was unique in establishing a Reform synagogue prior to an Orthodox house of worship.

The architecture of the Bradford Synagogue of British and Foreign Jews was oriental, a style popular in Europe at the time. It measured 44 feet long by 30 feet wide and was 27 feet high, with seating capacity for 140.[77] There was no women's gallery, the sexes were seated separately, on ground level. The exterior of the synagogue was, and still is, of a striking design, composed of horizontal courses of red sienna and white stone, with the Hebrew inscription over the main entrance, 'Open ye the gates that the righteous may enter'. Inside, the Ark of the Covenant, of eastern design in marble, stood under a blue-domed, star-studded background. Though not as awe-inspiring as the ultimate synagogue in Berkeley Street, the building must have been impressive, standing as it did in a row of 'bleak grey tenement houses'.[78] To the young Humbert Wolfe it was disappointing as it offered 'no reassuring pomp, no churchlike governing silences'. To the six-year-old boy it was 'At best a biggish square room with a gallery for harmonium at the back and with a few Saracenic windows obscurely glazed...an unambitious pulpit a few feet in front of the altar had an eternal light over it'.[79] This is an unfair and unflattering description of a house of worship which may not have been overwhelming by comparison to Anglican churches but one which, even in the late twentieth century, has an ambience which demands respect and elicits appreciation for its architecture.

The consecration ceremony was attended by Reform ministers from London and Manchester and Christian ministers from the local non-conformist, German Lutheran, Anglican and Dissenting churches. Strauss had developed an affinity with local socialist religious dissenters and German expatriates. The service, which reflected the 'advanced views of Dr Strauss and his congregants',[80] evoked criticism and correspondence in the *Jewish Chronicle*.[81] The procession to the synagogue had begun in a Christian public school. The ministers, wearing their canonicals and *tallit*, then walked through the streets to the Bowland Street synagogue. The service that followed was, for the most part, in English,[82] as opposed to 'the Ancient and Holy Tongue common to Jews throughout the world'.[83] The use of a Christian school from which to start the procession, the playing of classical music and the employment of the Bradford Choral Society for the choral accompaniment drew strong criticism. The *Jewish Chronicle* contested that 'Jews and Jewesses should have been sought to make up the choir, not Christians'. The opinions of the visiting Reform ministers are not recorded but the conservative Reverends Simmons, Marks and Lowy, though doubtless pleased at the birth of a new community, could not have been unaware of its radical nature. Dr Strauss replied to his critics in a letter to the *Jewish Chronicle*. He considered the accusations were unfounded. The school referred to was 'a day school used by all religions...the consecration ceremony conformed with continental tradition and was quiet and decorous' – this a fact which had been noted by the *Jewish Chronicle*. Strauss argued for the increased use of English, as it enabled his congregants to understand the service. He concluded by stating his belief that the 'Organ of British Jewry had demonstrated its intolerance by criticising the Christian members of the choir'.[84]

Dr Strauss was the hard-working, outward-looking, underpaid servant of the Bradford Congregation of British and Foreign Jews from 1873 until 1922. During the latter years of the nineteenth century he received a salary of approximately £250 per annum – the Reverend David Woolf Marks received £650. Strauss was plagued by the autocratic attitude of the governing laity. In his autobiography he refers to the 'somewhat dictatorial attitude of the leading members of the community'. Wolfe is more outspoken and provides us with the following insight into the life of the rabbi. He describes Strauss as:

> a paid servant...who had been bullied into a state of sullen stupidity by the Governing Body of the Synagogue. They permitted no interference with their consciences by their paid servant. The Rabbi's business was to interpret the ways of God to man in general, but to avoid the particular at all costs. His was by no means the place of honour accorded to the Rabbi in the poor Jewish communities...his learning did not interest a congregation the majority of which knew only enough Hebrew to repeat the main prayers by rote...The position of Dr. Strauss was precisely that of chaplain in the eighteenth century.[85]

Left to interpret 'the ways of God', Strauss combined the radical and the traditional. Following his appointment in 1873 he conducted *barmitzvah* services and in 1893 articulated his belief in, and support for, *shechitah*, which he considered 'a necessary adjunct to our religion'.[86] Under the terms of his office the minister of the Bradford Reform Synagogue was required to provide religious instruction for the children of the congregation, but he still found time to write and to involve himself with contemporary Jewish and secular issues. He was appointed Lecturer in Hebrew and Oriental languages at Airedale College – later Leeds University – in 1874. Two years later he published *Religion and Morals*, a short catechism of 42 questions and answers for use in Jewish schools. A man concerned about Jewish and Christian social issues, he was a member of the Bradford Committee of the Salvation Army and a founder of the Bradford Branch of the Anglo-Jewish Association. Strauss and his wife supported both the suffrage movement and the Zionist cause. The latter was one which divided the Jewish clergy, Orthodox and Reform.[87] Together with his wife, Dr Strauss attended the second Zionist Congress in Basle in 1898 and subsequently, as an ardent supporter of the Zionist cause, founded the Bradford Montefiore Zionist Society and became president of the Provincial English Zionist Federation.

Though he may have been subservient to the synagogue's governing body Dr Joseph Strauss created a Jewish community out of what had previously been a Jewish presence. When criticisms appeared in the *Jewish Chronicle* in 1906 about the 'advanced state of decay' of Judaism in Bradford, of the paucity of Sabbath morning synagogue attendance, and of the instances of drift and defection, the blame was placed on the 'disease of Reform Judaism in England' aggravated by Dr Strauss whose advanced views 'made defect to Christianity easier'.[88] The honorary secretary of the Bradford Congregation of British and Foreign Jews responded by stating that Strauss, 'far from helping members to join the Unitarian Church, actively drew people back to Judaism'. The article appeared in 1906, the year in which the Orthodox congregation consecrated its synagogue. Orthodox eastern European Jews had been present in the city since the mid-1870s. Initially, Strauss acted as their rabbi and preacher and even performed marriage ceremonies for a number of them in the Reform synagogue. The *Jewish Year Book* records that by 1900 the two small Orthodox congregations, one founded in 1886 and one in 1890, had amalgamated and were based at 25 Houghton Place.[89]

The theology of Bradford's first Reform rabbi is best summed up by the following quotation which appears in his autobiography:

> There is no central religious authority in Judaism, no single ecclesiastical dignitary who exercises a universal overlordship. The so-called slavery of the letter does not exist in Judaism, which has always been ruled by a spirit of high altruism, preaching goodwill to all men, irrespective of race or creed'.[90]

According to the official Bradford Reform Synagogue history the synagogue 'flourished and services were so well attended that between 1903 and 1906 it became necessary to engage the services of an Assistant Minister, the Rev. Shulman'. He departed for America in 1906 complaining that the Bradford services were insufficiently Orthodox. After seven years on the other side of the Atlantic Shulman revised his opinion, his reconsidered view being that services in Bradford were too traditional.[91] Joseph Strauss remained minister of the Bradford Reform Synagogue until 1922. Retaining his radical image, in his later years he became recognised as an elder statesman of Reform.[92] But he had been a critic of Reform Judaism's progress in Britain, in common with Zangwill he believed that it was stagnating. In 1893 Strauss voiced his concern that even 'the orthodoxy were reforming more rapidly'.[93]

By the close of the nineteenth century there were three active Reform communities in England. They had sprung from different beginnings even though there were some common factors. For the most part their founders were successful, middle-aged business men, interacting socially and commercially with their Gentile counterparts. Active in civic and community affairs, they needed, and looked for, a form of religious observance that was in keeping with their lives as Englishmen of the Jewish faith. Wolfe describes Bradford Jewry, so recently arrived from Germany, as 'very Anglicised, they used Yorkshire phrases and clipped their vowels'.[94] Indeed a number of Jews in the West Riding considered themselves first and foremost Yorkshiremen.

What nexus existed between the three Reform communities? Clearly, at the end of the nineteenth century it was somewhat tenuous. In 1893, in a letter to the *Jewish Chronicle*, Dr Strauss held West London responsible for a 'lack of brotherly connection' – a belief vindicated by the fact that the Council of Founders had earlier rejected a suggestion, made by Revd Lowy, that the Manchester and Bradford congregations be consulted over the revision of the Prayer Book. Strauss also criticised the Berkeleystreeters for not inviting any of the provincial rabbis to participate in the fiftieth anniversary celebration service held by West London in 1892 and for there being no reference to the provincial communities in the jubilee sermon. The sole acknowledgement came when London 'borrowed a few *Sefer Torah* from the provincial synagogues'.[95] Strauss asked why. Was it 'lack of true zeal for the case of reform, lack of courage, or too much lay control of government and management'? There was no published response from West London. Five years on there was an apparent change of heart. Morris Joseph, appointed second minister of West London in 1893, presented a paper to the West London Synagogue Association on 8 January 1898,[96] in which he proposed closer links between the three Reform synagogues in England. The meeting, which took place in London, was attended by the Revd Dr Strauss, Mr J. Moser and Mr M. Gottheil, all from Bradford. No representative from Manchester attended. It was an absence indicative of the prevailing climate of separateness. As a follow-up to his paper, Morris Joseph supervised the sending of letters to the two provincial communities. He asked them to approve the idea of a 'federation' based on the following principles:

> 1. That it be non-financial, its objectives being, (a) to afford opportunities for the discussion of questions of common interest (b) to strengthen the position of Anglo-Jewish Reform as a religious force.
> 2. The objectives to be promoted by periodical conferences to be held alternately in London, Manchester and Bradford and attended by representatives of the three congregations.
> 3. The conferences to have a consultative character only, each congregation maintaining its independence in respect of ritual and other matters.[97]

According to the West London Association's Annual Report for 1897/1898, 'An extremely favourable reply was received from Bradford and an extremely unfavourable reply from Manchester'. The lay council of the Manchester Synagogue replied saying that the synagogue's community and civic position was of far more importance than the proposed federation because:

(a) It did not want to disturb the harmony of the Manchester Jewish community.
(b) The formal establishment of a reform federation 'would highlight the differences within Anglo-Jewry and this could prove disastrous to the existence of the Manchester Reform Community'.
(c) As the Manchester Reform Congregation's leaders wished to work for the unity of the whole of Anglo-Jewry, federation would only redefine the factions that existed.[98]

Having been treated as a poor provincial relation in the past Manchester's Reform leadership was clearly not prepared to sacrifice its position of influence and leadership in the city for what, one can assume, it saw as second-class citizenship in a London-dominated federation. The plan for federation was abandoned and not reconsidered until 1942 when, significantly, the resolution to establish the Associated British Synagogues was passed at a meeting held in Manchester.

FAILURES

A chapter on provincial reform Judaism cannot be closed without considering those 'would-be' congregations that either never made it or were unable to survive.

Brighton

In the late eighteenth century Brighton became a fashionable 'watering hole', popularised by the patronage of the Prince Regent. The first reference to a Jewish presence in the town appears in 1670.[99] In 1789 the first synagogue was opened in Jew Street; 34 years later, in 1823, the synagogue, with a membership of 40, moved to Devonshire Place. There it remained until 1875.[100] The coming of the railway to east Sussex in 1841 made Brighton both more accessible and attractive as a retreat from London during the summer and early autumn months. West London members were among those who spent their summers away from the capital and synagogue attendance suffered accordingly. In order to bring religion to the holidaymakers, in

1867 the newly ordained third minister of London's Reform synagogue, Philip Magnus, suggested in a letter to the Council of Founders that, as there were no Reform services held in Brighton, West London should 'authorise one of its ministers to officiate weekly in rooms hired for the purpose', as there was a 'strong desire on the part of visitors and residents' to attend synagogue. He estimated that some 40 or 50 people would attend services, especially if these were reduced to a length of one and a half hours, as 'most persons at Brighton were anxious to spend most of their time in the open air'. Magnus also believed that West London would, as he put it, be able to 'spread the good to those who had not yet experienced the same'. As the services would only be held for three months in the year the temporary synagogue should not be considered as a branch but as a facility for London members and a way of ensuring that they preserved their religiosity. The archives provide us with no detail of the discussions that followed Magnus's request, all that exists is his letter of request and the attached note which reads 'not acceded to', dated 6 December 1867.[101]

It would appear that West London, as Strauss suggested almost 20 years later, 'lacked the true zeal' in the 1860s to spread the gospel of Reform through the provision of out-of-town services for members and other Reform Jews visiting or residing in Brighton. Was there a tinge of regret when, in September 1875, the new Orthodox synagogue, now located in Middle Street, was consecrated by Dr Adler? A note on the envelope containing the two tickets of invitation for the representatives of West London simply states 'none of the wardens able to accept'.[102]

Leeds

A Jewish presence was recorded in Leeds as early as the last quarter of the eighteenth century.[103] By 1820 there was the nucleus of a community which included artisans, professional and business men. By the 1870s the city's Jewish population, swelled by the arrival of eastern European immigrants seeking work in the sub-divisional tailoring workshops, had grown to some 5,000.[104] The city housed two synagogues plus several small *chevrahs* established by immigrants who did not find spiritual satisfaction in the Anglicised Belgrave Street synagogue which was rebuilt in 1878 with seating capacity for over 1,000 souls. The synagogue of the

Leeds 'Jewish establishment' was a 'lavish edifice which celebrated the affluence of its congregation'.[105] But behind the splendour was communal dissension, as the events surrounding attempts to establish a Reform synagogue reveal, though whether the differences were of a temporal or spiritual nature is not immediately clear. There were two secessions from Belgrave Street and two attempts to establish Reform congregations, neither of which was successful.

The first group to secede from Belgrave Street was led by Joseph Guttman Oppenheim, a middle-aged woollen merchant of German origin. In June 1880 Oppenheim wrote to the West London Council explaining that he had been in communication with David Woolf Marks for some time and wished, with others, to 'establish a synagogue in every way conforming with the ritual of West London'. He requested that West London consider his synagogue as 'a branch'. He went on to explain that he and the (unnamed) others had

> no desire to place your congregation [West London] under a pecuniary obligation...no synagogue that cannot be self-supporting should be sat on as fools. Our object in having our congregation identified with yours is that we may have the advantage of the spiritual direction of your Chief Minister and that we may be enabled to claim the authority of your congregation to nominate as registrar of marriages the secretary of a synagogue which adopts your ritual...As regards a Minister for our congregation Prof. Marks thinks he knows a gentleman. I may mention that there are 500 Jewish families in this town, the majority of whom never darken the doors of a place of worship but we confidently believe many of them would be attracted to a synagogue conducted in the same manner as Berkeley Street.[106]

In reply West London confirmed that it would hold 50 sets of Prayer Books – at a cost of £42.15s. 0d. – until the Leeds Reform community was ready to hold services. The Council was unable to confirm the constitution of the new Reform synagogue because the relevant people were on holiday.[107] In the August of that year Joseph Oppenheim announced the acquisition of what had previously been a Christian chapel in which the proposed Reform congregation, to be called the 'Congregation of British Jews, Leeds' intended to hold services. Impatience surfaced. In a further letter to West London Oppenheim complained that he had not yet had any details about the proposed minister. In addition, he asked if West London could provide the nascent congregation with *Sefer Torah*, as they 'couldn't get them in Leeds'.[108] Somewhat jumping the gun, in an article which appeared in the *Jewish World* on 20 August, Oppenheim announced that:

> A congregation of British Jews is being established in Leeds. Mr. J.G. Oppenheim and a committee of gentlemen have devoted themselves to the preliminary labours and a chapel ... has been secured for public worship and will shortly be consecrated by the Rev. Prof. Marks. All the preparations are complete and the building will be opened for the ensuing holidays.[109]

And there the history of the Congregation of British Jews in Leeds comes to an abrupt end. There appears to have been no further correspondence between West London and Oppenheim and no minister appointed. However, the Minute Book of the Belgrave Street synagogue provides us with a clue. It records the sending of a letter to 'J.G. Oppenheim and others', on 23 August 1880, which stated that a 'deputation wished to wait upon them for congregational matters'.[110] A week later it was proposed that Mr Oppenheim and Mr Brash (another seceder) be accepted as members of Belgrave Street by 'paying twelve months at 1/- per week and that D. Isaacs pay his arrears'. So the affair appears to have been settled. On 10 October that same year the Council of the Belgrave Street Synagogue received a letter from Messrs Oppenheim and Brash which confirmed their willingness to settle their twelve months' outstanding subscription on condition that 'their ladies were permitted to have front seats in the Synagogue'.[111] No more is heard of Oppenheim and Reform but, significantly, his fellow seceder Brash was appointed President of Belgrave Street in 1886!

Reform in late-nineteenth-century Leeds does not end there. On 1 January 1881, one S. Tannenberg wrote to the wardens of West London on notepaper headed New Hebrew Congregation (Leeds), stating that: 'The above congregation having been established some few months as an independent body are wishful to know upon what conditions they can be affiliated to the reform congregation. We number about 50 members and subscribers. I have written to the Rev. Prof. Marks who has referred me to you on the subject.' (The letter was signed J. Tannenberg, President.)

The only other information about that Reform congregation is to be found in a letter sent by D.W. Marks to his wardens on 5 January 1881. Without that piece of evidence it might have been assumed that Tannenberg had carried on where Oppenheim left off. In that letter Marks explains that in 'September or October' of the previous year he received a communication from 'Mr. Tanner' (as Marks referred to him) representing himself as President of the New Congregation that had seceded from the Orthodox synagogue. Marks explained that he did not think the schism was due to a difference of ritual, but he presumed it was the result of vestry disputes 'as are common enough in provincial congregations'. Tannenberg had asked if West London would certify the secretary of the new synagogue. Marks then refers to a second letter from Tannenberg in which he had stated that though the majority of the congregants supported the adoption of the West London ritual, some were 'differential'. In his letter to the wardens of West London, Marks further explains:

> I know nothing whatever of Mr. Tanner [sic] nor of the congregants whom he represents. I have had frequent letters from Mr. Oppenheim...Mr. Oppenheim and his followers appear quite independent of Mr. Tanner and his party. It would not be unreasonable to infer from all this that our brethren at Leeds are in a state of congregational disruption.

This would appear to be an accurate assessment. There is some corroboration of Marks's view. In August 1880 Simon Tannenberg, a Polish immigrant jeweller, resident in Leeds since 1850, was beaten in the contest for the position of Synagogue President. A vexed Tannenberg resigned from the synagogue. Reform was not his first option. On 30 September the Old Synagogue committee voted to recommend that Dr Adler withhold sanction for a *shochet* to Tannenberg and his 'party'. Clearly the initial break was from the synagogue but not from the Orthodox tradition, Reform was the second choice. Political differences within the Orthodox synagogue had acted as the catalyst in the attempts to establish Reform congregations in Leeds. Whatever Oppenheim and Tannenberg may have told West London, in reality ideology, theology and religious tradition had lesser roles in the fight for community status. Reform Judaism lay dormant in Leeds until a congregation was established in 1944.

South London

The failure to establish a 'South London Synagogue of British Jews' provides further evidence of the reluctance of the Council and wardens of Upper Berkeley Street to encourage new 'associates'. During the latter quarter of the nineteenth century the pattern of migration from inner London was one of a movement north, north-west, south and south-west. One choice for those looking for easy access to the City of London was the more salubrious areas of Clapham and Brixton. Among those who settled there was the Seligman family. In April 1874 Isaac Seligman told Francis Goldsmid that, as he was now living in Clapham Park, he wished to establish a local Reform synagogue.[112] In August of that year Seligman wrote to Philip Magnus asking if he would preach at what was being temporarily called the Brixton New Synagogue. The 'New' synagogue's council considered that the presence of Reverend Magnus would be 'beneficial for the young congregation'. It was further hoped that the Revd Prof. David Woolf Marks would deliver a sermon at the consecration of the synagogue, which was scheduled to take place on 6 or 10 September 1874, the exact date still to be determined. The request was premature. On 9 October the Council of West London received a letter from what was now being called the 'South London Synagogue of British Jews', explaining that at a meeting of residents of 'Clapham, Brixton and the neighbourhoods' it was decided to establish a synagogue which conformed to the ritual of West London. The lease of a plot of ground in Sudbourne Road, Brixton had been purchased and the temporary synagogue, which had been erected, was to be consecrated at the beginning of November that year, 1874. Requests were made for a minister occasionally to preach at the synagogue, for the loan of a *Sefer Torah* and for the Revd D. Woolf Marks to officiate at the consecration. The letter ended by saying that though the new synagogue would not have 'ornamental accessories' it was hoped that it would develop on a 'firm and enduring basis'. It was signed by I. Seligman of Clapham Park, H. Harding of Brixton and one E. Emanuel whose address was given as Lancaster Gate.

For a while the new synagogue received the support it wanted. David Woolf Marks agreed to officiate at the consecration, a *Sefer Torah* was provided on loan until the new synagogue could acquire one of its own and the Revd Lowy agreed to preach occasionally. In addition Joseph Simmonds's name was put forward as prospective preacher. Following his selection for the post Simmonds placed himself under the guidance of David Woolf Marks. However, neither the proposed consecration nor association with West London took place. Membership remained below the requisite 20 and, in October 1875, a request was made for the arrangements agreed the previous year to be held over. No further progress was made and at the beginning of 1877 E. Emanuel wrote to West London to clarify the situation. The problem was money. The Brixton Reform Synagogue's funds were dependent on 'less than a dozen gentlemen'. Death had resulted in the loss of some of the most 'eminent members' while others had left the neighbourhood. The synagogue was now faced with a deficit of £120. Unless help was forthcoming survival could not be guaranteed. Emanuel appealed to West London for help. The modest sum of £100 per annum for three years would enable the South London community to 'ultimately succeed'. The letter book of the West London Synagogue records that the request for help was refused. The wardens were not prepared to take a financial gamble which could have extended far longer than the estimated three years. A pathetic letter from the Revd Joseph Simmonds signals the end, in formal terms, of the short-lived South London Synagogue of British Jews. On 9 May 1877 he wrote to the wardens of the West London Synagogue explaining that on the advice of David Woolf Marks he had originally accepted the office of minister to South London, 'a fact which precludes me at once from any chance of becoming Minister of an Orthodox community'. He applied 'hesitantly' for help to fill any vacancy and offering to officiate in the absence of ministers. He added that a temporary salary of £50 per annum would be of considerable help.

The origins of the South London Reform Synagogue in some ways reflect those of West London. Location suggests that its membership, finding the Reform service to their liking but not the walk to central London, established a branch located nearer to their homes. What they lacked was the financial resources of Upper Berkeley Street. They did not attract a sufficiently large membership to ensure either survival or the prerequisite 20 members for association with West London. Without influence, finance and numbers, the desire for a Reform congregation could not become an enduring reality.

At the end of the nineteenth century there were only three Reform congregations in Britain: West London, Manchester and Bradford. Three other attempts had failed. The Reform breakaway in Liverpool – rumoured in the early 1840s – never materialised. In Birmingham there was to be only a temporary fracture, which occurred in the second decade of the twentieth century. Failure here was due to the flexible attitude of the city's Orthodoxy at the outbreak of the First World War. The available evidence suggests that the West London Synagogue of British Jews was little concerned with proselytising and missionary work. As the Bradford congregation discovered, the Berkeleystreeters had to be badgered into providing the formal documentation necessary for association. In cases of financial hardship, low membership or absence of credible identity, little or no encouragement was forthcoming. West London took on the mantle of 'mother' synagogue with reluctance and, as in the case of the celebration of its golden jubilee, with little regard for fledgling congregations.

In Manchester, the spiritual dimension of Reform was an important factor in the birth of the Manchester Congregation of British Jews – though decorum and reforms were also on the agenda. Without the presence of Tobias Theodores the appearance of a Reform congregation might have been delayed. In Bradford Reform was the only choice for the German-Jewish immigrant community. In neither city was synagogue location of concern. But it was always the newcomer that made the approach, never West London. Even when a minister from Berkeley Street suggested the creation of an out-of-town congregation, as Magnus had with regard to Brighton, his idea was quashed.

It is not surprising that Jews who were searching for something more than was on offer from the Orthodoxy should look beyond Reform, which by the century's end had progressed so little from its eventful beginnings. The Jewish Religious Union established in 1902 provided the stepping-stone to Liberal Judaism, its major protagonists being a Reform Jew, Claude Montefiore, who found little satisfaction in the more contained teachings of Berkeley Street and Lily Montagu, the daughter of the Orthodox Jew, Samuel Montagu, later Lord Swaythling, founder of the Federation of Synagogues. However, it was not until the 1930s that new dynamism and spiritual direction were injected into Reform Judaism in Britain. For some who were questioning

Orthodox Judaism in a world in which the storm clouds of Fascism and Nazism were gathering Reform provided the answer.

NOTES

1. Bill Williams's *The Making of Manchester Jewry* (1976) provides an excellently researched and finely detailed account of the origins and growth of Manchester's Jewish community between 1740 and 1875.
2. A Sephardi congregation was not established until the nineteenth century. The first Manchester Sephardi Synagogue was consecrated in 1874, 16 years after the consecration of the Reform synagogue. See Williams, op. cit. (1985 edn), pp. 319–24.
3. Williams, op. cit., pp. 18–19.
4. Williams, op. cit., pp. 31 and 50.
5. Williams, op. cit., p. 77.
6. Williams, op. cit., p. 260.
7. Williams, op. cit., p. 128.
8. R. Gottheil, *The Life of Gustav Gottheil* (1936), pp. 285–328.
9. Gottheil, op. cit., p. 294.
10. Gottheil, op. cit., p. 299. (Gottheil's diary has been translated from the original German by the author.)
11. Gottheil, op. cit., p. 321.
12. Gottheil, op. cit., p. 323.
13. Gottheil, op. cit., p. 281.
14. Ibid.
15. Williams, op. cit., p. 229.
16. T. Theodores, lecture, *The Rabbinical Law of Excommunication* (Manchester, 1854).
17. Williams, op. cit., p. 220.
18. Williams, op. cit., p. 222.
19. Williams, op. cit., p. 247.
20. Ibid.
21. Minute Book of the West London Synagogue of British Jews, 10 April 1859, loc. cit.
22. Williams, op. cit., pp. 240–7.
23. Minute Book of the West London Synagogue of British Jews, 28 Sept. 1856, loc. cit.
24. Ibid.
25. Ibid.
26. *Jewish Chronicle*, 9 April 1858, Supplement, p. 1.
27. Williams, op. cit., p. 255.
28. Ibid.
29. *Jewish Chronicle*, 9 April 1858.
30. P. Goldberg, *The Manchester Congregation of British Jews, 1857 –1957* (1957), p. 27.
31. Williams, op. cit., p. 262.
32. *Jewish Chronicle*, 14 April 1859.
33. Gottheil, op. cit., p. 14.
34. M. Meyer, *Response to Modernity* (1988), pp. 80–4.
35. Gottheil, op. cit., p. 15.
36. A practice discontinued in New York in 1855 and in Berlin and Hamburg at least ten years earlier.
37. Goldberg, op. cit., p. 34.
38. Williams, op. cit., p. 296.
39. Minute Book of the West London Synagogue of British Jews, 18 May 1862, loc. cit.
40. Meyer, op. cit., pp. 247–8.

41. Goldberg, op. cit., p. 35.
42. Gottheil, op. cit., p. 18.
43. Goldberg, op. cit., p. 37.
44. Meyer, op. cit., pp. 236–8 and 247.
45. Goldberg, op. cit., p. 45.
46. *Jewish Chronicle*, 1 Feb. 1895, p. 18.
47. Goldberg, op. cit., p. 40. (The Fast of Ab commemorates the destruction of the first and second temples.)
48. Goldberg, op. cit., p. 58.
49. *Jewish Chronicle*, 20 June 1890.
50. A. Briggs, *Victorian Cities* (1980 edn), p. 140.
51. Ibid.
52. G. Firth, 'The Bradford Trade in the Nineteenth Century', in D. Wright and T. Jowitt (eds), *Victorian Bradford* (1981), p. 13.
53. Briggs, op. cit., p. 152.
54. N. Grizzard, *Follow the Bradford Jewish Heritage* (1984), p. 2.
55. Williams, op. cit., p. 85.
56. Unna was an ancestor of the actress Dame Peggy Ashcroft.
57. *Jewish Chronicle*, 11 Aug. 1865.
58. *Jewish Chronicle*, 21 Oct. 1870.
59. *Jewish Chronicle*, 22 Nov. 1872.
60. In 1848 a wave of liberal revolutions swept across Europe. In Germany the realisation of total Jewish emancipation seemed a possibility under the terms of the new Prussian constitution. But the dream soon faded and by 1849 there was a reversion back to autocratic rule. Where a year previously there had been hope, there was now disillusion and a restoration of Jewish disabilities. For many Jews, revolutionaries and others, it was a signal to leave Germany and seek their fortune elsewhere. For details of the Jewish role in the European revolutions of 1848 and the after-effects, see H.M. Sacher, *The Course of Modern Jewish History* (1982 edn), pp. 107–12.
61. *Jewish Chronicle*, 1 April 1881.
62. *Jewish Chronicle*, 25 March 1881.
63. Letter from Dr J. Strauss to the West London Synagogue of British Jews, 15 Oct. 1880, AJ/A 59/6, Anglo-Jewish Archives, University of Southampton.
64. O. M. Stroud, *The Story of the Stroud Family* (1974), AJ/A 152, Anglo-Jewish Archives, loc. cit.
65. Stroud, op. cit., p. 26.
66. Stroud, op. cit., pp. 26–7.
67. H. Wolfe, *Now a Stranger* (1933), p. 118.
68. Wolfe, op. cit., p. 121.
69. Letter from Strauss, dated 15 Oct. 1880, AJ/A 59/6, loc. cit.
70. D.W. Marks's report on application for the position of Assistant Minister, undated, AJ/A 59/6, loc. cit.
71. Wolfe, op. cit., p. 124.
72. Stroud, op. cit., p. 27.
73. *Jewish Chronicle*, 1 April 1881.
74. See below.
75. *Bradford Chronicle*, 7 April 1880.
76. Semon died on 18 July 1877 at the age of 65, Calman died on 21 December 1880 at the age of 50 and Jacob Unna died on 7 January 1881 at the age of 80 – information from the Bradford Congregation of British and Foreign Jews, Register of Death.
77. *Bradford Chronicle*, 30 March 1881.
78. Wolfe, op. cit., p. 118.
79. Ibid.
80. *Jewish Chronicle*, 1 Sept. 1922.
81. *Jewish Chronicle*, 1 April 1881.

82. *Bradford Chronicle*, 30 March 1881.
83. *Jewish Chronicle*, 1 April 1881.
84. *Jewish Chronicle*, 8 April 1881.
85. Wolfe, op. cit., p. 120.
86. *Jewish Chronicle*, 28 April 1893.
87. See below, Chapter 4.
88. *Jewish Chronicle*, 29 June 1906, Supplement, p. IV.
89. *Jewish Year Book, 1900–1901* (1900), p. 109.
90. Stroud, op. cit., p. 15.
91. Stroud, op. cit., p. 64.
92. *Jewish Chronicle*, 1 Sept. 1922, p. 14.
93. *Jewish Chronicle*, 2 June 1893, p. 11.
94. Wolfe, op. cit., p. 126.
95. *Jewish Chronicle*, 2 June 1893, p. 11.
96. The Association was in fact a cultural society which invited members and distinguished guests to debate the issues of the day.
97. West London Synagogue Association 3rd Annual Report, 1897–1898, Archives of the West London Synagogue of British Jews.
98. Ibid.
99. D. Spector, 'Brighton Jewry Reconsidered', *Transactions of the Jewish Historical Society in England*, Vol. XXX, 1987–88, p. 93.
100. Spector, op. cit., p. 108.
101. Letter dated 6 Dec. 1867, Anglo-Jewish Archives, AJ/A 150, loc. cit.
102. Letter dated 23 Sept. 1875, Anglo-Jewish Archives, AJ/A 150, loc. cit.
103. C. Roth, *A History of the Jews in England* (1978 edn), p. 230n.
104. A. J. Kershen, *Uniting the Tailors* (1995), p. 36.
105. Ibid.
106. Anglo-Jewish Archives, AJ/A 59/6, letter dated 10 June 1880, loc. cit.
107. West London Synagogue of British Jews, Copy Letter book, 1879–80, 20 July 1880, p. 321, Archives of West London Synagogue of British Jews.
108. Letter from Oppenheim dated 18 Aug. 1880, Anglo-Jewish Archives, AJ/A 59/6, loc. cit.
109. *Jewish World*, 20 Aug. 1880.
110. Minute Book of the Leeds Old Congregation, 23 Aug. 1880.
111. Minute Book of the Leeds Old Synagogue, 10 Oct. 1880. The authors wish to acknowledge the help of Doug Chairing in providing the details of the Minute Book of the Leeds Old Synagogue and information from the *Jewish World*.
112. West London Synagogue of British Jews, Copy Letter Book, 16 April 1874, loc. cit.

4 Into the Twentieth Century, 1870–1929

By the end of the nineteenth century Reform Judaism had taken root in three of England's major cities; it did not cross the border into Scotland until 1937 when a congregation was founded in Glasgow. With certain exceptions, which included the common usage of prayer books, the congregations led independent and, some considered, élitist lives.[1] This chapter sets out to explore the path of Reform in Britain until the end of the third decade of the twentieth century, to the point at which the expansionary period in Progressive Judaism in Britain began.

The last years of the nineteenth century and the first 20 of the next were years in which the composition of British Jewry underwent a major transformation, one which would make a decisive impression on the future controlling structure of the community.

The assassination of the Russian Tsar Alexander II in 1881 heralded a renewed and virulent series of pogroms and increased to a flood the already growing number of eastern European immigrant arrivals; between 1881 and 1914 over 100,000 poor and largely unskilled foreign Jews settled in the East End of London. In 1895 Political Zionism first appeared in England in the figure of Theodor Herzl. In a political climate in which issues of national identity, eugenics[2] and Empire were, at the beginning of the twentieth century, taking centre stage, the mass of 'pauper aliens' in East London and the proposals for the creation of a Jewish State produced a feeling of unease within the minds of some, though not all, recently emancipated members of the Anglo-Jewish élite. In 1917 the Russian Bolshevik revolution once again fanned the flames of British anti-Semitism, glowing since the late 1880s. To many, 'Bolshie' and Jew were one and the same. All these developments were disturbing to an Anglo-Jewish establishment whose members considered themselves full and equal citizens of Britain. This chapter sets out to examine the reaction of Reform Jews to these major events.

Though national and international affairs were of vital importance, in London and the provinces there were issues which had to be addressed at local and community level. These included the nature of the relationship between the Orthodox and Reform synagogues, changes in Reform ritual and liturgy and the spiritual and intellectual discontent within the synagogues. This latter grew to such a level that the Council of West London was forced to acknowledge it as 'the crisis of Reform Judaism'. It was this that led to an articulation of those universalist beliefs that sowed the seeds of a schism at the end of the first decade of the twentieth century which resulted in the creation of the first Liberal Jewish synagogue in Britain. Closer to home the senior clerical figures, David Woolf Marks, Albert Lowy and Joseph Strauss, men who had gained the respect of all of Anglo-Jewry, were making way for those who would lead their flocks through the physically and emotionally devastating First World War and into the new order beyond.

We begin on a celebratory note, the occasion of the fiftieth anniversary of the consecration of Britain's first Reform Synagogue. The ceremony, which was reportedly magnificent, was held in the impressive synagogue in Upper Berkeley Street on 27 January 1892. The service was conducted by a now white-haired David Woolf Marks who carried the weight of his 81 years lightly. In fact it was his younger colleague, Albert Lowy, who at the age of 76, was the first of the original Reform ministers to retire from office. The occasion could have been an opportunity to heal the breach in Anglo-Jewry. Only a month before, the Orthodox Reverend Simeon Singer had appealed for the (re)establishment of a bond between the Orthodox and Reform.[3] Singer was not the only one to see the fiftieth anniversary as an opportunity to build bridges. In his editorial in the *Jewish Chronicle* the enlightened Orthodox editor, Asher Myers, criticised Chief Rabbi Adler and *Haham* Gaster for refusing to attend the jubilee service, one which was attended by Lord Rothschild, Philip Ornstein from the United Synagogue and by ministers from the constituent Great, Bayswater, Central, North London and New West End synagogues. In his editorial Myers asked whether Orthodox practice would really have been weakened by Adler's attendance at Upper Berkeley Street. After all, he wrote, 'Adler goes to Westminster Abbey for Queen Victoria's Jubilee but he doesn't become Christian'.[4] There was a positive need for Anglo-Jewry as a whole to 'secure the intelligence, culture and thinking power of the community' which, according to the *Jewish Chronicle*'s editor lay with the élitist Reformers.

In his anniversary sermon David Woolf Marks re-examined the events which had led to the 1840 schism and the subsequent development of West London. He declared that the recently improved decorum, liturgy and sermons which were noticeable in Orthodox synagogues were the result of the example set by West London, whose foundation had proved a 'service to Judaism', particularly as it had 'maintained the attachment of intellectuals... who might otherwise have drifted away'. The creation of the Jewish Religious Union and, a few years later, the Liberal synagogue, proved this to be a somewhat inaccurate assessment. The service also provided an opportunity for the first pronouncement, in Upper Berkeley Street, of the Royal Prayer in English; the Manchester Reform congregation had adopted the practice some years before. In concluding his sermon David Woolf Marks posed a rhetorical question: had Reform advanced or retarded spiritual Judaism? Marks posited his belief that, 'by letting light into the synagogue', Reform had brought 'amity, brotherhood and common sentiment...in support of every effort for the promotion of the community at large'.[5]

David Woolf Marks's sermon raises certain questions. First, though he made reference to the 'Reform Community', West London made no attempt to include representatives of the two provincial congregations in the service. Such an invitation would have been an overt announcement, however tenuous, of the existence of an English 'Reform Movement', something the Berkeleystreeters appear to have been reluctant to concede. West London's independent stance was further reflected in the fact that there is no record of an American or European Reform presence at the ceremony. This must be seen as a further example of how little European Reform had influenced the ritual and liturgy of West London. Second, Marks refers to the example set by West London to the Orthodox synagogues but ventures no criticism of the absence of their spiritual leaders. Co-operation and acceptance of one group by the other was a continuing issue. Following the consecration of Upper Berkeley Street in 1870 attempts had been made to draw the two closer together. Overtures were made and rejected. When Chief Rabbi Adler died in 1890, David Woolf Marks and Assistant Minister Isidore Harris attended his memorial service. At West London Harris gave a memorial sermon to the man he acknowledged as the 'ecclesiastical head of the great majority of English Jews' in which he referred to the 'divergence of religious standpoint between the Orthodoxy and the Reform'. Harris went on to say that though Adler had been 'intolerant at the outset of his career, time had smoothed the edges of difference'. In Manchester the Reverend Simmons went even further, saying that although there had been 'minor' differences Adler had been truly the Chief Rabbi of the whole community.[6]

None of these sentiments was sufficient to encourage West London to agree to the request made by the United Synagogue, for West London to send a delegate to the conference held to confirm the appointment of Adler's successor as Chief Rabbi. The invitation from the United Synagogue[7] exposed the divisions extant within the Council of Founders of West London. Philip Magnus, Frederick Mocatta and Albert Lowy were in favour of sending a representative. Mocatta and Magnus, together with Herbert Lousada had, two months earlier, written to the President of the United Synagogue suggesting that 'steps be taken to bring our [West London] synagogue under the guidance of the spiritual Chief [Rabbi]'. The West London Synagogue Council was highly critical of such an unprecedented and unauthorised step.[8] Reverends Marks and Harris, together with Julian Goldsmid, at that time Chairman and President of West London, supported a resolution requesting the sending of a reply which read as follows:

> The congregation, whilst desiring to maintain, and if possible, strengthen the cordial relations now happily subsisting between it and the United Synagogue, cannot be represented by delegates at a conference which is called to consider the appointment of a new Chief Rabbi.[9]

In that same year another opportunity arose for co-operation between Orthodox and Reform, this time in the establishment of a synagogue and provident society in the East End. Debate and dissension were the order of the day at West London. Philip

Magnus argued that the solution to the problem of the large number of pauper alien Jews, whose presence had drawn forth accusations that the aliens (eastern European Jews) were taking the homes and jobs of Englishmen, was not in the creation of large synagogues but in 'men with brains and hearts to live there and... to devote their time to the betterment of the condition of their foreign brethren'.[10] No doubt Magnus had in mind the university settlements, Toynbee Hall and Oxford House, which had been established in the East End in order that graduates from Oxford and Cambridge might live and work among the poor of east London giving those less fortunate moral uplift, spiritual guidance and education. Eventually, it was decided that Sir Julian Goldsmid would represent the London Reform Synagogue at the discussions with the United Synagogue. However, these ended in disagreement and the venture was not pursued. Eight years later, in 1898, the topic re-emerged when the West London Synagogue Association[11] debated the desirability of establishing a place of worship in the East End of London. The chief aim appears to have been to 'Anglicise the foreign element'. As Morris Joseph, at that time acting Senior Minister, explained, 'Russo-Jewish immigrants had to realise their duty was to leave behind them the ideas and habits that were tolerated in Russia but entirely out of place in England. The young should be saved from themselves.' The meeting was told that 'a great number of foreign Jews tramped to Berkeley Street on the festivals'. One view put forward at the meeting was that the establishment of a Reform Synagogue should be at the request of the East Enders. Joseph countered this by arguing that the Reformers had a duty to establish an East End synagogue. The majority were opposed to this and it was finally resolved that an East End synagogue should be opened only 'if it was requested'.[12]

The debate is indicative of the prevailing attitude of the Anglo-Jewish establishment. The immigrants must be Anglicised. They projected an image of Jewry that was disturbing to those who identified themselves as Englishmen who observed the Jewish religion. This belief was highlighted by Morris Joseph's reference to the 'duty' of the immigrants to their new-found homeland. Anything which identified the Jew as an outsider, as for example the persistent use of Yiddish, was to be discouraged and eradicated during the process of assimilation and acculturation.

In spite, or because, of the disagreements, Reform Judaism did not arrive in the East End of London until after the First World War. By that time Basil Henriques's Boys' Club, established before the outbreak of war, had blossomed into the St George's Jewish Settlement.[13] At the end of the war it was recognised that Jewish soldiers returning from the front to the East End might well prefer a religious service that combined tradition and progress. Henriques appealed to both West London and the newly founded Liberal synagogue for financial assistance. West London donated an initial £1,000 and the Liberal synagogue £600. A managing council was established, appointed by both synagogues, and it was agreed that a minister be made available by each. The Settlement's first warden was the six feet five inches tall Basil Henriques – the 'Gaffer' as he was known to the boys. Services were to be held along progressive lines following a ritual that conformed in character 'with the religious needs and desires of the congregation'. It was agreed that 'only when an ideal Minister is forthcoming – a man of deep spiritual feeling, ready to live amongst his flock...then should a separate East End Minister be provided'.[14] Services at the Settlement were a combination of the traditional – with two days of festivals observed and the retention of certain traditional prayers – and the progressive. The Settlement's 'custom-made' prayer book, in English and Yiddish, as well as Hebrew, mixed old with certain new English hymns and anthems in recognition of a membership which was largely of east European origin.[15]

Throughout the last years of the nineteenth century and the early years of the twentieth, attempts were made to bring the Reform and Orthodox factions closer together. It was generally felt that the differences were receding and that the two had 'drifted towards one another so nearly that the rill which divides is of the thinnest'. In the 1890s emphasis was on the narrowness of the divide and the need for communal fellowship. Perhaps this explains why the former Third Minister of West London, Philip Magnus, had his son's *barmitzvah* at the Orthodox New West End Synagogue where the minister, Simeon Singer, pronounced in July 1893 that there was 'no natural antagonism between the various elements which constitute our common Judaism'.[16] Singer made this statement two months after declining the offer, made by Julian Goldsmid, of the position of Senior Minster of West London. The Orthodox, but forward-looking, Singer, believed that he would be of more use 'to our common Judaism by remaining [at New West End] and fighting against the narrowness and intolerance of every kind', than by joining West London.[17] Singer's optimistic assumption of impending harmony was not generally shared. In 1895 Frederick Henriques commented that, while socially the division was narrowing, on doctrinal matters 'the severance was far wider'.[18]

Differences were set aside when David Woolf Marks died in Maidenhead in June 1909 at the age of 98. For 69 years he had served the Reform congregation of London and acted as the clerical point of reference for those of Manchester and Bradford. The sentiments expressed in the letters of condolence illustrate how at the time of his death he was revered and respected by the whole of Anglo-Jewry. The letter sent by the Council of the United Synagogue illustrates both the regard in which Marks was held and the help, unspecified, he had rendered. The letter read as follows:

> Many changes have taken place in the history of the London Jewish Community since he [Marks] assumed his high office ... It was his earnest desire to bring into close and friendly relations the United Synagogue and the West London Synagogue and to co-operate in matters of high communal importance while the public assistance which he at times rendered to the rabbinate must be gratefully remembered.
>
> The Council [of the United Synagogue] gladly recall the sympathetic help rendered by the Council of West London... and they fervently hope that unity and concord may always exist between the sister congregations to the benefit of the community as a whole.

The Committee of the Deputies of British Jews which, under the Presidency of Sir Moses Montefiore, had been so bitterly opposed to Marks and his synagogue, was explicit in its regard for his community achievements. In his letter of condolence David Alexander said:

> His tact and diplomacy were among the principal causes of the final obliteration of any feeling of bitterness occasioned by the initiation of the Reform Movement. He lived to see the complete amalgamation for all secular purposes of his congregation with the rest of the community and the triumph

> of the cause of harmony and concord among the Jews of this country which he had laboured so long and so zealously to secure.[19]

There was general agreement that David Woolf Marks had played a major role in narrowing the gap between Orthodox and Reform. The *Jewish Chronicle* looked back to the time when Marks had been 'the most hated man in Anglo-Jewry – a rebel'. However, as a result of his conciliatory attitude change had come about. Marks had stemmed the more extreme ambitions of the Reformers and had refrained from 'carrying on the traditions of the Reform Movement on the Continent'. The *Chronicle* believed that Marks had been the force and influence responsible for certain of the reforms carried out by the Orthodox synagogues. His high standard of pulpit eloquence was an undoubted factor in the decision to introduce English sermons into the United Synagogues, while the removal of *Piyutim* and the holding of services at more convenient hours also carried the hallmark of the Reform example. Marks's funeral manifested the distance travelled since the death of Benjamin Elkin in 1848. The Chief Rabbi first crossed the threshold of Reform in 1905, when he attended a memorial service for F. D. Mocatta at the West London Synagogue.[20] David Woolf Marks's burial brought together the Chief Rabbi, the *Haham*, Dayan Feldman, a broad representation of rabbinic and secular members of the United Synagogue and their Reform counterparts.[21]

The narrowing of the divide between Orthodox and Reform was reinforced by a common concern over the religious apathy manifest among late-nineteenth-century Jewry. The 'crisis of Reform' had been brought about in part by the stagnation referred to earlier. It was an environment ripe for the emergence of a form of Judaism suited to the intellectual demands of certain late Victorian English Jews. At the end of the nineteenth century a climate of indifference was permeating the institutions of Reform Judaism. In Manchester and London, no doubt Bradford too, synagogue attendance was poor. In 1885, a member of West London commented that 'if it were not for our women... the male attendance of themselves would be hardly sufficient to impart meaning to a public service'. In the decade that followed there was little improvement. A letter to the *Jewish Chronicle* in 1895 noted that even though 367 seats were let in the synagogue and 358 in the women's gallery 'on one Saturday in November the congregation of West London consisted of eight people on the right of the Ark, five with *tallit* and prayer books, three without and on the left six all wearing *tallit*'.[22] Including the officers a total of 18 males were in attendance. The 'enthusiasm' that had accompanied the birth of Reform was 'drifting away'.[23]

There was sparse attendance at Hebrew classes, which had finally begun in London as late as 1886. Even then prize winners were frequently children of the Orthodoxy. (It is unclear whether the children of the Reformers were receiving private Hebrew tuition or none at all.) Sir John Simon, presenting the prizes at West London Hebrew classes, commented that a considerable number of congregants of the synagogue retained membership for marriage and burial purposes only. Sir John, the man attributed with having introduced David Woolf Marks to Reform ideology, continued by saying that 'Reform meant nothing unless it meant progress and the only justification for those separated from the great mass of their [Orthodox] co-religionists was the belief that in so doing they were better promoting the cause of their religion'.[24]

The apathy and decline in worship manifest among Reform Jews was also apparent within Orthodox circles. Concern was expressed at the disregard for religious practice, dietary laws and marriage within the faith.[25] It was little different within the Christian Church where higher criticism of the Bible, the questioning of its authenticity, was undermining religious conviction. Little had changed since the religious census of 1851. The exception was in the East End of London where, in 1906, the *Daily News* recorded 50 per cent synagogue attendance by eastern European immigrants on the first day of Passover.[26] Allied to irreligion was desire for change. Following his formal installation as Chief Rabbi, after the death of his father in 1891, Hermann Adler did sanction certain modifications of the Orthodox *Minhag*. For some these were insufficient. Jews who had moved to the rarefied middle-class pastures of Hampstead in north-west London – where there was no 'local' synagogue or easy access to Sabbath morning services – were still dissatisfied, though it is unclear whether the problem was one of distance or of 'other commitments'. One solution was the introduction of Sabbath afternoon services in the Town Hall in Broadhurst Gardens, West Hampstead, in 1890. These attracted Jews 'of all shades of opinion', Ashkenazi, Sephardi and Reform. Significantly, a major portion of the congregation was female. In late Victorian England the status of women was a contentious topic and one considered a major issue by the female progenitor of Liberal Judaism, Lily Montagu.

Among those who attended the first Saturday afternoon service were Claude Montefiore, Lady Simon, Oswald Simon, Reverend I. Harris, the Third Minister of West London, and the Reverend Berliner from the Orthodox Synagogue in St John's Wood, north-west London. The *Jewish Chronicle*'s reporter noted that he 'could see at a glance that he [Revd Berliner] was not sympathetic'. Berliner was clearly antipathetic to the service which the Reverend Morris Joseph began at 3 p.m.[27] In his sermon Joseph explained why there was a need for such an unorthodox service, 'religion was ceasing to be the dominant factor', Judaism was perceived by many as medieval and this was leading to a 'gradual intellectual alienation'. Echoing the themes of 1840, he went on to say that services lacked spiritual uplift and were poorly attended. Judaism needed modernising. Change was justified if it made religion more effective. Joseph concluded by saying that 'progress is the one universal law to which even religions must bow'.[28] Here we have a glimpse of the theology of the man who, though trained as an orthodox minister, would later succeed David Woolf Marks as Senior Minister of Britain's first Reform synagogue.

The Sabbath afternoon services brought together, albeit briefly, those who had been separated by the schism of 1840. There were even those who ventured so far as to propose a union of Jew and Christian. That proposal was made by Baron de Rothschild's daughter, Constance Flower, later Lady Battersea.[29] In his letter to Mrs Flower, though Morris Joseph turns down her suggestion for a shared Christian-Jewish service, he does signal his search for a 'more liberal exposition of Judaism as well as an enlightened form of service, in short a new synagogue'. He goes on to express his determination not to succumb to the 'monopoly of Polish Rabbis' even though the Sabbath afternoon services were 'not flourishing financially'. There was a positive need for those he described as 'paying congregants'. Joseph was even prepared to sacrifice the acquisition of an organ if the St John's Wood committee would allow the synagogue to be used for services. In Joseph's view it would have been 'a distinct gain if, by the admission of the service into an Orthodox synagogue we would get some conservative recognition of our movement'.[30] Subsequent developments demonstrated that the committee of St John's Wood was not prepared to permit the predominantly female, Reform-Orthodox congregation to use its synagogue for services.

It was over the application for the use of an organ during the Sabbath afternoon services that the future religious pattern of Anglo-Jewry was decided. The inclusion of instrumental music during services was contrary to Orthodox practice and, not unexpectedly, the request for the use of an organ on the Sabbath was rejected. The issue split the supporters of the Saturday afternoon services. The majority, Orthodox in habit and in support of the rejection, established the Hampstead Synagogue and affiliated to the United Synagogue.

Morris Joseph supported the establishment of the new Orthodox synagogue and it was a foregone conclusion that he would apply for, and be appointed to, the position of minister of the Hampstead Synagogue. However, Joseph had advocated the use of instrumental music at the Sabbath service, had 'voiced his opposition to the revival of the sacrifices' and had 'published views at variance with traditional Judaism'.[31] His appointment was not sanctioned by Hermann Adler, the new Chief Rabbi. Instead, the Anglicised, East End born, Aaron Asher Green became the first minister of the Hampstead Synagogue. Joseph and Green, though representing different camps, did think along similar lines and thus were destined to co-operate in the next stage in the history of intellectual Judaism in Britain, the foundation of the Jewish Religious Union in 1902.

The Jewish Religious Union was the progenitor of the first Liberal Jewish synagogue. Looking back to 1840, it seems almost ironic that its foundation resulted from the 'conservative' attitude of the West London Synagogue Council and its clergy. The original concept of the Jewish Religious Union was as a medium through which to reawaken support for an intellectual and spiritual Judaism considered by some to have become dormant, and by others as on the verge of total disintegration. Following a series of meetings which had the support of thinking and concerned Jews across the spectrum of religious practice it was decided to continue in the style of the earlier Sabbath afternoon services with lectures, publications and services. The Jewish Religious Union was founded in February 1902. Claude

Montefiore, at that time a warden of West London, was appointed President, supported by a committee which included Morris Joseph, Israel Abrahams, the Reader in Rabbinics at Cambridge, Lily Montagu, daughter of the founder of the Federation of Synagogues, Samuel Montagu, and Orthodox ministers including Simeon Singer, who had taught the young Lily Hebrew, and A.A. Green of the newly founded Hampstead Synagogue. At the meeting held in February 1902 to establish the Union and set up its committee, Lily Montagu announced that most of the services would be in English, that there would be mixed seating 'to merge the family in the ideal of communal life' and that there would be instrumental music 'to quicken the spirit into corporate action'.[32] The services would be timed to accommodate those unable to attend Sabbath morning services. There was a suggestion that the service be held on Sunday mornings but this was rejected as too radical. The Chief Rabbi's reaction to the JRU's *modus operandi* was to issue a statement which said that the Union went against Jewish law.

Montagu and Montefiore, two of the three M's of Liberal Judaism – the third being Israel Mattuck, a graduate of Cincinnati Hebrew College who was appointed first Liberal minister in 1911 – were the forceful and ideological progenitors of Liberal Judaism in England. The new-style Sabbath afternoon services, at that time not intended as a separate religious group, conveyed their philosophy. Montefiore in his Hibbert Lectures of 1892 had revealed his radical, historically based, concept of Judaism. Encouraged by Benjamin Jowett, his tutor at Balliol, he revealed that he saw his religion as a spiritual, universal and progressive form of worship, something that was not immutable. If a section were outmoded it should be dispensed with. In 1899 Lily Montagu outlined her views on contemporary Judaism in an article in the *Jewish Quarterly Review*. She expressed her concern over the failure of the Orthodoxy, and no doubt West London, to stem the tide of drift and defection. She stressed the need to 'lift Judaism from its desolate position' and make it part of contemporary and enlightened life. There was a need to revitalise Judaism, to give it life, meaning and modernity. The article initiated the intellectual relationship between Montagu and Montefiore that was to provide the catalyst for Liberal Judaism in England.

At its outset, in spite of the Chief Rabbi's earlier

pronouncement, the JRU had the support of all streams of Anglo-Jewry. The inaugural service, which took place at the Great Central Hall, Marylebone Road, was conducted by Simeon Singer. According to a report which appeared in the *Jewish Chronicle* it bore very little relation to a synagogue service, there being little Hebrew, no *chazan* and no *Sefer Torah*. What there was, was solemnity and dignity. In his inaugural sermon Claude Montefiore asked why there should be only one type of Jewish service, Jews were drifting because they did not like tradition and the JRU was compensating for this.[33] A. A. Green, uneasy at the radical stance the JRU was adopting, resigned. While he had been in favour of reforms within the framework of the Orthodox synagogue he could not support a movement which went beyond traditional boundaries and made independent changes. On the eve of the inaugural service the founders of the JRU announced that, as their search for a synagogue in which to hold services had so far proved unsuccessful, they would use whatever facilities were available in order to cater for those who, though not versed in Hebrew or tradition, wanted to follow a Jewish service.

The search for a home continued. The Orthodoxy rejected the JRU outright. An approach was then made to West London for permission to hold services in the Upper Berkeley Street Synagogue on a Sabbath afternoon.[34] In the letter which outlined the request the JRU explained that 'for the successful working of the scheme the congregation may be permitted to sit together irrespective of sex and that modern English prayers may be included in the service'. The debate over mixed seating and increased English usage was heated and in 1903, to the majority of Berkeleystreeters, still unacceptable. It is therefore not surprising that this and other points were rejected. West London's Council drew up a provisional list of ten conditions under which the synagogue could be used by the JRU for Saturday afternoon services. These were:

- All preachers and readers to be Jewish.
- The sexes to be separate.
- The Ark to be opened, the scroll of Law taken out and elevated, the portion of the Law varying from week to week.
- All hymns and psalms to have been composed by members of the Jewish faith.
- All modern English prayers of Jewish authorship to be included

in the ritual to be approved by Council of the West London Synagogue.
- Sabbath afternoon *Amidah* included and a portion to be read each week.
- A *Kaddish* to be read once.
- The above only to take effect if and when the ritual proposed by the Union shall have been adopted by the synagogue in conformity with Law 169.
- Subject to the foregoing all else to be left to the control of the committee of the JRU.
- The sub-committee of the JRU to submit the ritual of the Union, with power to approve, to the sub-committee appointed by the Council of West London.

The West London Council debated the conditions throughout February and March 1903. On 23 March an amended scheme was submitted to the Council of the JRU.[35] At first it seemed as if the JRU would concede to the demands of the Reformers but, after further consideration, sent a formal letter to West London. It signalled the independent future of the JRU. The letter thanked the Council for the 'invitation it had extended' but explained that the JRU could not see its way to accepting the conditions laid down.[36]

With no spiritual roof over their heads the JRU continued to meet and hold services privately. It 'posed no communal threat to Anglo-Jewry',[37] and was perceived merely as an élitist intellectual movement which was retaining the interests of Jews who might otherwise have eschewed religion or defected to Christianity. As the ideological and theological gap between the Berkeleystreeters and the JRU widened, demands were made for the resignation of Claude Montefiore from the position of warden. No *cherem*, no demand for removal from the synagogue, but shades of the intolerance West London itself had exposed. Even the bond of fellowship and understanding that existed between Morris Joseph and Montefiore could not withstand the ideological pressures that the latter's universalist approach and use of the New Testament created. Joseph could not accept Montefiore's justifications for a 'licence to change'. But in spite of all the differences Claude Montefiore's emotional ties remained in Upper Berkeley Street. As he later explained, 'my heart is in the West London Synagogue and my head at the Liberal Synagogue'.[38]

In 1909 the JRU added the words 'For The Achievement of Liberal Judaism' to its title and began the search for a suitable site for what would be the first Liberal synagogue in Britain. In 1911 both a building, in Hill Street, Marylebone, and a minister were found. No longer just a group offering spiritual and intellectual stimulation and satisfaction, the JRU had now entered the communal arena and staked out a place for itself and those who would follow the path of Liberal Judaism.

Anglo-Jewry was concerned. Orthodox and Reform ministers were increasingly aware of the pressure for modernisation. It was ironic that what was seen as revolutionary in 1840 could, within 70 years, be viewed as conservative. Within both factions only minor changes had been made and these largely to accommodate an increasingly Anglicised and suburbanised community. One of Adler's more significant reforms was the introduction, in 1890, of Simeon Singer's Authorised Prayer Book. This brought uniformity to the Orthodox service. For the first time a full English translation was available for those who, though they followed the traditional service in Hebrew, were unaware of its true meaning.

During the first decade of the twentieth century Anglo-Jewry underwent a social transition. The Anglicisation process had accelerated and Jews and Gentiles now encountered one another in a diversity of socio-economic spheres. These changes were acknowledged by the publication of a pamphlet in 1912 entitled 'Proposed Reforms In the West London Synagogue and their Justifications',[39] which pinpointed entrance to 'public schools, universities and professions' as being particularly responsible for the increase in proselytism. The authors of the pamphlet, concerned at the growth of the Liberal movement and worried about the potential loss of membership and revenue if reforms were not introduced at West London, pronounced it necessary to 'make our religious practice accord with the spirit of the times'. Reference was made to David Woolf Marks's words, 'For Israelites to adapt ritual to the wants of its members', in the introduction to the 1841 Prayer Book, and to his sermon on the occasion of the golden jubilee of 1892, when he stressed that 'Judaism has nothing to fear from adaptation to the necessities of the times'. The pamphleteers acknowledged that 'there is a crisis in the community' and that the creation of the JRU was the 'result of withholding judicious reforms'. There was reference to the introduction of English into Orthodox services and the need to increase its usage at Upper Berkeley Street. The excuse that foreigners would be unable to follow was discounted, 'it was more important to retain English members than it was to accommodate the occasional foreign visitor', a sentiment that characterises the very 'English' nature of the membership of West London. There was a call for shortened Sabbath services – for these to commence at 11 a.m. and continue for only one and a half hours, thus making them convenient for those who had a distance to travel. There was also a renewed appeal for mixed seating. The pamphlet concluded with the warning that rejection of the proposals 'would be fraught with the gravest danger to this congregation and to the community'. Shorter services and an increased usage of English became part of the ritual before the First World War. The more radical step of mixed seating had to wait until 1930.

Even before the appearance of the pamphlet, demands for changes to the ritual and liturgy were being articulated in the United, Federation and Sephardi, as well as the Reform, synagogues, while changes were also being called for in secular institutions such as the Board of Deputies and the AJA. The foundation of the Liberal Jewish Synagogue, and its possible threat to the status quo, only served to highlight the issues and in December 1909 a conference of Anglo-Jewish ministers was convened by the *Jewish Chronicle*. The conference was held at Jews College in central London and attended by between 80 and 90 ministers from London and the provinces. The spread of religious practice, from Federation[40] through to Reform and Orthodox Ashkenazi, was covered. The unexplained absence of a Sephardi representative gave rise to considerable comment and a degree of covert criticism in the *Jewish Chronicle*'s reports of the conference.[41] However, in spite of the absentee, Liberal Judaism and increasing drift and defection appeared to be uniting those who decades before were virtual enemies.

In his opening address Chief Rabbi Hermann Adler appears to have gone out of his way to stress that the conference was not a reaction to the emergence of Liberal Judaism but had been convened in order to provide a forum for debate on the role of Jewish ministers in contemporary society, a society which had to contend with an increased alien presence and the rise of middle-class Jewish suburbia. Emphasis was placed upon the 'over Anglicisation' of the Jewish community. Papers presented covered a variety of related topics, from the sending of Jewish children to

Christian boarding schools to mixed marriages and the function and status of the Jewish ministry. In his paper on Sabbath observance, Harry Lewis, the radical minister of the Manchester Reform Synagogue, argued that in modern society not everyone could formally observe the Sabbath in the morning and therefore the time of public worship should be open to change. Mr Lewis, appointed to his ministry in March 1908, prefaced his paper by pointing out that he came 'from a different religious standpoint to the majority of his fellow conference members'.[42] In fact his appointment the previous year had been the subject of considerable debate at the Manchester Reform Synagogue. A number of members of the selection committee abstained from voting for Lewis because, in his application, he had requested the 'right to preach at the JRU... should he be asked to do so'.[43] The objections to the proposed appointment were eventually withdrawn but the bias of Lewis's religious feeling remained in evidence. The pro-Zionist Cambridge graduate was active in a variety of fields and certainly did not conform to the standard dog-collared image of an Edwardian Jewish minister. Four years after his appointment, frustrated by what he saw as the conservative attitude of the Manchester Reform Synagogue, Lewis tendered his resignation. As he put it, 'something was wanting to revive the synagogue'.[44] The final straw was the unwillingness of the Manchester congregation's lay leadership to sanction sermons given by Claude Montefiore and Israel Mattuck. There was a general feeling that Lewis's radical presence would discourage new membership. In 1913 he left for America to become chaplain and principal of the Jewish Institute of Religion in New York.

Henry Lewis represented the most radical form of Judaism at the conference, highly critical of what he termed the current practice of 'two Sabbaths', Sunday devoted to leisure and Saturday to prayer. Morris Joseph presented a paper on another facet of the assimilation process, marriage between Jews and non-Jews. In this he identified himself with the conservative faction of Reform Judaism. Joseph argued that 'We [West London] are as irreconcilably opposed to marriage between a Jew and an unconverted Gentile as is the most thorough-going adherent of *Shulchan Aruch*... on this question English Reform cordially joins hands with the Orthodoxy'.[45]

The conference ended with a stronger display of unity between those who had so harshly separated in 1840 than had been evidenced in the past 69 years. A conference constitution was drawn up and it was agreed that there should be a meeting every two years. Initially, the second conference, in 1911, appeared to be successful, delegates discussing issues as diverse as ritual slaughter of meat, the Shops Bill going through Parliament and conversionist propaganda. Its conclusion was marred, not by ideological and theological division, but by differences over the requisite qualifications of a preacher and of a *chazan*.[46] The outcome was that the preachers seceded and subsequently called conferences for themselves alone, under the collective of the Anglo-Jewish Ministers, co-opting Reform ministers as members and on the executive.

The turn of the nineteenth century brought with it the passing of some of the old brigade and the arrival of those who would take Reform Judaism into the twentieth century. In the lay world the death of Sir Julian Goldsmid, Chairman and President of the West London Synagogue, in 1896 at the untimely age of 56, was sorely felt. In its obituary the *Jewish Chronicle* referred to him as a 'Prince In Israel', a man of superior intellect, sound and solid judgement, with an unselfish and noble nature even if his religious views had been somewhat radical for the increasingly conservative West London Synagogue of British Jews. Three years before his death, in 1893, Goldsmid gave a sermon in which he advocated 'doing away with the present mode of separating male and female worshippers', an end to the sounding of the *Shofar* which was 'unmusical and not in harmony with the day in which we live', the removal of the hat – 'God sees no reverence in a covered head' – and increased use of English in the service to attract the young and others who did not attend – 'progress demands constant enlightenment and improvement'. Julian Goldsmid was indeed a Reformer in the truly progressive sense of the word. Like the Founders before him, he clearly wished the observance of Judaism to be in keeping with the demands and realities of modernity. Goldsmid had made considerable efforts to break down the divisions between Orthodox and Reform.[47] A past President and Vice-President of the AJA he guided the Association through its most 'brilliant period'. A regular attender at synagogue, he was a man admired and respected by all and his death marked the end of an era.

The following year saw the death of the man who, it has been suggested, was responsible for introducing David Woolf Marks to the Reform ideal. Sir John Simon, who at one time had considered becoming a minister in order to 'regenerate Judaism',[48] was one of the earliest to advocate the denial of the Oral Law, believing that it contradicted the scriptures. Following the foundation of West London Simon actively involved himself with both the ritual and the music of the Reform service. This was in addition to the demands of the legal profession which he served as both barrister and judge – he was the first Jew to sit as an English judge – and his position as Serjeant-at-Law in the House of Commons. Sir John's youngest son, Oswald, continued the family tradition and became actively involved with West London as both a member of the Council and a lay preacher. The latter in some way compensated for the fact that his application for the position of Assistant Minister, in succession to Philip Magnus, had been rejected.[49] It is worth noting here that, with the exception of the appointment of Philip Magnus for the years between 1904 and 1911, until 1925 the joint position of Chairman and President of West London remained with the descendants of the original Founders, that is with the families Henriques, Goldsmid, Mocatta, Montefiore and Lousada.

Change was also manifest within the clergy. In London David Woolf Marks, now in his ninth decade, found the mantle of Senior Minister weighing heavily upon his increasingly frail shoulders. The ministry of the Synagogue had been, since the arrival of Philip Magnus in 1866, in the hands of three ministers – David Woolf Marks (1841–1909), Albert Lowy (1842–93) and Philip Magnus (1866–80). Magnus resigned his post in 1880. His letter of resignation provides us with an insight into the role of the minister and the conflicting pressures it imposed with regard to pastoral and religious demands. In his letter Magnus expressed regret that he had been unable to exercise 'the influence which I had hoped... or utilise the energy which I was prepared to devote to the service of the members of my own congregation'. He felt that as a paid servant or, as he put it in his letter, 'salaried officer of a religious community', he was restricted in the way he could 'assist the cause of religion'. He believed that he could best serve the Reform community 'in the tradition of the ancient Jewish rabbis – in an honorary capacity'.[50] His subsequent achievements are proof of his success in serving not only the Jewish community, but the nation at large. In 1886 Philip Magnus was knighted for his work as a member of the Royal Commission on Technical

Education and in 1917 he was appointed Baronet. In 1906 he was elected Member of Parliament for the University of London. Opposed to the concept of political Zionism, Magnus was a member of the League of British Jews and a signatory to the Letter of Ten which rejected Bolshevism.[51] When he died in 1933, at the age of 91, the *Jewish Chronicle* wrote of Magnus that 'he made his own way and was awarded a knighthood, not because of amassed wealth and industry but as a result of ability and character'.[52]

With the exception of Oswald Simon, whose application, according to a member of the committee, was 'misunderstood', there were three applicants for Magnus's vacated position: Joseph Strauss, whose application we know was rejected, the Reverend Joseph Simmons, who had officiated at the short-lived South London Synagogue, and the Reverend Isidore Harris. Marks and Lowy both acknowledged that they were growing older and, 'as the congregation had grown very large', there was a need for a competent and relatively young assistant. If Magnus's resignation illustrates the differing attitudes towards the role of minister and the tensions that existed between employer and employee then the reports on the applicants for his successor denote the status West London afforded itself. Strauss was ruled out because of his strong guttural accent and Simmons 'might be suited to a small provincial community but hardly... adapted to the office for which he is now an applicant'.[53] It was agreed that though Harris's Hebrew reading and delivery of English left room for improvement he was a man of scholarship. Accordingly he was appointed Assistant Minister in January 1881 and, following the retirement of Albert Lowy and the appointment of Morris Joseph, Harris was elevated to the position of junior minister at a salary of £500 per annum. But though he was later considered suitable for the position of assistant minister and 'acting' Senior Minister until ill health forced his retirement in 1925, he was not in the league of senior ministers, a fact that was made quite clear to him on his appointment in 1893. In his letter of acceptance Isidore Harris expressed his wish to apply for the post of Senior Minister, 'should the vacancy occur'. This statement was met with 'regret and disapproval' by the Council, Harris being thought not the man to relieve the Revd Professor D.W. Marks of the more 'onerous duties' which because of his age he was now unable to perform with regularity.[54] What they really meant was that Harris was not the man to stand as the religious head of Reform Judaism in Britain. In his subsidiary position, Isidore Harris served West London for 44 years. He died in July 1925. His worth must not be underestimated. Harris was a scholarly man who wrote the history of the United Synagogue, was for long involved with Jews College and the Jewish Religious Education Board and carried out admirable work with Jewish deaf and dumb children. In his memorial sermon Reverend Livingstone, of the Golders Green (United) Synagogue, said of him, 'while Rev. Harris joined the Reform Community he never left the Orthodox Community'. Harris was a conservative Reformer, far removed from Liberal Judaism, and his appointment as a junior minister to West London in 1881 caused something of a sensation. But as Reverend Jacobs, successor to Joseph Strauss in Bradford, noted in his memorial sermon, 'His [Harris's] aim was to support harmony amongst the Jews of Britain'.[55]

At a meeting of the West London Council in December 1892 it was suggested that David Woolf Marks, by then in his eighty-second year, should become 'Honorary head of the congregation, preaching occasionally and taking part in the reading of the service'. It was further agreed that a 'Senior Minister be appointed to carry out active duties'.[56] The suggestion which, it may be assumed, had been intended kindly was misinterpreted by some as a slight. David Woolf Marks calmed troubled waters by issuing a formal letter denying such a suggestion and further acknowledging the 'great kindness and consideration I gratefully appreciate'.[57]

Different camps within the West London Council saw the Reverend Simeon Singer and the Reverend Morris Joseph as potential successors and each group encouraged their favourite to apply for the position. The choice of applicants highlights the divisions within the council over its aim and direction. Morris Joseph was invited 'to attend [a meeting] without obligation on either side'.[58] By chance, the timing of the meeting coincided with the publication of a collection of Joseph's sermons under the title, *The Ideal in Judaism.*[59] In this Joseph expressed his belief in a return to Israel without the restoration of the sacrifices and his belief that the 'Messiah is always moving amongst us'.[60] He believed in the rationality of religion, stating that 'True religion is reason'. Joseph's stated opinion on the role of women in society was strictly in keeping with contemporary English middle-class thinking. He considered the female 'ill-adapted to battle with men for supremacy in the political field' and that a woman's place was in charge of the home, where she became the 'power behind the throne...the character builder'.[61] The collection of sermons was favourably reviewed by the *Daily Chronicle*, the *Scotsman* and the *Record*. Solomon Schechter,[62] writing in the *Jewish Chronicle*, expressed the view that the sermons provided 'powerful aids to devotional faith and practical Judaism'.[63] However, Joseph's brand of theology did not find favour with all the Berkeleystreeters.

In recommending Morris Joseph for the position of Senior Minister Julian Goldsmid, at that time Chairman of the Council, was highly enthusiastic. He had an obvious empathy with Joseph who, if not as radical as himself, had expressed progressive views which might revitalise a synagogue which was seen by some at that time more 'as a Burial Club for Jews than a place of worship'.[64] Sir Julian Goldsmid provided the following reference for his candidate:

> Mr. Joseph is a man of great energy and ability. He has published a volume of sermons which have received the highest commendations...he is anxious to enter upon the wider field of usefulness which is open to a metropolitan minister. Mr. Joseph has long known the Rev. Prof. Marks and has been received by him on terms of cordial friendship. Under all the circumstances of the case therefore the Committee believe the selection of Mr. Joseph would be acceptable to him and the great majority of members of the synagogue.
>
> Julian Goldsmid.[65]

In spite of Goldsmid's support, certain of the West London congregation were disturbed by *The Ideal In Judaism*. It exposed a theology which was too progressive. As one explained, Joseph's sermons were 'interesting but not Jewish'. Conversely, others considered the sermons to be 'an honour to Judaism' and stated that Joseph would be 'an honour to any congregation'.[66] Joseph was not the universal choice and it was not until Simeon Singer had formally rejected the position of Senior Minister made to him by West London on 15 May 1893 that a final decision was reached. In his letter of rejection, sent to Julian Goldsmid, the Reverend Singer outlined the reasons for his refusal. They were as follows:

- During his 14 years as minister of New West End Synagogue Singer had experienced no serious differences and had been permitted to exercise such religious influences over his congregation as legitimately claimed.
- Singer believed he could be of more use in the 'interests of our common Judaism' fighting against 'narrowness and intolerance of every kind' if he remained where he was. As he explained, 'It is some comfort to think I have been labouring long and not altogether unsuccessfully in this direction'.
- He considered that unity and understanding in the cause of 'a broader spirit of Judaism' were more likely to occur if he remained at St Petersburgh Place.

He concluded by saying:

> If there were any real danger of the disruption or collapse of a congregation with so splendid a record as that of the West London Synagogue of British Jews...which have had far-reaching and beneficial effects among British Jews generally ...would perish for lack of clerical support and guidance, the calamity would be one that would involve not your body alone but the whole of the Anglo-Jewish Community. I am persuaded that a successor of able and devoted ability will be found to render such a contingency impossible. 'The war will call forth the man.'[67]

Morris Joseph was that man and, having been kept waiting by the Council for some months, his appointment was finally confirmed in July 1893 by a majority vote of 45 to 20. His election to the position of Senior Minister was initially for one year at an annual salary of £600.[68] In his inaugural sermon Morris Joseph promised to 'toil for the individual members of the congregation and for the congregation as a whole'. His stated intention was to make the synagogue a 'rallying point for the dormant beneficent activists' and to narrow the divisions within the community. There should be no religious barriers, 'Reform and Conservatism should work together'. Joseph concluded with a rallying call to arms: 'reform is a life...it is the watchword for those anxiously seeking after God...congregants should be devoted to the principles of enlightened religion.'[69]

Morris Joseph (1848–1930) served West London as its Senior Minister until 1925, although in the last four years Isidore Harris took over the majority of his duties. Joseph was born into an Orthodox, clerical family, his father having been the minister of the Maiden Lane Synagogue. In 1868, when his studies at Jews College were completed, Morris Joseph joined the newly established North London Synagogue as minister-secretary. There followed a seven-year period with the progressively inclined Princes Road Synagogue in Liverpool which was brought to a close in 1881 due to his ill health. An enforced period away from active religious life enabled Morris Joseph to stand back and examine his beliefs and consider his future direction. As one of the founders of the Sabbath afternoon services he chose to draw closer to the progressive elements of Judaism and subsequently interpreted his denial of the ministry of the Hampstead Synagogue as a means of 'being set free' to work for the benefit of all of Anglo-Jewry. During his term of office at West London the divide between Reform and Orthodox Judaism was at its narrowest. When Chief Rabbi Dr Hermann Adler died in 1911 the honour of delivering the memorial sermon (*Hesped*) was given to Morris Joseph who, in an impressive address, said of Adler that 'others will succeed him, but none will take his place'. Joseph was renowned as a forceful preacher who 'delivered literary gems of sermons with an out-of-the-ordinary style'.[70]

At the end of the nineteenth century an issue entered the Anglo-Jewish arena which divided not only Jews in England, but communities throughout the Diaspora. The debate surrounding the establishment of a Jewish State in Palestine went beyond sermonising or drawing-room discussion, it went straight to the heart of the Jewish people. Reform attitudes may well have been predictable, bearing in mind the background and social status of its adherents and, though 'Political Zionism gained very few converts among Reform elements within Anglo-Jewry',[71] it was a strictly personal matter and not subject to the censorship of synagogal bodies.

Initially, leading Reformers adopted a reserved attitude towards the concept of Political Zionism, one which was overtly in conflict with the ideal of citizenship as well as at odds with the universalist belief of Progressive Judaism. In one of his early sermons David Woolf Marks had delegated the 'restoration of Judaea' to matters spiritual. He believed that in the real world Jews should remain dedicated to the priority of citizenship and should give their allegiance 'to the land of our birth';[72] here he was in harmony with

American and central European Reformers of the time. In the forefront of Anglo-Jewish anti-Zionists was Claude Montefiore who in fact met Theodor Herzl on his first visit to England in 1895. One year later Montefiore gave a sermon fiercely opposing Zionism. He could neither accept its relevance to Jews who were emancipated citizens nor see it as a solution to anti-Semitism, the latter, he posited, an attitude which could be overcome by universal Judaism. Montefiore told the congregation of West London that they should 'set against the political idea of Jewish nationalism, the religious idea of Jewish universalism...if every community advanced to the level of Berkeley Street and not further then anti-Semitism would be smaller'.[73] The ideal of Political Zionism was in direct conflict with the thinking of a man who confessed that at times he just wanted 'to live exclusively among my English neighbours...my own people'.[74] Even in those early days, a year before the first Zionist Conference, a number of Berkeleystreeters were overtly anti-Zionist. Oswald Simon, writing in the *Jewish Chronicle*, emphasised the dangers inherent in the founding of a Jewish State.[75] F. D. Mocatta dismissed the idea as 'utterly impractical'. Three generations of the Magnus family openly expressed their antipathy, son and grandson following the example of Philip who, in 1891, had outlined his views in *Jewish Activities and Jewish Ideas*. Only months after Claude Montefiore's sermon, Magnus again spelt out the dangers inherent in the Zionist thesis. Opposition to Zionism yes, but no denunciation of religious loyalty, he was 'bound to Judaism by religious and spiritual ties' that could not be broken.[76]

The Reform clergy were divided in their views on Zionism. The universalist Morris Joseph was totally opposed. In common with Philip Magnus, he 'abhorred the notion of a militant Jewish state'.[77] Political Zionists, he argued, denied the missionary role of the Jews, by suggesting it was a 'new notion'. Joseph posited that it was 'some thousands of years old', the Children of Israel were dispersed in order to 'extol Him before all the living'.[78] Opposition to Political Zionism also created unexpected bedfellows. Chief Rabbi Hermann Adler and the Reverend Morris Joseph jointly attacked activists at the universities of Oxford, Cambridge and London.[79] Adler also joined the future founder of Liberal Judaism, Claude Montefiore, in condemning the Zionist thesis. Such antipathy was not manifested by other Reform clergy. In the provinces the mood was distinctly pro-Zionist. The

Reverend Dr Wolf, minister of the Manchester Reform Synagogue from 1901 to 1908, preached that it was 'the duty of all true Jews to support the Zionist cause'.[80] In Bradford, Joseph Strauss's enthusiasm was evident. As a founder of the Bradford Zionist Society and provincial Vice-President of the English Zionist Federation, he travelled throughout the nation giving lectures on Zionism and, in 1903, published an article in support of the movement in the *Gentlemen's Magazine*. His fervour encouraged a number of members of the Bradford Reform congregation, including Jacob Moser, to follow the Zionist path. At West London, Isidore Harris adopted an ambivalent, though benevolent, stance, stating that, 'though I am not a Zionist, Political Zionism was propounded as a remedy for anti-Semitism and Political Zionists should be allowed to express their views'.[81]

As the first decade of the twentieth century progressed anti-Semitism[82] was increasingly drawn into the Zionist debate. In England, during the early years of the decade, the presence of a large number of eastern European Jews gave rise to a number of expressions of anti-alienism. In 1895 the Trades Union Congress passed a resolution demanding a halt to the entry of pauper aliens; in 1901 the British Brothers League, led by the overtly anti-Semitic Major W. Evans-Gordon, was founded in the East End of London; and in 1905 the Aliens Act, the first act of legislation to restrict alien entry in peacetime, was passed. Lucien Wolf[83] called Zionism 'the natural and abiding ally of anti-Semitism'.[84] He viewed national separateness as a dangerous tool in the hands of those who expressed a clear dislike of the Jewish people. The creation of a Jewish State would provide the anti-Semite with a justifiable reason to demand the removal of Jews in the Diaspora to their 'own' land. Palestine would become the 'ghetto of the world'. For those Anglo-Jews concerned to adhere to the emancipation contract, Political Zionism was an unwelcome spectre on the horizon, a backtracking on the advances made in the Diaspora. At a meeting of the West London Synagogue Association held in 1913, in a climate still recovering from the implications of the Jewish involvement in the Marconi and Indian Silver scandals and the suggestions of Jewish profiteering during the Boer War,[85] the growth of anti-Semitism was debated. The Reverends Joseph and Harris called for Jews to curb 'their more unpleasant characteristics', as a means of avoiding anti-Semitism. In this Morris Joseph was repeating an earlier plea, made in 1902, for Jews to eschew vulgarity and extravagance and adopt a more sober way of life.[86] Isidore Harris focused on the facts that the influx of 'foreign Jews' had 'excited prejudice' and that there were too many Jews in Parliament, adding that those that were there were of a 'lower quality'. He stressed that religion – as opposed to Jewish nationalism – was the weapon with which to tackle anti-Semitism. Oswald Simon reminded his audience that England was the least anti-Semitic country in the world. The meeting ended with the chairman, Claude Montefiore, joining with the speakers in encouraging the community to adopt a circumspect attitude.[87]

In 1917 two events took place which served to emphasise the divisions within the Anglo-Jewish community over the proposed creation of a Jewish national state. Throughout that year the British Government had been debating the issue.[88] There can be no doubt that the need to gain the support of Jews in America and Russia[89] – Britain's allies against Germany – during a period of heightened pacifist and socialist propaganda, was a major factor. The Government, before issuing a statement of opinion, consulted a number of leading Jews, including Claude Montefiore and Sir Philip Magnus. In spite of the latters' negative opinions, on 2 November 1917,[90] Arthur Balfour, in a letter to Lord Rothschild, pledged the British Government's support for the eventual establishment of 'a national homeland for the Jewish people in Palestine'. A few weeks earlier, concerned at what might lie ahead, a group of leading Anglo-Jews met at the New Court headquarters of Rothschild's to establish a League of British Jews. They were determined to oppose the Zionist thesis that 'the Jew was an alien in the land of his birth' and declared their intention to 'uphold the status of British Jews professing the Jewish religion'.[91] The League counted among its number the following members of the West London Synagogue of British Jews: H.S.Q. Henriques, H.G. Lousada, Philip Magnus, Laurie Magnus, Alfred Waley, Philip Waley and, of course, Claude Montefiore. The League was not opposed to Jews settling in Palestine, in fact it supported the setting up of the Jewish Territorial Organisation (JTO) – a body which sought to settle victims of Russian persecution – but, as Laurie Magnus explained, the exchange of 'religious heritage for a political state...made a mockery of revealed Judaism'[92] and endangered the emancipation contract. In a sermon he gave at the time of the Balfour Declaration, Morris Joseph pronounced that 'the less political the new Jewish order in Palestine proves to be the nearer it will approach the ideal one'. Palestine was the spiritual home, not the political base; if it became the latter then, Joseph believed, Jews would not be accepted as true citizens elsewhere.[93] The Balfour Declaration encouraged more open support for the Zionist cause. In an effort to counter this the Leaguers, who though few in number wielded considerable influence,[94] founded their own anti-Zionist journal, the *Jewish Guardian*, which was published from 1919 to 1931, under the editorship of Laurie Magnus.

Within weeks of the Balfour Declaration an event took place which changed the course of the world and which, more specifically, added to the concerns of the Anglo-Jewish establishment. In March[95] the first Russian Revolution, that which overthrew the oppressive tsarist regime, took place. There was unanimous pleasure throughout the Jewish community. However, certain members of the Board of Deputies urged caution. Philip Magnus suggested that the Revolution should be regarded as a 'political matter' and thus, while the Board should proffer Prince L'vov its congratulations it should avoid all mention of 'the revolution', however beneficial it was to the oppressed Jews of Russia; a recommendation the Board of Deputies followed. On 25 November[96] affairs took a more ominous course. The Bolsheviks staged their successful coup. The Jews of Britain reacted in differing ways. The Anglo-Jewish establishment was dismayed, conscious of the increased anti-Semitism the event must arouse. The Jewish populace of the East End was overjoyed. An end to the repression and exploitation of their families and friends in the *Heim* was in sight.[97]

Zionists were worried that the Bolsheviks' intended policy of assimilating Russian Jewry would run counter to their ambitions for the creation of a Jewish homeland. Anti-Zionists, including Morris Joseph, were concerned on two counts, first, that the Bolshevik disregard of ownership and their practice of expropriation were at odds with the 'Mosaic sacredness of property'[98] and second, at the likelihood that increased anti-Semitism would result from the growing, albeit unfounded, belief, that the revolution was a 'Jewish conspiracy' and that Jews, particularly alien Jews (Jews who had recently arrived from eastern Europe), represented a threat and were part of the world-wide conspiracy referred to in the *Protocols of the Elders of Zion*.[99]

As reports grew of Jewish complicity in the assassination of the

Tsar and of the perpetration of atrocities by Jewish-Bolsheviks, certain leading members of Anglo-Jewry adopted a programme of 'communal self-defence'. For Jews who considered themselves Englishmen, the intervention of Britain on the side of those with a history of Jewish persecution – the White Russians – posed a moral dilemma, particularly when a Day of Mourning was called, on 28 June 1919, for Jews suffering at the hands of the Poles. Communal differences were once again put aside and Morris Joseph joined Chief Rabbi Hertz in a service held at the Queen's Hall in Central London. Philip Magnus, with divided loyalties, was uneasy and informed the Foreign Office of his misgivings – a move for which he was condemned by the Board of Deputies and the *Jewish Chronicle*.[100] The reprimand came close on the heels of the furore that followed the publication of the 'Letter of Ten' which appeared in the *Morning Post* on 23 April 1919. The letter was an outspoken repudiation of the Bolshevik ideology as it conflicted with the 'tenets and teachings' of Judaism. It was signed by ten of the leading members of Anglo-Jewry including Lord Rothschild of the United Synagogue, Lord Swaythling of the Federation, Claude Montefiore of both Liberal and Reform and Philip Magnus of West London. The letter was not only a response to the tensions and accusations which had so recently appeared in the English press, it was also a means of distancing the writers from the sentiments of Leopold Greenberg, pro-Zionist editor of the *Jewish Chronicle* who, in the spring of 1919, had published an article which could have been interpreted as being in support of Bolshevism. Greenberg warned that the revolution might be viewed as the 'hope of humanity', as a warning of what could overtake western society if it did not address its inherent weaknesses. Not surprisingly the Letter of Ten did not go down at all well with the immigrant Jewish community in the East End of London. Nor was it well received by the Board of Deputies who hurriedly approved a resolution condemning its divisive nature.

The tensions created by the 'Bolshevik threat' eased after the signing of the Anglo-Soviet Trade Agreement in 1921. But the years between 1917 and 1921 were disturbing and traumatic for British Jews, especially the more influential members of Reform synagogues. The issues involved were those at the very heart of Reform Judaism – Messianism and nationalism. Reformers believed in the universal dimension of Judaism. This did not make them lesser Jews. They saw their role as missionary and the creation of a political, as opposed to a spiritual, Jewish homeland in a world that was still reeling from the chaos and inequality of war was, to their minds, ill-timed and unacceptable. They could not support the creation of a Jewish 'political State' as was propounded by 'race' Zionists. Politically most, if not all, the Reformers, in common with many middle-class Jews, were supporters of either the Liberal or the Conservative party, so in purely ideological terms Bolshevism would have been unacceptable. Added to this was the fear that, as some Reformers saw it, Bolshevism and Zionism posed a threat to the perceived security, prestige and power they believed they had secured in the years since 1858.

The outbreak of the First World War forced many Jews in Britain to choose between patriotism and roots, religious and national. For some it was a hard choice: those of German origin, particularly those in Manchester and Bradford, were faced with dual loyalties.[101] Recent arrivals from eastern Europe were equally pressured, unwilling to join the armed forces and fight alongside an ally who had been responsible for the harsh and cruel existence they had endured in Russia and Russia-Poland. They were stigmatised by the host society for their cowardice, profiteering and alien identity. Once war was declared the Anglo-Jewish establishment recognised its place and, urged on by the columns of the *Jewish Chronicle*, which only three weeks previously had recommended Britain's neutrality, enlisted in their hundreds. King and Country came first. Approximately 10,000 British Jews volunteered for military service before the introduction of conscription in May 1916.[102] All three Reform synagogues suffered losses during the war, the memorial boards listing officers and men alike, founder members and those more recently arrived at Reform Judaism. The clergy too played their part in the war effort. Vivian Simmons, appointed Assistant Minister of West London Synagogue in December 1913 – he was the sole applicant for the post[103] – took up military duties at Aldershot, a commitment he honoured until 1919.[104] In Manchester, the Reverend Jacob Phillips, Harry Lewis's successor, was appointed assistant chaplain to the Forces for Western Command. He worked unsparingly to cheer wounded Jewish soldiers.[105] All the Reform clergy ensured that special services were held for military personnel.

The idealism of young Jewish males fighting for their country was shattered by the harshness of war and the volume of losses. More than 2,000 Jewish soldiers died in the trenches. For those who returned it was hardly a 'land fit for heroes'. The post-war years were depressed and racked by high inflation and unemployment. West London received countless letters asking for help from demobbed soldiers, more often than not wounded and unable to survive on their pension of 5s. 6d. per week.[106] In a lighter vein, inflation proved to be a problem for the synagogue choir which as 'part of the general suffering due to the high level of inflation' complained that their recent increase of five per cent was insufficient.[107]

The post-war years brought little change in the hierarchy of West London. The same names appeared on the list of members of the synagogue council: Montefiore, Henriques, Lousada, Mocatta, Magnus, Simons, Lowy and Elkin, shades of 1842.[108] In 1924, in Manchester, the death occurred of Moritz Schlesinger, the sole surviving member of the group that had attended the meeting at the house of Horatio Micholls when it was resolved to establish the Manchester Congregation of British Jews.[109] The elder statesmen were dying. When Joseph Strauss died in 1922 the Bradford Reform Synagogue was in straitened financial circumstances. A report in the West London Council Minutes the following March agreed to 'a subvention not exceeding £200... on condition that their [Bradford Reform Synagogue] choice of a Minister be approved by the Council or a Committee thereof'.[110] The appointment of the Reverend Jacobs met with approval but his period of office was short. His ministry ended in 1927 and for the following 13 years the community was without a minister. This, added to the effects of the Depression, which were hard felt in the industrial North, nearly brought about the demise of the Bradford Reform Synagogue and it was only due to the hard work of 'a small dedicated group of people'[111] that it survived.

In 1925, Isidore Harris, the man who had been acting Senior Minister at West London since Morris Joseph's retirement from office, resigned for medical reasons.[112] The search began for a replacement. Vivian Simmons was ruled out as a possible candidate for the helm of the cathedral of Reform Jewry and, with no college for Progressive rabbis in Britain, the Berkeleystreeters turned to America. They had been told that Dr Joel Blau, the rabbi of the Temple Pen El of New York was 'an ideal candidate'. A selection committee composed of H.S.Q. Henriques and H.C.

Marks[113] was despatched across the Atlantic to consult a number of 'specialists'. Their first meeting was with the Chief Rabbi of Montreal and then they travelled to New York to confer with a number of Jewish academics including Richard Gottheil, son of the former minister of the Manchester Reform Synagogue, Gustav Gottheil. Dr Morgenstern of Cincinnati was also consulted. Morgenstern was president of the Hebrew Union College, an intellectual keen to put Reform Judaism in America on a new path, one of synthesis and unity.[114] It is not surprising therefore that certain of Morgenstern's recommendations were considered 'too reform' for the conservative West London Synagogue of British Jews. In the end there was 'only one suitable man' for the position, Rabbi Dr Joel Blau. After discussions with Henriques and Marks, Blau agreed to a 'stipend of £1,500 per annum plus the cost of transporting him and his family to England'. At first Blau refused to sign a contract as, for some unexplained reason, he was under the mistaken impression that West London was an Orthodox synagogue.[115] The search had taken one month. Henriques and Marks returned to England in October 1925.[116]

Hungarian-born Joel Blau was 45 when he took up the position as Senior Minister of West London. Educated in Cincinnati, he followed the conservative school of American Reform. His power as a preacher was reported by the Selection Committee to be 'beyond what even might be supposed'. According to Israel Zangwill he had published 'the most daring book [*The Wonder of Life*] ever written on religion by an American ecclesiastic'. In his induction sermon Blau, in no uncertain terms, criticised the divisions in Anglo-Jewry. A clear disciple of Morgenstern, he saw no room for secularism in Judaism. The *Jewish Chronicle* approvingly considered his moderate stance to be 'far removed from the vagaries of Liberalism'.[117] Though at times 'paradoxical, Blau was always profound' with a brilliant analytical ability.[118] Tragically the promise of the man was not fulfilled. His health was failing, and once again Vivian Simmons found himself 'carrying the load'.[119] In October 1927, at the age of 47, Rabbi Dr Joel Blau died.

The funeral of the incumbent Senior Minister of the West London Synagogue of British Jews was once again an occasion for a display of clerical unity. Chief Rabbi Hertz and the *dayanim* of the United Synagogue attended the funeral of a man who, in common with others who had held the position before him, was seen, not just as a loss to Reform Judaism, but to the Anglo-Jewish community as a whole. In the short period of Blau's ministry revision of the Reform Prayer Book had continued.[120] Now a new Senior Minister was urgently needed to steer the congregation out of the 'depressed' twenties and into a new and hoped-for prosperous and expansionary decade ahead, a man whose role it would be to fulfil the promise held out by Joel Blau.

NOTES

1. See P. Goldberg, *The Manchester Congregation of British Jews, 1857–1957* (1957), p. 67.
2. The term 'eugenics' as relating to the sustained improvement of the human race was coined by Francis Galton in 1883. The English Eugenics movement never developed the extremes of race and class bias that were to emerge in the United States in the 1920s and, to its most perverted extreme, in the Nazi regime.
3. *Jewish Chronicle*, 26 Dec. 1891.
4. *Jewish Chronicle*, 26 Jan. 1892.
5. *Jewish Chronicle*, 26 Jan. 1892, Supplement.
6. *Jewish Chronicle*, 31 Jan. 1890, pp. 15 and 16.
7. For the history of the United Synagogue see A. Newman, *The United Synagogue 1870–1970* (1977).
8. Minute Book of the West London Synagogue of British Jews, 27 April 1890, loc. cit.
9. Minute Book of the West London Synagogue of British Jews, 22 June 1890, loc. cit.
10. *Jewish Chronicle*, 28 March 1890, p. 8.
11. The West London Synagogue Association was founded on 27 January 1895. Its object was to 'increase the usefulness of the West London Synagogue as a religious and philanthropic centre and as a forum for debate of topical issues which were of relevance to Reform Jews and Anglo-Jewry as a whole'. A range of guest speakers were invited from the provinces, Europe and the United States.
12. West London Synagogue Association Reports, 3 April 1898, Archives of West London Synagogue.
13. The Settlement was called St George's after the ward in the East End in which it was located. For a history of the Settlement see A.J. Kershen (ed.), *150 Years of Progressive Judaism* (1990), pp. 29–37.
14. *Jewish Chronicle*, 10 March 1919.
15. Kershen, op. cit., p. 30.
16. *Jewish Chronicle*, 14 July 1893.
17. Letter from Reverend S. Singer to Julian Goldsmid, dated 30 May 1893, Archives of West London Synagogue.
18. *Jewish Chronicle*, 22 March 1895.
19. Letter from United Synagogue dated 9 June 1909, letter from Board of Deputies dated 16 May 1909, Archives of the West London Synagogue.
20. D. Philipson, *The Reform Movement in Judaism* (1931), p. 205.
21. *Jewish Chronicle*, 7 May 1909, pp. 18–20.
22. *Jewish Chronicle*, 22 March 1895.
23. Ibid.
24. *Jewish Chronicle*, 5 July 1895, p. 5.
25. S. Bayme, 'Claude Montefiore, Lily Montagu and the Origins of the JRU', *Transactions of the Jewish Historical Society*, Vol. XXVII, 1979, p. 61.
26. *Jewish Chronicle*, 13 April 1906, p. 23.
27. At this time Joseph, whose health had broken down in 1881, was not attached to any synagogue. He earned his living by private teaching and writing for the *Jewish*

Chronicle. He was formally appointed to the West London Synagogue in 1893.

28. *Jewish Chronicle*, 28 Feb. 1890, p. 61.
29. Constance Rothschild Battersea was the daughter of Baron (Anthony) de Rothschild. Although Constance rejected Orthodox Judaism she never converted to Christianity, even after her marriage to Cyril Flower, later Lord Battersea. She was an active social worker and founder of the Jewish Association for the Protection of Girls and Women.
30. Letter from Morris Joseph to Lady Battersea, dated 6 Jan. 1892. West London Synagogue Archives.
31. *Jewish Chronicle*, 13 April 1906, p. 23.
32. Bayme, op. cit., p. 64.
33. *Jewish Chronicle*, 24 Oct. 1902, p. 10.
34. West London Synagogue Letter Book, 17 Feb. 1903, Archives of West London Synagogue.
35. Council of Founders Minute Book, 23 March 1903, Archives of West London Synagogue.
36. Council of Founders Minute Book, 20 April 1903, Archives of West London Synagogue.
37. Bayme, op. cit., p. 67.
38. M.J. Goulston, 'The Theology of Reform Judaism in Britain', in D. Marmur (ed.), *Reform Judaism* (1973), p. 68.
39. Anglo-Jewish Archives, AJ/A 246, University of Southampton, loc. cit.
40. The Federation of Synagogues was created in 1887 under the direction of Samuel Montagu. It was composed of the small *chevrahs* which had been set up all over the East End of London by eastern European Jewish immigrants who were uneasy with the Anglicised and cathedral synagogues of the longer-resident Ashkenazi Jews.
41. *Jewish Chronicle*, 31 Dec. 1909, pp. 30–1 and 37–8.
42. *Jewish Chronicle*, 31 Dec. 1909, p. 37.
43. Goldberg, op. cit., p. 71.
44. Goldberg, op. cit., p. 76.
45. *Jewish Chronicle*, 31 Dec. 1909, p. 37.
46. *Jewish Chronicle*, 16 June 1911, pp. 24–39.
47. *Jewish Chronicle*, 10 Jan. 1896.
48. *Jewish Chronicle*, 2 July 1897, p. 21.
49. Letter to West London dated 12 Dec. 1880 in Anglo-Jewish Archives, AJ/A 59/6, loc. cit.
50. Letter to West London dated 9 Dec. 1880 in Anglo-Jewish Archives, AJ/A 59/6, loc. cit. Magnus subsequently became Secretary and Director of the City and Guilds Institute.
51. See below.
52. *Jewish Chronicle*, 30 Aug. 1933.
53. Minutes of Council of West London Synagogue, 26 Dec. 1880 in Anglo-Jewish Archives, AJ/A 59/6, loc. cit.
54. West London Synagogue Council Minutes, 12 Feb. 1893.
55. *Jewish Chronicle*, 24 July 1925, pp. 9–11.
56. Council Minutes of the West London Synagogue of British Jews, 14 Dec. 1892.
57. Letter from D.W. Marks to the West London Synagogue Council, dated 18 April 1893.
58. West London Synagogue of British Jews Council Minute Book, 19 Feb. 1893.
59. M. Joseph, *The Ideal in Judaism* (1893).
60. Joseph, op. cit., p. 13.
61. Joseph, op. cit., p. 167.
62. Solomon Schechter (1847–1915) was Romanian born. He was brought to England in 1882 by Claude Montefiore whom he had taught at the *Hochschule* in Berlin. He was appointed Reader in Rabbinic at Cambridge in 1892. He later went to America where he was appointed President of the Jewish Theological Seminary in 1901.
63. *Jewish Chronicle*, 17 Feb. 1893.

64. *Jewish Chronicle*, 21 July 1893.
65. West London Council Minute Book, 19 Feb. 1893, loc. cit.
66. *Jewish Chronicle*, 21 July 1893.
67. Letters from Julian Goldsmid to Simeon Singer, 15 May 1893 and letter from Simeon Singer to Julian Goldsmid dated 30 May 1893, West London Synagogue of British Jews Archives.
68. West London Synagogue of British Jews Council Minutes, 6 July 1893, loc. cit.
69. *Jewish Chronicle*, 15 Sept. 1893.
70. *Jewish Chronicle*, 25 April 1930.
71. S. Cohen, *English Zionists and British Jews* (1982), p. 184.
72. Mark's sermon quoted in H.J. Cohn, 'Progressive Jews and Zionism', in D. Marmur (ed.), *A Genuine Search* (1979), p. 175.
73. *Jewish Chronicle*, 1 Feb. 1896.
74. Cohen, op. cit., p. 165.
75. *Jewish Chronicle*, 1 May 1896, p. 7.
76. *Jewish Chronicle*, 7 Nov. 1913.
77. *Jewish Chronicle*, 15 April 1898, p. 28.
78. Morris Joseph, *The Spirit of Judaism* (1930), pp. 41–51.
79. Cohen, op. cit., p. 130.
80. *Jewish Chronicle*, 9 Oct. 1903, pp. 14–15.
81. West London Synagogue Association Report for the meeting dated 5 Feb. 1899.
82. The term 'anti-Semitism' as meaning 'Jew hatred' was coined by the German racist journalist, Wilhem Marr, in 1879 when he produced a pamphlet on the power of German Jewry.
83. Lucien Wolf was a journalist who became secretary of the Conjoint Foreign Committee (the Joint Foreign Committee) from 1917. Known as the 'Foreign Secretary' of Anglo-Jewry he attended the Versailles Peace Conference and was active in presenting the case of the persecuted Jews of eastern Europe.
84. Quote in S. Cohen, 'First World War Anglo-Jewish Opposition to Zionism', *Transactions of the Jewish Historical Society of England*, Vol. XXX, 1987–88, p. 156.
85. See C. Holmes, *Anti-Semitism in British Society, 1876–1939* (1979), chapter 5.
86. Report of Meeting of the West London Synagogue Association, 1 July 1902.
87. Report of Meeting of the West London Synagogue Association, 26 June 1913.
88. The motives behind the Balfour Declaration have been dealt with in depth in S. Cohen, *English Zionists and British Jews*, op.cit., and S. Kadish, *Bolsheviks and British Jews* (1992).
89. Following the revolution in Russia in February 1917 those Jews active in Kerensky's Liberal regime became of importance to the allies.
90. Historians differ as to whether the meeting took place in late October or early November 1917.
91. S. Cohen, *English Zionists and British Jews*, op. cit., p. 305.
92. L. Magnus, *New Lamps for Old*, quoted in S. Cohen, *English Zionists and British Jews*, op. cit., p. 183.
93. Joseph, *The Spirit of Judaism*, op. cit., p. 66.
94. Kadish, op. cit., p. 132.
95. The revolution which overthrew the tsarist regime took place in February 1917 and the second, Bolshevik, revolution, in October. When the western calendar was adopted these became respectively March and November.
96. See note 95.
97. The *Heim*, the home, be it town or village.
98. Kadish, op. cit., p. 76.
99. *The Protocols of the Elders of Zion* had appeared in Russia in 1905 and in England in 1920: it purported to expose a world-wide conspiracy for the Jews to take control of the world.
100. Kadish, op. cit., p. 116.
101. See V.D. Lipman, *A History of the Jews in Britain since 1858* (1990), p. 139.

102. Of that number 1,800 were officers, of whom 300 were killed in action. In all some 41,500 British Jews served in the armed forces during the First World War. See Lipman, op. cit., pp. 140–1.
103. West London Synagogue Council Minutes, 14 Dec. 1913, p. 480, loc. cit.
104. Anglo-Jewish Archives, AJ/A 78/31, loc. cit.
105. Goldberg, op. cit., p. 81.
106. Anglo-Jewish Archives, AJ/A 78/31, loc. cit.
107. Ibid.
108. West London Synagogue Council Minutes, 2 April 1922, p. 526, loc. cit.
109. Goldberg, op. cit., p. 82.
110. West London Synagogue Council Minutes, 25 March 1923, p. 236, loc. cit.
111. Bradford Synagogue Foundation Centenary Dinner Booklet, 23 April 1980.
112. West London Synagogue Council Minutes, 8 Feb. 1925, loc. cit.
113. H.C. Marks was the grandson of the Revd Professor David Woolf Marks.
114. M. Meyer, *Response to Modernity* (1988), pp. 297–8.
115. A.J. Kershen's conversation with the late Hyman Symon, 1 July 1990.
116. Report of Selection Committee to West London Synagogue of British Jews, 8 Nov. 1925, loc. cit.
117. *Jewish Chronicle*, 22 Jan. 1926, pp. 11–12.
118. *Jewish Chronicle*, 28 Oct. 1927, pp. 11–12.
119. West London Synagogue Council Minutes, 3 April 1927, p. 560, loc. cit.
120. West London Synagogue Council Minutes, 4 March 1927, p. 571, loc. cit.

PART TWO

Reform as a Movement, 1929–1995

5 A New Era, 1929–1942

The decade of the 1930s – the central period of this chapter – was to witness major political and social developments nationally and internationally that were to help create the conditions for Reform to change from a few isolated synagogues with little co-ordination to an association of like-minded congregations united by a common purpose. These included the process of suburbanisation within London Jewry, which facilitated the creation of Reform communities in new areas of Jewish settlement; the rise of Fascism in Germany, leading to an influx of Jewish refugees to Britain, many from Reform backgrounds, including rabbis, who boosted the growth of Reform synagogues; the upheavals caused by the outbreak of the Second World War, particularly to the Jewish education of children, and the joint response of Reform congregations this prompted. In addition there was the forceful personality of a newcomer from the United States, Rabbi Harold Reinhart.

On 16 March 1929 Rabbi Harold Reinhart was installed as the Senior Minister of the West London Synagogue. There was a large congregation in attendance and those present may have been conscious of the similar pomp and ceremony that had taken place only three years earlier at the induction of Rabbi Blau. However, the high hopes that never materialised then owing to the short-lived nature of Blau's ministry were to be more than fulfilled in that of Reinhart. His appointment was to prove a turning-point in the fortunes of the synagogue as well as a key factor in the establishment of the Reform movement in Britain.

In his first message to members of the community in the West London magazine Reinhart enthused over the splendour of the synagogue's architecture and the history 'that breathed within its walls'.[1] Some of his readers might have felt that these passive attributes were the only distinctive features of the synagogue, for the awesome character of the building and the weight of past glories had stultified any new developments. For several years the congregation had seemed to be experiencing more difficulties than successes.

There was concern over the poor attendance at services, both on Friday evenings and Saturday mornings, with even members who were prominent in communal affairs being among those absent. In addition, the Children's Services at the High Holy Days had been so poorly supported that it had been decided to discontinue them, while the once fulsome gifts of flowers and foliage with which to decorate the synagogue at *Shavuot* had fallen considerably.[2] The spirit of apathy that prevailed was epitomised by the repeated failure of the West London Synagogue Association to stimulate the social and cultural life of the congregation. This led to the formation of a new committee in 1924 and the introduction of a series of public meetings and lectures. However, after four years of effort it was admitted that these were 'no more than partially successful' and there was yet another appeal for new ideas and greater involvement by the membership, only a small fraction of whom belonged to the Association.[3] One of the achievements of the Association was publishing the monthly magazine, but that too suffered from lack of support and no issue appeared between November 1928 and the following June. An additional problem, and one that boded ill for the future of the congregation, was the lack of accommodation for the religious education of children. Unlike most other Metropolitan synagogues, West London had no suitable premises for such instruction, with the result that a large number of members' children were taught privately. While attention had been drawn on several occasions to this major omission, the matter had still not been resolved.

In view of such difficulties in the internal life of the congregation it is not surprising that there was little enthusiasm for carrying the message of Reform to the wider Jewish community. A public debate in 1924 on whether 'in the interests of Judaism, an extension of the Reform Judaism was much to be desired' found the motion opposed by both religious and lay leadership. The consensus was that it would be better not to 'waste their energies in attempting to establish other synagogues, which must be a constant and increasing drain on the forces of Berkeley Street'.[4] Indeed, the only new congregation to be established since Bradford in 1873 had been the Settlement in 1919, although even this had been founded through the personal initiative of Basil Henriques, arising from his work locally at the Settlement. No effort by the Reform leadership was made to foster new communities and the next Reform synagogue was not established until 1933. This may be contrasted with the more active spirit among the Liberals, who oversaw new synagogues in North London (1921), South London (1927) and Liverpool (1928).

Relations between the existing Reform synagogues were cordial, although there were no attempts at formulating a concerted policy and certainly no talk of any federation. At the time of Reinhart's appointment Bradford had been without a minister for almost a year following the departure of Revd Nathaniel Jacobs for Kingston, Jamaica. As a result Bradford was experiencing difficulties in maintaining communal interest and there were fears that it might have to close.[5] Manchester was in a stronger position, but its complete independence is highlighted by the fact that not once had any news of the congregation been included in the West London magazine until a few months after Reinhart's arrival.

It is noticeable that the eulogy delivered on Blau's death had not only mourned the loss of him personally but also lamented the failure of the attempt to revive the congregation: 'What might have been the future of the Synagogue with Joel Blau as its chief minister is useless to speculate. There is very little doubt that, under his leadership, Jewish Reform in England would once more have become a Movement and British Jews as a whole enriched by a giant driving force.'[6] The situation before Reinhart's arrival, therefore, was very different from the heady days in the 1840s when new ideas and a sense of mission had characterised Reform. As Vivian Simmons himself admitted, Reform was[7]

> Isolated and aloof from the rest of Jewry... Enthusiasm was frowned upon and decades passed away without any change, except very minor ones, in organisation or ritual. Jewish reform was not a flowing stream, but a silent pool – good to drink from, with sweet and pure water for a time – but hedged round with undergrowth and fences – choked and impenetrable.

In the hunt for a successor to Blau it was quickly established that no Englishman was available, whilst the other minister of the congregation, Simmons, had written to the Council asking not to be considered for the position. When eyes turned to the United States advice was sought from Rabbi Stephen Wise, one of the leaders of American Jewry and President of the Jewish Institute of Religion in New York. He recommended Reinhart as a candidate whom he had known since childhood, having been minister at the congregation in Portland, Oregon where Reinhart had grown up. Reinhart's name may have been known already as he had been invited to become Assistant Minister to Rabbi Israel Mattuck at the Liberal Jewish Synagogue in 1921. However, Reinhart had declined to take up the position owing to his reluctance to be so distant from his parents and the synagogue's declaration that it could not guarantee any financial assistance for visiting them.[8] Had he accepted, the relative growth of the Reform and Liberal synagogues might have been very different.

In January 1928 Philip Waley, President of West London, wrote to Reinhart suggesting that he become the Senior Minister of the congregation. In his reply Reinhart expressed his delight at the invitation but voiced two reservations: he queried whether West London was more akin to a Conservative synagogue in America, something 'I could not conscientiously serve'.[9] He also wondered how successful he would be at adapting to a different national climate. Waley went to America and met Reinhart. The two men took to each other immediately and were to remain close friends for the rest of their lives. Waley reassured Reinhart on both reservations – the former was not the case while the latter could be remedied with time and effort. He also guaranteed him leave of absence and travelling expenses to visit his family in America. The appointment was confirmed.

Reinhart came to West London aged 37 and immersed in American Reform Judaism. As a child he had been brought up in the Reform Temple in Portland and had been greatly influenced by Wise who was its minister at the time of his *barmitzvah*. Having obtained his undergraduate degree at the University of Cincinnati and his M.A. at Chicago University, Reinhart returned to Cincinnati to study for the rabbinate at the Hebrew Union College. He was ordained in 1915 and then served three Reform congregations, starting in Gary, Indiana, then going to Baton Rouge, Louisiana, and later to Sacramento, California. Throughout this time American Reform was dominated by the principles of the 1885 Pittsburgh Platform, which concentrated on the prophetic tradition within Judaism and placed much greater emphasis on personal conduct than on ritual observances. It stressed the spiritual and ethical in the Jewish message, and gave priority to the moral demands of Judaism. The right to initiate was fundamental, and Judaism was viewed as a 'progressive religion ever striving to be in accord with the postulates of reason'.[10] There was no hesitation in discarding the legalisms of the past and maintaining 'only such ceremonies as elevate and sanctify our lives, but reject all such as are not adapted to the views and habits of modern civilization'.[11] The Jewish people were regarded not as a racial group but as a religious community and all thoughts of returning to the Land of Israel were renounced. The ultimate task of Jews was to work for the reign of justice, truth, righteousness and peace. The Pittsburgh Platform was to be replaced in 1937 by the Columbus Platform which expressed greater attachment to tradition, to the Land of Israel and to historical precedents, but Reinhart himself was to remain devoted to the earlier set of principles.

The style of Reinhart's ministry often seemed to owe more to the 'Bible-punching' Protestantism of Western America than to the Judaism developed by the rabbis through centuries of debate and study. His deep faith was founded on the Hebrew Bible, which he quoted frequently in his sermons and articles. The Book of Psalms, in particular, was his constant reference point. He did not value rabbinic texts highly and, save for the *Ethics of the Fathers*, rarely mentioned them. For Reinhart the essence of Jewish life was communion with the Deity and the act of prayer. Although it was invariably the precursor of action, he regarded it as having the most important effect of any kind of human effort in the world. It was to be said of him that 'He never reads prayers *to* his congregation, but prays aloud in their presence'.[12]

Reinhart's passionate belief in prayer was matched by his certainty in the truth of other convictions that he held and which he maintained staunchly whether or not they were popular. He was a committed pacifist and had antagonised many in his Baton Rouge congregation in 1917 when America entered the First World War by treating the Stars and Stripes as an emblem of war and refusing to allow the flag in the synagogue. He was an early opponent of capital punishment and whenever a hanging took place he would demonstrate outside the gaol concerned, silently holding up a placard of condemnation. He was highly critical of Zionism and even refused to attend wedding receptions if there was to be a toast to the President of Israel. He was opposed to Ladies Guilds on the grounds that they were divisive and, long before the term became fashionable, sexist.

In these and other issues Reinhart never saw the need to trim his sails according to popular opinion. He regarded his ministry as a 'holy office' and was to declare of it: 'I have tried to fight for principles and to teach the service of truth within the Jewish community, even though it might not always be comfortable for the Jewish community.'[13] He regarded his rigid stance as the natural duty of a rabbi and was to urge it upon colleagues when inducting them into office:[14]

> God's word will I speak, God's word that is clean and sure, that knows no hesitancy and compromise, that burns like fire, that breathes life and hope. The true rabbi is he who has a heritage from the prophets, with a lively passion for justice and a quick courage to drive the message home. That passion and that courage must be unmistakable. Every rabbi must be a marked man, because it must be known that he is incorruptible not to be persuaded by interest or advantage, but motivated solely to advance the holy cause. His word must be an application in the living present of the ancient and eternal truth.

This characteristic of inflexible rectitude could also make him a difficult person with whom to work, and some were to find his dogmatic assertiveness unacceptable. Several decades later it was to lead to his departure from West London under a cloud of mutual acrimony.

Although West London had been used to the 'Mosaic-centredness' of David Marks and the 'conservative Reform' of Morris Joseph, Reinhart's inspirational approach to Judaism was not considered too far removed for everyday purposes. On the contrary it was precisely the breath of air that was felt to be needed. His arrival had the desired effect and soon galvanised the congregation out of its torpor. According to one contemporary observer,[15]

> the new spirit began to permeate the 'ancient stillness', and a new enthusiasm and fresh discontent began to replace the old

complacency and policy of *laissez-faire*...a new missionary spirit with the desire to spread reform amongst those no longer loyal to the old ways – all these influences began at last to give new promise and hope.

A year after taking office Reinhart published his definition of Reform Judaism, which was both a personal declaration of faith and a manifesto for his ministry to West London and beyond:[16]

THIS IS REFORM

To be Jewish enough to have faith in the inner resources of the Jewish people, and its capacity for universal ideals and human service; and so to identify Jewish destiny with broad and progressive paths;

To be Jewish enough to believe that truth is the seal of God, and so to allow the light of reason to play upon our past, our present and our future, and to pursue that light with confidence and with courage;

To be Jewish enough to feel that man is the partner of God in the work of creation, and that it is our task to build the kingdom of heaven here on earth through the perception and fulfilment of God's living will progressively revealed through human history;

To be Jewish enough to seek to love the Lord our God, not with formula and ritual, but with heart and soul and might, and to strive after that true and simple spiritual exercise which releases and nourishes the divine within us.

THIS IS REFORM

His words were intended not merely as a description of Reform but as a recipe for action. This included instituting changes in the letter of Jewish law in order to maintain its spirit. For Reinhart, Judaism was in a state of constant flux – it could not be conserved, only developed – and was answerable not just to the past but also to contemporary situations. Whereas Orthodox rabbis also recognised the need for change they were often constrained by what they felt to be their own lack of authority or by the absence of any universally accepted mechanism for change. Reinhart, however, had no such inhibitions and, in the true style of classical Reform, asserted a subjective justification for initiating reforms:[17]

> The authority for our ultimate decision is the voice of God in our own hearts. 'To thine own self be true', say we, and not only 'thou canst not then be false to any man', but also, thou canst not be false to God himself... Orthodoxy with its completed code and its lack of living authority sufficient to deal with any matter of radical significance must exalt conformity into the place of prime importance. We may respect this attitude. But it is not ours... Ours the task to revive the creative side of Jewish faith and practice. Ours to hew the channels through which may flow the waters of a new and freshening faith.

On the first anniversary of his arrival at West London Reinhart preached a sermon rejecting 'the middle way' that the synagogue was pursuing as 'halting between two opinions, failure to believe in the old, but lacking sufficient spirit and power to seek the new'. He challenged the congregation to 'be in the vanguard... we must emphasise anew that we stand for a definite point of view... In order to achieve today we must spread abroad... This is the hour of our development.'[18] Reinhart's call to action led to many changes in the congregation, both internally and in its relations with other Reform communities. One concerned the building, which had been designed to provide for services and occasional Council meetings only, and was inadequate for the congregation's needs. There was no provision for social and cultural activities, while the Religion School met in corridors and ante-rooms. Launching the scheme in 1930 to erect additional premises, Waley described the situation of the synagogue 'as that of one waking from a long sleep, trying to stretch its limbs and finding no space available'.[19] Property in Upper Berkeley Street and Seymour Place adjacent to the synagogue was acquired, rebuilding work began and the new building was opened on 27 May 1934. In addition to meeting rooms, secretarial offices and classrooms there was a library and a large hall, named after Sir Edward Stern, one of the major donors, who had died shortly before it was completed. Although many people had contributed to planning and financing the new building, it was recognised that Reinhart had been the moving spirit and had 'goaded' the membership to ensure that no expense was spared in meeting the communal needs. The concept of the synagogue as a community centre was a feature of American Jewry but was a novelty in Britain and owed much to his influence. It involved a major re-orientation in the focus of synagogue life, serving no longer just for worship but for all aspects of Jewish life and involving all age-groups. Moreover, the new facilities were to serve purposes never envisaged at the time, catering for the exigencies of war and providing a home for the Reform movement for many years.

Another significant step taken in 1930 was the decision to join the World Union for Progressive Judaism (WUPJ). The organisation had been founded in 1926 as a link between Progressive communities in order to exchange ideas and work for the furtherance of Progressive Judaism. Its prime mover had been Lily Montagu of the Liberal Jewish Synagogue. West London had declined to join at the time amid fears that it might lead towards Liberal practices and prevent any *rapprochement* with the Orthodox. However, this policy was reversed at the Annual General Meeting held on 6 April 1930 when the Council recommended affiliating to the World Union. Speaking in favour of the motion Reinhart declared that it was time for the congregation to end its isolation and to join forces with other like-minded religious bodies. He and other speakers asserted that the fears of becoming unduly Liberal were unfounded, while the possibility of links with Orthodoxy were equally illusory. Some still opposed what they regarded as a 'drastic measure', but the motion was passed by a large majority. Nevertheless, many of the reservations remained and for a long period West London's involvement in the World Union was cautious.

The expansion of Reform horizons was evident, too, in the attempts to strengthen links with other British Reform congregations. Starting in November 1929 the *West London Synagogue Magazine* carried monthly reports of news and activities in Manchester, while details of the Settlement and Bradford now appeared more regularly. There was also a noticeable increase in the attention paid to European Reform: Dr Leo Baeck's books were reviewed in the *West London Synagogue Magazine* and articles by German Reform rabbis appeared. The only interruption in the flow of energy and progress that now characterised the synagogue was the death of Morris Joseph on 17 April 1930, a few weeks before his eighty-third birthday. He had never ceased to serve West London after his official retirement and had made a major contribution to the new prayer book that was to appear the following year. He assisted with certain responsibilities in the two-year interregnum between Blau and Reinhart and was still regarded as 'the ultimate appeal upon all matters affecting the religious welfare of the congregation'.[20] His death was mourned not only by the congregation but by Anglo-Jewry as a whole. His reputation as a preacher crossed all religious boundaries, and his *Judaism as Creed and Life* had been hailed as the finest presentation of Judaism in the English language. Chief Rabbi Hertz attended the memorial service, while tributes came from many parts of the world from those who had never met him but had come to regard him as their teacher from the three books of his collected sermons. Church leaders were also among the mourners, attesting to the high regard in which he was held by the wider community. He was cremated – a custom forbidden by the Orthodox but permitted by Reform – and his ashes buried in the Hoop Lane cemetery.[21]

A religious innovation, both for the congregation and for British Jewry generally, was the introduction in April 1931 of a 'communal *seder*' designed to cater for strangers and for members without families: 'For a ceremony so intimately associated with the home as the *seder*, there must always be a certain diffidence in arranging a communal celebration, but it is the function of the Synagogue to provide hospitality for the wayfarer and how more appropriately than by gathering together in festive mood on this great night.'[22] It proved a great success and not only became an annual event but was imitated by other congregations from all denominations. A further development that same month was the establishment of the Junior Membership (JM) for the 16 to 23-year-old age group. Its object was to give young people a definite status in the congregation and to provide them with a representative voice in synagogue affairs. The report on the first meeting was correct in suggesting that 'in the distant future [it] may be looked back upon as an important milestone in the history of the Synagogue',[23] for it was to prove an invaluable source of future leadership. Meanwhile the size of the community was expanding, both in numbers and in radius. In September 1931 the Wigmore Hall had to be hired for the first-ever High Holy Day overflow services, while a branch of the Religion School was opened in Eton Avenue to cater for the large number of members living in the Hampstead area. At the beginning of 1932 the membership stood at 1,300 adults.

The Settlement Synagogue was also experiencing a great

expansion at this time, catering for the religious needs of the Settlement's large membership. The prayers said at the end of club evenings had developed into regular Sabbath services. No attempt was made to wean children away from the religious traditions of their parents, but inevitably many preferred to attend synagogue with their friends. There were also many adults who no longer went to the local Orthodox services held on Friday afternoons in winter when they were still working and were glad to attend services at a later, more convenient, time. The use of English was also an attraction. In October 1929 the synagogue published its own prayer book, compiled by Basil Henriques. It combined material from the liturgies of both its sponsoring bodies, West London and the Liberal Jewish Synagogue, and occasionally used translations from the Singers (Orthodox) Prayer Book. A special feature were the 30 'special prayers' in English grouped under headings such as 'For Faith, For Unselfishness, For Courage, For Understanding'. Some were new compositions, others were extracted from the *Fratres Prayer Book* compiled for club use by Henriques in 1916, or from *Prayers for Trench and Base* which he had published for Jewish troops in 1918. The new prayer book also included 21 English hymns. In addition some of the prayers were changed substantially in content in their English translation, although the Hebrew text itself remain unaltered. Thus the prayer at the opening of the Ark, *Va'ye'hee binso'a*, which was translated normally as 'Arise, O Lord, and let thine enemies be scattered, let those who hate thee flee before thee', was instead rendered as 'Arise, shine forth, O Lord, that those who have forsaken thee may find thee'. Such instances in which the original sense was transformed totally was justified in order to ensure that 'there is no prayer which conflicts with the thoughts and aspirations of that type of Judaism for which the Synagogue stands'.[24] The prayer book proved highly popular and was to serve the Settlement for several decades, being used in preference to the new prayer book published by West London two years later and still being used today in tandem with the revised edition of 1977.

The services at the Settlement attracted remarkable attendances, with 400 people coming on Friday nights, while over a thousand were present at the High Holy Days. Its success was due to a combination of factors: during the inter-war period there was still a large Jewish population in the East End, although at the same time the process of Anglicisation of the children of the immigrants meant that many were receptive to a more modern approach to Judaism. In addition, the disillusion caused by the First World War and the lessening attachment to traditional religious authority resulted in many seeking new forms of Jewish expression. The style of the service was very similar to that at West London, the spiritual home of Henriques, with the few variations being longer periods of silent meditation and greater recitation of prayers in unison. In deference to the traditional background of most members a second day's service was held at the New Year. The synagogue itself moved in June 1930 from its original location at Betts Street to the new purpose-built Bernhard Baron Centre at Berner Street, which was opened by H.R.H. the Duke of Gloucester. The previous year it had been recognised for purposes of marriage registration, with the sub-warden, Abraham Pulverness, being appointed the first secretary for marriages. A further development in its communal facilities was the opening of a religion school in 1931; within a year its roll had increased from 11 to 60 pupils.

The Manchester Congregation was still served by Revd Phillips and maintained a full range of social and cultural activities. However, the lack of any growth in membership caused tensions within the Council, with calls for reforms by some members being resisted fiercely by others. Indicative of the problem was the small size of the religion school, which consisted of only 20 children. A motion to appoint a second minister who might attract younger couples and organise youth activities was proposed at a general meeting in July 1930. However, it was defeated by those unwilling to take any financial risks in the wake of the Depression of the late 1920s and early 1930s and by the supporters of Phillips who wished to see no change in the religious leadership. The result of this opposition to any positive measures was that the following decade witnessed increasing stagnation and decline in the congregation. Moreover, the economic problems experienced by many businessmen within the community during the Depression resulted in a number moving away from the city and a depletion in the congregation's membership.

The West London form of worship was followed, save for the timing of the Friday evening services which was not fixed but varied according to the season. There was also Second Day service at New Year. Like West London, many of its leading members played an influential role in Manchester's other Jewish institutions: thus, amongst others, Annie Henriques was honorary secretary of the Manchester Jewish Ladies' Visiting Association, Sydney Frankenburg was president of both the Jewish Amateur Operatic Society and the Manchester and Salford Jewish Ex-Servicemen's Association, Mrs Dorothy Quas-Cohen was vice-president of the Manchester Victoria Memorial Jewish Hospital, and Harold Behrens was president of the Jewish Board of Guardians. The regular reports of Manchester's news in the *West London Synagogue Magazine* from 1929 onwards was an assertion of their common identity. Reinhart visited Manchester periodically to preach at the synagogue in a deliberate attempt to strengthen the links between the congregations, and declared that he viewed his ministry as not only concerned with Upper Berkeley Street 'but also in the great movement of which it is part'.[25]

On the other side of the Pennines, Bradford Synagogue was still experiencing many problems from the lack of a minister. Services and other religious functions were undertaken by a team of lay members: J. Hirschell, O. M. Strauss, H. D. Drucquer, A. Shapira and M. Arensberg. The other two Reform congregations provided considerable support. Vivian Simmons made periodic visits and sent Mr S. Jamaiker, an Oxford graduate who had been appointed as a temporary assistant to him, to take the High Holy Day services. Revd Phillips assisted by sending sermons to be read out at services, and he also officiated at many of the funerals.

One of the most tangible examples of the new developments within British Reform was the publication of a sixth and substantially revised edition of the prayer book in 1931. The fifth edition, which was used before that, had been issued in 1898 and, like its predecessors, was essentially the same as that originally published by Marks in 1841, with only a few modifications. In the 90 years since then, the Reform congregation had undergone enormous changes, with the initial act of rebellion against the geographical restraints imposed by the *Ascamot* developing into a reformation in theology and practice. However, this was not reflected in the existing prayer book and it was failing to cater for the religious needs of congregants. Complaints of absenteeism at both Friday evening and Saturday morning services have already been noted. By way of explanation critics argued that the current service was too passive in character and did not encourage worshippers to join in sufficiently. There was concern, too, that it was too rigid, preventing any variety or enthusiasm, and that this was responsible for the widespread feeling that the service was 'cold'. The over-complicated melodies sung by the choir were held to be additional bars to congregational participation.[26]

The new prayer book was the result of several years work and reflected the efforts of many individuals, including three successive senior ministers. The Council of West London appointed a committee to revise the prayer book in 1923 under the chairmanship of Harry Marks, a grandson of D.W. Marks. It was typical of the authority structure of the community that it consisted entirely of lay members. The three ministers (Joseph, Harris and Simmons) attended only at the invitation of the committee.[27] After many debates and trial services using draft versions, the new prayer book made its public debut in April 1931 and was used exclusively thereafter. A revised hymnal was issued in November, containing new material and a larger selection of texts and music. Neither Manchester and Bradford synagogues nor their ministers were invited to participate in the revisions, although they did purchase the new publications for use in their services.

The prayer book was a watershed in the religious development of Reform and served not only as a liturgy for its members but also as a public declaration of its principles. It was radically different from its predecessor, although based upon it, and reflected a conscious desire to tailor the prayers to the lifestyle and beliefs of the modern worshipper. Thus while the Preface referred to 'the deathless spirit which inspired the pious founders of our Congregation' and reprinted in full the Introduction to the first edition, the differences were enormous. Conscious of the realities of current patterns of worship, the new edition began with the Sabbath service, whereas the old one had started with the daily services. Moreover the latter were no longer even provided in full, but merely summarised by a short table referring to pages suitable for the morning, afternoon and evening midweek services. It was indicative of the shift to Sabbath services as the main occasion for communal prayer in Reform and wider circles, and was a vivid pointer to the growing secularisation of British Jewry.

Another structural change was the inclusion of services appertaining to the range of ceremonies for the cycle of life, such as for circumcision, marriage, dedication of a new home, funerals, tombstone consecration, and prayers on visiting a grave. Two further additions reflected new trends in synagogue life: the service on naming a girl indicated the desire for a specific public ceremony for the birth of girls. The service upon admission to the Jewish faith mirrored the more favourable attitude towards receiving converts and the growth in the number of cases arising. Conversely, the lessening impact of the terrors of the past meant that of the three separate prayers in the old edition – for setting out on a journey, on going to sea and during a storm at sea – only the first was retained in the new edition.

The most dramatic change of all was an additional section, which was devoted entirely to the Psalms and which occupied over half the size of the prayer book. It contained 80 of the 150 Psalms, although some were considerably edited, omitting material that was considered to be inappropriate for modern worship. Thus calls for the destruction of one's enemies, along with references to the evils done by the wicked and the retribution due to them, were deleted. Another reform concerned the layout of the Psalms, along with all other instances of poetry, with both the Hebrew and English texts presented in verse form, as befitting the original composition. The object of the section was both to provide greater variety in the content of public services and to be a source of inspiration for home use.

Another new feature was that some prayers were given only in English, such as the service for a mother after childbirth, as well as the prayers to be said at night, in the morning, when setting out for a journey, and those recited by the sick. The omission of a Hebrew option for such moments was to be criticised by some, but the assumption was that the use of the vernacular would be preferred for such instances of personal prayer. Even more revolutionary was the inclusion of a hymn in English, and which, after much experimentation by the Prayer Book Committee, was placed immediately after the *Amidah*. Some simple structural changes within the services also had great impact, such as reversing the order at the end of services and making the concluding hymn, be it the *Yigdal* or *Adon olam*, follow the *Kaddish* rather than precede it and thereby finishing on a more uplifting note. Equally dramatic was the change in character brought to the Priestly Blessing by having it recited by the minister at the conclusion of the *Shabbat* morning service rather than by the congregation at the very beginning. It was thus revitalised from being a historical memory into a new act of blessing, albeit by a modern non-priestly leadership, and gave a solemn finale to the service.

Among the public services themselves there were also many changes. There was no provision for *Torah* readings at midweek morning services. The *Shabbat Musaf*, in the previous edition a truncated version of the traditional original, was abandoned altogether. Many individual prayers were omitted, such as the opening *Kaddish*, the second and third paragraphs of the *Shema* on the Sabbath evening, the paragraph *Ata kiddashta* in middle of the *Amidah*, and the *Oseh shalom* at the end of it. The Song of Moses was removed from the Sabbath morning service, although printed at the end of the Psalter so that it could still be used occasionally. Other prayers were shortened, as in the Grace after Meals which was reduced to half its previous length, or the *Emet v'emunah*. However, the reforms did not just entail a rejection of the past, but consisted of a genuine re-evaluation of what was appropriate for a modern prayer book. Thus the deletions were balanced by the reintroduction of traditional passages that had been abandoned by previous reformers. The song *L'cha dodi* was restored, albeit in a shortened form, as was the prayer *Ribon ha'olamim* for the Sabbath. The original Aramaic form of the *Kaddish* made its return as an option alongside the Hebrew version. More significantly the blessings for the Sabbath candles reappeared, as did prayers for the celebration of *Chanukah* and *Purim*. Their inclusion represented a theological shift, for they had been omitted by Marks on the grounds that there was no biblical basis for their assertion that God had 'commanded us' to light the Sabbath and *Chanukah* candles or read the *Purim* scroll; they were merely rabbinic enactments. Their restoration in the new edition indicated that such distinctions were no longer held to be of overriding importance and that other criteria would be applied to judge what was suitable for modern Judaism.

There were many other alterations arising from theological considerations, which reflected a concern to make the new prayer book correspond as much as possible to the beliefs of those who would be using it. Any remaining references to the sacrificial system were edited out, as in the phrase in the *Avodah* paragraph of the *Amidah* alluding to the service of the Temple. Similarly deleted were any mentions of the coming of a personal Messiah, as distinct from the Messianic age, such as the call for God to hasten 'the advent of His anointed' in the Hebrew *Kaddish*. Allusions to the Jewish people being superior to others were also found unacceptable. The *Alenu* therefore lost the sentence declaring that God 'hath chosen us from amongst all peoples'. Conversely, any disparaging references to Gentiles were removed, as was the declaration in the *Ribon ha'olamim* that 'the nations of the world are as a drop from the bucket'. This sensitivity applied equally to historical references that appeared to be over-triumphant. As a result, praising God for slaying the first-born of Egypt and drowning the enemies of Israel in the Red Sea was excluded from *Ezrat avotenu*. The desire to achieve a pure and inspiring atmosphere for worship extended to omitting the misdeeds of Israel herself, and the removal of the third stanza of *Maoz tzur* which confessed the idolatry and drunkenness in which Israel had indulged during the Babylonian exile.

Political considerations can be detected in certain of the revisions and in the way Jewish life is presented. All petitions to 'gather us from among the nations' or 'from the four corners of the earth' were deleted as unwarranted suggestions that Jews in England were in a state of exile and in a place other than their natural home. This was at a time when Zionism was a major public issue and there was much debate over practical implementation of the British Government's promise via Lord Balfour to facilitate 'the establishment in Palestine of a national home for the Jewish people'. For the same reason there was a meticulous removal of all suggestions of political independence associated with the restoration of Zion. The daily *Amidah* suffered in particular, with the complete omission of the paragraphs *Geullah, Kibbutz galuyot, Birkat mishpat, Boneh Yerushalayim* and *Birkat David* calling upon God respectively to 'Look upon our affliction...and hasten to redeem us', 'Sound the great horn to announce our freedom', 'Restore our judges as aforetime', 'Speedily establish the throne of David' and 'Cause the offspring of thy servant David speedily to flourish'. In the Sabbath service the end of the *Avodah* which previously blessed God for restoring His divine presence to Zion now blessed God for causing His holy spirit to rest upon Zion, and thereby changed a political programme into a statement of spiritual regeneration. Even mention in the *Av ha'rahamim* of rebuilding the walls of Jerusalem was excised, while there was no doubt about the fate of the last line of the *En kelohenu* calling for God to arise and favour Zion when the appointed time arrived.

In the many prayers where the Hebrew text was left unaltered there was still the issue of how best to render the translation. This was not just a matter of style but also of theology. Thus the paragraph *Gevurot* in the *Amidah* concluding with *m'hayeh ha'metim*, translated previously as 'who revivest the dead' now became 'who quickenest the dead' in an attempt to distance the prayer from a literal belief in physical resurrection of the dead and to substitute belief in the immortality of the soul. A similar attempt lay behind changing the end of *Elohy n'shammah* from 'who restorest the souls unto the dead' to 'who quickenest the dead to everlasting life'. In other prayers the English translation was sometimes used as an opportunity to present a more universalist character than was in the actual Hebrew version. Thus the *Oseh shalom* at the end of the *Kaddish* calls upon God to 'grant peace to us and to all Israel', but was rendered instead 'grant peace unto Israel and unto all mankind'. A similar desire for universalism led to the substitution of Isaiah 2: 2–3 and its vision of international harmony for the decidedly particularist passage before the *Ki mi'tzion* about scattering Israel's enemies.

Equally radical was that some prayers were entirely new compositions, written specially for the prayer book. Written largely by Morris Joseph, they included six options at the start of the Sabbath morning service and prayers for private devotion. These served a dual purpose, both giving fresh input to the service, and allowing variations to take place. The prayer for the Royal Family was rewritten, as were the night prayer and that recited at *Chanukah*. New in concept were the prayers for the bereaved and for the sick inserted after the *Torah* reading.

Another aspect of the new prayer book was the increased influence of the Ashkenazi service. Marks's editions had primarily been based upon the Sephardi service and reflected the religious background of most of the early members of West London. By the 1920s the synagogue had evolved its own tradition, no longer referred automatically to its Sephardi roots, and catered for a membership that was of more mixed origins. The minutes of the Prayer Book Committee reveal the willingness to adapt from the Singers Prayer Book, such as introducing the *Ma tovu* at the beginning of the service and including at the end of the service parts of the second paragraph of the *Alenu*. The 'Ashkenazification' process can also be seen in the abandonment of the Sephardi tradition of reciting Psalm 23 at the end of the Sabbath eve service, which had been emulated in the previous edition, while the shorter Ashkenazi version of the *Adon olam* was now preferred over the Sephardi one used beforehand.

The new edition of the prayer book received a generally warm welcome from the congregation. Particularly appreciated was the greater level of participation which had been achieved by the increased number of prayers recited by the congregation, including the reading of the latter portions of the *Amidah*, which previously had been read silently. Another significant step was the reintroduction of the reading of the *Haftarah* by members themselves. Nevertheless, criticism was expressed over a few specific points, such as certain translations and the greater use of English prayers, while those who were attached to the old edition resented the suggestion that change was necessary at all. The most serious general accusation came from Reinhart himself who admitted that it was guilty of theological inconsistencies. Thus despite concern over mention of a personal Messiah and the deletion of 'the advent of His anointed' in the Hebrew *Kaddish*, a similar reference was retained in the *Yigdal*. Equally inconsistent was the omission of the *Vay'chulu* from the home service for Sabbath evening on the grounds that it reinforced the now discarded belief of Creation in six days, yet the even more explicit *V'shamru* was retained. This theological confusion arose because no attempt had ever been made by the original committee to draw up articles of belief upon which to make the revisions. Each prayer was considered separately and other considerations, such as their popularity and their overall effect, were also used to judge them and might take precedence. There were some instances of firm direction, as in the case of rehabilitating rites sanctioned by the Oral Law or that of abandoning belief in the resurrection of the dead. The result was a new liturgy that left many question marks over the precise principles of Reform, but produced a combination of the familiar and the refreshing that satisfied the needs of most worshippers at whom it was directed.

The early 1930s was also notable for the birth of three new Reform congregations, which, discounting the special circumstances of the Settlement, was the first such development for 60 years. The Glasgow Synagogue was formed in 1933 following a visit by Reinhart to a group of Reform-minded individuals who had been holding services very successfully for several months. It was hoped that the city, with a population of approximately 14,000 Jews, could support the first Reform congregation in Scotland. West London loaned prayer books and paid for its then temporary Assistant Minister, Theodor Gaster (son of the former

Haham, Moses Gaster) to make regular visits to Glasgow. To help the small congregation establish itself fully, West London also agreed that it would pay the cost of a minister for his first year. Premises were acquired at 33 Queen Square and by the end of the year it had a membership of 50 families. Rabbi Joseph Levine was inducted in July 1934 and helped to double the size of the congregation. After he returned to the United States in mid-1938, his compatriot Rabbi Samuel Baron took office. West London continued to give financial help, as well as encouraging the community to persevere in its endeavours.

At the same time a number of Jews in Golders Green were also looking for a modern interpretation of Judaism. They were part of a general move by Jews to the area following the extension of the London Underground's Northern Line there in 1907. It resulted in Golders Green and its environs becoming a favoured suburb among Jews wishing to live in easy access of the West End or East End where they worked, but out of the city. Their initial approach to the Liberal Jewish Synagogue met with little encouragement, so they contacted West London. Once again, Reinhart responded enthusiastically, attending the first committee meeting in May 1933 and leading the first service the following month. Originally known as the Hampstead Reform Synagogue, it later adopted the title the North Western Reform Synagogue, and was more colloquially referred to as 'Alyth' once it acquired premises in Alyth Gardens, NW11. It, too, received great support from West London, including financial help, the loan of two scrolls, and, most importantly, the grant of unused grounds at the Hoop Lane cemetery in order to erect a synagogue. Reinhart personally wrote to all West London members in the area and invited them to become involved in the new community. It was also fortunate in having its own minister from the very start, Rabbi Solomon Starrels, who had previously served at the West Central (Liberal) Synagogue. Membership rocketed, leaping from the 19 founders to 303 members in two and a half years. Among them were many German Jewish refugees who moved into the area during that period. Starrels remained with the congregation until 1938 when he returned to the United States, his duties being taken over by Revd Maurice Perlzweig.

In 1924, the Northern Line was extended to Edgware and helped turn it into another area of Jewish settlement as Jews increasingly became a suburban population. Indeed, partly thanks to the development of the underground transport system in the first decades of the twentieth century, north and north-west London had replaced the East End as the main area of London Jewish residence by the 1930s.[28] Towards the end of 1934, 13 members of Edgware (United) Synagogue resigned over a dispute concerning communal organisation and discussed the formation of an independent congregation. They did not originally intend to establish a Reform one, but following a visit to West London, they felt it was more in keeping with their religious aspirations – 'Just what we were looking for' – and they founded the Edgware and District Progressive Jewish Fellowship.[29] In December, Reinhart addressed them on the principles of the Reform approach to Judaism and made a deep impact on them. He also offered to provide free religious education for the children of members. The following February they established themselves as a congregation and decided to designate themselves as Reform, changing their name to the Edgware and District Reform Synagogue. They received much support from West London, with regular visits from Reinhart and Simmons, as well as lay readers. Perlzweig also took services. The almost accidental way in which the congregation became a Reform one was typical of the lethargic religious nature of most British Jews, who were content to retain their Orthodox affiliation unless jolted into reconsidering their position by some external event. This might have applied to thousands of others who would probably have felt more at home in a Reform synagogue had they explored the different religious options available to them and made the effort to change.

The demographic changes affecting London Jewry were a significant, though not crucial, factor in the growth of Reform. As Marshall Sklare has shown in his study of American Jewry in the same period, 'suburbanisation brought with it problems of the maintenance of Jewish identity'.[30] Many in America whose attachment to Orthodoxy was superficial took the opportunity afforded by their physical move into new surroundings to effect a religious transition as well. This occurred in Britain in the 1930s, and was continued in the following decade by new Reform communities in Hendon and Wimbledon. However, it was on a more modest level and did not, as in the United States, signal the predominance of non-Orthodox Judaism. One reason for the difference was that in America, Orthodoxy failed to react to changing demographic patterns and was often left behind, quite literally, in the urban centre. In England, by contrast, the United Synagogue was quick to move out with the first signs of new settlements. Thus the United Synagogue had established a congregation in Golders Green as early as 1917 and one in Edgware in 1932. The fact that the United Synagogue was the first to colonise the suburbs meant that Orthodoxy continued to enjoy the affiliation of many Jews who did not subscribe to its tenets. The lack of unity between the few Reform synagogues and the absence of any programme for expansion meant that British Reform was unable to take advantage of a critical moment that offered enormous potential for growth; instead it merely expanded at a slow rate and never emulated the success of its American counterpart.

There was a modest growth in existing Reform congregations too, leading to other ministerial appointments. Once again West London felt the need for a third minister and in January 1936 invited Rabbi Louis Cashdan to accept the position. The appointment of an American was because efforts to find a suitable English candidate had failed. The following year, the Settlement Synagogue appointed Rabbi Camillus Angel as its minister – another American – and both he and Cashdan also visited the Edgware Synagogue, with the assumption clearly being that a new Reform community was the responsibility of the established ones. Another new departure from the élitist and disinterested attitude of the Reform synagogues of previous decades towards others was the initiative taken by Angel to spread the message of Reform Judaism throughout the East End of London. He inaugurated and widely advertised a series of special sermons about Reform's basic principles. Meetings were also held to welcome prospective members and initiate them into the meaning of Reform Judaism.

Not every venture was successful. An attempt by H. D. Drucquer in 1930–31 to find others in Leeds willing to establish a Reform community met with failure. He received encouragement from Reinhart, but lacked local support, and it was not till 1944 that a Reform synagogue was formed there. Nevertheless, the mid-1930s saw the number of Reform congregations virtually double. It was no accident, therefore, that in December 1934 the monthly newsletter previously known as the *West London Synagogue Magazine* suddenly changed to the *Synagogue Review*, with the sub-title 'Organ of the following Associated Congregations', listing all the Reform communities.

Amid these developments in the 1930s, there were also changes affecting Reform's religious perspective. It was recognised that if Reform was to be loyal to the dynamic character of Judaism that it professed to uphold, it would have to be willing to re-examine its own practices and beliefs. Thus in 1930 it was felt that West London's early abolition of *barmitzvah* and its replacement by confirmation was no longer appropriate and the ceremony was reintroduced. However, a communal confirmation for all 15-year-olds was retained. Another West London custom that was abandoned was the wearing of a *tallit* at the Friday evening service, a practice which was not necessary according to Jewish tradition, but had been adopted out of a desire to harmonise ritual at services. Changed too was the celebration of *Simchat Torah*. Originally it had been discarded by the early Reformers as part of the general abolition of the extra days of festivals. Its popularity was such that it had been brought back by being made part of the afternoon service of *Shemini Atzeret*. Now it was changed to the morning of that day, combining the two festivals together. The Settlement held a Second Day service at *Rosh Hashannah*. It was the only congregation at that time to retain an extra day apart from Manchester, and the practice reflected its location in the heartland of traditional Jewish life. The *Haftarah*, previously limited to readings from the Prophets, was extended to include extracts from the Writings. The New Year service was abridged by half an hour to two hours, the existing services being considered too long. Sabbath evening services now lasted 45 minutes and the morning ones an hour and a half. These moves reflected the concern first expressed in 1840 that services should not be burdensome but inspire decorum and concentration. Indeed, when the ceremony of *kiddush* was introduced, it was only on the condition that another prayer be omitted so as not to elongate the service. The nature and length of the weekly sermon had also changed considerably from Marks's day: 20 minutes rather than 45, and no longer thundering down about congregants' faults but more direct and intimate. West London introduced daily evening services in 1934 and also Children's Services, an innovation imitated by many other Reform congregations. The issue of freedom of the pulpit had also been raised. At West London Reinhart had successfully opposed attempts in 1934 to ban him from introducing politics into his sermons, but at Manchester Revd Phillips had far less independence. The Executive asked him 'to refrain from delivering sermons more often than once a month, unless specifically requested to the contrary'.[31]

Greater use of English was evident, even in the most traditional prayers, such as the *Amidah*, and the *Torah* portion was translated immediately after it had been read. This was not merely a matter of facilitating comprehension, but predicated on the rigorous re-evaluation of the Bible, outlined by Vivian Simmons. Reform now accepted 'the inequality of its various revelations and of its literary and religious character' and therefore only used in worship those parts 'whose teaching is universal, or in other respects appeals to us, leaving alone those parts which are definitely of poor quality, or of temporary character. We have even established the principle, unheard of in the past, that nothing should be read or taught from the Hebrew Bible which cannot be fittingly read or taught in English translation.'[32] Simmons further suggested that 'If the day comes when we Progressive Jews shall decide to use a smaller Bible, one which shall contain only the great teachings and sources of inspiration for our religious life, I, for one, will be neither disappointed nor surprised'.[33] While radical attitudes such as this may have been consistent with the thrust of Reform thinking, they gave vent to the criticism that Reform was simply a departure from Judaism. Reinhart, for instance, acknowledged that Reform 'is grossly misunderstood – thought of as an effort to destroy rather than develop and preserve. The essential contribution of the Reform movement in modern Judaism is the placing of the emphasis where the emphasis belongs. Not ceremonial but righteousness!'[34]

Equality was gradually extended to women, reflecting both the principles of Reform and the influence of wider social trends which had seen women being given increasing responsibility in the workplace during the First World War and gaining political enfranchisement in 1928. Separate seating was abolished by 1933, with women released from the gallery upstairs and free to join the men in the main body of the synagogue. The fact that women had to return upstairs at High Holy Days was due to practical considerations, as the majority of seats were still owned by men from the days before mixed seating was allowed. Mixed seating was permitted, however, at the overflow services in the Stern Hall. During the war, *force majeure* completed the equalisation process when the possibility of air raids made it more practical for families to sit together at all times. Girls participated equally in confirmation ceremonies and could read from the scroll or the Prophets, but could not do so at ordinary Sabbath services. In response to a complaint that women were still not fully integrated, the West London ministers declared that there was no objection to them wearing a *tallit* and that it was up to the women themselves to do so. It was an offer that was not taken up for almost 50 years! Not all synagogues were so accommodating, and a motion to permit mixed seating at Bradford was defeated at an Extraordinary General Meeting as late as 1950.

The differences in religious policy applied to other spheres of synagogue life and sometimes even within the same congregation. Thus one community decided that it was inappropriate to hold a sweepstake for the benefit of the synagogue, but did permit a boxing tournament. Other debates centred over the permissibility of driving to synagogue on the Sabbath, and although there were some who objected, it was commonly accepted. In fact, it may be inferred from a motion that 'no meetings should be held and no work in the Synagogue offices be allowed after 6.30 p.m. on Friday and Festival evenings' that strictness in Sabbath observance was not always a priority.[35] Music remained an important element of services. A suggestion that West London reintroduce the position of a cantor was rejected and it continued to rely on its very proficient choir. However, some felt that 'the very artistry of the choir causes the congregation to be struck dumb and converts the service into a performance'.[36] When, by contrast, North Western appointed Rabbi Werner Van der Zyl as their minister in 1943, he brought with him from Germany a more informal and tuneful approach to synagogue music, encouraging the congregation to participate rather than listen. Variations occurred in the matter of head-coverings: in 1938 Glasgow decided to modify the wearing of hats by male worshippers by the introduction of *kippot* on the grounds that they were more aesthetically pleasing, while women were not obliged to cover their heads. West London wardens still retained their traditional headgear of top-hats, but they had long ceased being worn by the rest of the community. These and other changes were regarded as continuing the momentum created in 1840. At a special service in April 1940 celebrating the centenary of West London, Reinhart summed up the openness to change that was inherent in Reform Judaism when he told the assembled congregation, 'We honour them [our founders] not by repeating their words parrot-like, or by imitating their actions monkey-like, but by answering in their spirit the needs of our time'.[37]

Meanwhile, moves were afoot to strengthen relations within British Jewry by bringing the West London Synagogue, the Liberal Jewish Synagogue and their associated congregations closer together. There was much that they had in common: despite differences in the conduct of their services, both shared a modern approach to Judaism, assuming the right to implement change on their own authority, whether jettisoning old traditions or introducing new ones. They subscribed to a historical interpretation of Judaism, valued sincere faith over ritual observance, and did not consider themselves bound by the dictates of Jewish Law. Three factors had led to the attempt to draw the two groups together. First, there was the personal contact that had developed over the years, for the Liberal Jewish Synagogue was only a short distance away in St John's Wood and the ministers met together on numerous occasions to discuss matters of mutual interest; they had also preached at each other's synagogues. A second factor was that West London had joined the World Union for Progressive Judaism, of which the Liberal Jewish Synagogue was a founder member; thus there now existed a formal link between the two congregations, which became stronger as the Union sought to expand its activities. A third factor may have been a reaction to the horrors being unleashed on German Jewry and the desire to promote as much domestic unity as possible.

The initiative came from the ministers of the two congregations, Reinhart and Mattuck, who had suggested to their respective Councils that active steps be taken to ensure greater co-operation between them. A committee was established in October 1936 consisting of the ministers and three lay representatives from each synagogue, as well as Basil Henriques representing the jointly sponsored Settlement. The committee's first decision was to elect Claude Montefiore as chairman. He outlined an ambitious set of aims, in which a new organisation might be created, linking all existing Reform and Liberal congregations and helping to found new ones, although without interfering with the internal autonomy of individual congregations. One of the consequences would be the demise of the Jewish Religious Union – the association of Liberal synagogues. Others concurred with his vision, albeit expressing themselves more cautiously, while they also emphasised that the committee was only an advisory one without any executive power.

A difficulty that emerged was agreement on a mutually acceptable name for the new organisation, and for the form of Judaism that it espoused. After the meeting the West London lay representatives issued a statement declaring that although they welcomed 'the purpose of advancing the cause of what is at present known as Progressive Judaism, they could not recommend for the approval of their congregation any scheme that seemed, however indefinitely, to envisage the abandonment of the West London's own presentation of Judaism or the fusion of the governing bodies of the two institutions'. [38]

At the second meeting a sub-committee was formed, consisting of Dr Mattuck and Mr J. G. Lousada (of West London) to draw up recommendations as to the function and constitution of the new body. They proposed a federation entitled the Association of Liberal and Reform Synagogues promoting a modern interpretation of Judaism, and funded by all associated congregations. Reinhart produced a memorandum of his own, suggesting that it be called instead the Associated British Synagogues – a name he was later to use for the Reform movement itself – and listing largely similar aims. After a long deliberation the committee chose the unwieldy title Joint Committee of Progressive Congregations for the Advancement of Judaism. It was a compromise between those who wanted to stipulate what form of Judaism was being proclaimed and those, led by Reinhart, who were opposed to limiting their form of Judaism by the addition of any qualifying adjectives. However, there was an even greater dispute that could not be overcome: the fear by West London that the body's governing council would be dominated by the Liberal members; for even though the seats would be equally divided among both groups, they feared that as the Liberal synagogues were already associated together through the Jewish Religious Union, they would act as a bloc and always outvote the representatives of Reform synagogues who had no such association and would vote independently of each other. West London's lack of trust in its putative partners meant that little progress could be made. The personality clash between Reinhart and Mattuck also caused difficulties. Montefiore issued 'an eleventh hour appeal' to prevent the breakdown of the talks: 'It seems most regrettable and even absurd, that we should not be able, because of trivial minor differences, and, I fear, I must add, trivial minor suspicions and jealousies, to come together and work for our common cause.'[39] He also claimed that all the concessions made in the discussions so far had been by the Liberals, and that West London had made none. The fifth and final meeting of the committee took place on 27 May 1937 but the impasse remained. Two obstacles – the desire to preserve each party's own existing organisational structure and the fear of being taken over by the other side – proved more powerful than the ideals of a common future, and were to characterise similar debates in future decades. Upon Dr Mattuck's proposal, it was agreed to abandon plans for closer union, although co-operation would continue and the committee would arrange periodic conferences. One of these occurred in November 1938 on the theme of religious observance, but subsequent efforts were impeded by the outbreak of war.

There was never any question of any formal link between West London and the Orthodox establishment, but everyday relationships were mutually cordial, both on a personal level and institutionally. The Chief Rabbi's Court, for instance, had no hesitation in sending would-be converts to the Reform when appropriate. Writing in 1930 to Revd Simmons about a female applicant who was engaged to a nominally observant Jew, *Dayan* Gollop stated:[40]

> The fact that the gentleman concerned is not a strictly Orthodox Jew, would seem to point that she would be more at home with you than with us. It would be almost absurd to train an applicant for strictly Orthodox Judaism, when the man she proposes to marry does not observe the religion she is presumed to undertake. I see no reason why you should not deal with the case if he wishes to place it in your hands.

In turn West London ministers occasionally referred cases to the Chief Rabbi's Court that were felt to belong under Orthodox auspices. The willingness of the two authorities to recommend proselytes to each other indicates a degree of mutual respect and goodwill. It reflected the esteemed position that West London had acquired in the general community. Despite its schismatic origins and fears that it would be a source of heresy and anarchy, the synagogue had earned a high reputation for its decorous form of worship and its philanthropic activities. The close family ties between many of its leading members and those occupying important roles in the Orthodox community contributed to the amicable regard in which it was held. The relationship also reflected the tolerant liberal tradition of Orthodoxy at the end of the nineteenth century and in the first three decades of the twentieth. It consisted of extending the boundaries of the permissible to the maximum in order to promote harmony within Anglo-Jewry and to encourage those on the fringes to stay within the communal framework. As was shown earlier, Reform ministers were allowed to participate in Orthodox institutions and ceremonies. For its part, West London sought to promote good relations, and even determined that the times of *Kol Nidre* services should begin at the same time as the Orthodox ones so that the entire community should join in prayer at the same time. When attempts were made to start a Reform congregation in Leeds, express instructions were given not to do 'anything that might appear to be propaganda against the Orthodox, of which certainly none of us want to be guilty'.[41]

Individual Orthodox rabbis agreed to preach at West London, with Revd Arthur Barnett of the Western Synagogue and Revd Dr Abraham Cohen being occasional guests. Hertz's visit to West London to deliver a lecture there in 1925 was hailed as 'a sign that the old bitterness which existed in the past was now buried forever'.[42] When Hertz returned in 1934 to be the guest of honour at the opening of West London's extension – along with Rev David Bueno de Mesquita, minister of the Spanish and Portuguese Congregation at Lauderdale Road – he affirmed the *rapprochement*:[43]

> I feel that my presence here requires some words in explanation. It is certainly not due to the fact that I dismiss the religious issues that led to the formation of this Synagogue ninety-four years ago as of trifling importance. I am the last person in the world to minimise the significance of religious difference in Jewry. If I have nevertheless decided to be with you this morning, it is because of my conviction that far more calamitous than religious difference in Jewry is religious indifference in Jewry.

He went on to praise the Reform community's contribution to Jewish life and presented it as his ally rather than his enemy:

> Your co-operation is especially welcome at the present day, when there is need for emphasising the religious nature of Anglo-Jewry, in face of the exaggerated racialism proclaimed

> by some Jews. For you are of those who maintain that Anglo-Jewry is far more than a racial group with certain social and civic interests; and that Israel is first of all a spiritual community, to whom the God of our Fathers in the days of old entrusted a Law of Truth, and thereby planted everlasting life within us.

It was a remarkable speech that epitomised a mood of religious tolerance that would never have been imagined at the time of West London's inception. He returned the following year to give a lecture in the Stern Hall. The close relations may have been encouraged by the clouds of Fascism menacing Jews at home and abroad, with Hitler terrorising German Jewry while Oswald Mosley and his Blackshirts were threatening British Jews. In May 1939 Rabbi Israel Brodie, later to be Chief Rabbi himself, addressed West London's Senior Discussion Group on 'The Mystical Approach to Judaism'. However, that date not only marked the last spring before Europe plunged into war, but also the end of the *rapprochement*. Hertz reversed his former policy of co-operation, while Brodie was to become a fierce opponent of Reform.

The change in the relationship was due primarily to changes within the United Synagogue. One important development was the arrival in England in 1932 of the renowned Lithuanian scholar, Rabbi Yehezkel Abramsky. Three years later he was appointed the senior *dayan* of the Chief Rabbi's Court. He saw it as his task to combat the United Synagogue's preference for easy-going compromises and to promote instead a much stricter interpretation of Jewish law. Thus 'right-wing pressures' were brought into the very leadership of the United Synagogue. His efforts were considerably aided by the influx of Continental Jews fleeing from the growing Nazi oppression in Europe. Although there were many who gravitated towards the Reform community, there were also a substantial number from strictly traditional backgrounds who bolstered the new Orthodoxy in Great Britain. Their number included many rabbis who began to serve as congregational ministers throughout the country or to sit on the Chief Rabbi's Court. They not only brought a very different approach to communal life but were also adamantly opposed to Reform Judaism and any contacts with the Reform that might appear to be condoning it. Moreover, the position of Hertz himself was to change owing to events in his personal life. In January 1940 his daughter, Judith, married Dr Solomon Schonfeld, who was the presiding rabbi of the Union of Orthodox Hebrew Congregations. The two men became very close, working together on the Chief Rabbi's Religious Emergency Council for German and Austrian Jews, which Dr Schonfeld spearheaded. With Hertz still grieving the loss of his wife and despondent over his own ill health, he came to rely increasingly on his son-in-law for advice and altered his previously hostile attitude to the right-wing camp.

The impact of these changes soon became evident communally, in, for example, the tightening of regulations concerning the dietary laws, particularly hindquarters, and a sharp decrease in conversions. There were no overt attacks on the Reform community, but links with it began to decline. Previously friendly Orthodox ministers now turned down invitations to preach at West London, albeit apologetically. One was Abraham Cohen, who refused because of the delicate political situation he faced: 'I am just now arguing a few points with the [London] *Beth Din*. I have the feeling that my appearance in Berkeley Street may prejudice the chances of a successful outcome for those people whose affairs I have taken up.'[44] In Glasgow the editor of the *Jewish Echo* was instructed by the local *Beth Din* not to accept any advertisements from the Reform congregation, which, it was claimed, was 'pregnant with the dangers of assimilation'.[45] The Sephardi congregations were equally affected by the new spirit of retrenchment, and Mesquita wrote regretfully: 'I know that a goodly number of my Congregation would be deeply disturbed if I preached at Berkeley Street, and peace within the Congregation is of paramount importance.'[46] It was not appreciated at the time, but the changes that led to the gulf between Orthodoxy and Reform were also to be responsible for the growth of Reform as a movement of national consequence.

However, it was an external threat that proved much more painful, for this period was overshadowed by the clouds of Nazism which had been gathering since Hitler came to power in 1933. The agony of German Jewry was appreciated from the start by West London Synagogue and shared throughout the decade. Shortly after Hitler acquired power, Reinhart drew the congregation's attention to 'the organised contempt of liberty, justice and the recognised process of civilisation'.[47] A series of public meetings was organised to raise public consciousness and to orchestrate protest, both by Jewish leaders such as Leonard Montefiore (in his capacity as President of the Anglo-Jewish Association and joint President of the Joint Foreign Committee with the Board of Deputies) and non-Jewish public figures such as the Bishop of Durham or Robert Bernays MP. The fond hopes uttered that world opinion would prevent a tragedy developing indicate how impossible it was to foresee then the full brutality of the Nazi regime: 'We enjoy the active sympathy of people everywhere... The help of such will be a strong shield because it bespeaks the aroused conscience of humanity. The positive and beneficent forces in society will not all fail.'[48] The congregation responded very generously to the massive fund-raising efforts that were launched in mid-1933. By August, the Central British Fund for German Jewry, which had been established as a direct response to Nazism, had collected £163,000, of which West London had raised £20,000. It included the efforts of the children at the Religion School who were asked to bring weekly contributions.

Even more significant were the initiatives that West London took for those German Jews who had already arrived in England and who now, rootless and impoverished, sought to establish a new life for themselves. In November the newly formed Refugees Committee held an 'At Home' at the Synagogue for all refugees, and it then became a regular monthly event. Its popularity and the growing number of refugees led to the opening of a permanent club, known as the Thirty-Three Club, open daily from 3.00 p.m. to 10.00 p.m. at 33 Seymour Place. It offered a reading room with English and German books and periodicals, a lounge for social gathering, chess and draughts, while light refreshments were available. Founded by Daphne Haldin and Esme Henriques, it also featured both an English-speaking and German-speaking host or hostess each day. The club opened on 1 March 1936 as the Nazi oppression of Jews in Germany worsened and it immediately became a centre for refugees throughout London. Facilities such as table tennis and English lessons were added, while rambles and visits were also organised. Initially it attracted 150 members, growing to 350 the following year. By May 1939 there were 574 members and it was so crowded that non-members were only admitted twice a week. It was open every day of the year except *Yom Kippur*, and provided a place of welcome where weary souls could be refreshed, old friends could be reunited, and ways of adapting to their new environment could be learnt. The only restriction placed on them was when a request for a room in which to hold German classes was denied.

Equally active was another West London group, the Hospitality Committee under the energetic leadership of Elsa Goldschmidt, which gave practical help to individual refugees. In December 1935 an appeal was issued to the congregation asking for volunteers for a variety of tasks: to take a child or young person for a limited time into one's home, or for the school holidays; to invite young people for hospitality and meals; to help students complete their education by giving lessons; to be financially responsible for the care and education of a child; or to make regular financial contributions towards such care. The concentration on children and young adults reflected the high percentage of youngsters who had come over by themselves on the *kindertransporte*, or whose parents were also in Britain but were unable to look after them because of their impoverished state or lack of accommodation. The appeal earned the ire of Otto Schiff, who had wanted all efforts to be co-ordinated by the Central British Fund's sub-committee, the Refugees Committee, which he headed, but West London had been determined to initiate its own campaign. A report in May 1936 outlined the range of services undertaken by the Hospitality Committee:[49]

> TWO BROTHERS AGED 16 AND 15. A member of the Congregation has furnished a room on the premises and is giving a home to these two boys. They have both secured opportunities to learn a trade and are making splendid progress.
> GIRL AGED 13. Parents without means. Refugees from Germany. The Committee is sending her to a residential school in the provinces.
> BOY AGED 15. Father, a professional man, has applied to the General Medical Council to practise here. Boy entered next term at a provincial school paying half-fees. Parents paying part, member of the Committee paying part, some clothing coming from Germany and the balance of incidental expenses borne by the Committee.
> BOY OF 14. The son of a man who is at present imprisoned in a fortress. Committee is keeping the boy at school for a further half-year and will then give him technical training.

> YOUNG QUALIFIED DENTIST. Permitted to practise in England, without means. Can obtain no money from Germany. The Committee has agreed to make him an allowance for three months, during which period he is trying to get some appointment.

Regular reports thereafter highlighted the many demands made and the personal tragedies with which the committee was able to assist. By 1944, it had 'adopted' 150 refugee children. On a more spiritual front – and in keeping with Reinhart's strong belief in the power of prayer – a special service of solemn intercession 'for Jews and all who suffer from persecution' was held on 17 July 1938. Other Reform communities held similar activities: the Bradford and Manchester ministers devoted Passover sermons to the plight of Jews oppressed by 'the German Pharaoh'. North Western established a Refugees Aid Committee, while Glasgow adopted a 'refugees levy' amounting to almost half the normal membership subscription.

Many of these efforts mirrored the response of British Jewry in general, horrified by the events overtaking German Jewry and rallying to raise funds and provide practical help. It had pledged to look after German Jewish refugees and not to put any burden on the State. Community leaders were also concerned with the Jewish education of the refugee children who had come to Britain. A Joint Emergency Committee for the Religious Education of Jewish Refugee Children was established by the Board of Deputies with the active participation of the Chief Rabbi, Dr Hertz, and with Owen Mocatta (West London) representing the Reform synagogues. Its aim was to ensure that their Jewish education continued, and that, where possible, it should be in harmony with their religious affiliation. The committee had been created solely because of the havoc unleashed by the Nazis, but in fact the possibility of such co-operation had been greatly enhanced by completely unrelated moves in 1934. The West London Synagogue Education Committee had organised a conference to arrange for Jewish instruction in public and secondary schools. It was supported by the United Synagogue, Sephardi congregations and the Liberals, who agreed to meet regularly and who later produced a joint syllabus acceptable to all four sponsoring bodies. It was the first time that all sections of the Jewish community in London had met to confer on a purely religious question, and indicative of the tolerant sentiments then prevailing. However, by 1939 this climate had changed and Reform leaders often felt that refugee children from Reform backgrounds were not being treated fairly. Thus lists of refugee children and their addresses were sent by the Joint Committee only to Orthodox synagogues, and not to Reform or Liberal ones, on the assumption that 'the overwhelming majority of the children are Orthodox'.[50] As a large percentage of German Jewry were members of Reform-style congregations (although known as 'Liberal' in Germany) this was highly tendentious. Moreover, there was a breakdown in the agreement that Orthodox representatives who found children subscribing to Reform Judaism would refer them to Reform synagogues. In June 1939 West London was informed of only three refugee children in the London area, while in Bradford it was reported that many Reform refugee children were receiving an Orthodox education. Lack of proper resources to monitor the whereabouts and religious affiliation of refugee children undoubtedly contributed to the problem, but there was little doubt that the Orthodox establishment, used to a dominant position in Jewish affairs, was either unaware of, or chose to ignore, the much greater religious pluralism among the refugee population.

The arrival of the German Jews – some 60,000 in all between 1933 and 1939 – may have been seen as a heavy responsibility for British Jewry, but it was to become a significant influence, particularly on the Reform community. It was Germany that had been the birthplace of the Reform movement at the beginning of the nineteenth century. Since that time, it had attracted wide support, had become well established and its rabbis enjoyed a high degree of respect among the general Jewish community for their combination of Jewish and secular scholarship. Unlike Reform Judaism in England, which had broken away from Orthodox congregations and was seen as a peripheral group, in Germany Reform manifested itself within old established communities which altered their religious allegiance. It was much stronger and more accepted than in England. Many of the refugees, therefore, were sympathetic to Reform and their arrival swelled existing congregations and helped lead to the foundation of new ones. There were also those who were nominally Orthodox and might have remained within the Orthodox fold had the Chief Rabbi and honorary officers of the United Synagogue been able to put into practice a scheme of special services – that started late on a Friday evening and included a sermon – designed specifically to attract them. However, their attempts were thwarted by the Council of the United Synagogue, and refugees who were used to such services could find them only in a Reform synagogue.[51] It was a situation the importance of which Reinhart realised at the time, and he wrote to other Reform synagogues urging them to make every effort to respond positively to the newcomers:[52]

> It is a well known fact that a much larger proportion of Germans are sympathetic to a progressive interpretation. If by catering a little to the particular needs of the refugees at the moment, I think that the congregation should not only be rendering a service to the individual refugee, but at the same time will be discovering a source of new strength for the congregation in time to come.

Even more important was the fact that the Continental refugees included some 35 Reform rabbis. Their arrival was to prove crucial for the expansion of the movement. There was at that time no facility for training Reform ministers in England. Home-grown lay preachers might appear, such as Basil Henriques, while some Jews' College graduates switched allegiance and served Reform synagogues, such as Selvin Goldberg and Philip Cohen. The more usual source for obtaining ministers was importing Americans who had graduated from the Hebrew Union College. This accounted for Reinhart and Cashdan at West London, Baron at Glasgow and Starrels at North Western. The sudden mass immigration of the German Reform rabbis (along with the Czech, Dr Arthur Katz) provided the movement with a quality of leadership to which it could not otherwise have aspired. Some were congregational ministers, others were scholars and academics. Their commitment to Reform Judaism gave British Reform a new strength and distinction. Much of the credit for channelling this talent to the good of the movement lay with Reinhart, who was active on their behalf when they were in difficulties in Germany and gave them a warm reception on their arrival in England. Most obtained jobs through him, while their posts were often funded by West London. Curtis Cassell, Bruno Italiener and Arthur Katz were appointed as Assistant Ministers to the synagogue, while Michael Curtis, Max Katten, Jakob

Kokotek, Simon Lehrman, Gustav Pfingst, Arthur Rosenthal and Hermann Schreiber were employed as teachers there. Others, such as Lederman, Henrique Lemle, Georg Salzberger and Warschauer were asked to contribute articles to the *Synagogue Review* and thereby both exercise their talents and supplement their income. Positions were created for the former leader of German Jewry, Leo Baeck, at the Society for Jewish Study, along with Arthur Loewenstamm. When synagogues needed ministers, or even when small embryonic groups began to arise, it was the refugee rabbis who began to serve them from 1940 onwards. Gerhard Graf went to Bradford, Werner Van der Zyl to North Western, Ernest Sawady to the Settlement, Curtis Cassell to Glasgow, Ignaz Maybaum to Edgware, Charles Berg to Bournemouth and Bruno Italiener to Southport. Michael Curtis became the clerk and linchpin of the new Reform *Beth Din*; its formation would have been impossible without the refugee rabbis to man the courts. For the next two decades they dominated not only it, but also the Assembly of Ministers, and they provided many of the lecturers for the Leo Baeck College, including Arieh Dorfler. It is highly unlikely that the future Reform movement could have developed in the way it did without the rabbinic support that it was able to call on as a result of Hitler.

The issue of children's education during the war became increasingly acute. There was the general problem of the disruption caused by the evacuation and by the absence of teachers away on war-service. At the beginning of 1942, Basil Henriques gave a stark warning of the consequences:[53]

> The Jewish soldiers of the last war came back to homes in which the routine had remained undisturbed...Today there is a very different state of affairs. The women and children have been evacuated into areas where Jews had perhaps never been seen before, they have been billeted in non-Jewish homes, and they have perforce been unable to keep up many of their old practices, especially the dietary laws...The teaching in the religion school has in no way been adapted to this changed environment. The children are muddled!...The fearful tragedy of Anglo-Jewry is that, with the rarest exceptions, the leaders of Judaism are not taking account of, and planning for, this changed attitude.

Many religion schools were noting a speedy fall in their attendance register. This included West London, which had a proportionate increase in pupils receiving correspondence course lessons. In December 1941 it was providing such tuition for 170 children; by the following month the number had risen to 200.

Nevertheless, an even greater concern was the sense of injustice at the policy of the Joint Emergency Committee for the Religious Education of Jewish Refugee Children. It was felt that the fair treatment promised to the Reform community had not materialised, and that Reform children were being denied education along Reform principles. It is an open question as to whether this had been deliberately jettisoned, or was just the result of being a low priority for a grossly over-stretched and under-funded body. However, there was no mistaking the anger in Reform circles: all hope of communal progress 'was dashed to the ground when the ultimatum of orthodox ecclesiastical authorities to the effect that all teachers and all courses of study had to be subject to the approval of the orthodox Chief Rabbi, was accepted'.[54] It meant that members of the Reform community were excluded from the committee and were debarred from acting as teachers. Insult was added to injury when the Board continued to maintain publicly that its efforts were for the whole community and urged Progressive synagogues to make a financial contribution to its appeal on behalf of the committee.

Reinhart was particularly incensed and wrote to Leonard Leonard, treasurer of Manchester, proposing a special conference of all Reform congregations to discuss the education issue. It was agreed that Manchester should be the venue, although as Leonard declared that 'Manchester do not feel competent to take a leading part',[55] the invitations were issued by West London. All six congregations responded positively and representatives of Bradford, Glasgow, Manchester, North Western, St George's and West London went to the Midland Hotel on 4 January 1942 for a meeting of the Associated British Synagogues. Edgware did not participate as the community had disbanded in 1939 because of the wartime disruption and did not resume activities until 1945. It was the first time that such a gathering of Reform synagogues had occurred and was in itself a historic occasion. Still, the fact that it did happen was not a foregone conclusion. A similar idea of building closer relations between individual Reform synagogues – proposed by P. M. Quas-Cohen of Manchester in 1934 – had failed to materialise despite West London's backing. The lack of any obvious cause to bind them together may have been a factor, as well as the undeveloped state of the newly founded North Western and Glasgow communities. This time, however, there was both a powerful *raison d'être* and a growing assertion of Reform identity. It was sufficient, moreover, to overcome the logistical difficulties of organising a conference during wartime and delegates being able to travel to it.

The 26 delegates appointed as chairman Harry Marks, then President of West London. As the debate on education progressed, it was clear that there was widespread dissatisfaction with the Board of Deputies, and agreement that separate arrangements should be made to cater for the needs of Reform children. Common policy was emphasised and the need to speak with 'a united Reform voice'. A motion by Reinhart that the six congregations should co-operate to provide religious education for children was strongly echoed by Leonard Mendel and Sam Rainsbury (both from North Western) and carried unanimously. Further discussion indicated that such a policy would involve establishing and financing a complex range of activities: training teachers, formulating curricula, studying educational problems, providing textbooks and organising classes. It was clear that an organisational structure was necessary to implement such tasks, and a motion by Revd P. Selvin Goldberg was passed recommending the formation of the Education Committee of the Associated British Synagogues. It would consist of two delegates from each congregation and be financed by a central fund of contributions from each synagogue proportionate to their size. This simple motion contained the key elements of the Reform movement's way of operating from then onwards: a central body that was both controlled and funded by autonomous constituents.

Having tasted the benefits of co-operation, the delegates were unwilling to limit themselves to matters of education. They backed the call by A. Lewes (Manchester) to maintain contact by establishing a standing conference that would meet at least annually, and more often if necessary, to discuss issues of mutual concern. There was general consensus that the meeting was an outstanding success and had combined enthusiasm of intent with harmony of policy. Many shared Reinhart's view that its impact was important for the wider Jewish community:[56]

> We believe that the Reform interpretation of Judaism not only is the truest and best, but also is especially required by our age...thousands of Jewish children who receive no religious lessons and who have no attachment to any Synagogue will respond best to the Jewish spirit of which the progressive Synagogues are the custodian. To disavow responsibility for such teaching on an ambitious scale, would be to stultify our position in the Jewish community and before the bar of history.

The conference signalled the birth of Reform as a national grouping. It also marked the transition of Reform Judaism from being a common feature of disparate synagogues to becoming the ideological thrust of an active association. What had started as a protest meeting against the Chief Rabbi's ruling on matters pedagogic ended as the foundation of a new movement in British Jewry. There was an ironic parallel with the establishment of the first Reform synagogue: just as West London had not been a deliberate breakaway premeditated from the outset but had been pushed into existence by the refusal of the Bevis Marks authorities to countenance a branch congregation, so the Reform movement came into existence accidentally in reaction to moves by the Chief Rabbinate limiting the scope of Jewish education.

The broader aims of the new association anticipated at the Manchester conference was well in evidence that November when the second meeting of the Associated British Synagogues took place, this time at West London. Goldberg urged more missionary work, both to boost smaller congregations and to set up new ones. Reports were given on the internal affairs of existing congregations, and the advice and help of others was sought. The importance of energetic spiritual leadership for Jewish youth was emphasised. There was also a call to establish a *Beth Din* that would not only deal with the reception of proselytes – until then dealt with by individual congregations under their own auspices – but pronounce upon Jewish matters in accordance with a Reform viewpoint. The enthusiasm of the first conference was turning into a purposeful programme of action.

Progress had already been achieved in the educational concerns that had initiated the Associated British Synagogues. An invitation had been extended to the Liberals to participate in their efforts and led to a jointly sponsored Council for Progressive Jewish Education under the chairmanship of Leonard Montefiore. By May 1942 an appeal for £10,000 had been launched for its work, which included both actual classes and correspondence courses. A pamphlet on Passover was produced and distributed to all children. However, despite the enthusiastic start, there were major difficulties with which to contend, and which reflected the tensions that had nullified earlier attempts at closer union between the two movements. These included the personality clash between two key members, Reinhart and Mattuck, as well as matters of principle, such as whether Hebrew was a compulsory subject. As a result it was decided not to have a joint syllabus, but to work independently in harmony. Even this proved impossible and the Council was disbanded in 1945, having been lambasted as 'an association in which the parties concerned agree only in this: that they won't agree to anything'.[57] Once again the two movements went their separate ways, and there was no joint effort to take account of the new provisions for religious education in schools outlined in the Education Act of 1944. Attempts to achieve some co-operation with the Orthodox were made but met with even less success.

Two new committees were established – although later amalgamated into one body – with an ambitious agenda that developed radically both the work and concept of the new movement. The task of establishing a central fund to provide financial assistance to constituent synagogues in need of help, and the proposal to examine ways of enlarging the Reform community in Glasgow, meant that the synagogues were not only engaged in joint ventures but also accepted responsibility for helping each other. Equally significant was the decision to consider the establishment of a *Beth Din* and a ministers' assembly – both of which heralded the creation of authority structures that would at least have some moral force even if they were to be advisory bodies. Perhaps most remarkable of all was the brief to examine ways of bringing into closer harmony the forms of service used in the constituent synagogue. It might not impinge on an individual community's right to pray as it pleased, but it implied that being part of a movement was not just a matter of consulting with others on external affairs but carried ramifications for a congregation's internal life. The nascent Reform organisation was growing up fast.

NOTES

1. *West London Synagogue Magazine*, June 1929, p. 55.
2. *West London Synagogue Magazine*, Dec. 1924, p. 2; Feb. 1925, p. 2; May 1925, pp. 1 and 3; Sept. 1927, p. 3; Oct. 1928.
3. *West London Synagogue Magazine*, Sept. 1924, p. 2; Sept. 1927, p. 1; May 1928, p. 31.
4. *West London Synagogue Magazine*, Nov. 1924, p. 1.
5. Bradford Synagogue Foundation Centenary Dinner Booklet (1980), p. 7.
6. *West London Synagogue Magazine*, Oct. 1927, p. 6.
7. V. G. Simmons, *Reform in Judaism* (1942), p. 11.
8. Minutes, Liberal Jewish Synagogue Council, 21 March, 19 June and 26 Sept. 1921; at Liberal Jewish Synagogue.
9. Harold Reinhart to Philip Waley, 8 March 1928, Reinhart Papers, Anglo-Jewish Archives, Parkes Library, Southampton University.
10. Pittsburgh Platform, Sixth Principle. The full text of the eight principles drawn up at the 1885 Pittsburgh Conference, can be found in E. Borowitz, *Reform Judaism Today* (1977).
11. Pittsburgh Platform, Third Principle.
12. Silhouette in *Jewish Chronicle*, 26 March 1954.
13. Sermon delivered at West London Synagogue, 28 March 1954; quoted L. Golden and J. Golden, *Harold Reinhart* (1980), p. 171.
14. Sermon delivered at North Western Reform Synagogue on the induction of Rabbi Van der Zyl, 11 July 1943; quoted Golden and Golden, op. cit., p. 116.
15. Simmons, op. cit., p. 12.
16. *West London Synagogue Magazine*, Feb. 1930, p. 83.
17. *West London Synagogue Magazine*, April 1930, p. 118.
18. Idem .
19. General Meeting, 7 Dec. 1930; quoted *West London Synagogue Magazine*, Jan. 1931, p. 74.
20. *West London Synagogue Magazine*, March 1933; *Jewish Chronicle*, 26 March 1954, p. 19.
21. For the Reform attitude to cremation see Jonathan Romain, *Faith and Practice* (1991), p. 67.
22. *West London Synagogue Magazine*, May 1931, p. 151.
23. Ibid., p. 44.
24. Preface, *Prayer Book of the St George's Settlement Synagogue*.
25. Reinhart to Dorothy Quas-Cohen, 17 Jan. 1930, Reinhart Papers, loc. cit.: File: 20; Manchester 1930.
26. *West London Synagogue Magazine*, Nov. 1924; Prayer Book Revision Committee, Memorandum 2.
27. Other members were W. Elkin, H.S.Q. Henriques, Julian Henriques, Laurie Magnus, Claude Montefiore, Leonard Montefiore, and Philip Waley. Others who served subsequently included E.D. Lowy, M. Keyser, Dr H. Simonis and S. Hands. It should be noted that Claude Montefiore had also assisted with the Singers edition of the (Orthodox) Daily Prayer Book, while Magnus had played a role in the High Holy Day Prayer Book issued by Chief Rabbi Hermann Adler.
28. V. D. Lipman, 'The Development of London Jewry', in Salmond S. Levin (ed.), *A Century of Anglo-Jewish Life 1870–1970* (1970).
29. A. J. Kershen, interview with Cicely Barnett, a founder member, 23 Aug. 1989.
30. Marshall Sklare, *Conservative Judaism* (1972), p. 256.
31. Minutes, Manchester Executive, 8 Jan. 1940; at Manchester Synagogue.
32. *West London Synagogue Magazine*, Aug. 1931, p. 191.
33. *West London Synagogue Magazine*, Sept. 1931, p. 5.
34. *West London Synagogue Magazine*, Oct. 1934, p. 32.
35. Minutes, West London Synagogue Wardens, 15 Nov. 1933, Archives of the West London Synagogue of British Jews.

36. *Synagogue Review*, June 1939, p. 148.
37. Sermon by Reinhart, 15 April 1940, quoted *Synagogue Review*, May 1940, p. 99.
38. Minutes, Committee on Co-operation, 16 Feb. 1937, Archives of the West London Synagogue of British Jews.
39. Minutes, Committee on Co-operation, 10 May 1937, loc. cit.
40. Gollop to V. G. Simmons, 30 Oct. 1930, Reinhart Papers, loc. cit.: File: Proselytes S–Z.
41. Reinhart to H.D. Drucquer, 23 March 1931, Reinhart Papers, loc. cit.: File: Leeds.
42. Words of greeting to Hertz by H.S.Q. Henriques, Chairman of West London; quoted *West London Synagogue Magazine*, March 1925, p. 2.
43. Speech delivered 27 May 1934; quoted *West London Synagogue Magazine*, July 1934, p.172.
44. Cohen to Reinhart, 6 Oct. 1938, Reinhart Papers, loc. cit.: File: Correspondence.
45. Z. Golombok to W. Mundlake, 24 Aug. 1937, Reinhart Papers, loc. cit.: File: Correspondence 12.
46. Mesquita to Reinhart, 28 Oct. 1938, Reinhart Papers, loc. cit.: File: Correspondence 12.
47 *West London Synagogue Magazine*, April 1933, p. 117.
48. Edward Henriques (then Senior Warden of West London) at the Synagogue A.G.M., 9 April 1933; quoted *West London Synagogue Magazine*, May 1933, p. 133.
49. *Synagogue Review*, May 1936, p. 132.
50. Henry Isaacs (Secretary, Joint Committee) to Reinhart, 9 June 1939, Reinhart Papers, loc. cit.
51. Aubrey Newman, *The United Synagogue 1870–1970* (1977), pp. 107 and 133–4.
52. Reinhart to Alex Levy (Chairman, Manchester Synagogue), 14 July 1939, Reinhart Papers, loc. cit.: File: Provincial Reform Synagogues: Manchester Congregation of British Jews.
53. *Synagogue Review*, Jan. 1942, p. 123.
54. *Synagogue Review*, June 1942, p. 170.
55. Leonard to Reinhart, 13 Nov. 1941, Reinhart Papers, loc. cit.: File: Manchester Congregation of British Jews.
56. *Synagogue Review*, June 1942, p. 170.
57. Reinhart to L. G. Montefiore, 31 May 1943, Reinhart Papers, loc. cit.: File: Correspondence; Minutes A.B.S., 22 Feb. 1945.

6 The Association, 1942–1957

The establishment of formal links between the Reform synagogues in 1942 was to prove the beginning of a hectic period in which the new association faced several struggles: to assert its own identity; to match its ambitious plans with its limited finances; to support existing congregations and nurture new ones; to create its own institutions such as a *Beth Din*, rabbinical college and youth movement; to develop relationships with other Jewish bodies, particularly the Liberals and the Board of Deputies, and overcome periodic differences with them; and to combat the increasingly hostile attitude of the Orthodoxy. All these tasks were set against a background of the economic difficulties and social disruption during the war years and afterwards. Amid it all, Zionism was a major issue with which to contend, both before and after the founding of the State of Israel.

For the first three years of the existence of the Associated British Synagogues, the country was at war and the new organisation had to struggle with all the limitations on personnel, resources and activities that this entailed. There was also the difficulty of appealing to a civilian population who had little time or energy for religious innovation. The impact of the war was felt even more by the individual congregations. Very often the venue of services was altered for the sake of greater safety, whether from the synagogue to the hall, as at West London, or had to be abandoned, as with Edgware. Services occurred earlier in the winter months to avoid contravening black-out regulations, while the maximum permitted number of 250 worshippers meant that some synagogues held identical consecutive services over the High Holy Days. Families were urged to sit together to minimise panic in the case of an air raid. Some synagogues did fall victim to the bombs, although none when services were in progress. West London was hit in November 1940, but the damage was not widespread and repair work did not prevent normal activities continuing. Both its cemeteries – Balls Pond Road (Islington) and Hoop Lane (Golders Green) – were also hit, with some tombstones destroyed. More devastatingly, Manchester's Park Place Synagogue was completely burnt out in June 1941. The community lost all its scrolls and prayer books, and it had to find temporary accommodation for seven years until moving back to Park Place in a pre-fabricated building. The loss of their 80-year-old synagogue and the disruption that ensued could have led to the disintegration of the congregation, but it was to its credit that it persevered, maintaining existing activities and retaining its membership. Substantial war damage funds were received by West London from the Ministry of Works as compensation, while Manchester's allocation helped build a new synagogue at Jacksons Row, eventually consecrated in 1953.

Another result of the war was that many synagogues developed activities to cater for the new needs. West London led the way by turning Seymour Place into a club for Jewish service personnel, providing a canteen, reading room, entertainments and social facilities. Over the course of the war an estimated 200,000 servicemen and women attended. When German air strikes on the East End led to local schools being closed, the Settlement Synagogue started day-school activities on its premises. As in the First World War, ministers also took on extra duties, such as Goldberg who became Visiting Chaplain to the British and American Forces in his area. Local initiatives often extended to the general community, as in the help given by Glasgow to survivors of the torpedoed liner *Athenia*. Patriotism and fortitude was encouraged by a series of stirring wartime prayers that appeared in the *Synagogue Review* as well as a lectionary of daily readings from the Bible on the themes of courage and direction. At West London the Council decided that the national anthem should be sung on all festivals and the first Sabbath of each month. The war was also in evidence from the drastic reduction in size of the *Synagogue Review* after 1940 and the periodic obituaries for those killed on active service from within the Reform movement.

Despite the many difficulties presented by the war, long-term strategic inspiration was provided in a paper delivered by Edward Henriques to the 1944 conference. The author described it as a way 'to get our minds clear' and was concerned primarily with the promotion of the movement. He drew attention to the low rate of increase of the Reform community since its inception and called for an acceleration in growth. Estimating the Reform membership to be around 8,000 individuals out of a total Jewish population of around 400,000, he set a target of 80,000 members. He did not wish to poach those who were happy with Orthodoxy, but pointed out that there were large numbers who were dissatisfied with it, or who had no affiliation at all. Not only would they boost Reform synagogues, but Reform could help them realise their spiritual aspirations, while it would also change the picture of Anglo-Jewry and influence it 'to show a more sensible outlook in public affairs than it does at present'.[1]

Henriques considered publicity to be essential, with the best way of achieving it being through pamphlets. Modern men and women needed clear, concise and easily digestible answers to the questions they asked about Judaism and how it related to their own lives. He criticised the articles written by ministers in the *Synagogue Review* as being too erudite and lacking simplicity of style. On the theme of funding these and other projects of the movement he warned that synagogue contributions carried potential disadvantages: they could cause resentment among synagogue treasurers hard-pressed to balance their books and complaints by members that their subscriptions were being used for objects other than local needs. He proposed instead a voluntary contribution that each individual member should make in addition to the synagogue subscription.

The suggestion was never adopted; the difficulty of planning a budget for the movement without knowing the amount of annual income to expect made it impractical, but his warnings about discontent over central dues were prophetic and they were to remain a constant theme of the movement.

One of the many changes that occurred following the end of hostilities was a change to the title under which the Reform movement had been born – the Associated British Synagogues. In 1942 the country had been at war; patriotism and Britishness were characteristics to be emphasised. Yet by 1946 there was general agreement that the name was not the most appropriate, particularly because the movement included many refugee members who did not have British status. During the war they had suffered from the label of 'aliens', while many had been interned. There was a desire to have a title that avoided offending their susceptibilities and as well, one that brought to the fore the religious nature of the movement. During the debate the question of including the words 'progressive' or 'reform' was mooted. However, this was vigorously opposed by many, led by Reinhart who argued that the progressive quality of Judaism was traditional and had always been inherent in its very nature. Any attempt to qualify the movement's form of Judaism would limit it and question its authenticity. This view was accepted at the time, although the issue was to resurface more controversially in the future. Edward Henriques' suggestion that the body be known as the Association of Synagogues of Great Britain (ASGB) was carried unanimously.[2] The name was to hold sway for the next 12 years until new factors led to yet another change.

The year 1946 also witnessed another important milestone when the Association's first constitution was drawn up, although it was not adopted formally until the conference the following April. The document laid out the 14 objects of the ASGB (see Appendix 1 for a full list). At its core was the desire 'to promote and foster a robust and virile Judaism which will contribute to the life of the entire Jewish Community, and which will play its part, together with other religions, in the physical and spiritual betterment of mankind'. More immediate tasks included mutual aid among member congregations, establishing new synagogues, training rabbis and teachers, educational activities for children, adults and youth groups, and sponsoring a rabbinic court and rabbinic meetings. By then the original six congregations had been joined by Edgware which had re-formed after disbanding during the war (see Appendix 2 for a full list of synagogues).

The bulk of the constitution dealt with matters temporal rather than spiritual such as definition of membership, honorary officers, and management of meetings. One crucial paragraph characterised the grass-roots and essentially lay nature of the movement: Paragraph 9 stated that the governing body of the Association was Conference, the body made up of delegates from the constituent synagogues. It emphasised the difference between the ASGB and the United Synagogue, with the latter being controlled centrally by an elected council that could then implement major decisions without any further ratification. Moreover, the United Synagogue was subject to the authority of the Chief Rabbi in questions of a religious nature. The ASGB might well take advice from its rabbis, but ultimate authority was still vested in Conference.

The issue of how the congregations were to be represented fairly given the enormous variation in size among them was resolved by each having two delegates, with those consisting of more than 100 members having an extra delegate for each additional 200 members. The financial contribution was also established per capita, with every congregation being expected to pay ten shillings for each member – although provision was made to exempt those congregations which were not self-supporting. Until then the movement had existed on an annual budget of £600, raised by West London providing two-thirds, Manchester and North Western paying one-sixth each, while Bradford, Glasgow and the Settlement made token payments. The new method did not necessarily alter those percentages, but did allow for future growth and change. The architects of the constitution were E. F. Q. Henriques (then treasurer), E. E. Mocatta (a member of the executive) and M. A. B. King-Hamilton, all from West London.

Finance was all-important, for a constant concern was that the more active the Association became, the greater its financial needs. The £600 required in 1942 had doubled by 1946. Moreover the ability to fund initiatives was not just a matter of raising income, but begged the question of whether the Association had an executive role or was to be only an advisory body. Beneath any discussion of principle lay the fact that while one synagogue – West London – provided the bulk of the money, it was inevitable that it would exert powerful control on the expenditure and general direction of the movement. This was particularly evident in the case of the *Synagogue Review*. As was often pointed out, although it bore the subtitle 'the organ of the A.B.S.', it was financed and owned entirely by West London, with Reinhart as the editor. There was little complaint by the other synagogues about its content, and certainly no suggestion that they would assume its cost, but all were aware of the anomalous position and that one day the Association should take responsibility for its own publication. However beneficial West London's moral and financial support, it meant that the movement lacked real independence and for many years it reflected the aspirations of Upper Berkeley Street.

Another recurring problem was that lofty ideals and financial reality often conflicted. Conference endorsed Reinhart's suggestion that the executive raise a fund from which capital loans

8 The service to commemorate the Golden Jubilee of the West London Synagogue of British Jews in 1892 *(courtesy The London Museum of Jewish Life)*

9 Morris Joseph
(courtesy The London Museum of Jewish Life)

10 Joseph Strauss
(courtesy The London Museum of Jewish Life)

1

Conference of the Associated British Synagogues

Sunday, 4th January, 1942, Midland Hotel, Manchester

delegates

The following were present:

Congregation	Delegates
Bradford Reform Synagogue	Mr. M. Arensberg Rabbi L. Gerhard Graf Mr. J. Hirschel
Glasgow Progressive Synagogue	Captain A. E. Barnett Mrs. Barnett Mr. Maurice Olsberg, J.P.
Manchester Congregation of British Jews	Mr. G. de Lange Mrs. N. Fine The Rev. P. Selvin Goldberg Mrs. B. Harris Miss A. Q. Henriques Mr. W. Komrower Mr. B. Kuit Mr. A. Lewes Mr. L. H. Leonard Mrs. Leonard Mrs. D. Quas-Cohen Mr. I. Stoller Mr. M. Wansker
North Western Reform Synagogue	Mrs. R. Lawton Mr. E. L. Mendel Mr. S. Rainsbury
St. George's Settlement Synagogue	Rabbi Dr. Bruno Italiener
West London Synagogue	Mr. H. C. Marks Lady Nathan Rev. Harold F. Reinhart

prayer

Rabbi Dr. B. Italiener opened the proceedings with prayer.

Mr. de Lange welcomed the delegates to Manchester, and expressed the hope that the Conference would be the first of many meetings in the service of Reform Judaism. He then proposed that Mr. H. C. Marks take the chair; and this proposition was unanimously approved. Mrs. R. Lawton was asked to act as Hon. Secretary of the Conference.

Background of the Conference

Mr. Marks gave a brief resume of the events that had led to the calling of the Conference. He told of the long negotiations between the West London Synagogue and the Jewish Board of Deputies and of the failure of the Synagogue to persuade the Deputies that their scheme should not be confined to sponsoring orthodox teaching. The West London Synagogue was, of course, pursuing its own Educational programme; but it was felt now that concerted effort by the Congregations here represented would be of great value for the common good. At the suggestion of the Chair, it was agreed that the meeting should be considered as confidential to the Councils of the Congregations represented.

Cooperation for Religious Education

The Rev. Harold F. Reinhart spoke of the special problems of religious education caused by the war; and he suggested as the appropriate joint responsibility of all the Reform Congregations, three classes of children: (1) Evacuated children of the Congregations themselves, (2) the large body of children who received no religion lessons, and many of whom would doubtless be responsive to our teaching, (3) refugee children from "progressive" homes.

Mr. E. L. Mendel suggested that the unhappy result of the negotiations with the Jewish Board of Deputies was due in

11 Minutes of the opening meeting of the Associated British Synagogues, 4 January 1942

12a Rabbi Harold Reinhart

12b Robert Henriques

13 Conference of the Youth Association of Synagogues in Great Britain, Hawkshead, 1947 *(photograph by Victor Leighton)*

14 The Presidents of the RSGB: Leonard G. Montefiore (above left), Rabbi Dr Leo Baeck (above right), Rabbi Dr Werner van der Zyl (bottom left) and Rabbi Hugo Gryn (bottom right)

15 Exodus participating in a Soviet Jewry demonstration in London

16 Akiva, the first Reform Jewish day school

17 The Centre for Jewish Education – teaching the teachers

18 The Assembly of Rabbis in debate

19 Members of the RSGB's 1991 Israel Tour meet new Ethiopian immigrants

20 The Sternberg Centre for Judaism at the Manor House, north London

21a Rabbi Jacqueline Tabick

21b Peter Levy and Sir Sigmund Sternberg

22 Dry Bones sums up the problems facing reform Jews in Israel, 1977
(reproduced by kind permission of Kirschen)

Greater London congregations

Beit Klal Yisrael
 – North Kensington
Bromley and District
Buckhurst Hill
Edgware and District
Finchley
Hampstead
Harlow
Hendon
Kol Chai – Hatch End
Middlesex New
Mill Hill, Kingsbury
 and District
North Western
North West Surrey
Radlett and Bushey
Settlement
Southgate and District
South West Essex
West London
Wimbledon and District

Greater Manchester congregations

Manchester
Menorah Synagogue
 – Cheshire
Sha'arei Shalom
 – North Manchester

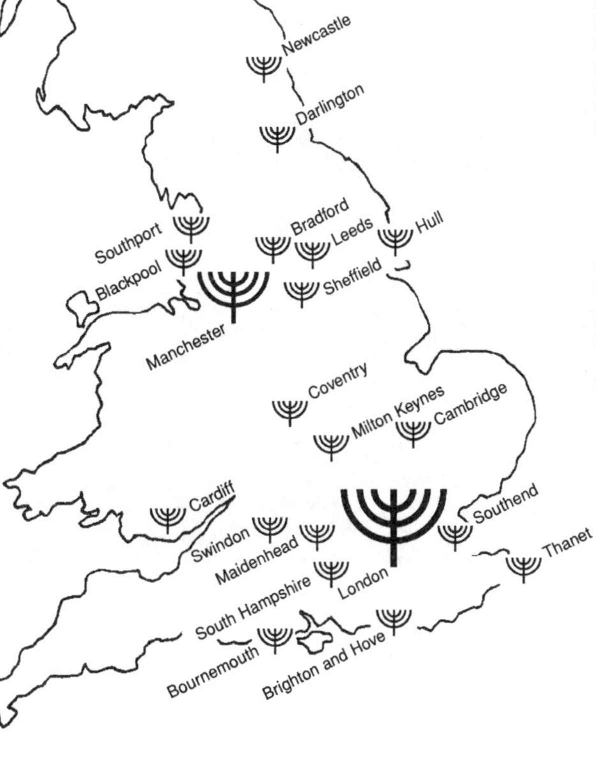

23 The congregations of the RSGB

24 Raymond Goldman hands the *Torah* to his successor, Rabbi Tony Bayfield
(photograph by Hugh Noble)

could be made to congregations which could not otherwise finance their development. Yet the executive struggled to meet existing demands let alone provide for special projects. An estimated deficit of £800 for 1948 spurred the executive into raising extra funds, but also imposing more stringent control over expenditure. An appeal committee was established, while the treasurer, Edward Mocatta, proposed that:[3]

1. No more than 50 per cent of the budget be expended in support of needy congregations.
2. The grant made to any congregation should not exceed the income it had raised locally the previous year.
3. Grants should be considered loans, although this might not apply during the first two years in the life of a new congregation.
4. Payments made to general Jewish causes for prestige reasons should be paid from special appeals rather than from ordinary per capita income.

The latter clause applied to charities such as the Association of Jewish Ex-Servicemen or the Association for Jewish Youth, which the ASGB felt obliged to support, albeit by asking for contributions from individual congregations and forwarding them in the name of the movement as a whole.

A much bigger drain on resources was the financial assistance given to ASGB congregations, particularly Glasgow. The community's problems had been a matter of concern from the very first year of the Association. It lacked rabbinic leadership, its membership had declined from 100 to 60 individuals, and it was making hardly any impact on a city of 14,000 Jews. Two obstacles to progress were its inability to offer burial facilities to members, and the arrival in Glasgow of an eloquent Orthodox communal rabbi who lost no time at his first public meeting in telling the large audience that Reform synagogues were churches for Jewish Christians. There was also a more fundamental problem that was to face future attempts to establish Reform synagogues in the provinces, such as Leeds and Cardiff: the decline in Orthodox practices among Jews was not accompanied in similar measure by a drift to Reform synagogues. Whereas Reform took hold among the already Reform-minded Bradford Jews and gained adherents from some of the more assimilated Jews of Manchester, it found it much harder to attract members of the biggest constituency, the non-committed Orthodox. Thus, despite the large Jewish population, the Reform synagogue in Glasgow made relatively little impact locally. Nevertheless, its chairman, Captain A. E. Barnett, was confident that a suitable minister would lead to substantial growth and only lamented that there was no one available. He subsequently suggested that West London was better equipped to find a candidate for Glasgow. He dismissed objections that it would be wrong for one congregation to select a minister for another by replying that as West London was the main part of the Association, it should carry out the policy of expanding Reform communities. It was a good example – often repeated elsewhere by others – of smaller congregations being happy to depend on West London and seeing little distinction between it and the Association as a whole.[4]

The appointment of Rabbi Curtis Cassell in April 1945 gave Glasgow the confidence and direction it needed. His first year's salary was paid substantially by the Association. Membership returned to the 100 mark, although attempts to reduce the grant in the second year proved impossible as the congregation was still not financially viable. The lack of progress was becoming an increasing burden on the Association, while other congregations questioned why Glasgow alone had failed to grow. At the end of 1947 the community was given a year to improve its affairs dramatically or lose any further support. The sale of the Albert Road premises – forced upon them by extensive dry rot – raised a capital sum that contributed to the acquisition of new premises in Albert Drive in 1951.

A very different proposition was presented by Leeds where, despite some tentative moves in the 1930s, no Reform community existed. Now there was a much greater level of local interest in forming one and the Association was keen to assist. This was a departure from the practice of West London before 1942, which had supported already established Reform congregations, but had never intervened to promote a new one. The initial work done in the area by Rabbi Graf, then serving Bradford, was welcomed, but there were fears that the Association could not afford 'another Glasgow'. However, once a small group was established in January 1944, known as Sinai Synagogue, funding was given and Leeds became regarded as 'a test case' for the Association's ability to foster new communities. When one of its founders, Edgar

Isaacs, expressed fears for the future, he received a typically encouraging and abrasive letter from Reinhart:[5]

> I do not fail to appreciate your disappointment over the paucity of response to the initial appeal – but beginnings are hard! And we know that the people are slow and cowardly and unimaginative. The *first hundred* members will be difficult. After that it will be another story.

By October 1946 Sinai had grown to 60 members and the offer of an interest-free loan of £1,000 by West London to help purchase a building reflected the confidence in its future. The movement itself undertook to contribute towards a minister's salary once an appointment had been made.

Existing constituents were given much less financial support and were encouraged to be self-sufficient. Thus Bradford was refused a grant, while Edgware was told its education budget could not be accepted. Other new congregations received financial assistance from the movement, but on a much more modest and occasional scale, such as to help the newly formed Bournemouth Synagogue with a minister's salary. The latter was another example of a locally inspired initiative taken by Reform-minded Jews. They established their own group and then turned to the Association for guidance. After visits by Rabbi Van der Zyl, Robert Henriques and Robert Galan to ensure that the group was viable, serious and in harmony with Reform principles, Bournemouth was admitted as the ninth member of the ASGB in April 1947. Within a few months it had grown to 200 members, acquired a burial plot and appointed Rabbi Charles Berg as minister.

The arrival of Reform in Bournemouth was met by fierce opposition from the Orthodox, as had happened in Glasgow. Refusal to share part of their cemetery meant the new community had to obtain facilities from the Borough Council, although the independence they thereby gained was probably to their advantage. When a marriage took place between a woman from the Reform community and a man from the Orthodox, the bride's father was invited to receive an *aliyah* at the *aufruf* in the groom's synagogue, but then refused on the day on the grounds that he was not Orthodox. Rabbi Berg was also shunned by the local Jewish leadership: a communal brains trust was cancelled because he had been invited to sit on it, while he was even excluded from membership of the local B'nai Brith group, which was supposed to unite all Jews and bridge religious differences. It was a very similar story in Cardiff – another local initiative: rapid growth, hostility from the Orthodox, and the speedy appointment of a rabbi, in this case Graf. It also typified the by now standard policy of the movement of making rabbinic leadership a priority for any new community. Money was much more readily given to pay for a minister's salary than to acquire premises. A permanent building undoubtedly had its benefits, but a minister who could bind together the community, develop a range of religious, social, cultural and educational activities, and attract new members was even more valuable.

Another feature of Cardiff was that they had originally approached the Liberals for help, but had afterwards decided that they preferred the Reform approach. It highlighted the delicate issue of the Association's relationship with the Liberals. Sharing a modern interpretation to Judaism and having very similar aims, there was much that two movements had in common. Both movements had expansionist aims and, inevitably, they were both interested in similar groups in similar locations: Jews who were dissatisfied with Orthodoxy in areas of a reasonably large Jewish population. The question was whether the two movements would act in competition with each other or recognise each other's spheres of influence. When Edgware's activities were suspended during the war, the Union of Liberal and Progressive Synagogues (ULPS) had been approached by individuals interested in forming a Liberal synagogue in the area. However, on learning that the original members of Edgware were about to restart the community, Lily Montagu recommended the enquirers to support Edgware and 'avoid overlapping'.[6] It is unclear whether the ASGB displayed the same charitable spirit. When Mattuck broached the idea of a Liberal community in Hendon, he was informed that as North Western was still gaining members in the vicinity there was no room for a Liberal synagogue. However, within a few months Hendon Reform Synagogue had been founded, although admittedly it began as a local initiative to which the ASGB then responded positively. Indeed, many years earlier, North Western itself might have been a Liberal congregation, for the founder members had intended to associate with the Liberal Jewish Synagogue. However, their overtures met with a cool response, and when they turned instead to Reinhart at West London they were welcomed warmly.

A different scenario occurred in Brighton in 1955, where a request for the ASGB to assist a small group of Reform individuals upset the Liberals as one of their synagogues already existed there. Reinhart justified ASGB support on the grounds that it was merely responding to an appeal for help and that 'in the circumstances we do not feel that we can refuse their request for a trial'. The Liberals also expressed concern when a public meeting entitled 'What is Reform Judaism?' was held not far from Southgate Liberal Synagogue in 1956, although it was another six years before a Reform community was established there. Relations with the ULPS continued along the path of wary friendship. Thus when ULPS notified ASGB of plans for a new congregation in the North Finchley–Mill Hill vicinity, they were informed that three existing Reform synagogues (North Western, Edgware and Hendon) already served the area. However, when ULPS decided to go ahead with its project, the ASGB executive wished them every success. There was no agreement to avoid direct competition even in locations in which one movement already had a community, and the ASGB did not feel that it was precluded from expanding in areas in which small Liberal groups existed but had not realised the potential for growth. When the ASGB did notify ULPS of plans to set up congregations in certain locations it is hard to know whether it was a genuine sharing of information or a move to pre-empt any competition. In 1956 Rabbi Edgar, Mattuck's successor at the Liberal Jewish Synagogue, proposed a meeting to discuss a common policy regarding new congregations. It was agreed that if either body were approached by a group seeking to establish a local community, they should notify each other. A subsequent suggestion by the ULPS that no action should be taken by either body until they had discussed the matter together was rejected by the ASGB. It is clear that at that time the ASGB had a much greater missionary spirit than the ULPS. Moreover, the availability of a large number of refugee Reform rabbis and the generous financial support of West London meant that the ASGB was better equipped to respond to the requests of new communities. Between 1942 and 1957 twelve Reform congregations were established, compared to six Liberal ones. Moreover, whereas most of the Liberal communities were in the London area, less than half of the new Reform synagogues were, a reflection of the Reform movement's much wider national outreach.

The application of Maidenhead to join the Association in 1953 presented a novel situation, for it was an independent Orthodox synagogue that had already been established for 13 years and possessed its own premises. A visit to a Reform synagogue in the United States convinced a leading member, Sidney Rich, that a modern approach to Judaism was better suited to the community and he led a successful campaign to change its affiliation. Maidenhead was an example of countless congregations outside the metropolis which were nominally Orthodox but whose lifestyle and beliefs corresponded with the Reform. Unlike most other such communities, Maidenhead was not tied to the United Synagogue through trusts, loans or ownership of its building and was therefore able to change its allegiance after a special meeting of its members. The constraints faced by similarly-minded communities was one of the factors in the slow growth of the Reform membership – given a British Jewry that was largely Reform in attitude – and a reason why it compared so poorly to the enormous strides made by Reform synagogues in the United States.

Other new ASGB congregations during this period were Southport (1948), Wimbledon (1949) and South West Essex (1956). In part they reflected the continued Jewish exodus from city centres in London and the provinces which carried on apace after the Second World War. Wimbledon was the first instance since the formation of Bradford the previous century of Jews coming together to establish a Reform synagogue in an area that did not already have an Orthodox congregation. However, not all local initiatives met with success. Establishing a Religion School in Letchworth did not lead to a Reform community being formed. Periodic contact with the Association by a group in Nottingham between 1945 and 1955 did not result in any developments, although a Liberal community was established there in 1965. A request for assistance came from some families in Sheffield in 1949 but the ASGB's offer of help was not taken up – although another attempt almost 40 years later was more successful. The same occurred in Eastbourne the following year. A potentially dramatic gain came in a letter from the President of the Aberdeen (Orthodox) Synagogue, who said his members were interested in the Reform movement and requested information, but that request also ended without resolution.

At the same time as responding to all these enquiries, the ASGB had its own programme of growth. The 'Expansion Committee' was established in June 1948 to fulfil one of the original objects of the Association. Its efforts to issue suitable propaganda material were initially thwarted when all seven pamphlets presented by ministers of the ASGB were considered unsuitable.[7] Subsequent editing saw the publication of 'Judaism as a Way of Life' by Van der Zyl later that year – the first of many to present the Reform viewpoint in a clear and easily accessible fashion. Its success prompted the decision to print 10,000 copies of subsequent pamphlets. Their effect was both to boost the confidence of existing members and to be a source of information for potential recruits.

The work of the Expansion Committee was not only to develop new congregations but also to support existing ones; there were complaints that some had been 'allowed to drift without proper guidance'. Morale-boosting efforts included holding occasional executive meetings in the provinces, executive members making individual visits to congregations and attending their council meetings or other events, and organising brains trusts of prominent lay and rabbinic personalities at different communities. Further pamphlets were issued, presenting the Reform position on a range of ethical, theological and practical issues. Display advertisements appeared in the *Jewish Chronicle* each month, listing constituent synagogues and information about their services, religion school and other activities. Copies of the *Synagogue Review* were sent to libraries in Jewish areas in London and the provinces for display in their reading rooms. In addition conditions for communities wishing to affiliate to the Association were reviewed so as to ensure that membership was only granted to those that were clearly viable and would not impose a drain on finances and energy of the movement. It was defined that a congregation had to be established for a minimum of a year, consist of 40 adults and to hold regular services in order to qualify for admission.[8]

An early attempt at boosting a sense of solidarity among constituents was the recommendation in 1951 that the letterhead and literature of each should carry the words 'Affiliated to the Association of Synagogues in Great Britain'. Equally significant was the decision for the movement to employ Rabbi Dr Schreiber as a 'roving rabbi' to take services at different synagogues at least twice a month. Over the next two years he officiated at Edgware and Hendon, although the majority of his work was with Wimbledon. The success of the venture was reflected in the fact that when Wimbledon sought a full-time minister of their own, the ASGB agreed to make a contribution to his salary. Less simple to organise were attempts to transfer membership rights for those joining one Reform congregation from another. Despite detailed suggestions from a special sub-committee, no progress was made on the matter until the Joint Jewish Burial Society was formed in 1968. The ASGB was occasionally requested to give assistance when local disputes had reached an impasse and needed outside adjudication. Thus the executive was asked to heal the breach that had arisen between Rabbi Graf and the wardens at Cardiff in 1951. A deputation was sent to meet both parties and helped bring the matter to an amicable solution.

Inter-congregational help was also in evidence. North Western had originally tried to dissuade families in Hendon from establishing a separate community. However, once it was clear that the group was determined to proceed, North Western gave it every support and formally offered Hendon the opportunity to participate in its Saturday morning services when the latter held only Friday evening ones. Still, neighbourliness could also occasionally turn into competitiveness. When Hendon found a site in Danescroft Avenue on which to build its synagogue, the council of North Western was most concerned at its proximity to their catchment area. A special meeting of the ASGB executive was called to discuss the problem, but no solution was reached. Hendon went ahead with its plans, regretting they could find no other land available, and leaving North Western to record its disapproval. In the event, there was a sufficiently large Jewish population to support each synagogue, both of which grew substantially. Nevertheless the incident highlighted the lack of central planning or control exercised by the Association. It was also the first of various minor rivalries that were to recur between some nearby synagogues in future years.

The sense of solidarity between the sister congregations was most evident in the frequent ministerial exchanges, with rabbis from one congregation often guest-preaching at another. Although this was partly the result of friendships between individual ministers who extended invitations to each other, it also applied to communities that temporarily lacked a rabbi or that were in the process of establishing themselves. Thus Reinhart took the first service at Edgware and Goldberg travelled much further for the inaugural service at Bournemouth. A rota of eight different ministers took services at Cardiff when it was formed, and similar rosters were arranged for other congregations when their ministers were absent on holiday or through sickness. It was evidence of the communal responsibility that Robert Henriques had urged in 1946 whereby 'we are each "our brother's keeper" ...and the dry rot that threatens the structure of the Glasgow Synagogue affects indirectly the congregation in Manchester'.[9]

The overall result of these and local efforts was moderate success in the general expansion of the movement. At the 1951 conference all synagogues reported increased membership, particularly Bradford and Edgware. At the same time Cardiff, Manchester, North Western and Wimbledon were all erecting new buildings. The following year Edgware and Leeds joined the number engaged in obtaining new premises. Continued growth was again reported by all at the 1953 conference, with increases of around 10 per cent by Cardiff, Edgware, Hendon and North Western. The fact that virtually all synagogues reported increased attendances at their religion schools indicated that much of the growth was in the crucially important sector of young families, many of whom were concerned that their children should be brought up in a religious environment that corresponded to their lifestyle and beliefs. It also reflected the effects of the changing nature of British Jewry: those who were born as second-generation English were mainly brought up Orthodox, but were much more willing to change their affiliation than their parents had been.

The growth of the movement – doubling the number of its congregations from 6 to 13 within its first decade – also led to some problems. One was the uneasy balance between central leadership and local autonomy. It was a constant theme that permeated every debate, but was bluntly expressed at the 1953 conference by the North Western delegate and executive member, Sam Rainsbury. In a speech that was to be echoed by others for many years afterwards, he rebuked the constituent synagogues for their disinterest in the Association, giving it little material support and displaying no general enthusiasm. He also criticised the ASGB executive for not making any effort to acquire the authority that would enable it to work effectively, strengthen the movement and supervise member congregations. The fundamental weakness of the Association, he asserted, was the insistence of all parties on the absolute individualism of each congregation. The lively debate that followed his remarks was not conclusive, with many arguing that increased centralisation would be a dangerous and unwelcome step, and carry with it the stagnation of deadening uniformity.

Any changes in the direction and policy of the Association were often the result of a lengthy process of debate that was conducted both centrally and locally. It usually arose after some minor innovations had proved to work in practice and to be not too threatening in principle. An important instance of this was the establishment of a central finance committee that would enable congregational treasurers to meet and exchange ideas. In particular, it was intended to tackle common problems over membership fees, building costs, loans and expenditure on synagogue equipment. In 1954 all congregations were asked to submit a copy of their annual accounts to the committee. Was this a case of engineering central control or of enhancing local expertise? Most congregations felt it was the latter and agreed to the proposal, although some, such as Bradford, dissented and refused to submit their accounts, claiming that it would serve no useful purpose. The committee was duly formed, with representatives of those congregations that wished to participate, and was generally acknowledged not only to have benefited them but to have highlighted the individual advantages that could arise from concerted action. An idea that did not meet with the same approval was that the ASGB executive should give guidance to constituent synagogues as to the selection of ministers. This was seen as crossing the thin border between help and interference.[10]

A second continuing problem faced by the ASGB was the perilous state of its finances. The increased income arising from new congregations and the general expansion of membership was always counter-balanced by expenditure to assist synagogues experiencing difficulties or to fund new projects that the movement wished to initiate. The per capita payment in 1951 was ten shillings, although this was scaled down to 5s. or 2s. 6d. when appropriate. The anticipated expenditure for that year reflected the priorities and work of the Association:

Publicity (including the *Synagogue Review*)	£ 450
YASGB grant	£ 300
Secretarial services	£ 300
Conference expenditure	£ 200
Minister's salary (Schreiber)	£ 200
World Union contribution	£ 50
Ministers' expenses (Assembly, *Beth Din*)	£ 50
Printing, stationery	£ 20
Audit	£ 10
	£1580

There was a suggestion at the conference by North Western that subscriptions be changed and be based instead on a percentage of the annual subscription income of each synagogue. However, this was not adopted, while the treasurer's own proposal that the per capita amount be raised to 12s. 6d. to cater for the extra demands being placed on the Association was also rejected. The result was that the budget was left unbalanced, and this not only brought criticism from delegates but also calls, particularly from Manchester, that ASGB accounts should be scrutinised to ensure that expenditure was only on the objects of the Association. This was one of many warnings from Manchester that the Association was taking on responsibilities beyond its original mandate. Equally vociferous, however, was the view by the joint treasurers that 'the existence of the ASGB as a useful and virile force in Anglo Jewish life must of necessity be jeopardised if its activities are curtailed by lack of financial support'.[11] The harsh realities of tailoring income and expenditure were put aside in the question of loans. When Hendon offered to pay a rate of interest of two per cent on the loan of £1,200 (repayable over ten years) that it had been granted, the executive decided that the ASGB, as a religious organisation, should not charge interest to constituent synagogues.[12]

The issue of loans was itself a matter of significance. In the early days of the Association there had simply been no funds available and all loans had come from West London, at first as a direct arrangement between it and the other synagogues concerned and later via the good offices of the ASGB. In this way Cardiff, Edgware, North Western and Leeds had all received significant grants, primarily to assist in financing building projects. However, in 1950 West London declared that it could no longer offer further loans as it needed to preserve funds for repairs to its own building. A subsequent request for a loan from Glasgow was answered through the personal generosity of three West London members, but there was clearly a need for a more permanent solution. In January 1950 Robert Henriques proposed that a capital fund of £10,000 be raised and invested to provide a source for future loans. It was yet another step in the process whereby the Association was gradually weaning itself away from dependence on West London. Wimbledon became the first recipient of the fund when it sought help to finance its new building the following year. However, the high hopes for the fund did not materialise as fully as was expected. Launched at the April 1951 conference it had raised only £1,500 a year later, largely thanks to individual donations, and had not been supported by any major fund-raising by congregations. A further problem was the decision at the 1952 conference to establish a fund in the name of Rabbi Dr Leo Baeck upon his eightieth birthday for the endowment of scholarships for training ministers and teachers. The burden of this also fell upon constituent synagogues and the two funds competed with each other for subscribers. The target for the Leo Baeck Fund was £20,000 but it, too, raised little more than £1,000 after a year of appeals. Nevertheless this was sufficient to make grants to two students then studying under the supervision of the Ministers Training Board, Lionel Blue and Michael Leigh, both later to become major figures in the movement.

The growth in its size and activities meant that there was an increasing need to reassess the workings of the Association. A reorganisation sub-committee was established in May 1954 under the chairmanship of Sidney Kingsley (Hendon). It had a wide-ranging brief to consider the objects, administration, powers and finances of the ASGB with a view to its better practical progress. After seven months' deliberation it presented an interim report that urged a variety of changes to the constitution. One recommendation was to delete the pledge to co-operate specifically with the ULPS and substitute a more general commitment to act in harmony with all fellow Jews of whatever affiliation in the best interests of the Jewish people. It reflected the view that the difference between the two movements' approach was too wide to permit anything but administrative co-operation. The amendment was accepted by the executive, although there was more debate over the suggestion that ministerial representation on the council be limited as its work was purely administrative. It was pointed out that the Association was a religious body, and how important it was for lay members and ministers to work in close harmony.

A proposal that was welcomed was the establishment of standing sub-committees that could deal more effectively with administrative issues. Among them would be one for metropolitan synagogues and another for provincial ones to resolve their particular problems. The final governing body of the Association would remain the Conference, although, to protect the smaller congregations from the sway of the larger ones, no synagogue should be entitled to be represented by more than six delegates. It was also agreed that any constituent in arrears with its contribution to the Association would lose its membership after 12 months rather than two years. There were no recommendations on the financial policy of the Association owing to the difficulty in obtaining replies from constituents to a questionnaire that had been distributed to them. Many had refused to answer questions relating to their financial affairs or had given incomplete answers.

This reticence to respond to central requests anticipated the most controversial aspect of the report: the attempt to enforce a much greater degree of solidarity and obligation on the congregations. It was proposed that the constitution be changed so that member synagogues not only agreed with, but were also 'bound by' the rule of the Association and the decisions of its council. Responding to objections that this would threaten the autonomy of the congregations, Kingsley pointed out that they were trying 'to build up a movement throughout the country and that it only brought ridicule on the movement if there was no unity of purpose'.

What appeared to be a familiar debate was overtaken by a bombshell delivered by the Manchester representative, Alexander Levy. Manchester felt that it no longer wished to remain part of the Association as it currently existed. Manchester considered that the ASGB should be an association purely for the exchange of ideas and should not be an authority to govern all the subsidiary activities of the movement as a whole. It also felt that the ASGB was a London body and did not cater for, or represent, Manchester's needs. Manchester suggested that the existing basis of a per capita assessment be changed to an annual affiliation fee of 20 guineas.

The announcement presented the executive with a grave dilemma. If Manchester's definition of the ASGB was accepted it would completely alter the nature of the Association as it had developed, while the severe drop in income would limit its role automatically; if the proposals were rejected and Manchester resigned its membership, the movement would be greatly weakened by the loss of the second-oldest and second-largest Reform congregation in the country. It led to a special meeting between the ASGB honorary officers and the Manchester council at which it transpired that the congregation's main concern was financial. Manchester wanted to be able to determine how its contribution was spent and proposed that the annual amount be dependent on the objects of expenditure envisaged for the year and subject to each congregation's approval. Many felt that this would be unworkable, but the reorganisation sub-committee agreed to consider the matter. In the meantime the executive passed an amended version of the sub-committee's proposal, whereby a member congregation should 'by its membership be deemed to comply with the rules of the Association' – a wording that expressed the idea of common action and mutual responsibility, albeit less strongly.

The position taken by Manchester was not a new one, but reflected discontent that had simmered for some time. In 1949 they had complained about receiving insufficient space for reports of their activities in the *Synagogue Review* and six years later objected to contributing to the salary of the religious director of the Association for Jewish Youth when he largely served London communities and was of no benefit to them. The rift reflected the fierce independence that Manchester had maintained from the very beginning of its existence in 1856, when it had pursued different policies from West London in matters such as the observance of the Second Days of festivals and had seen no reason to adopt a common practice. The conscious pursuit of a separate identity was also part of north–south rivalry between Manchester and London in general. This had continued in the congregation's relationship with the ASGB, which it often identified as an extension of West London. There was also a liturgical controversy which, though not decisive, added to the strain on the relationship. Manchester felt strongly that a prayer for the State of Israel should be included in services, and was impatient with West London's opposition to it. It reflected the gulf between the generally supportive attitude towards Zionism in the provinces and the more reserved, if not frosty, views that prevailed in parts of the capital. Indeed, it was Manchester that in 1954 not only raised funds to donate an ambulance to Magen David Adom, the Israeli equivalent of the Red Cross, but did so in the name of the ASGB. Nevertheless, despite the many grievances that Manchester expressed, it is noticeable that the other provincial synagogues did not view the ASGB with such frustration and hostility. This may have been due to the fact that they were smaller in size and so more reliant on the Association for help, be it financial, or the supply of ministers or the need to be part of a national movement. In addition, being largely newer congregations, they did not have the same sense of their important historical role and were amenable to losing some independence in order to co-operate better with other congregations. In this respect Manchester was not the leader of a provincial rebellion, but was an isolated figure swimming against the tide.

The 'Manchester problem' raised its head again two years later when the congregation proposed a radical change in the direction of the ASGB. It suggested that the annual contributions from constituent synagogues should only be to cover secretarial and administrative expenses. Estimated costs for all other items – such as support of youth, the World Union, the *Synagogue Review*, advertisements and publications – should be circulated to constituents who would then decide of their own accord which to fund and to what extent. The motion would have jeopardised many of the ASGB's projects by making them subject to the support of each individual synagogue council, with no guarantee of sufficient funding for any one of them, nor any guarantee of continuity from one year to the next. Intentionally or not, it struck at the heart of the ASGB as a motivating force with a definite and co-ordinated programme of action. As before, the council wished to accommodate Manchester's concern and a 'trial budget' on the lines suggested by Manchester was sent out – separating administrative items from other projects – alongside the real budget for that year so as to see what impact it might have.

Presenting Manchester's case at the Special Conference called to debate it and other urgent matters in November 1956, Vivien

Steinhart declared that 'The Association was first formed as a consultative association for the benefit of its members. During the period of its existence, however, it had attained some rather extravagant ambitions which were not visualised when the Constitution was originally drawn up.' Some support was given by Edward Henriques, then treasurer of West London, who was worried that Conference could vote expenditures that synagogues were then expected to pay even though they had not been authorised by that synagogue's council. However, the majority of delegates considered that the Manchester proposals would weaken the ASGB and render it ineffective. Mr W. L. Michaelis of Bradford summed up the mood of most congregations when he declared that autonomy was fundamental, but synagogues could still pull together in the same direction and contribute to the financial support of the ASGB. A compromise resolution was passed, which agreed that annual dues should cover the Association's basic administrative expenses, but including all the other intended projects in that definition. Effectively this maintained the status quo. However, another of Manchester's proposals was adopted, for at the same time a change was made in the way that contributions were assessed – no longer by a certain amount per capita but calculated on the basis of a fixed percentage of each synagogue's income from subscriptions and seat rentals. It was an attempt to simplify the method of assessment, and also to rectify the existing situation in which some synagogues paid annual amounts that did not increase or decrease, and were not in accordance with any principle. It also bypassed the problem of the different ways in which synagogues computed their membership. Despite these agreements, the difficulties with Manchester resurfaced the following year when the congregation protested over the increase in the ASGB's running costs and called for expenses to be curtailed to a realistic level – a concern prompted by the publication of a budget of £7,458 for the rabbinic college at the same time as Manchester had made a large financial commitment to build a local youth centre. Alexander Levy felt that his dual role as a Manchester delegate and chairman of the ASGB was incompatible and resigned from the chair. When it was explained that the college budget was not to be financed by the Association's general fund but through other avenues, Manchester felt reassured but Levy adhered to his personal decision.[13]

Amid all the structural and financial problems faced by

constituent synagogues, questions of identity periodically arose, with calls both for the addition or the omission of the word 'Reform' from their names. Bradford's original title – the Bradford Congregation of British and Foreign Jews – reflected the high proportion of immigrants among its founders. In later years, when the foreignness of the members was no longer the case, nor a historical trait that they wished to emphasise in the wake of the xenophobia of the First World War, the shorter title of Bradford Reform Synagogue was used. However, in 1949 this was changed to Bradford Synagogue. The North Western Reform Synagogue considered a parallel move the following year but decided not to go ahead. Sinai Synagogue debated whether to become Leeds Reform Synagogue, but eventually opted to maintain its existing Hebrew title, both for sentimental reasons and to avoid fresh controversy. Glasgow faced an additional problem in that its full title – Glasgow Progressive Synagogue – meant it could be mistaken for a Liberal synagogue, and so in 1950 it adopted the name of Glasgow New Synagogue. The lack of any general consensus was reflected in the variety of titles adopted by the 11 synagogues founded between 1942 and 1957: four used the neutral term 'New', referring primarily to the date of their establishment, rather than the nature of their approach, although perhaps intending one to gently imply the other – indeed the nomenclature was seldom employed by Orthodox synagogues (Brighton, Cardiff, Middlesex and Southport); three included the word 'Reform' in their name (Bournemouth, Hendon and South West Essex); three used no adjective at all, being the only synagogue in the area, and so declined to have a term that might limit their appeal (Harlow, Maidenhead and Wimbledon); and one chose a Hebrew name that conveniently avoided such issues (Sinai).

The question was more than one of semantics but touched on the very nature of Reform. Was it a new form of Judaism that was a departure from the past and highly distinctive? Or was it a continuation of past traditions, thoroughly rooted in the faith and practice of previous generations? Nor was this only a matter of theology; it had practical ramifications for the direction of the ASGB. Should it promote itself as offering a new and appealing form of Judaism that would be attractive to the many who were disillusioned with Orthodoxy? Or should it claim to be the real heir to a tradition that became stultified in Orthodoxy and that had been revived through Reform? There was also the question of relations with Orthodoxy itself, which still accounted for the vast majority of synagogue-members in Britain and represented the Jewish establishment. Did Reform wish to pursue an independent line that would distance it from the establishment and make co-operation in non-religious areas more difficult? Or did it want to work towards being accepted by the general community as a minority partner in the life of British Jewry?

The issue, which arose at various times among the constituent congregations, came to the fore in the movement as a whole in May 1952. Sinai asked the ASGB executive to provide a directive as to the desirability or otherwise of the use of the word 'Reform' in synagogue titles. Edgware proposed a resolution at Conference that, while recognising the autonomy of congregations, its inclusion was recommended as desirable. Two different approaches emerged in the ensuing debate by the executive. John Chapman of Edgware argued that the use of 'Reform' was a matter of honesty and clarity. As members of the ASGB, congregations were all Reform synagogues and should be proud to declare their allegiance to a Reform approach to Judaism. Reinhart, by contrast, claimed that the term 'Reform' had a limiting effect, implying that the movement was less than wholly authentic. He also appealed to the origins of Reform in Britain, when his synagogue had deliberately used the title 'The West London Synagogue of British Jews' to efface distinctions within the community between different types of Jews. Using 'Reform' would turn the association into a sectarian group and he proclaimed his belief in 'non-adjectival Judaism'. The others ministers present were divided in their opinion: Goldberg (Manchester) and Maybaum (Edgware) favoured the term 'Reform' while Berg (Wimbledon) and Van der Zyl (North Western) opposed its use. Voting on the motion, the ASGB executive rejected it by 13 votes to 7, but it was agreed that the motion could still be presented to Conference. Similar arguments were expressed there, although some delegates called for the movement itself to incorporate 'Reform' into its title. At the end of the debate the Edgware motion was again defeated, albeit by the smaller margin of 22 to 16. Of course, being autonomous, congregations were still at liberty to determine their own name and policy. A proposal to add the word 'Reform' to the ASGB's own title was debated at the 1954 conference, but was not voted upon. The issue subsided for a while, but was not resolved, and was to resurface later with a different conclusion.

Far less contentious was the decision at the 1950 conference to adopt a Hebrew name for the Association. The title proposed initially was *Kehillot Ha'kodesh Tomchei Torah*, meaning 'Congregations who hold fast to the *Torah*'. The suggestion arose because it was considered important to have a logo on letterheads in Hebrew characters that immediately emphasised the Jewish nature of the organisation. It also allowed a statement of belief that complemented the purely functional title of the Association of Synagogues in Great Britain. Theology would be added to geography. Of course, it is open to debate whether it was entirely legitimate to claim that the ASGB synagogues did 'hold fast to the *Torah*' – many inside and outside the movement would have contested the claim, although it could be upheld in a figurative sense. However, no further discussion was necessary as it was discovered that the use of this title might lead to possible confusion with another body. It is noticeable that the amended title unanimously passed at the 1953 conference avoided any theological implications and was a literal translation of ASGB – *Chever Batei Haknesset B'britannia Ha'gedolah*. The ministers' assembly subsequently felt that it would be better to use the more traditional term for the formal title of a synagogue, and so the final version became *Chever Kehillot Kedoshot B'britannia Ha'gedolah*. It was used on the official seal of the ASGB which was devised by the College of Arms. On a background that displays olive leaves as symbols of Judaism and oak leaves representing Britain, there is a scroll with the Hebrew inscription of Psalm 16: 8, 'I have set the Lord always before me'.

Among the objectives boldly proclaimed in 1942 there were two which concerned primarily the ministers but involved much lay discussion too: the establishment of a rabbinical conference and a rabbinic court. The former was created officially in 1947, although it was largely a formalisation of the *ad hoc* meetings of the ministers serving ASGB congregations. It became known, however, as the 'Assembly of Ministers', so as to avoid any confusion with the ASGB's governing body, the annual conference. The idea of a rabbinic court presented more difficulties. It was most keenly advocated by Reinhart, who was anxious to avoid the anarchy over status issues he had witnessed while in the United States; he also felt it was an essential institution if Reform was to be considered normative Judaism and serve the needs of its members. However, owing to the new movement's preoccupation with establishing itself and supporting its constituent congregations, proposals for a *Beth Din* were not put to the ASGB Conference until April 1947. They generated considerable controversy. Opposition was based on the feeling that this was a 'retrogressive step' and an undesirable return to the 'rabbinical authoritarianism' of Orthodoxy. This fear was more a reflection of the origins of British Reform than a slight on current ministers. There were still memories of the Ashkenazi and Sephardi rabbinate combining to issue a *cherem* against the founders of West London. Moreover, Reform was initiated by the laity and, although subsequent ministers such as Marks and Joseph had exerted great influence, the lay members had always been involved in decisions on religious matters. The lack of an organised Reform movement until 100 years after the first synagogue was established meant that individual congregations were accustomed to both administrative and religious independence. The thought of a central rabbinic authority with wide-ranging powers that would diminish local autonomy was of particular concern to Manchester. It had maintained a strong sense of independence ever since its foundation, while it also shared the resistance of the city at large to any form of control by Londoners, be it economic, political or religious.[14]

There were differences among the ministers too. Goldberg – who did not have *semichah* at that time – was concerned that a Reform *Beth Din* manned by rabbis would effectively debar him from participation. Maybaum had theological objections, considering that the role of Jewish law in the Reform movement required clarification and that having a Reform *Beth Din* was 'playing Orthodoxy'.[15] Frustration at his continuing inability to gain either rabbinic or lay agreement led Reinhart to unilaterally establish the Reform *Beth Din* in February 1948, appointing Rabbi Michael Curtis as its clerk. The lack of official recognition was circumvented by issuing any certificates in the name of the particular congregation from which the case came. Effectively the court served the ASGB *de facto*, albeit not *de jure*. Lengthy debates and a number of compromises ensued before the Reform *Beth Din* was recognised by the ministers' assembly in March 1950. It was agreed to separate issues of marriage and divorce from proselyte cases, with the former being under the exclusive jurisdiction of the court, whereas the latter could still be dealt with by individual congregations if they so wished. It was also determined that ministers without *semichah* could adjudicate on proselyte cases, although not matters of divorce, while any litigant dissatisfied with a court's decision had the right of appeal. These changes secured the general approval of most synagogues, with the result that they relinquished their own procedures and transferred all their cases to the Reform *Beth Din*. However, Manchester, for which the compromise formula had largely been devised, insisted on maintaining its own courts for proselytes. When, in 1954, it too decided to refer proselytes to the Reform *Beth Din*, it meant that the court's authority in all status issues was at last recognised by the ASGB as a whole. It was also a major development in the process of centralisation, whereby individual congregations sacrificed some of their local autonomy to strengthen the movement as a whole. In this respect British Reform was unique, by comparison with Reform movements elsewhere in the world, all of which had local or regional courts, but not a central one commanding national jurisdiction.[16]

The nature of the Reform *Beth Din* differed markedly from the main Orthodox *Beth Din*, the Chief Rabbi's Court. It operated on different principles, based on a Reform interpretation of Jewish law, and seeing its primary duty as being to help the individuals that appeared before it rather than to adhere to predetermined rules. It was not served by a permanent *dayanim*, but all ministers of the Association sat in rotation, although continuity and consistency was provided by the presence of the clerk. The court's establishment also coincided with the reintroduction of the granting of a *get* following a civil divorce. The necessity for a *get* had been abandoned in the nineteenth century by the early reformers, but was now a condition before a re-marriage in synagogue could take place.

The fact that the Reform *Beth Din* had been recognised by all constituents did not result in an end to controversy. Proselyte cases were heard by the court but tuition was organised by the sponsoring community, and this led to concerns over the considerable variations in the length and depth of the courses. Another problem was that some congregations felt that proselytes should be vetted more closely as to their motives, particularly those converting for the sake of marriage, while fear was also expressed that Reform was seen as a 'dumping ground' for converts refused by the Orthodox authorities. Moreover, certain synagogues had experienced problems assimilating proselytes socially within their communities. Heated debates led to the calling of a special conference to discuss the unification of proselyte procedures. Recommendations were drawn up by the Assembly of Ministers to establish a unified procedure for the application, preparation and examination of proselytes. It included a preamble that emphasised the welcoming approach to converts that had become the hallmark of Reform: 'In accordance with Jewish Tradition we recognise the right of Gentiles, who are able to prove their fitness, to be accepted into the Jewish Community, and we desire, in charity, to give such assistance as we can.'[17]

The recommendations were accepted by all the congregations save Manchester. The latter's attempt to change the minimum period of tuition suggested, from nine months to 18, resulted in Conference's passing a compromise resolution that tuition be a minimum of 15 months and urging that the Ministers' Assembly concur. After further deliberation the Assembly rejected the idea, insisting that its original formula allowed sufficient flexibility for shorter or longer periods depending on individual circumstances. This provoked a constitutional crisis: Manchester accused the ministers of challenging the ultimate authority of Conference by refusing to accept the resolution it had passed. The chairman of the ASGB, Alexander Levy, was a member of Manchester and felt obliged to resign over the conflict of interests. In the event, both sides made conciliatory gestures and confrontation was avoided. The ministers accepted Conference's paramount role in all matters, while Manchester tacitly agreed to the Assembly's recommendations. Levy returned to the chair although, as was described above, he was to resign again a few months later, this time permanently, over the Leo Baeck College budget.[18] Nevertheless, the underlying tension over who determined religious issues – the rabbis or the movement – remained unresolved and was to surface in later decades over questions such as liturgical change and the introduction of the *mikveh*.

In fact there was talk early on of revising the liturgy. The question arose in 1944 after Manchester reported that they had failed to locate any new festival prayer books following the destruction of all their old copies when the synagogue had been bombed. A decision to reprint extra copies for present needs was accompanied by an agreement to revise all editions of the prayer book. Among the criticisms made of the existing liturgy was that prayers in the Day of Atonement were constantly repeated; inadequate provision was made for *Chanukah, Purim* and weekday prayers; and no Reform *haggadah* had been printed. It was pointed out that in the past prayer books had been edited and published by West London and simply adopted by other congregations, but now they should be involved in the process and it should be a co-operative enterprise. The Assembly of Ministers was given the responsibility of making the revisions, although it proved to be a major enterprise that took much longer than anyone envisaged. The ministers only met three or four times a year and had many other issues that also needed urgent attention – particularly conversion and divorce procedures. As a result they found it extremely difficult to devote sufficient time to the liturgy and accelerate its revision. By 1952 there was the added problem that many congregations were seriously short of High Holy Day prayer books, with both Wimbledon and Hendon reporting that they only possessed one book for every four worshippers. In order to speed up the process, Rabbi Dr Dorfler was employed to assist the Assembly on a part-time basis. However, his subsequent illness, along with the changes he suggested which required considerable discussion by the other ministers, had the effect of delaying the revision even further. The debate over one particular prayer – that for the State of Israel – also hampered the pace of progress, as will be seen below.

Nevertheless, progress was being made in other areas and during that year there was the publication of both an Evening Service prayer book and a Funeral Service prayer book. It was the first time that prayer books had appeared under the imprimatur of the Assembly of Ministers. In the past, the West London liturgies had shown a strong Sephardi influence; but now, with most of the current rabbis being refugees from central Europe and with many members of new Reform synagogues coming from Ashkenazi backgrounds, certain changes were in evidence: the second paragraph of the *Alenu* was included, *Kaddish* was rendered in its Aramaic form, and the blessing after reading the Scroll of Esther was introduced.

Apart from liturgy, the Assembly was concerned with a host of extraneous matters. Thus in 1950 it debated the Movement for Calendar Reform which horrified, among others, Orthodox Jews by its proposal to reorganise the world calendar into a standard year of exactly 52 weeks, which would have entailed shifting the date of the Sabbath. The Assembly decided not to support it, albeit not because its members objected in principle but out of solidarity with the Orthodox and in deference to Jewish tradition. When the dinner celebrating Leo Baeck's eightieth birthday was being planned, the Assembly ruled that although the meal should conform to the requirements of *kashrut*, it was not necessary to have the supervision of the Kashrut Commission. The same was to apply to any other function organised by the ASGB or constituent synagogues.[19] Another issue was the financial situation of ministers, concerning which Bradford proposed the establishment of a ministers' pension scheme. Upon investigation it was found that the high average age of the ministers meant that any scheme would be prohibitively expensive for the Association. Instead ministers were advised to join a contributory scheme. It was ascertained, however, that ministers were classified as employees rather than self-employed persons, and would therefore be entitled to extra benefits in the event of unemployment or sickness.

One of the other aims outlined at the beginning of the movement was the provision of rabbinic leadership for the future. The only initiative since then had been West London's own decision to help sponsor Hugo Gryn pursue his studies at university and then at the Hebrew Union College in Cincinnati. Gryn had survived Auschwitz as a child and was considered 'a likely candidate for the ministry' according to a council report. An ASGB sub-committee was given the responsibility of both locating 'young men' desirous of studying for the ministry and establishing the means of training them. It led to the formation in 1945 of the Society for the Advancement of Jewish Knowledge (later changed to the Society for Jewish Study), which was intended to be the forerunner of a school for rabbis and teachers. The principal was to be Dr Leo Baeck, with Dr Loewenstamm as his assistant. It would be housed at West London, which would also bear most of the costs involved, although the ASGB made a token contribution so as to retain its connection. In 1949 the Ministers' Training Committee was formed under the chairmanship of Reinhart to speed up the process of finding suitable candidates, but failed to make any headway. Discussion turned to co-operating with the Liberals and establishing together a theological college at Oxford or Cambridge. The idea was rejected by the ASGB executive partly on practical objections over the financial implications, but primarily for reasons of principle. It was feared that ULPS would use the joint venture for 'propaganda' purposes and the venture would be detrimental to the ASGB's image, making it appear 'sectarian' rather than mainstream. It was thought better to co-operate with the University of London and the Society for Jewish Study. In the meantime, Charles Berg, who had left Germany while training for the rabbinate at the *Hochschule*, had been completing his course in England through private studies with individual teachers. In October 1952 he was examined by Baeck, Loewenstamm and Katten, and awarded *semichah*. It was the first rabbinic ordination in England by a non-Orthodox authority.[20]

The decision to have a rabbinic course independent of the Liberals was accepted by the 1953 conference, despite the regret of the chairman himself, Edward Mocatta, and in the face of a resolution from the youth representatives lamenting the lack of joint action. Moreover, the Settlement Synagogue felt that the divisions between the two movements – its two parent bodies – placed it in a difficult position and resolved that its delegates should henceforth attend council meetings as observers rather than voting members. Following the application of two candidates in 1952 a course was devised consisting of a degree in Hebrew studies at University College London supplemented by lessons from tutors at the Society for Jewish Study. The arrangements were largely overseen by Reinhart and Van der Zyl and funded by their synagogues. It was increasingly obvious, however, that there would only be real progress in recruiting ministers if the ASGB had a proper college of its own. The launch in 1952 of the Leo Baeck Fund for the training of ministers and teachers was the first step to securing financial backing for the project. The proposal at the 1955 conference for each congregation to add five shillings to every member's bill emphasised the responsibility of the movement as a whole to fund its own future. It coincided with a growing awareness of the importance of qualified rabbinic leadership. A resolution from Wimbledon shortly afterwards urged the Assembly of Ministers to establish standards for admission, including possession of a minister's diploma.

The crucial role of Van der Zyl in nurturing the idea led to his appointment as the first director of studies in May 1956 when Conference finally agreed to establish a college. The Jewish

Theological College was inaugurated on 30 September at West London with Lionel Blue and Michael Leigh being joined by Henry Brandt, Michael Goulston and Dow Marmur. There was an impressive list of lecturers, including Rabbi Dr A. Dorfler (Talmud and Liturgy), Dr J. Heller (Philosophy), Rabbi Dr M. Katten (Midrash), Dr E. Littmann (Bible), Rabbi Dr I. Maybaum (Comparative Religion), Dr E. Rosenthal (History) – all of whom had been refugees. In his inaugural address Dr Leon Roth described the college as an 'act of faith and an act of affirmation'. Following the death of Dr Baeck in November it was renamed the Leo Baeck College. Until that point all the ministers who had served congregations in the ASGB had received their training either from Orthodox institutions or from Reform seminaries abroad, primarily in Germany and also in the United States. Their studies had been complete before they had received any contact whatsoever with Reform synagogues in Britain. Now, at last, British Reform ministers could be trained specifically for the congregations they would be serving. Moreover, with the destruction of the Berlin *Hochschule* and the Breslau Theological Seminary during the war, the Leo Baeck College rekindled the light of Jewish learning in Europe and became the training ground of religious leadership for Reform communities throughout the Continent. Van der Zyl, himself a graduate of the *Hochschule* and then a refugee, was not only the prime mover behind the re-creation of his *alma mater*, but went on to guide its progress for the next ten years as director and to be responsible for much of its success.[21]

The concern for children's religious education that had prompted the founding of the Association was also a constant theme after its inception. Particular attention was given to improving the level of religious teaching. Following a highly successful teachers' refresher course at West London in July 1950, a teachers' conference was formed the following January. Its first chairman was Mr D. A. Shavreen and its aims were to organise commissions on textbooks and instigate training courses. That same month, the ASGB established a central committee of education under the chairmanship of Albert Polack, housemaster of the Jewish house at Clifton College. Its object was to co-ordinate existing activities in the various synagogue religion schools, liaise with the Assembly of Ministers and the teachers' conference, and promote new ideas in Jewish education. By that time the Association was providing Jewish instruction for some 800 children. The ambitious programme was initially subject to the limitations imposed by lack of finance, but it received a considerable boost at the 1952 conference. The launch of the Leo Baeck Fund for the training of both ministers and teachers indicated the movement's determination to turn intentions into action, while the creation of three annual teaching scholarships gave immediate help. For many years the annual teachers' refresher courses were organised by Rabbi Cassell and attracted leading educationalists and academics as speakers, such as Raphael Loewe, Chaim Rabin and Cecil Roth.

By 1954 almost 1,000 children were receiving religious education via ASGB synagogues; within two years the number had risen to 1,500 – an indication of the number of young families being attracted to the Reform movement. It also emphasised the importance attached to education, as does the fact that almost every synagogue had its own adult education classes. In September 1956 the ASGB appointed its first education officer – a part-time salaried post that was taken by David Kelner, the headmaster of a secondary modern school in Manchester. His brief was to visit the different religion schools, discuss the methods of organisation and instruction with the head-teachers, and prepare an overall syllabus. The report he issued a year later was greeted with acclaim, although the post was terminated owing to the Association's financial troubles and the need to fulfil its commitment to the Leo Baeck College.

It was recognised that just as important as the years a child spent at religion school was what happened afterwards. Many, although not all, congregations had their own youth club and it was suggested that a 'Junior Membership Association' be established to link existing groups, help found new ones, and provide activities for individual youngsters without local facilities. This was achieved with the formation of the Youth Association of Synagogues in Great Britain (YASGB) in October 1946, catering for the 16–23 years age-group. Its first president was Ernest Bello. The importance attached to YASGB by Conference was indicated not just by making an initial grant but by agreeing that it should be represented on the executive. YASGB threw itself into a host of activities – organising the first of many weekend conferences at Hawkshead in the Lake District, adopting children in a camp in Germany, sending parcels to a hundred French and Belgian children. It was clear that YASGB could not be self-supporting and it was readily agreed that it was the permanent financial responsibility of the Association and 'one of the first claimants on the ASGB funds'.[22] In the autumn of 1948 YASGB held a joint conference with the Federation of Liberal and Progressive Jewish Youth Groups (FLPJYG) at Heacham, Norfolk. Despite an appeal by Basil Henriques that the two groups merge, this was opposed by YASGB owing to the difference in viewpoints between them. Nevertheless, friendly relations were maintained and a joint committee was established.

A year after its formation, YASGB had grown to nine groups with a total membership of over 500 individuals. Part of its appeal lay in its strong sense of direction and purpose: a movement for intelligent young people, committed to a modern form of Judaism and furthering their own Jewish awareness. Social activities alternated with study groups; weekends away meant not only doing their own cooking but taking their own services. For some, it was the first time that they had been introduced to a vibrant Jewish atmosphere or a traditional celebration of the Sabbath. There was close contact with ministers of the ASGB, and their involvement in both local groups and weekends away played an important role in developing the character of the youth movement. One such highlight was when 130 members attended the summer school in 1952 at the Beatrice Webb House, near Dorking and heard Dr Leo Baeck address them. At the 1953 summer school the 130 participants were visited by no fewer than ten ministers for various talks and study sessions. It became customary for student ministers to participate as part of their course, a pattern started by the first trainees, Lionel Blue and Michael Leigh, leading sessions at the summer school the following year. Strong religious input also came from Jacob Petuchowski, a refugee from Berlin then pursuing his rabbinic studies in England, who initiated many study projects and was responsible for publications aimed at YASGB members on the beliefs and practices of Reform Judaism. These first appeared in 1948, entitled 'Judaism – Past and Present: An Introduction to the History of Jewish Life and Thought' which covered topics ranging from biblical times to the modern period. In addition he helped provide regular Jewish content in the monthly magazine *Y.A.S.* (established that same year). The enormously positive impact made by the youth groups was evident also in the decision taken at the 1956 conference to establish a younger branch of youth clubs to cater for those aged 13–16 years. Much of the success of the early years was also due to one of its early chairman, Raymond Goldman, who instilled the movement with a sense of religious responsibility as well as organisational efficiency. His marriage to fellow YASGB member, Joy Cohen, was one of many marital unions that arose from those involved. Not only did many YASGB members of the 1950s become leaders of the parent movement in subsequent decades, but they produced a generation of children who were born into the movement and became the next layer of committed participants.

Wider horizons were developed when YASGB members met youth delegates from several other European countries at a special conference in London in September 1950. It was part of an attempt to revitalise a devastated European Jewry whose communal structures had been annihilated by the war. It also served to assist Continental communities in which Reform Judaism was much less developed than in Britain. The success of this led the World Union for Progressive Judaism (WUPJ), at its conference in July 1951, to form a youth section, with Ernest Bello as the first chairman. WUPJYS, as it became known, was designed to help support the activities of WUPJ, arrange joint projects and holiday schemes between the national youth movements, and provide hospitality to students visiting different countries. WUPJYS was also to play a significant role in providing a channel for the future leadership of the respective movements and was especially influential in encouraging men and women from both Britain and elsewhere in Europe to train for the rabbinate.

Youth work was just one of many areas in which the Reform and Liberals had failed to co-operate as fully as might have been expected of two Progressive movements. There were many who felt that this was both regrettable and counter-productive. A committee was established in March 1946 to investigate how closer co-operation could be achieved, and a standing committee to enable the two groups to take joint action when desirable was proposed, but there were no further developments. In the same year Basil Henriques launched a campaign for a Federation of Progressive Synagogues, comprised of ministers and lay representatives of all non-Orthodox synagogues. Its aim was to answer the spiritual needs of those no longer attracted to

Orthodox Judaism, particularly those returning from the Forces, who were searching for a sense of faith and new ways of being involved in Jewish communal life. 'We must not puzzle these men and women by making them think that there are three forms of Judaism, the Orthodox, the Reform and the Liberal, whereas in fact there are only two, the Orthodox and the Progressive.'[23] However, as with all the other initiatives, the differences in approach prevented any real progress. The uneasy relations with the Liberals was an important factor in the ASGB's attitude to the WUPJ. In 1945 the Association joined the Union, of which individual Reform synagogues had been members for several years already. Nevertheless, there were constant urgings by some within the Association for it to resign from the Union. They generally arose when the ASGB's annual contribution was due or when its hard-pressed financial situation resulted in calls for outgoings to be curtailed. However, beneath the monetary argument lay the deeper motive of not wishing to be publicly aligned with the radical theology of the Liberals and their rejection of many traditional customs. The concern came to the fore in 1952 in the blunt question that the ASGB executive asked the Assembly of Ministers to consider: 'Does being identified or closely connected with the World Union tend to give a misleading understanding or false complexion of the ASGB?' The ministers returned a divided opinion. Some praised the work of the Union – helping overseas congregations, supporting the Leo Baeck School in Haifa, and playing a role at UNESCO – and considered that severing the link would be isolationist. Others denied that the Union had any real effect and felt that affiliation limited the ASGB from drawing together with wider Jewry. With the ASGB executive itself being equally unable to reach a clear decision the matter was left to debate at Conference. The delegates there gave a forceful verdict in favour of continued co-operation and voted 37 to 5 to maintain active membership of the WUPJ. It was not to be the final word, and two years later the executive again raised the question of resigning from the Union. As Dr Leo Baeck was president of both organisations it was resolved to present the arguments for and against disaffiliation to him personally and seek his reaction. He sympathised with many of the ASGB's reservations but considered it the wrong time to take any action or to act divisively, and his advice was followed. Nevertheless, the Association's lack of enthusiasm was still evident: in 1956 Lily Montagu drew attention to the sparse interest shown in the World Union by the ASGB and complained that it did not shoulder its financial responsibilities, with ULPS paying £375 per annum and the ASGB £200.

The coolness between the two Progressive groups paled in comparison with the hostility displayed by the Orthodox. The harmonious relations that had existed in the 1930s had long evaporated, both because of the more uncompromising stance of the Orthodox rabbinate and because the growth of the Progressives had turned them from an aberration to be tolerated into a threat to be combated. For a while the brunt of the Orthodox attack was directed against the Liberals, to whom Hertz was vehemently opposed The Reform movement may have received less attention, but it was not exempt. Shortly before his death, Hertz denounced Reform as 'a malignant growth' and 'as a structure built on quicksand'.[24] Fierce criticism at a local level, already seen in Bournemouth and Glasgow, occurred in Cardiff when plans to establish the Reform community there were announced in 1948. When Chief Rabbi Brodie inducted Rabbi Weisz as Senior *Dayan* of Manchester the following year, he took the opportunity to attack strongly the inroads of Reform Judaism. Another Mancunian leader, *Dayan* Golditch, used his New Year message to condemn 'misguided Jews who, in their ignorance and presumption, set up splinter sectarian synagogues...proposing to reform Judaism and not themselves...giving the sanction of religion to the vain imaginings of their own heart'.[25] The ASGB usually advised constituents not to respond in kind. Reinhart's letter to the Cardiff chairman echoed that policy:[26]

> Because I have had so much unhappy experience in these matters, may I be so bold as to suggest that you warn your co-workers against replying to unseemly and bigoted statements or making counter-recriminations, or any expression that will lead to, or intensify, communal quarrelling. I feel sure that to ignore vituperation and to concentrate solely on positive, constructive efforts is the right policy for our congregations.

When some members of Southport reacted by vilifying their local Orthodox counterparts, Reinhart warned the council that 'crude and unsympathetic attacks on sections of the Community other than our own...[are] quite contrary to the tradition of Berkeley Street'.[27] Nevertheless, there were still some contacts between the different groupings. In February 1946 North Western had a joint meeting with Finchley Synagogue, at which the latter's minister, Revd M. Bloch, put the case for Orthodox Judaism and Van der Zyl explained the Reform perspective. Ministers from the United Synagogue – such as Arthur Barnett, Solomon Goldman and Ephraim Levine – along with its President Sir Robert Waley Cohen, as well as representatives of the Federation, Sephardim and the Union of Orthodox Hebrew Congregations attended West London's reopening service in 1952 following the repair of war damage. However, these tended to be isolated instances that belied the increasing hostility shown by the Orthodox, which extended also to educational efforts. Thus the Chief Rabbi sent an Orthodox teacher to Marylebone Grammar School to teach Jewish studies to Jewish children there, even though a Reform Jew had provided such tuition there satisfactorily for many years; similarly he established a special class at another local school so as to rival the class previously offered at West London to Jewish pupils attending this school. Nevertheless, the ASGB council decided not to respond to attacks on Reform that appeared in the *Jewish Chronicle* in June 1956, on the grounds that it would serve no useful purpose and merely intensify the discord.

Religious issues also affected the ASGB's standing *vis-à-vis* the Board of Deputies. The difficult relationship that existed initially between the Board and West London upon its inception had never been wholly resolved and affected other non-Orthodox congregations too. The Liberal synagogues were given representation at the Board, but refused certification for performing marriage ceremonies. Years of fruitless discussion over the Liberals' request to be granted their own marriage secretary came to a climax in 1949 when the Board voted on the issue. They had been urged to refuse certification by the Chief Rabbi on the grounds that the Liberals married women who had not performed *chalitzah* and who had not received a *get*. When deputies voted against the request, albeit by a narrow margin, the Liberal delegates resigned in protest and there was a division of opinion among Reform congregations as to how best to react. Some felt they should remain part of the Board to argue the case for the Liberals and continue the debate on their behalf. The majority, however, felt it was best to resign from the Board as a matter of principle to show solidarity with the Liberals and to object to the implication that non-Orthodox synagogues did not profess the Jewish religion fully. It was also recognised that, but for having an

Act of Parliament granting them marriage rights independently of the Board, the Reform community would be in the same unenfranchised position. West London therefore withdrew from the Board, as did North Western, Glasgow and Bournemouth. Most of the other Reform synagogues did not belong to the Board, but some which had considered affiliating, such as Edgware, decided not to do so 'until there is a change in its present attitude towards Progressive Judaism'.[28] The only Reform community to remain at the Board was Manchester, largely because at the time they were in the midst of a campaign to recover certain funds from the Board, although there may also have been a desire to show their independent attitude.

Over the following months there was a series of private meetings with representatives of the Board and with the Chief Rabbi in an attempt to effect a reconciliation. Negotiations for the Reform were led by Percy Cohen of the West London Synagogue. The matter was discussed at length at the Association's 1951 conference and although it was noted that each congregation had the right to define its own relationship with the Board, it was agreed that no congregation should take any action to return to the Board without consultation with the others. The unilateral decision of West London shortly afterwards to re-affiliate caused some resentment among other congregations. It had followed agreement between the Board and the Liberals that the question of marriage secretaries should be settled via Parliamentary legislation, resulting eventually in the 1959 Marriages Act. The issue also led to questions as to whether it was still appropriate that West London should be the authority for certification of Reform synagogues that wished to appoint a marriage secretary. It was time, argued Glasgow, for the ASGB to be regarded as the parent body of the Reform movement. Nevertheless, in view of the inconvenience of obtaining a new Act of Parliament, West London retained its power of authorisation for other Reform congregations, as it does to this day. By 1953 all Reform synagogues had returned to the Board or affiliated for the first time. There was no attempt to form a bloc group, although common action was taken when appropriate. At that year's conference there was a call for the ASGB itself to be represented at the Board. It was an indication both of the *rapprochement* between the Board and the Reform community, and of the growing awareness that, as a significant institution within British

Jewry, the ASGB's voice should be heard at the highest communal level. The Board agreed to the proposal and Sidney Kingsley was nominated as the first deputy to represent the movement as a whole. While staunchly promoting ASGB interests, he and other Reform delegates supported the freedom of religious practice for Orthodox Jews whenever external events posed a threat to it. Thus in April 1955 they urged ASGB synagogues to assist the Board's protest against a Parliamentary Bill that would have prohibited the provision of *kosher* food.

It must be recognised, however, that the row over marriage secretaries was only one of the reasons for withdrawal from the Board. As will be seen below, another and more important factor was the question of Zionism. The issue caused much controversy even within Reform circles. Some welcomed Jewish nationalism, be it as a fulfilment of the ancient dream of returning to the land of Israel, or as a practical solution to the age-old anti-Semitism faced by Jews in many parts of the world, a concern given particular urgency with the rise of the Nazis. Others opposed Zionism vehemently, either fearing it would bring into question the loyalty of Jews to their host country, or objecting that it was a crude distortion of the essentially religious nature of Judaism, degrading spiritualism into nationalism. The divide merely reflected the ambivalent attitude amongst British Jewry in general.

The tendency for the older 'established' synagogues to be less enthusiastic towards Zionism was also mirrored in the position of West London, which was much less sympathetic than some of the newer congregations. It was epitomised by Reinhart himself who considered that the universal spirit of Judaism was being hijacked by political exigencies and being squeezed into a geographical straitjacket. Prayers that hinted at favouring a Jewish homeland were omitted from the service and attempts to find a haven in Palestine for German Jews were resisted and described as 'a scandal'.[29] Explaining his position, Reinhart wrote: 'We believe that the Jews constitute not a nation like other nations, but a world-wide community of believers, a universal people who possess a common religious tradition and a common spiritual destiny... they are not seekers of a "national home".'[30] The real object was to build instead a living creative Judaism in Britain. He and many others supported the foundation of the Jewish Fellowship at West London by Basil Henriques in November 1944. It was designed to be 'the appropriate organ for the representation of all Jews for whom

Judaism did not centre in Palestine, but within their own hearts as citizens within this country'.[31]

Under Reinhart's editorship, the *Synagogue Review* attempted to ignore most developments connected with Zionism, however important. No mention, for instance, was made of the establishment of the State of Israel in the May or June 1948 editions. When Zionism did merit attention, it was usually an opportunity for condemnation, such as the instances of Jewish terrorism during the last stages of the British Mandate. The most far-reaching criticism came during the renewal of hostilities after the United Nations peace terms in 1949 in which he denounced Israel's responsibility for the sufferings of Palestinians:[32]

> Whatever the extenuating circumstances the bitter and ineluctable fact remains that because of the aggression of Jews hundreds of thousands of innocent men, women and children have suffered the pitiful fate of which so many millions of the House of Israel have been the victims...This indeed is a hideous price for any Jewish victory.

However, this continued antagonism was not shared by all members of 'the establishment', as epitomised by Robert Henriques, for whom 1948 was a turning-point: 'I was against a Jewish state, until it was created. Once it was created, there was no more room for argument.'[33] Moreover, Henriques then visited Israel, flew out to lend his military expertise during the Sinai campaign, and later built a house for himself in Galilee.

Among the rabbinate, both Maurice Perlzweig, when he was serving North Western, and Baron, at Glasgow, took a positive view and advocated the Zionist cause. The reality of the State's existence also persuaded many to re-evaluate their attitude. Charles Berg, who considered that the prophetic ideals were being realised in some of the *kibbutzim*, gave a religious defence of the new State. The real danger to Progressive Jews, he declared, would be for them to cut themselves off from the new-born hopes.[34] Manchester had long been a centre of Zionist activity and Goldberg was a robust supporter of Zionism. He described the birth of Israel as 'a feat of incalculable historic momentousness' and asserted that one could be loyal to Britain without approving of Ernest Bevin's foreign policy.[35] The tensions over Zionism surfaced within the affairs of the ASGB itself and the issue was debated in 1945 at the fourth conference following an article in the *Synagogue Review* critical of Zionism. Henry Lefridge, a North Western delegate, not only queried the appropriateness of the piece but complained that 'there is an impression that anti-Zionism is part of the Progressive faith'. It was left to the chairman, Edward Henriques, to declare that the Association included many shades of opinion and should 'pursue its work without the intrusion of contentious discussion on Zionist matters'.[36] This was to remain the policy for many years, although the image that Reform was either opposed or indifferent to Zionism also persisted.

The Zionist controversy spilt over into religious fields too. Reinhart led those opposed to the introduction at services of a prayer for the State of Israel, while he campaigned against the use of the Star of David on synagogue buildings because of its Israeli associations.[37] He even refused to attend wedding receptions if the President of Israel was to be toasted. Another anti-Zionist suggested that prayers such as the *Kaddish* be emended to avoid using the word 'Israel', for after 1948 it was incompatible with the theme of Jewish universalism.[38] Others urged the inclusion of a prayer specifically for the State and felt that it was improper that Reform services included prayers for the leaders of Britain, but not for the leaders of Israel. With Israel surviving the War of Independence and developing year by year, there was a gradual change to a more positive attitude towards Zionism. It manifested itself in a vote at the 1951 ASGB conference to add a prayer for the State. Despite the usual warnings that it would lead to charges of dual loyalty and that current references to Zion were sufficient, the motion was passed by 41 votes to 26. A special sub-committee was made responsible for composing an appropriate prayer and it was printed for insertion into prayer books for those congregations that so wished. The question arose again with the publication of the draft version of the new Festival Prayer Book in 1954 which did not include the prayer in the text. Manchester and North Western led the campaign to instate the prayer, rejecting the suggestion that a slip be inserted and claiming that it would be seen as a poor reflection of the Association's attitude. Their view was countered by those who felt that as there were already numerous prayers relating to the land and people of Israel, it would be wrong to introduce political leanings into the liturgy. The executive was evenly split on the issue, and the matter was referred to the Assembly of Ministers to draft a prayer acceptable to all congregations. This eventually resulted in a prayer for 'the Land of Israel' which did not pray for a sovereign State but did pray for Jews living within Israel specifically. In words that could be interpreted either politically or spiritually, it uttered the hope that 'Zion may proclaim the message of righteousness and peace to all mankind'.[39] Further evidence of the gradual shift towards Zionism came in the decision to invite the Ambassador of Israel to the ASGB dinner to mark the tercentenary of Anglo-Jewry – albeit on a majority vote.[40]

The reservations, if not hostility, towards Zionism held by many West London members played a significant part in the break with the Board of Deputies. There was a long-held disquiet at the pro-Zionist policy among the Board's leadership, particularly after Selig Brodetsky's election as President of the Board in 1939. It was perceived by many as a 'Zionist take-over', while Brodetsky's Russian origins meant that it also represented the wane of the old Anglo-Jewish establishment and the transition of power to the 'new community' of the east European immigrants. They had a different agenda, tended to have more left-wing political leanings and were more enthusiastic about Jewish nationalist aspirations. There was much resentment of this within the circles who felt that they were being displaced, and a variety of accusations were made: that the Board was in the control of a Zionist caucus, that it no longer represented the views of British Jewry but took orders from the Zionist Organisation, and that undemocratic methods were used to influence committee decisions. In 1946 many delegates formed an 'independent deputies' group within the Board to fight against 'the use of the Board as a spear-head for official Zionism'.[41] When West London and other Reform deputies resigned from the Board it was admitted that the dispute over the Liberals was subsidiary; indeed, representatives of the Spanish and Portuguese Congregation and the Anglo-Jewish Association left at the same time because of the Zionist issue. Under the terms of agreement that led to the return of all parties, changes were made to the Board's constitution to ensure that meetings were not held nor resolutions passed without due notice being given and without substantial quorums being present. Moreover a declaration was added, stating that 'The Board of Deputies, as the representative organ of British Jewry, while free to co-operate with other organisations, is independent of any form of outside control, and its policies should reflect the largest possible measure of common agreement'. The wording of the formula was a tacit admission of the real basis of some of the accusations against the Board, and Percy Cohen heralded the return of West London and other delegates as a succcssful conclusion to 'the fight against regimentation of opinion and the trampling on the rights of minorities'.[42] Despite the claim of victory, however, the non-Zionist element was increasingly described by contemporary observers as a 'minority', both within British Jewry and within Reform communities.

By 1957 it was evident that another influence was beginning to wane, although it would still be in evidence for some years to come: that of the German refugee rabbis. Many had passed away in the two decades since their arrival, during which time they had made an important contribution to British Reform Judaism. Caesar Seligmann (died 1950) had been a leading member of the Society for Jewish Study. Herman Schreiber (died 1954) had assisted several congregations and also played a significant role in building up the reputation of the Reform *Beth Din*. Bruno Italiener (died 1956) had served the Settlement Synagogue and then spent ten years as minister at West London. Ernest Sawady (died 1956) was rabbi of the Settlement Synagogue at the time of his unexpected death at the age of 40. Max Katten (died 1957) was guest preacher at many congregations, sat regularly on the Reform *Beth Din* and was one of the main lecturers at the Leo Baeck College. Gustav Pfingst (died 1957) conducted correspondence courses at West London for children evacuated during the war and later served as minister to Sinai Synagogue.

Most keenly felt of all was the passing of Leo Baeck on 2 November 1956. He had already become a world-renowned figure in pre-war Germany for his scholarship, his pastoral care and his courage in standing up to the Nazis. His decision to return to Germany after bringing some of his flock to England in August 1939 was typical of his outstanding devotion to his community. The leadership he displayed while in Thereisenstadt concentration camp – whether his own personal dignity in dealing with the daily hardships or the inspiring series of lectures he gave by night as a form of spiritual resistance – made him a legend in his own lifetime. After the war he settled in England and allied himself to the Reform movement, worshipping generally at North Western, of which he was the President, and at West London. He became a living symbol of Jewish survival and used his immense stature to promote the cause of Reform Judaism, serving as president of both the ASGB and the WUPJ. Reunited with many of his former pupils from the Berlin *Hochschule*, he gave regular lectures at the weekly seminars for rabbis on Monday mornings at West London, as well as at many public forums. He helped tutor the first trainee ministers and gave valuable support to the proposed rabbinic college, later to be named after him. Although he was not involved in the day-to-day affairs of the Association, his moral influence was crucial, and he had immense influence on the whole generation of rabbis who served the movement before and after his death. In a unique tribute to his greatness, Baeck's body lay on a high bier in the Stern Hall at West London for two days, attended by members of the Burial Society. At the funeral service the coffin was brought into the synagogue and set before the Ark before being taken to Hoop Lane cemetery.

Another key figure was lost to the movement in July 1957 when Reinhart resigned as Senior Minister of West London. His departure was due to disputes over internal synagogue policy and the direction of the congregation, with Reinhart feeling that elements in the congregation who lacked spirituality and vision were taking over, while many members considered Reinhart was becoming increasingly autocratic and out of touch with their needs. Matters had worsened after the appointment of Revd Alan Miller as religious education adviser, seen by some as injecting a new vigour into the congregation, but regarded by Reinhart as a challenge to his authority. After Reinhart's resignation, a group of supporters from West London established an independent Reform synagogue, Westminster, under his leadership. Cassell, who resigned in sympathy at the same time, left England to become minister in Bulawayo, Rhodesia. Van der Zyl was appointed as the new Senior Minister at West London. As Reinhart was no longer serving an ASGB congregation he felt obliged to resign as vice-president of the movement and from his many other positions, including the Assembly of Ministers, Leo Baeck College, Reform *Beth Din* and numerous committees, even though he was urged to stay in office. The many glowing tributes to his work – both from individuals within the ASGB itself and from many synagogues – was testimony to the crucial role he had played in helping create the movement, nurturing several new congregations and supporting many existing ones. He had been 'father and founder of the Association. A great debt of gratitude was due to him which could never be repaid.'[43] Yet there were also tensions, with Reinhart being increasingly dissatisfied about the direction in which the movement was going: 'emotion has gained ascendancy over intellect...there is an accent on blood and soil, with all the narrowness and obscurantism that accompanies it.' He complained about the weakening of faith, that the ASGB was becoming an organisation for managing religion and that 'we should be a little more fearful of our numerical growth and a little more concerned for our individual loyalty to our high and holy task'.[44] These sentiments were by no means shared by all and the tributes to him also included the observation that 'we have witnessed the tragedy of the over-possessive parent who gives all for the child, little realising that although father knows best, the child grows up and must loose the yoke if it is to develop normally'.[45] In many respects Reinhart's departure from the ASGB marked the final moment of an era in which both the original founders of the Association made way for new leaders and West London lost its pre-eminent influence. A few weeks earlier, Leonard Mendel of North Western Reform Synagogue had been elected chairman of the ASGB, the first time that someone not from West London or Manchester had headed the movement. It was as if the 'founding synagogues' which had pioneered Reform Judaism in Britain were giving way to the 'new synagogues' which were barely a few decades old.

NOTES

1. Minutes, ABS, 5 March 1944, Reform Synagogues of Great Britain Archives, the Sternberg Centre for Judaism, London.
2. Minutes, ABS, loc. cit., 23 and 24 July 1946.
3. Minutes, ASGB, 16 April 1948, Reform Synagogues of Great Britain Archives, the Sternberg Centre for Judaism, London.
4. Minutes, ASGB, loc. cit., 22 Nov. 1942, 5 March 1944.
5. Reinhart to Edgar Isaacs, 10 Feb. 1944, Reinhart Papers, Anglo-Jewish Archives, Parkes Library, Southampton University; File: Leeds.
6. Lily Montagu to Reinhart, 18 Feb. 1946, Reinhart Papers, loc. cit., File: Edgware.
7. Minutes, ASGB, loc. cit., 24 Aug. 1948.
8. Minutes, ASGB, loc. cit., 18 Oct. 1949.
9. *Synagogue Review*, Sept. 1946, p. 10.
10. Minutes, ASGB, loc. cit., 4 Nov. 1951.
11. Minutes, ASGB, loc. cit., 3 May 1953.
12. Minutes, ASGB, loc. cit., 22 July 1954.
13. Minutes, ASGB, loc. cit., 29 Aug. 1957.
14. See Bill Williams, *The Making of Manchester Jewry* (1985), pp. 221 and 340.
15. Minutes, Assembly of Ministers, 7 Dec. 1949, 15 March 1950, Reform Synagogues of Great Britain Archives, the Sternberg Centre for Judaism, London.

16. Jonathan Romain, *The Reform Beth Din* (1992), p. 13.
17. Minutes, ASGB, loc. cit., 3 Sept. 1956.
18. Minutes, Assembly of Ministers, loc. cit., 12 Dec. 1956, ASGB Executive, 15 May 1957, Reform Synagogues of Great Britain Archives, the Sternberg Centre for Judaism, London.
19. Minutes, ASGB, loc cit., 19 Feb. 1953.
20. *Synagogue Review*, Dec. 1952, p. 109.
21. For further details of the college, see Ellen Littmann, 'The First Ten Years of the Leo Baeck College', in D. Marmur (ed.), *Reform Judaism* (1973), pp. 160–9.
22. Minutes, ASGB, loc. cit., 10 Feb. 1948.
23. *Synagogue Review*, July 1946, p. 101.
24. *Synagogue Review*, July 1946, p. 107.
25. *Jewish Gazette*, 13 April and 23 Sept. 1949.
26. Reinhart to L. Corne, 17 June 1948, Reinhart Papers, loc. cit., File: Cardiff.
27. Reinhart to Sampson Goldstone, 1 June 1951, Reinhart Papers, loc. cit., File: Southport.
28. Minutes, ASGB, loc. cit., 13 Sept. 1949.
29. Minutes, West London Synagogue, 29 March 1931, Archives of West London Synagogue; *West London Synagogue Magazine*, June 1936, p. 146; Reinhart to L.G. Montefiore, 22 Aug. 1938, Reinhart Papers, loc. cit., File: Correspondence.
30. *Synagogue Review*, April 1945, p. 58.
31. *Synagogue Review*, Dec. 1944, p. 26.
32. *Synagogue Review*, March 1949, p. 119.
33. S.J. Goldsmith, *Twentieth Century Jews* (1962), p. 54.
34. *Synagogue Review*, Oct. 1948, p. 25.
35. *Synagogue Review*, April 1949, p. 147.
36. Minutes, ASGB, loc. cit., 22 Feb. 1945.
37. Reinhart to B.M. Adler, 14 Jan. 1957, Reinhart Papers, loc. cit., File: West London Synagogue 1957; Reinhart to P. S. Goldberg, 13 Nov. 1951, Reinhart Papers, loc. cit., File: Manchester.
38 H. Gordon in *Synagogue Review*, Jan. 1949, p. 76.
39 The prayer book itself did not appear till 1965 because of editing and printing difficulties.
40 Minutes, ASGB, loc. cit., 12 May 1956.
41 Percy Cohen; quoted in the *Synagogue Review*, July 1949, p. 220.
42 *Synagogue Review*, Sept. 1951, p. 23.
43 Alexander Levy, then chairman of the ASGB; Minutes, ASGB, loc. cit., 27 June 1957.
44 *Synagogue Review*, Dec. 1955, p. 104.
45 *Synagogue Review*, Sept. 1957, p. 8.

7 Growth and Development, 1958–1980

The growing affluence and self-confidence that marked Britain as it emerged into the 1960s from the economic and social strictures of the post-war period affected British Jewry as a whole, but was particularly evident in the Reform. It expanded its congregations, developed a professional staff, and asserted its rights at the Board of Deputies. The traumatic experience of the Six Day War in 1967 helped complete the revision of its once hesitant attitude to Zionism and turned the movement into an active supporter of Israel. Moreover, it began to take the lead in certain aspects of Anglo-Jewish life, such as the efforts on behalf of Soviet Jewry. The decision at the end of this period to move from West London Synagogue to new and independent headquarters was an inevitable result of this process of enlargement and transformation.

The most tangible sign of the Association's growing confidence in its own purpose and direction was the decision – yet again – to change its name. The desire to incorporate the term 'Reform' into the movement's title was gaining increasing support. For some it was a matter of honest self-description: an association of Reform synagogues should be called Reform. For others it was a method of self-advertisement: Reform was an attractive concept and so every opportunity should be used to publicise it.

At a special conference on 17 May 1958 it was proposed by M.J. Hart-Leverton (West London) that the name be changed to the Association of Reform Synagogues in Great Britain. Many still had the same reservations as had been expressed in previous debates. Van der Zyl held that as the policies of ASGB were now well known there was no need to highlight its Reform character, while the addition of labels would encourage sectarianism. Revd

Cahn of Southport declared that it would be a 'sign of weakness' to change. However, a new mood was in the air and the recommendation was accepted by 25 votes to 13. In an unusual move the debate was reopened the following day on the grounds that the new name was open to criticism. A. S. Diamond proposed instead that it be changed to the Reform Synagogues of Great Britain – which attracted even greater support than its predecessor, being passed by 28 votes to 10. Once the inevitability of change had been accepted, it was a case of choosing a name that was both pronounceable and to the point. The Hebrew title was altered in parallel to express also the ideological stance of the movement; it became *Ichud Kehillot Kedoshot Mitkadmot B'britannia Ha'gedolah*.

Not everyone was satisfied and at the 1959 conference Bradford attempted to change the name back to the ASGB on the grounds that the movement had established itself under that name and it would lose the benefit of the reputation it had so carefully built up around it. Bradford also pointed out that only three synagogues actually used the word 'Reform' in their own titles. The resolution was defeated by the substantial majority of 35 votes to 13. It was partly as a result of this issue that Conference went on to pass a resolution that 'Except at the discretion of the Executive of the RSGB an amendment to the constitution shall stand for three years' – which was designed to avoid repetitious debates on the same subject every year.

Another aspect to the name-change that was particularly important for some was that it changed the emphasis of the movement from an organisational union ('Association of...') to a body with a theological stance ('Reform...'). It was part of a wider attempt to lift the movement above the necessary but mundane tasks of administration and finances, and dedicate more attention to its spiritual *raison d'être*. Thus the 1958 special conference saw another amendment to the constitution: that the first of the objects listed in Rule 2 should be 'To promote and foster a robust and virile Judaism which will contribute to the life of the entire Jewish community, and to co-operate with fellow Jews in whatever congregation or association they may be in order to promote and assist the religious and educational betterment of the Jewish people and mankind'. A similarly worded statement had been part of the 'Aims and Objects' published in 1946,[1] but what had previously been a lofty hope was now given the authority of constitutional status. The fact that it was accepted without dissension did not alter the tribulations of future treasurers, but did help to assert the religious priorities of the movement.

Despite this enthusiasm there was some dissatisfaction initially with the main vehicle for religious developments, the Assembly of Ministers. The lack of scholarly output was bemoaned in an editorial of the *Synagogue Review*:[2]

> In this generation we have neither a Claude Montefiore, an Israel Abrahams nor a Morris Joseph... The re-issue of *Judaism as Creed and Life* is a commendable step, but it does bring out the fact that with all our advances in numbers and organisation our ministry has not managed to produce a work of religious thinking responsive to the shattering events of the intervening half-century.

The remarks may have ignored the pastoral and educational strengths of Reform ministers, but did highlight their limited literary achievements.

In addition many lay members felt that the everyday guidance they needed was lacking. Criticisms were made in the early 1960s on the silence of the Assembly on contemporary moral questions, be they domestic or world-wide: such as over Apartheid, the status of illegitimate children, the hydrogen bomb and family planning. Those responses that did emerge were often long after issues had been raised. This was partly because the hard-pressed ministers had little time for the research and deliberation involved, and partly because the divergent views of members made reaching a consensus very difficult. The call was often made for 'a systematic guide on what should be Reform Jewish practice in this country'.[3] However this was usually resisted by the ministers themselves who feared the creation of a Reform rule-book. Thus Rabbi Lionel Blue declared that 'Religion is always in danger of being identified with ritualism...I regard religion as a questioning of the spirit... This spiritual freedom should not be sacrificed to conformism.'[4] Similarly Rabbi Michael Goulston warned of the danger of stultifying debate: 'Our Reform search for new meanings, deeper spiritual insights and quest for religious truth in the prophetic tradition would be called off.'[5] The laity were not necessarily persuaded but had to wait another 30 years for the self-confidence that made possible the publication of *Faith and Practice*, which provided the guide they wanted.

Another worrying aspect was that several of the most promising rabbis did not remain in England. Salary scales were much higher in the United States, and possibilities of career advancement were much greater. When Rabbi Alan Miller announced that he was moving to New York, an open letter of protest was issued by seven leading members of the YASGB: Raymond Goldman, Ronald Jacobs, Jerome Karet, Jack Lynes, Donald Salinger, Neville Sassienie and Ralph Stern. Citing the departure abroad not only of Miller but also of Hugo Gryn, Jakob Petuchowski and Andre Ungar, they wrote: 'We younger men and women of the RSGB are beginning to wonder how much longer the Reform Movement will continue to squander the spiritual future of our generation... We dare no longer ignore anymore the reason for this trend. Our congregations have not been able to offer these men sufficient spiritual and financial inducement to cause them to stay.'[6] A public meeting was called to address the problem. The 35 people who attended established a group called the RSGB Forum the aim of which was to work within the RSGB and strengthen its religious efforts, both centrally and within the congregations. It should be noted in passing that all of the letter's seven youthful signatories went on to be involved in the RSGB in later years and reflected the value of the YASGB in providing future leaders for the parent movement.

Despite these criticisms, there was a modest level of rabbinic productivity that, although slow to start, gathered momentum over the next two decades. In 1962 Rabbi Dr Dorfler issued a responsum on the question of donating eyes for an eye bank, concluding that such donation was permissible, a recommendation that was then adopted by the Assembly. Three years later, in the wake of the widespread availability of the contraceptive pill, the Assembly declared itself to be in favour of birth control. An article by Rabbi Goulston explained that although the family was the keystone of the Jewish faith, 'Parents have the right to determine the number and to space the births of their children in accordance with what they believe to be in the best interest of their families...The Ministers' Assembly only asks that this responsibility be exercised in the light of the ethical and moral teaching of Judaism, which places a strong emphasis on the blessing of family life.' Another small innovation came in 1964 when Rabbi Michael Curtis produced a two-year calendar of *Torah* and *Haftarah* readings instead of the usual annual ones. A further change came in 1968 when a triennial calendar was published, which better reflected the triennial system of readings that had long been adopted by the movement. The main books to be published came from the prolific pen of Rabbi Dr Ignaz Maybaum: *Jewish Existence* (1960) examined the Jewish contribution to civilisation, *The Faith of the Jewish Diaspora* (1962) was a collection of sermons on the chosen role of the Jews, *The Face of God after Auschwitz* (1965) grappled with theology after the Holocaust, and *Creation and Guilt* (1969) was a theological assessment of Freud's father–son conflict and its consequences for inter-faith relations. All were issued by commercial publishers – albeit with the RSGB agreeing in advance to purchase a certain number of copies – as they demanded an expertise and distribution skill that was far beyond the RSGB's capabilities. However, the movement recognised the value – both financial and in terms of prestige – of being able to publish the work of its own rabbis and in 1967 published a small book by Rabbi Michael Leigh entitled *Jewish Observance in the Home* which included a gramophone record of Sabbath songs. Intended as a guide to home practice for RSGB members it was highly successful and within a year almost 4,000 copies were sold.

The 1970s witnessed a much larger and more varied literary output. Foremost among these was *Reform Judaism* (1973) edited by Rabbi Dow Marmur. It was a series of essays by leading rabbis and lay members addressing theology, *halachah* and other issues facing the Reform movement. Many of the matters that it did not have the space to cover – such as Zionism, new trends in religious thinking and developments in religious education – were addressed in a companion volume, *A Genuine Search,* which appeared in 1979, also edited by Marmur. In the intervening years, various pamphlets were published in a series entitled *Judaism In Our Time*. They covered more immediate and practical topics such as intermarriage, dietary laws, mourning, vegetarianism, women's role and worship. Not everything written was printed. A pamphlet on education consisting of essays by two ministers within the Assembly which expressed markedly opposing stances was rejected on the grounds that neither position was acceptable to the general membership and that publication would be 'dangerous and unnecessary'.[7] An anthology of High Holy Day readings by Jonathan Magonet, *Returning* (1975) added to the growing library of RSGB authors, along with further books by Maybaum: *Trialogue Between Jew, Christian and Muslim* (1973) and, posthumously, *Happiness outside the State* (1980) exploring further the relationship between the three monotheistic faiths. Even greater impact was made by Lionel Blue. His first book, *To Heaven with Scribes and Pharisees* (1975) on the realities of Jewish communal and domestic life not only won the *Jewish Chronicle*'s Book of the Year award, but proved a best-seller among the wider public. It led to a series of other books, notably *Backdoor to Heaven* (1979), along with the texts of his highly popular radio broadcasts, as well as cook-books with June Rose and anthologies with Jonathan Magonet. The greater literary productivity of the rabbis, as compared to former years, reflected not only individual talents but also the fact that the 15 members of the Assembly in 1958 had grown to over 40 by 1980. In 1976 it had changed its name from the Assembly of Ministers to the Assembly of Rabbis in recognition of the fact that the vast majority of its members had received *semichah*. Indeed, the Assembly had become the largest Progressive rabbinic body in the world outside the United States.

Despite these achievements, the most important area of religious creativity was liturgy. Moves to revise the Pilgrim Festival Prayer Book had been mooted in 1944. The last edition had been edited by D.W. Marks and there was considerable discrepancy between its approach and that in the 1931 Daily and Sabbath Prayer Book. However, the small number of ministers, the long gaps between Assembly meetings, and the many demands both arising from their own congregations and relating to the movement as a whole meant that work was painfully slow. Enquiries from council members as to when the new liturgy could be expected became increasingly impatient. Dr Dorfler and Reverend Solomons of Bournemouth were delegated by the Assembly to finalise the Hebrew text and provide the English translation respectively. The former was responsible, too, for the new layout, which was designed to reproduce the poetic form and rhythmic character of the prayers. He also added aids for correct pronunciation of the Hebrew, with symbols to illustrate which syllable was to be stressed and when the easily-overlooked vowel, *kamats katan*, occurred. Eventually *Prayers for the Pilgrim Festivals* was published in 1965.

The prayer book continued the more traditional trend in the Reform way of worship and reflected the influence of the

Continental rabbis. Among the restored prayers were the hymns for the procession of the scrolls at *Simchat Torah*, the *Havdalah* ceremony, a fuller version of the *Kedushah*, and the Aramaic version of the *Kaddish*, which was now being used in nearly all RSGB synagogues in Sabbath services. There were a few new compositions, including a prayer after kindling the festive candles which used light as its central motif: 'May the radiance of these lights kindled in honour of this Festival illumine our hearts, and brighten our home with the spirit of faith and love. Let the light of thy Presence guide us, for in Thy light do we see light.'[8] Its popularity was such that it was to be incorporated in the next edition of the *Daily and Sabbath Service*. The memorial prayer after the *Yizkor* was greatly expanded, resulting in a lengthy section that combined lofty idealism with warm spirituality, and that blended the particular with the universal. A prayer for Israel was at last included in the text of the prayer book, having been an inserted slip for so long. However, it still referred only to 'the Land of Israel' and, mindful of the non-Zionists in the movement, spoke of 'Zion' proclaiming its message of righteousness, preferring to couch the prayer in religious imagery rather than make direct reference to political realities.

The English translation of the prayers was an attempt to be both truer to the deeper intent of the Hebrew text, rather than its literal meaning, but also more in keeping with Progressive religious teaching. Thus a verse in the Song of Moses at the Red Sea had been translated previously as 'The Lord is a man of war, the Lord is His name' – which implied God delighting in war and strife, a portrayal abhorrent to those who had recently witnessed the horror of war and the annihilation by nuclear weapons. Now it was altered to 'The Lord was victorious, Lord Almighty is His name'. Some expressions were changed so as to convey better the meaning of metaphors now no longer significant: 'My horn dost Thou exalt like the horn of a wild ox' (Psalm 92: 11) became 'But Thou, O Lord, hast strengthened me abundantly'. Archaic phrases were clarified, such as 'Lord of hosts' becoming 'Lord of all creation'.

Theological considerations were responsible for certain other changes. The second paragraph of the *Amidah* previously ended 'Thou art faithful to quicken the dead' – implying a belief in the physical resurrection of the human body to which most Reform Jews did not subscribe. It was therefore altered to 'Thou wilt surely grant eternal life to the souls of the departed', which echoed the general Reform belief in the immortality of the soul. References to a personal Messiah were reinterpreted as a hope for a messianic age of universal peace and religious fulfilment on earth. In place of the *Yigdal*'s assertion 'He will send our anointed at the end of days', the new version declared 'Our Messianic hope He will fulfil'. The revisions were largely welcomed, and the few objections that arose were on sentimental grounds rather than theological, with dismay at changes to favourite phrases with which worshippers had grown up. Indeed, such was the opposition to the altered first line of the *Shema* in the draft version – changed from 'Hear O Israel, the Lord is our God, the Lord is One' to 'Hear O Israel, the Lord is our God, the One and Eternal' – that it was amended to 'Hear, O Israel: The Lord our God, the Eternal, is One'.

The new festival prayer book met with general approval, not to mention relief at its appearance. However, the 20 years that had lapsed between it being commissioned and being published meant that certain assumptions made at the beginning of the process were not necessarily valid by the time it appeared. This applied particularly to the type of English used. The 'thee's' and 'thou's' style of the King James Bible had been acceptable in the 1940s, but was no longer in vogue in the 1960s. In this respect, it was part of a general change in the cultural climate of British society at large, as was also being discovered in the Christian world and epitomised by the enormous success of 'vernacular' translations such as *The Good News Bible* which was published in 1966. The other problem with the Festival Prayer Book was that it ignored completely the enormous impact of the two historic events of the twentieth century that took place while it was in preparation: the Holocaust and the birth of the State of Israel. They may have been too momentous to react to at the time, but two decades later they cried out for attention.

Work on a revised Daily and Sabbath Prayer Book began in 1964 and although it too took much longer to complete than was envisaged originally – finally being issued in 1977 – it marked a radical departure from previous Reform liturgy. It was primarily the work of Lionel Blue and Jonathan Magonet, who, unlike the previous editors, were English-born and graduates of Leo Baeck College. The most obvious change was the use of modern English in translations. Initially this aroused vociferous objection by those attached to the form of words with which they were familiar. They argued that the language of prayer benefited from an 'archaic' or, more positively, a 'refined' style of English distinct from that of everyday speech. Blue defended the new approach on the grounds that the prayer book was a pipeline to the past, but it was in danger of being blocked; it needed language that spoke to today's Jews: 'There are many things in the world that deserve our tears – let us not waste them on "Thou" and "Thee" and seventeenth century grammar. We are not dressed in doublet and hose, and God does not ask us to masquerade as our forefathers.'[9] In a series of wide-ranging substitutions, Victorian Gothic English was dropped: 'Thou' became 'You', 'hast' became 'has', 'verily' became 'truly', along with many other modifications. Moreover, the new translation tried to express ideas in a meaningful manner, so that 'A woman of valour', in the Sabbath eve home service, became 'A true wife'.

In fact, notice of this new approach had already been served by the new *Funeral Service* printed in 1974 and edited by Blue and Magonet. Modern English had been used, along with a simple and direct style of phraseology. The booklet also contained early signs of sensitivity to the different situations of different users. Thus there were alternative readings for an adult death, child death and an unexpected death. A series of mood-setting meditations at the start of the service was another pointer to the direction of the new *siddur*.

There were considerable structural changes to the *siddur*. The object was both to overcome the problem of the liturgy becoming routine, and to bring back some traditional prayers without lengthening the service. The solution was to give the Sabbath evening service four alternative introductory sections, each containing a different prayer, song and psalm. The Sabbath morning service had six different opening sections, each with a different theme: tradition, life and death, the future, the just society, the community and the family of Israel, after which all services converged into the *Amidah* and the *Torah* service. Within each service new forms of worship were included via responsive readings and passages for silent study. The effect was to maintain a regular structure yet add freshness to it. In addition a series of meditations were provided at the beginning of the *siddur* to help set the mood for the service. A Sabbath afternoon service – previously given only in outline – was included in full, along with a large selection from the *Sayings of the Fathers* which is traditionally studied at that time in the weeks between *Pesach* and *Shavuot*. Full daily services were another innovation. The number of prayers already existing for special life-cycle occasions was expanded with the inclusion of prayers to be said upon a *barmitzvah* or *batmitzvah*, and upon an anniversary (be it for a birthday or wedding), while the service for a mother was gently altered to a thanksgiving service for parents. The anniversary prayer was particularly innovative in that birthdays and wedding anniversaries hold no official place in Jewish tradition, yet are important to most Jews – which the new prayer book both recognised and brought into a synagogue context. Part of the prayer declared: 'On this day I come before You with my private memories and thank You for my own experience, and for companionship and love. Whatever the future brings, may this day always renew my spirit, giving me happiness on my journey through life.'[10]

Another innovation that reflected marvellously the realities of Jewish communal life was a prayer for committee meetings. Moreover, it not only helped introduce a moment of religion to discussions that often concerned very secular matters, but also helped establish an atmosphere appropriate for synagogue business: 'Let us listen to each other with respect, and treat each other with wisdom and generosity, so that we witness to the master whom we serve and justify His choice of us. May none of our controversies rise up like those of Korach, from ambition and self-seeking. Let them only be for the sake of heaven, like those of Hillel and Shammai.'[11]

At the same time there was a strong attempt to make the prayer book used as much at home as at synagogue. It was recognised that in previous decades the balance of ceremonies for many Jews had shifted from private practices to public observances, and that a more balanced approach needed to be restored. The section on home ceremonies was expanded; evening and morning prayers for children were provided, as well as full versions of the three daily services, which few RSGB synagogues held and which were left to individual discretion. There was a large anthology of songs, containing many Sabbath and other table songs, designed to encourage domestic usage. There was also a powerful educational thrust to the *siddur*, with an extensive study anthology that could be used both in synagogue and for home reading. This in itself was a treasure-chest of Jewish teaching, with a wide range of sources, from rabbinic passages to contemporary writers, and encompassing both secular and religious Jewish thought. It was intended as a doorway to the riches of the past combined with the insights of modern Jewish creativity.

The prayer book also sought to take account of the momentous events of recent Jewish history. Rabbi Hugo Gryn, who had succeeded Van der Zyl as Senior Minister of West London, declared in the Preface:[12]

> Since the sixth edition of the Daily and Sabbath Prayer Book two generations have lived through both history-shattering and history-making periods in Jewish existence... We are living under the still impenetrable cloud of the Holocaust and in the century of the refugee. We have witnessed the rebirth of the sovereign State of Israel and the spiritual horizons of Zion fill us with high expectations. We have the feeling that our generation is participating in the shaping of Jewish destiny itself. The pace is swift and the responsibilities very great.

The Holocaust was commemorated by a special memorial service for the six million which mourned 'the genius and the wit that died, the learning and the laughter that were lost'.[13] The prayer book also contained several illustrations, a unique feature which distinguished it both from previous Reform liturgies and from those of other Jewish groups. Many of the drawings were of European synagogues that were destroyed in the Second World War and whose inclusion not only decorated the prayer book but also ensured that their memory was kept alive.

The impact of the State of Israel was acknowledged in a *Yom Ha'atzma'ut* service that celebrated 'the hope that was born out of suffering, the springs that came to the dry sad valley, the rose that blossomed in the desert'.[14] In addition, there was a new prayer for the State of Israel during the Sabbath morning services, reflecting both the hopes and worries associated with it. It asked that 'peace may reign on its borders and tranquillity in its homes. May the spirit of friendship and understanding remove all fears and heal all wounds.'[15] Unlike the controversies surrounding previous versions of the prayer, there was now no longer any hesitation in referring to 'the State of Israel' by name. Yet the prayer did not challenge the validity of the Diaspora, and it managed to express pride in

Israel without assuming that all Jews should live there. It was only to be expected, therefore, that the alteration made to the Hebrew text of the *Avodah* prayer in the 1931 and 1965 editions – the translation of which is 'Blessed art thou, O Lord, who causest thy holy spirit to rest upon Zion' – was abandoned in favour of the traditional text, 'who restores His presence to Zion'. Similarly, many other sections that had been omitted because of the opposition to Zionism found their way back in the prayer book, such as the *Uv'neh Yerushalayim* paragraph in the thanksgiving after meals.

Another change in Jewish life that was reflected in the prayer book was that an age of faith had given way to an age of secularism. Many Jews experienced doubts about their beliefs, and were confused about the role of religion. This also meant that prayer itself, once automatic, was often problematic for many people. These difficulties were acknowledged in new compositions: 'There are times when it is hard to hear You, and times when it is hard to follow You; and I know that this is my loss. In the quietness of this Sabbath I turn my thoughts to You. Help me to hear Your voice, to find Your image in my soul, and to be at peace.'[16] In this way the prayer book took the radical step not only of recognising religious uncertainties but of allowing people to express them in synagogue. At the same time, there was an awareness that the nature of Reform thinking had altered, no longer embedded in the nineteenth-century belief in the mastery of reason and in the inevitable progress of humanity. The sufferings of two world wars and the question-marks hovering over the future resulted in greater openness to the emotional and mystical elements of Judaism. Quotations from the *midrash*, *Chasidic* masters or mystical excerpts from the writings of Martin Buber and Rav Kook all found a place in the prayer book.

The additions to the liturgy also included a restoration of traditional prayers omitted in previous editions. The second paragraph of the *Alenu* and the *Havdalah* ceremony were restored. The new edition went even further in reviving the act of putting on *tefillin* at midweek services, and in providing blessings before and after the *Haftarah* on the Sabbath. Yet the return to tradition was not accompanied by any inward-lookingness and there was no lessening of the prophetic vision. The prayers for peace and harmony were extended beyond the family of Israel to all humanity. Special prayers were also composed for inter-faith meetings and for international understanding, echoing and endorsing the contemporary moves towards religious and political harmony in the world.

Underlying the new prayer book was the awareness that while it was an attempt to answer the religious issues of its day, it would not be the last revision ever made. It was the logic of a 'contemporary' prayer book 'that it must sooner or later be superseded when another generation finds itself dissatisfied with that which is needed today'.[17]

A four-page supplement in the *Jewish Chronicle* on the new prayer book coincided with its official launch among RSGB congregations on 30 September 1977. The supplement not only gave much publicity to the prayer book itself but took the message of Reform Judaism into many non-Reform homes. The first print-run of the *siddur* was sold immediately and a second was sold out in advance. The book was greeted with enthusiasm among synagogue members and also received wide critical acclaim in a Jewish press that largely catered for members of Orthodox synagogues. The *Jewish Chronicle* review described it as 'an event of considerable communal as well as literary moment' and praised its value for both synagogue and home use: 'In this respect, certainly, it stands head and shoulders above any similar work published in this country.'[18] The *Jewish Gazette* also hailed it: 'The impact of the sheer poetry in Jewish prayer, presented in simple modern form, impinges sensitively into the mind to make the Reform Synagogues of Great Britain's just published volume "Forms of Prayer" a premier source of Jewish knowledge and prayer.'[19] It received considerable attention in the general media too, being widely and sympathetically reviewed in papers ranging from *The Times* to the *Catholic Herald* to *Ha'aretz* in Israel. Thus a significant incidental effect of the prayer book was to serve as a powerful advertisement for the Reform theology, and to put the RSGB on the religious map of England.

Another key area of rabbinic activity was the *Beth Din*. The steady growth of the RSGB was reflected in the increasing demands made upon it. The 40 proselytes (and nine children) who had appeared before the Court at its inception in 1948 had grown to 109 proselytes (and 39 children) by 1965. Adoption cases had been non-existent for the first few years of the Court's existence but reached 15 cases in 1965. Only in divorce cases was there little change, with the 18 cases heard in 1948 remaining a fairly constant figure. The figures also reflect other trends affecting British Jewry at large. The rise in intermarriage can be seen in the fact that the vast majority of those seeking conversion had a Jewish partner. Indeed, over half of that number were already married and there were many cases of mothers converting along with young children. Not surprisingly, over half of the converts were in the 21–30 age-group, and three-quarters were under 40 years of age. In 1968 a standing committee was established to assist the Court in dealing with unusual cases not covered by existing regulations. It also came to serve as a forum for recommending changes of procedure to the Assembly when appropriate.

It was also noticeable that the great majority of the cases coming before the Reform *Beth Din* were from partners of members of Orthodox synagogues who had failed to receive any help from the Chief Rabbi's Court. The Orthodox authorities largely opposed conversion, regarding it as a loophole for sanctioning intermarriage. If an applicant had a relationship with a Jew, it was usually regarded as grounds for automatic disqualification. An additional problem was that the demands made on applicants accepted for tuition were extremely rigorous, and they often presented considerable difficulties for even the most sincere of candidates. The Reform *Beth Din* pursued a different approach. Although knowledge and observance of Judaism (according to the Reform understanding) were valued, sincerity and identity were the main criteria. The Reform *Beth Din* was aware that many cases arose out of love for a Jew rather than out of love for Judaism, but felt that what was important was not the way the person had been introduced to Judaism initially but the subsequent attitude that developed. The best policy was to rectify an undesirable situation by bringing the non-Jew into the faith. As the Clerk to the Court, Michael Curtis, explained:[20]

> In principle we are against proselyte marriages. We share the fears of Jewish parents, we agree with the marriage counsellors and warn applicants against the inherent difficulties...but when the applicants come to us they have already made up their minds. It would be short-sighted to suppose that by refusing to accept the non-Jewish partner for conversion, the marriage could be prevented... We must meet the applicants on their merits, with an open and unbiased mind.

There was also a concern for the children of such unions and a desire to allow them to be part of the Jewish community if that was the wish of the parents. In the same vein, the Reform *Beth Din* also gave sympathetic treatment to several Jewish couples who had adopted non-Jewish children and wished to acquire Jewish status for them. Many of the families had been rebuffed by the Chief Rabbi's Court, which was unwilling to accept cases unless the adopting parents lived a strictly Orthodox life.

The differences between the Orthodox and Reform approach accounted for many of the divorce cases, most of which came from outside the ranks of Reform members. This applied particularly to women whose husbands refused to grant a *get* even though they had been divorced civilly for some years. The Orthodox authorities felt that they were unable to intervene, leaving many women with the alternatives of giving financial inducements to their ex-husbands or being unable ever to remarry in synagogue. The Reform *Beth Din* considered that in cases of malice or blackmail it had the right to award a *get* without the husband's consent and thus free the woman. It was a radical departure from Jewish law that was felt to be fully justified morally:[21]

> When the husband refuses to give the *get*, or his whereabouts are unknown, or he is presumed to be dead, or he resorts to bribery and makes payment of money a condition of his consent, the Chief Rabbi's Court cannot help... Is not the hardship of the frustrated wife undeserved and unjust? Under such circumstances our *Beth Din* dissolves the marriage and issues a document which allows the wife to remarry in any of our synagogues... We depart in these cases from the practice of the Orthodox Court, which condemns these unfortunate people to lifelong celibacy in the name of Jewish Law.

It should be noted that during the period under consideration the rate of divorce rose both nationally and among Jews. Yet there was little corresponding increase in the number of applications for a *get* at the Reform *Beth Din* during this time. Nor was there any increase via the Orthodox authorities. The reason is that many Jews did not bother to obtain a *get*, considering the civil divorce sufficient and not wanting the extra trouble of arranging a religious divorce too. Those that remarried often either married a fellow Jew in a Registry Office or married out of the faith. The paucity of cases at the Reform *Beth Din* and their minimal increase subsequently attests to the tendency towards religious indifference within the community at large and the growing assimilation.

It is clear that although the Reform *Beth Din* was intended to serve the status questions of RSGB members, it inadvertently acted as an important source of recruitment for those wanting a conversion, divorce or adoption, with the result that both the applicants and their families then joined the Reform movement. One study shows that 15 per cent of the growth in membership of Reform synagogues in London during the period 1940–60 can be accounted for in this way. Moreover, those using the Reform *Beth Din* had an even more considerable impact on the number of marriages performed in Reform synagogues, which increased dramatically during this period, whereas Orthodox marriages decreased. Of all Reform marriages, 45 per cent resulted from conversion or divorce cases heard at the Reform Court.[22]

The extremely large number of cases from Orthodox members also highlighted the growing gulf between the rabbinic leadership and the lay membership of the United Synagogue, which led many to change to RSGB synagogues – not from motives of status but simply because they no longer felt at home in Orthodoxy. It reflected the influence of the Continental rabbis from strictly traditional backgrounds who had come to England in the late 1930s and who had brought to an end the 'middle-of-the-road' Judaism of the United Synagogue. They not only served leading pulpits around the country but also came to dominate the Chief Rabbi's Court. They brought a very different approach to communal life and established a new type of Jewish clergy:[23]

> The Reverend X whose Jewish studies terminated when he was 18, who dressed like an Anglican clergyman, carried his umbrella on the Sabbath and was very broadminded about the dietary laws, was the real religious guide of his congregation. Owing, however, to changes within the community, the Reverend X has frequently been replaced by Rabbi Y who eats with very few of his congregants and generally comports himself in an Orthodox fashion. This is not a development which has found universal favour.

Many members of Orthodox synagogues felt that they could no longer relate to the Judaism of their rabbis. The 'progressive conservatism' espoused originally by Chief Rabbi Hertz had turned into a rigid Orthodoxy that had little in common with their lifestyle and beliefs. When they moved to a new area, they considered joining a Reform synagogue rather than automatically affiliating to the nearest Orthodox one. When a new Reform congregation was established in their vicinity, they deliberated about transferring to it, even though it meant losing burial rights with the United Synagogue or their provincial counterparts. The growth of RSGB membership can be said to be due as much to the Reform movement winning members as to the Orthodox losing members. Not only did RSGB congregations prove very attractive for many, but United synagogues appeared to have very little to offer.

Nevertheless, there were occasions when the Reform *Beth Din* seemed in danger of antagonising its own membership. A relatively minor controversy was whether to charge fees of applicants to the *Beth Din*. The services of the Court had always been free, with the costs and the salary of its clerk being borne by West London, which also housed the Court and initially provided most of its manpower. West London continued to pay for Curtis when responsibility for the Court devolved onto the ASGB in 1963. However, other costs rose as sittings of the Court increased, as did travel and administrative expenses. Suggestions from the movement that fees should be introduced were resisted by the Assembly on the grounds that it was a service to the community, while fees might discourage applicants. However, owing to financial pressures on the RSGB, a motion was passed at the 1967 conference to introduce modest charges and it was accepted by the Assembly. Provision was made for fees to be reduced or dispensed with in cases of hardship. In 1978 the RSGB treasurers recommended that the amounts be substantially increased so as to make the *Beth Din* self-supporting. It was argued that applicants would be willing to pay for the excellent service that the Court provided, which was efficient, helpful and sensitive. One factor for the rise was that Curtis had retired in 1972 and had been replaced by Lionel Blue, with the position of clerk now being supported by the RSGB. It was eventually agreed that fees should cover 80 per cent of the costs of the Court and RSGB would bear the balance.[24] The right to waive fees was maintained.

Of much greater consequence was the question of ritual immersion (*tevilah*) in a *mikveh* for converts. The matter had been raised by Dow Marmur in 1975 and an Assembly working party was established to discuss it. The recommendation in favour of the issue was based on four reasons: first, that it would bring RSGB procedure in line with rabbinic tradition; second, that it would allow applicants to be accepted in the time-honoured manner of Jewish tradition and be a more meaningful ceremony; third, that it would be a positive step towards the long-term goal of Jewish unity; and finally, that it reflected the more traditional stance of the Reform movement, both in England and abroad. The proposers were keen to point out that immersion for proselytes was a very different concept to immersion for women after menstruation (even though the same *mikveh* was used), and that reintroduction of the former did not imply restoration of the latter. It was also made clear that the new regulations would only apply to future applicants and would not affect the validity of converts accepted previously, although they could always undergo immersion if they so wished. Nevertheless, the proposal proved highly controversial. The rabbis themselves were divided, with opponents arguing that it was a regressive step, that the ritual carried offensive connotations, and that the hope that it would lead to Orthodox acceptance of Reform converts was illusory. It would also have the effect of separating Reform procedures from other Progressive bodies, such as the ULPS in England and the Reform movement in the United States. After lengthy consideration and many passionate speeches for and against the proposals, the matter was passed at the Annual General Meeting of the Assembly in January 1978 by 18 votes to 4. A resolution that *tevilah* be optional for a period of two years – intended to allay the fears of opponents and restore unity to the Assembly – was defeated on the casting vote of the chairman, Michael Standfield.

The issue also caused severe problems in the relationship between the Assembly and the rest of the RSGB. It had been assumed by the Assembly executive that their recommendations would be accepted without debate as it was purely a religious matter requiring rabbinic consideration only. However, the matter raised much anxiety among some lay members, who took exception to the proposal, be it on theological grounds or for emotive reasons. Furthermore it begged an important question of procedure: who was the supreme religious authority for the RSGB? For many, the Assembly seemed to be acting as if it occupied that role, whereas according to the constitution it belonged to Conference. Much of the difficulty was due to misunderstanding and lack of communication. Following considerable debate it was accepted that, in religious matters, the Assembly must be the final arbiter, but only after a full process of consultation and after giving due consideration to the views of the laity as expressed through both synagogues and the Council. As a result, a number of measures were implemented to bring closer relations between the rabbis and lay leaders: a second Assembly representative would sit on RSGB executives; all rabbis would receive council minutes, while RSGB executive members would periodically attend Assembly meetings. These developments proved successful and led to a much greater sense of partnership between rabbis and laity.

The acceptance of the Assembly proposals did not end the saga, as there then emerged a practical problem of implementation. Orthodox authorities were unwilling to permit the use of Orthodox-controlled *mikvaot* by applicants to the Reform *Beth Din* lest it imply endorsement of such conversions, which they still regarded as totally invalid. In the absence of a *mikveh* the old procedures were continued. Eventually it was discovered that, for historical reasons, the *mikveh* in Cardiff was owned by the local authority and was therefore available for use despite the protests of the local Orthodox community. From September 1980 ritual immersion became mandatory for all proselytes appearing before the Reform *Beth Din* and for the next 12 years applicants from all corners of the country made their way to Cardiff. The only exceptions were those attached to synagogues on the coast or by a river who were prepared to dip into colder waters nearer home, an equally acceptable form of *tevilah*.

At the same time as the immersion proposals were under consideration, the policy regarding a *get* was also changed. The nineteenth-century reformers had dispensed with the need for a *get*, considering a civil divorce sufficient. When it was reintroduced in 1946, there were several departures from the traditional regulations: the text was written with an ordinary pen rather than a quill, and on paper rather than parchment; the document was given by the man to the woman, rather than dropped into her hands, and there were no cuts made on it; witnesses tended to be anyone present in the building at the time, very often secretaries at West London. It was now agreed that the writing, witnessing and delivery of *gittin* would follow rabbinic tradition as part of the general move towards harmonisation of procedures. This meant that women could no longer be witnesses, although it did not prevent female rabbis being members of a *Beth Din* that permitted the *get* to proceed. Those who hoped that these changes might make the Reform document acceptable to Orthodox authorities were to be disappointed. Others regarded it as a development that was necessary for purely internal reasons and Reform's integrity as movement combining tradition with modernity.

An essential part of this role was Jewish education, both of adults and children. While many synagogues had their own adult education programmes, the Central Education Committee sought to boost these efforts with supplementary activities. It proved thorny ground: attempts at holding a residential study weekend in 1967 failed through lack of interest, while a bid to start a Jewish book club two years later also foundered. Their lack of success mirrored the widespread inertia with regard to Jewish learning among British Jewry as a whole. A small advance was made, though, in the wake of Lionel Blue's acclaimed keynote address on spirituality to the 1975 Conference. A religious renewal programme was established with a series of retreats organised by him. Most of the Central Education Committee's work concerned children's education: providing syllabi for religion schools, organising day seminars for teachers, refresher courses, as well as co-ordinating teachers' training courses with Leo Baeck College. Under the chairmanship of Rabbi Michael Goulston from 1967 it sought a more pro-active role, developing audio-visual aids and new methods of teaching. It sought to bring modern teaching theories into religion schools and utilise the best techniques available to promote Jewish learning. The series 'Jewish Heritage in Sight and Sound' was produced, while Ben Bardi's new Hebrew system, *Sha'ar Zahav*, became used in many RSGB religion schools, as well as ULPS ones. Following Goulston's death in 1972, the Michael Goulston Education Foundation was established in his memory to continue his pioneering educational work. The result was a series of publications on different themes for different age-groups during the next two decades, including *Prejudice* by Tony Bayfield, *The Jews of England* by Jonathan Romain, and *Mishnah Kadimah* by Andrew Goldstein. The following year saw the birth of the teachers' magazine, *New Ideas* under the joint editorship of Bayfield and Goldstein, which catered for both Progressive movements.

The enormous effort put into these and other educational activities helped raise the level of religion school tuition and instil a sense of enthusiasm that had highly beneficial effects. At a time when the religion schools of many Orthodox synagogues lacked properly trained teachers or curricula, those at RSGB synagogues enjoyed a high reputation in the wider Jewish community and became a reason for many to join Reform congregations. The name by which the schools were known was in itself an important indicator: not '*cheder*', with all its negative associations of ill-equipped rooms and poor standards; not 'Hebrew School', with its assumption that rote learning of the Hebrew language was the main aim; but 'Religion School', with its clear statement that the object was to become knowledgeable in the Jewish faith as a whole. It was part of the Reform ethos that girls were entitled to as much Jewish education as boys. They were encouraged to remain in classes till the age of 13 (rather than leave at 12, the traditional age of religious maturity for women) and it became natural in the great majority of Reform synagogues for them to graduate with a *batmitzvah* ceremony that was the same in every detail as *barmitzvah*. An increasing number of religion schools sought to encourage a longer period of Jewish education, extending classes till the age of 15 or 16. A number of synagogues also brought forward the age of commencing Jewish learning by establishing nursery schools.

The numerical growth of the Reform movement resulted in the increasing need for educational resources for a wide range of ages, and the realisation that voluntary efforts were insufficient to meet the demand. Some 4,000 children attended Reform religion schools. At the 1974 Conference an education department was proposed, along with the appointment of a full-time director of education. The idea was welcomed, but faced the immediate obstacle of funding, being totally beyond the already stretched budget of the RSGB. It would only be possible if financial backing could be found from external sources. Much time and energy was spent defining the exact terms of reference of an education department and submitting proposals. Happily the efforts coincided with an awareness elsewhere in the Jewish community of the need for a more professionally based approach to education and providing the means to finance it. In 1977 the then Chief Rabbi, Immanuel Jakobovits, had established the Jewish Educational Development Trust (JEDT) in the wake of research showing that only a third of all children in Anglo-Jewry received any formal Jewish education. When the RSGB was invited to participate and submit schemes there was some concern as to whether they would receive unbiased treatment, but it was agreed to respond positively and request funds to establish the education department. In the event, the JEDT made a grant of £12,500 for three years, while the L. A. Pincus Education Fund for the Diaspora, part of the World Zionist Organisation, awarded $25,000 for the work of Leo Baeck College Teachers' Training Department, which could be renewed in future years.

The position of Director of Education and Youth was widely advertised and of the 22 applicants who applied, Asher Amir was appointed in May 1980. He came from a senior post in one of Israel's leading teacher training colleges. It was a major step in the development of the RSGB, both a recognition of its success so far and a spur to future achievements. The Central Education Committee was disbanded after long and productive service, being replaced by a Department of Education and Youth. Its three major responsibilities were formal children's education, informal education and youth work, and adult education. A Council of Education and Youth was formed to set policy, while a management team carried out day-to-day work, assisted by specialist committees. The impending existence of the new department had also raised another issue: location. It was not possible to have the Education Department and the Teachers' Resource Library at the existing RSGB premises at West London. Alternative premises would have to be found.

Even more ambitious were calls for a Reform Jewish day school. The idea had first been raised by Rabbi Selvin Goldberg at the 1965 Conference, but was only taken up by a working party four years later under the chairmanship of Sigmund Schwab. Its interim report painted an overall reaction of apathy and disinterest: a questionnaire sent out with *Living Judaism* was returned by only four per cent of readers, and of these, only 30 per cent were in favour of a Jewish day school, and of that number only half said they would be prepared to send their own children to it. However, the idea was kept alive by the enthusiasm of Rabbi Dow Marmur and others, who held a series of meetings in north-west London for interested parents and sought the assistance of the Borough of Barnet. Although there were no immediate developments the goal itself was not abandoned and received added impetus at the 1977 Conference in the chairman's speech. In it, Jeffery Rose pointed out that with a third RSGB synagogue, Edgware, establishing a nursery school, the educational climate was changing and perhaps it was time to look again at the possibility of founding a Reform Jewish primary school.

The dramatic expansion in the RSGB's religious and educational activities was in response to and a consequence of the enormous growth of its membership. The 16 congregations which formed the ASGB in 1957 had been joined by another 14 by 1980. Many were in the north-west of London and the surrounding area – Southgate, Finchley, Radlett, Hampstead, Middlesex New and Wembley – reflecting the demographic concentration of London Jewry and the move to new settlements in the 'leafy outer suburbs' of Pinner and Bushey. But unlike some other synagogue organisations, whose membership was geographically limited, the RSGB also developed on the outskirts of London wherever Jews congregated, opening communities in Harlow, Bromley and north-west Surrey. Moreover, the RSGB maintained its role as a national movement with new synagogues in Blackpool, Cheshire, Newcastle, Southend and North Manchester.[25] Westminster enquired about affiliating to the RSGB in 1963 but decided to maintain its status as an independent Reform synagogue. However, in 1973, four years after the death of Reinhart, it agreed to make an annual donation to the RSGB for the use of the Reform *Beth Din* and other facilities. The establishment of provincial communities was sometimes more of an achievement than those in London, as there was often considerable prejudice against Reform. In areas where local Jewish social and cultural life was very tight-knit, joining a Reform congregation could be socially difficult and took much courage.

In most cases the congregations had arisen when a small nucleus of Reform-minded Jews had banded together, started to hold services and turned to the RSGB for help. Nurturing them was the responsibility of the Expansion Committee, giving assistance with the provision of prayer books, securing the services of guest preachers and lay readers, and sending committee members to advise on organisational matters. Despite the many flourishing synagogues that this led to, there were also instances of failure, usually because local support was insufficient. Approaches from small groups in Guildford, Middlesbrough, Gateshead, Ealing, Edinburgh and Barnet all ended inconclusively. In the case of

Nottingham, the nascent community approached both the RSGB and the ULPS for details of membership, but decided to join the latter. The Midlands Reform Synagogue Movement held services for two years, but failed to grow in size and merged with Birmingham Liberal Synagogue in 1970. The precarious nature of similar provincial ventures was epitomised by the small Reform group in Chelmsford, which disbanded in disarray after a survey of members showed that eight wished to affiliate with the ULPS, seven with the RSGB and five with the United Synagogue. A referendum of Harlow members, however, led to its joining the RSGB. A rare approach from an existing independent Orthodox synagogue came from that in Potters Bar which enquired about possible affiliation in 1964, but nothing resulted from it.

The Expansion Committee sometimes sought to establish a new congregation on its own initiative if it thought that a particular area had the potential to make one viable. Thus efforts were made to found a group in Highgate in 1967, and although this proved unsuccessful a similar attempt in Hampstead six years later gained a better response. An important consideration in such ventures was the impact they might make on established Reform synagogues in the vicinity. When the Committee canvassed views on starting a congregation in Swiss Cottage in 1959, it was informed by West London that it was one of the main sources of their own membership and they would not view any developments with favour. The project was dropped. At other times, neighbouring Reform synagogues were happy to sponsor new communities, such as the support of Radlett by Edgware. Occasionally, matters had to take their own course, as when several families formed the Wembley community even though it was part of the catchment area for Middlesex New.

Another consideration was the effect of new communities on Liberal synagogues, for while the RSGB reserved the right to respond to calls for assistance, it did not wish to clash needlessly with other Progressive synagogues. When attempts were made to establish a Reform group in Leicester in 1973, care was taken not to invite any members of Leicester Liberal Synagogue lest there be allegations of tempting members away. In the event the Reform group closed three years later. However, there was no avoiding a conflict of interests when two Liberal congregations transferred to the RSGB. Blackpool had been founded in 1947 and joined the ULPS. Yet many members soon found the gulf between their

Orthodox background and the Liberal form of service problematic. After contact with Rabbi Goldberg in Manchester, they decided that they felt more at home with the Reform approach and joined the RSGB in 1961. A similar pattern occurred in Southend, where many of the members had long been dissatisfied with the Liberal theology and transferred to the Reform in 1971. The friction this caused between the two movements was exacerbated by Liberal fears the following year that the new Radlett congregation might impinge on Stanmore Liberal Synagogue. In fact, for their part, the Liberals had held trial services in Edgware in 1968 close to the Reform synagogue there, which had led to the establishment of Stanmore. A courtesy notice had been sent to Stanmore about the Radlett project, although not to the ULPS itself. Addressing a council meeting on 23 January 1972, the chairman of the RSGB, Bernard Davis, indicated that the 'gentleman's agreement' of previous decades might have to be reassessed owing to new factors:

> The time has come to accept that most future development will take place in the relatively few high density areas of the Jewish population. Inevitably, therefore, Reform and Liberal synagogues will be established in adjacent areas. In our opinion experience has shown that more than one non-Orthodox congregation in an area results in their both becoming more readily acceptable.

His last point was a reference to the hostility from Orthodox communities to any Progressive congregation, which was combated best when there was a range of religious alternatives locally. It was noticeable, though, that long before this fracas, the RSGB had insisted on promoting Reform interests whenever an opportunity arose. Despite the many other joint committees that were established with the ULPS, such as those dealing with social issues or chaplaincy, the suggestion that the Expansion Committee hold joint meetings with its Liberal counterpart was rejected as far back as 1964, even though it was recommended by a joint meeting of the respective ministers. The attraction of the RSGB to some Liberal members was shown also in approaches made by North London Progressive and Liverpool synagogues. The former engaged in extensive negotiations in 1960 to have dual affiliation, while the latter considered leaving the ULPS entirely four years later. In the event, neither option was pursued, partly because the

RSGB made what were considered 'excessive demands' over the status of those who had remarried or converted through Liberal procedures.

The Expansion Committee's change of name in 1967 to the Congregational Development Committee signalled the role it had carved out in not only promoting growth but advising on financial management, youth activities, religious education, conducting services, drawing up a constitution and developing communal life in general. Under the leadership of Larry Ross, it also initiated seminars to deal with congregational issues, swap expertise and train new committee members. Its role was not limited to new communities but increasingly devoted to any RSGB congregation that needed assistance in a particular aspect.

The growth experienced by the RSGB was also evident within existing congregations, many of which saw a surge in their membership. The 190 members of North Western in 1934 grew to 500 in 1945, to 1,343 in 1958, and to 1,730 in 1962. The number of families belonging to Edgware during the same period increased from 30 to 54 to 320 to 800. Synagogues outside North West London also registered steady progress, with Wimbledon's 63 families in 1951 becoming 225 in 1961, while Sinai's 100 members in 1947 grew to 345 in 1965. The increases were all the more impressive because the size of British Jewry itself was declining. According to figures released by the Board of Deputies in 1979, the RSGB was the highest growth sector within the whole community, with a growth of 1.8 per cent at a time when overall synagogue membership within British Jewry decreased by 2.6 per cent. The RSGB had shown a net growth of three per cent, which, taking into account deaths and resignations, meant that the gross figure was in excess of five per cent – equivalent to 1,000 new members joining Reform synagogues a year in 1978. The RSGB's total membership stood at 21,000 adults.

It was vital for the RSGB to maintain effective communication between its ever-enlarging constituents. The resignation of Reinhart had meant that the *Synagogue Review* lost the editor who had guided it for the last 28 years. After a brief tenure by Sefton Temkin, responsibility for the magazine was transferred from West London to the RSGB in 1958 and Dr H. Bach of the North Western was appointed editor. A new format was adopted three years later, giving it a larger page and a more modern layout. Even more significant was that it was printed on lighter paper so as to be sent out with individual synagogues' own bulletins without incurring an increase in postage. Congregational news, once a major part of the *Review* was considerably reduced now that most synagogues were developing their own magazines. Instead there were articles of Jewish learning and book reviews, often written by leading Jewish figures world-wide such as Rabbis Bamberger, Freehof and Petuchowski. However, there was increasing dissatisfaction with its relevance to RSGB members and in autumn 1966 it was replaced by *Living Judaism* under the editorship of Dow Marmur. This was intended as a quarterly, which would have more popular articles and would act as a forum for discussion of issues relevant to the Reform movement. Its first issue covered the themes of education, Israel, marriage and conversion, Jewish–Christian relations and the nature of Reform Judaism. Those with a more intellectual bent found their needs answered by *European Judaism* which was founded the following year by Michael Goulston as a biannual journal to stimulate intellectual cross-currents amongst European Jewry. A method of publicising the RSGB's own activities was still needed, along with the news that the movement itself generated. This led to the publication, in October 1972, of *Inform*, initially as a monthly newsletter devoted to the work of the RSGB and selected news from the constituent synagogues. The existence of two periodicals emanating from the RSGB often led to concerns being expressed at council meetings over the costs involved, but the importance of keeping congregations in touch with each other and with developments at the centre was held to outweigh financial considerations.

The changing nature of the RSGB was very welcome but presented an enormous burden on the primarily volunteer administration. At the 1962 conference the honorary secretary, Sigmund Schwab, made a call for the appointment of a full-time secretary for the movement. Financial constraints postponed any immediate action, but it became increasingly obvious that a more professional approach was required to ensure that the office organisation functioned efficiently and to be available for the needs of congregations and committees. When the post was agreed upon and advertised in 1965, Schwab (now chairman) declared that 'the man we would want should have roots in the Movement, wide administrative experience, be mobile, a good speaker and persuasive'.[26] He would also need to be religiously committed; a rabbi could apply but would not necessarily be selected. The position was entitled 'General Secretary' – a suggestion that it be called 'Executive Director' having been rejected by a majority vote on the grounds that the nature of the post was to provide administrative back-up rather than to be responsible for policy, which was the prerogative of the elected leaders. Out of the four applicants, Raymond Goldman was selected and took up appointment in April 1966. He had been a member of North Western since he was six years old and had been thoroughly involved in all aspects of the synagogue – acting as a religion school teacher, youth leader, synagogue warden and lay reader. He had also become a prominent figure in the movement, being one of the founder members of YASGB and then its chairman in 1950. He had represented YASGB and later the North Western on the RSGB Council since then, and was at the time the synagogue's vice-chairman. He had been involved in several RSGB projects, and had been appointed convener of the *Synagogue Review* committee which was responsible for transferring it from West London to the RSGB.

On taking up his new post, Goldman stated that his ambition was 'to make RSGB articulate to its own membership and to build a movement of committed Jews' and to see it 'playing the full and influential role which was its right in Anglo-Jewry'.[27] The appointment was a historic milestone in the development of the RSGB. Not only was the position itself essential if the RSGB was to maintain its cohesion and continue its expansion, but in the personality of Goldman it found exactly the right person to help achieve this. His dedication to his task was such that two years later the executive suggested to him that in view of the number of weekend and evening meetings he attended he should not appear in the office on Mondays. Over the next three decades he worked tirelessly in a variety of areas: expanding the administration to meet the aims of a growing religious organisation; helping translate into action good ideas expressed in committee and bringing them to fruition; establishing greater links between the constituent congregations; building up a sense of RSGB as a movement; developing the publicity of the RSGB externally so that it became a familiar name both to its own members and to British Jewry at large; and promoting the religious principles upon which it was based – which sometimes included disabusing the Jewish public of misconceptions that arose from ignorance or that were planted deliberately. The move towards greater professionalism of the RSGB was both a sign of its progress and a spur to future expansion. An important ingredient in Goldman's success was his ability to work with the hundreds of different council members and synagogue representatives with whom he had contact. Equally impressive was the patience and tact he displayed throughout the thousands of hours of committee meetings he attended. Yet despite his decisive input into the movement, he always remained its servant, totally dedicated to supporting the decisions of the Council and implementing whatever was asked of him. There were no hesitations, therefore, in 1979 when it was decided to change his title to Executive Director – a move occasioned partly to bring the RSGB into line with the titles increasingly used by professionals in other Jewish organisations, and partly to match his title with the impending appointment of a Director of Education for the RSGB. There was no change in his actual job specification.

The variety of changes within the RSGB held particular concern for the northern congregations, which considered that their distance from London put them at a disadvantage. Although Conference was nearly always held in the north, most RSGB council and committee meetings took place in the south, which involved considerable inconvenience for northern delegates and often meant that their synagogues were under-represented. The northern communities faced the added difficulty that the majority were smaller in size than most of the London synagogues and they also encountered a more hostile response from the surrounding Jewish community, which increased their sense of isolation. The 1960 conference resolved to set up a regional council to address these problems and shortly afterwards members of Bradford, Sinai, Southport, Manchester and Blackpool met in Leeds. A Northern Regional Committee was established under the chairmanship of Roy Stroud, with the aim of co-ordinating youth and social activities among the northern synagogues, shortly afterwards changing its name to the Northern Provincial Committee. This in turn promoted greater awareness of their needs within the RSGB. Two tangible results were that it was decided to appoint a third vice-chairman who would always come from the provinces – the first incumbent being Mrs Louisa Librowicz of Bradford – while the RSGB council meetings were changed from late afternoon midweek to Sundays so as to facilitate better attendance by provincial representatives.

Another northern concern was the lack of rabbinic leadership, as several congregations were too small to afford a rabbi and thus suffered from the lack of religious guidance. The Association of North-Eastern Reform Synagogues was formed in 1967 by Bradford, Leeds and Newcastle for the purpose of jointly employing a minister. Their efforts were eventually rewarded with the appointment of Rabbi Henry Brandt. There were still periodic complaints of the lack of interest shown in the North by the RSGB, and requests for rabbis and executive members to visit more often. However, by 1970 it was decided to disband the Northern Provincial Committee as it was felt that the divisions between the metropolis and the provinces had been removed. Much of this was due to the efforts of the general secretary whose visits to congregations answered many of their concerns, and whose ongoing relationship with their council members helped make them feel part of the RSGB family. Moreover, with the greater professionalism of the RSGB administration, problems that had previously been brought to the Northern Provincial Committee were now taken direct to the RSGB office, and often dealt with more speedily.

With the increasingly active role being assumed by the Congregational Development Committee, it was felt that northern synagogues could be more efficiently served by a similar local committee. As a result the Northern Development Committee was set up in 1975 to assist local congregations. Among its innovations was an annual Northern Seminar weekend, the first of which took place later that year in Blackpool and was attended by nine communities. The presence of several enthusiastic rabbis serving northern synagogues and seeking closer links with each other led to the re-establishment of the Northern Regional Committee in 1980.

The work of the RSGB itself became increasingly devolved to specialist committees that drew widely on the talents within individual congregations. Mention has already been made of the Central Education Committee and the Congregational Development Committee, as well as the results of the Publications Committee, which oversaw the production of pamphlets along with RSGB journals. The vital role of the Youth Committee will be dealt with below, as will the Israel Committee. The long-established Music Committee maintained and extended its music library, helping to make music available that matched the Reform liturgy and Sephardic Hebrew pronunciation. It acted also as an important resource for congregations seeking to vary and improve both instrumental and choral music. Newer committees reflected the RSGB's concern to confront national and international political issues. The Race Relations Committee was formed in 1968 against a background of increasing tension in Britain over levels of immigration and the integration of newcomers. Spearheaded by Edie Friedman, it focused on the need to combat racial prejudice and to promote harmony among the different elements in society. Four years later it changed its name to the Community Relations Committee in an attempt to broaden its horizons. It concerned itself with Jewish–Christian relations, dialogue with the growing number of other religious and ethnic groups and social action. Projects were developed, such as teaching English to immigrants, recording books on tape for the blind and monitoring local press to rebut racist tendencies. It also urged congregations to become involved with local community relations councils.

The plight of Soviet Jewry had been appreciated by members of the RSGB long before it became a communal byword. As far back as 1963 Selvin Goldberg had raised the issue in Council. As the situation of Russian Jews worsened, the RSGB was in the forefront of efforts on their behalf. In 1969 the chairman, Harold Langdon, received national attention when he led an RSGB delegation to the Russian Embassy and presented a resolution passed at Conference urging the Soviet government to give Jews freedom of religious and cultural expression, permit the reunification of families separated by the Second World War, and allow those seeking to emigrate to go to Israel or elsewhere. His request to meet the Soviet ambassador was refused, although he was seen by another official. The large number of Reform synagogues with groups working for Soviet Jewry resulted in the creation of a Soviet Jewry Committee in 1974 under the chairmanship of Eva Mitchell, to co-ordinate the efforts and disseminate information. In this respect the RSGB was far ahead of other sections of the community, and the committee organised visits, letter-writing campaigns, public protests and lobbying of MPs. Some of this work had also been undertaken by the RSGB Association of Women's Guilds, which linked the guilds in all the constituent synagogues. Established in 1962 under the leadership of Ray Braham it quickly became involved in all aspects of the work of the RSGB, including Jewish adult education and social issues. Among its many valuable contributions was its annual fund-raising for the Leo Baeck College Scholarship Fund. At that time the £1,000 it provided each year amounted to ten per cent of the RSGB's share of the College expenses. It was later to raise equally handsome amounts towards youth development. Of all the groups within the RSGB, it was the one which had the most wide-ranging involvement in the movement's activities. It also proved a training ground for many future leaders, including the first woman to become chairman of the RSGB, Eva Mitchell, who assumed office in 1973.

Another important facet of the Reform movement, although not technically a committee of the RSGB, was the Jewish Joint Burial Society (JJBS). It was clear that the Hoop Lane cemetery used by Reform synagogues in London – shared with them by West London – was inadequate for their future needs, while a funeral insurance scheme was also required, particularly one in which rights could be transferred when congregants moved from one RSGB synagogue to another. In 1964 the RSGB established a committee to plan the provision of burial and cremation facilities, although in the event the congregations involved decided to form an independent burial society, JJBS, four years later as a company limited by guarantee. They were Edgware, Finchley, Middlesex New, North Western and South West Essex. They acquired rights of burial at the Cheshunt cemetery, which belonged to the Western Synagogue, an independent Orthodox congregation. It was not a commercial enterprise but a service to RSGB congregations at the smallest possible cost. After initial loans had been paid off, surplus profits – largely through fees paid by non-members – were used for charitable purposes and funded many projects within the RSGB, including Leo Baeck College. By 1980, 20 out of RSGB's 29 synagogues participated in the JJBS.

The vast expansion of activity within the RSGB had also led to the Communications Study Group being formed in 1972. It was deployed not only to assist communication between the RSGB and constituent synagogues, but also to improve members' own administrative procedures. Meetings were arranged for synagogue secretaries to discuss matters of common interest, and similar gatherings of treasurers were organised. In 1975 the Research and Demographic Unit was established as an advisory body for the executive. Its brief was to carry out feasibility studies, pinpoint priorities and make recommendations. Its first task was to examine the possible role of a development rabbi in the light of Jewish population distribution. Although the unit did not enjoy a long life, it was indicative of the realisation that the RSGB needed to look beyond day-to-day affairs and develop a long-term strategy. Concern over the proliferation of committees and the responsibilities they enjoyed led to 'General Guidelines' being issued in 1977, both to improve their efficiency and to maintain control over them. The guidelines reminded them of the need to abide by the RSGB constitution, to keep proper minutes, that decisions involving the Council or synagogues needed to be discussed in advance with the chairman of the RSGB, that decisions involving expenditure in excess of an agreed budget had to be discussed with the RSGB treasurer before action was taken. The RSGB Council itself began to change its procedures in response to the growing demands made of its time. Not all committee reports were taken at each meeting and in 1978 'Question Time' became a regular item on the agenda as a way of raising matters of information or immediate relevance. Three years earlier another small but significant addition had been introduced when it was decided that instead of a prayer each meeting should start with a *d'var torah* – some words of Jewish teaching – as part of bringing the heritage of Judaism and religious issues into the forefront of the Council's and the executive's work. Moreover it was not to be limited to rabbis, but delivered by lay members as well, who could be equally committed to Jewish study – the first being given by executive member, Alf Strudwick, in November 1975.

Changes were also made regarding Conference to take account of the great increase in the number of people attending, which had reached 200 by 1968. Until then it had always been held in the close vicinity of an RSGB congregation, visiting a different one each year, serving both as a morale boost for the community concerned and providing a synagogue for Sabbath services. That year saw the first time when size dictated that it move to a large conference-style hotel – the Palace Hotel in Buxton, which was to be the home of many future annual gatherings before rising numbers necessitated a switch to the Majestic Hotel in Harrogate. By 1977 attendance had grown to 300 people and the format of Conference also needed altering. Committee reports could no longer be discussed effectively in plenum and were instead discussed in three separate commissions. Congregational reports – the number of which had also multiplied – were now presented together and analysed for changing trends. At the same time the religious character of Conference was given added weight by the introduction of an *Oneg* on Friday evening and a *Torah* breakfast early on Sabbath morning. The absence of an organ at services reflected the more traditional form of worship common to many congregations. These changes built on the decision taken some 15 years earlier to separate the administrative and spiritual aspects of Conference. Whereas previously business meetings had taken place on Saturday afternoon, they were now limited to Friday afternoon, Saturday evening and Sunday morning, with the Sabbath devoted exclusively to lectures and discussions on religious topics, as well as the services themselves.

Although some welcomed the way in which the RSGB was forging ahead on many fronts, others were concerned at the financial implications. As was seen in the previous chapter, the burden of RSGB expenditure fell entirely on the constituent congregations, some of which had their own financial difficulties and even those that did not became alarmed at the extra costs they were being asked to fund. In 1958 Manchester voiced particular concern over the financing of Leo Baeck College and the World Union. In fact, the College costs were outside of synagogue assessments and were raised by a different appeal, while the WUPJ contribution was made voluntarily by individual congregations. However, the debate resulted in an agreement at Conference that year that while synagogues were obliged to pay whatever amount was determined by Council, it was subject to an upper limit of three per cent of their income from membership subscriptions. Two years later the ever-increasing work of the RSGB led its treasurer, Bernard Davis, to suggest the formal change to an annual percentage 'as shall be determined from time to time by the Council'. This raised fears of too much central control over individual synagogue budgets. It 'would turn us into a United Synagogue', declared Edward Henriques of West London. Protest came also from South West Essex, whose compromise resolution was passed, raising the maximum amount to five per cent of congregational income.[28] This ceiling was soon reached, standing at 4¾ per cent by May 1963, but the next time the executive proposed a higher assessment it was rejected by Council in May 1965 and the budget had to be trimmed to stay within the existing limits.

A sub-committee was set up to examine the RSGB's financial difficulties and to see how they could be most equitably shared by all constituents. Among the problems was the paucity of funds available for loans to congregations, usually towards building programmes. This was exacerbated by some existing loans that had not been repaid, such as the £500 long-overdue from Brighton. Nevertheless, the RSGB felt obliged to respond in some way and took money from its own General Fund to make modest loans to Finchley, Harlow, Newcastle and South West Essex. However, Blackpool's request for assistance to pay off its bank overdraft of £10,000 had to be refused. One solution attempted was a Development Committee established by Robert Henriques later that year, with the aim of raising £70,000 for the Capital Fund to cover projects over and above the regular activities financed by the assessments. However, his subsequent illness meant that plans were aborted and one of the most pressing problems of the movement – its inability to fund major developments and invest for the future – had to wait several years before being addressed seriously. Sporadic efforts at fund-raising – such as a gala performance of the film *Fiddler on the Roof* – proved disappointing, while a proposed RSGB lottery failed to see the light of day. Another result of the investigation was the decision to change the method of assessment back to a per capita rate, with synagogues paying an amount in respect of each full member as determined by Council and approved by Conference. It necessitated audited membership figures and was set at 25s. 0d. when it was introduced in the fiscal year 1966/67.

The new system proved satisfactory for most congregations, but some still voiced concerns, although usually relating to their own problems. Brighton were experiencing particular difficulties. They had completed a building whose cost had been grossly under-estimated and their fund-raising appeal had been unsuccessful as it coincided with the period of the Six Day War. From mid-1968 their attendance at council meetings evaporated and questions were raised over their commitment to the RSGB. Efforts at involving Brighton more in RSGB affairs – such as by holding a council meeting there in October 1969 – did not produce any positive response. Negotiations over the debt still owed to the RSGB failed to reach a solution in that Brighton questioned both the amount outstanding and the time limit in which to repay it. Apart from the strain on RSGB finances, this presented the potential problem of being a precedent for other synagogues to challenge and reduce their financial obligations. Subsequent meetings between the executive and Brighton delegates also ended in deadlock. By July 1972 it was reluctantly felt necessary to act and a resolution was passed that through continued non-payment Brighton had by default ceased to be a constituent member of the RSGB. There then ensued considerable debate as to whether the RSGB should start litigation against Brighton to recover its debts, totalling £5,000. In the end it was felt that it would be morally wrong to take a synagogue to court and that no action should be taken. For their part, Brighton felt that they had been treated unjustly and their rabbi, Erwin Rosenblum, joined the Liberal rabbinic body. It was the first, and only, time that a congregation was expelled from the RSGB, and although they returned to the fold 12 years later, it caused considerable heart-searching and distress at the time.

An earlier crisis, also financially based but more quickly resolved, had arisen with Manchester. The 1950s had witnessed many disputes with the RSGB, ranging from opposition to its fiscal arrangements to resistance to the establishment of the Reform *Beth Din*. At root was Manchester's insistence on a degree of autonomy so great as to prove incompatible with being part of a wider movement. It went far beyond the north–south divide that was an additional factor in the conflict. It culminated in Manchester's resignation in December 1958 – a threat made in previous years but never carried out. In a rash of complaints, Manchester criticised the RSGB for its high level of assessments, its acceptance of Liberal proselytes and generally 'moving to the left'. These accusations were rejected by the RSGB, but to no avail. However, perhaps because of its position as the second-oldest Reform synagogue in the country, there was clearly a will to seek a reconciliation. Manchester sent two representatives to attend the June 1959 conference as 'observers' and there were soon meetings to discuss terms of readmission. The RSGB insisted that 'constituent synagogues are expected to abide by the decisions taken at Conference and Council meetings' and would not negotiate changes to the budget until Manchester had rejoined. They did so in January 1961, and Conference that year was held in Manchester as a gesture of reconciliation.

No such breakdown in relations occurred with other congregations, but several experienced difficult periods. At that same time, both Southport and Glasgow were in arrears to the RSGB, while in 1972 Sinai's financial woes led them to request a 50 per cent reduction in assessments for five years. In response Manchester proposed a 50 per cent reduction in the assessments of all provincial synagogues in view of what it claimed was the reduced services they received from the RSGB by reason of their distance from the metropolis, citing as examples the lectures, youth activities and teachers' training courses. When this was discussed in Council, the general secretary pointed out that provincial synagogues received an equal, if not disproportionately high, amount of RSGB effort and attention, and the request was withdrawn. Hendon was more concerned with cutting the RSGB's own budget and proposed that Conference be biennial, and that *Inform* and *Living Judaism* be discontinued and replaced by an annual report. Despite the temptingly substantial savings these measures would have entailed, Council rejected them as inimical to the progress of the RSGB.[29]

The ongoing problem of several synagogues being in arrears over their assessments led to a reform of the method used. In 1974 it was agreed to combine the past and current system by a three-year arrangement under which the RSGB would levy a £2 per capita rate, with additional sums required being raised by means of a 2.7 per cent levy on subscriptions. The 1975 budget also contained a new feature – a one per cent contingency reserve for items of exceptional expenditure that might arise or for unexpected inflation. Until then the RSGB had always faced the problem that it had no access to funds other than those specifically allocated in the previous year's budget. Nevertheless, great difficulties were faced in 1977 when an inflation rate of 15 per cent hit synagogue finances very hard, obliging the RSGB treasurer to prune down the budget substantially and ask only for an extra 0.2 per cent increase in the percentage rate and none in the per capita rate. The problems in the national economy continued to have a deep impact on RSGB finances. In 1980 Wimbledon expressed concern at the 'financial irresponsibility' of the RSGB. It questioned the role of the RSGB as a central body with a life of its own, rather than being simply a forum in which constituent synagogues exchanged ideas, and declared that it would be reconsidering whether it wished to remain part of the movement.[30] At the same time a similar motion was brought to Conference from six of the northern congregations (Sinai,

Sha'arei Shalom, Cheshire, Manchester, Southport and Blackpool):

> Believing that the development of Reform Judaism in Great Britain must take place principally at grassroots level by the strengthening of our constituent synagogues, the Annual Conference of RSGB views with concern the continual and continued growth of the Budget of the Central Organisation, which increasingly threatens the limited resources of individual synagogues.

The motion went on to propose that future capitation assessments be limited to the 1980 budget, and that there also be no increase in the subscription percentage. Any additional expenditure requirements would have to be derived from other sources. Another conference motion from Middlesex New called for a reduction in the proposed budget, as did a similar one from West London. After a tempestuous debate the West London motion was withdrawn and the other two were defeated by a substantial majority. However, this was much more than an annual argument over figures. It was an issue of philosophy and the future direction of the movement. The six northern communities were correct in their perception about the expanding role of the RSGB and the increasing responsibilities of the movement. Yet at the same time the constituent synagogues always retained total control – collectively, if not individually – through Council and Conference. If their motion had succeeded it would have put the RSGB in a financial strait-jacket and forced the cancellation of many of its programmes, including the new Education Department, and cut-backs in its staff. Autonomy was still a bedrock principle. It was not so much a case of centralisation, but of professionalisation of the movement. Almost 20 years earlier, the then chairman, Richard Norton, had told delegates: 'My greatest disappointment so far is my manifest failure to weld the Council into a body which thinks RSGB instead of thinking "my local Synagogue".'[31] Five years later Sam Rainsbury lamented the same point: 'Whereas we should have been a Movement, we had become a collection of synagogues.'[32] Gradually, however, the obvious success of the RSGB, and the benefits it brought to its constituent members, persuaded them to 'think RSGB' and, even more importantly, fund RSGB.

One of the greatest areas of pride was the youth movement, the

YASGB. As well as assisting local synagogue groups develop, it promoted a host of supplementary activities, including a football club – somewhat incongruously named 'YAS United', a baby-sitting service and a communal *seder* (for which a special YASGB *hagaddah* was produced). A junior section for those in the 13 to 16 years age-group was established in 1960 and quickly proved successful, both at local level and centrally. The following year saw the establishment of the YASGB Society (for Jewish Study and Action) which met weekly at West London both to continue Jewish learning and to offer practical social help. It was also intended as a bridge between the YASGB and the RSGB, and a means of keeping the involvement of those who might otherwise have left the movement. A less positive feature was the decline in the involvement of ministers, previously always present in great number at residential weekends and camps. When attention was drawn to this in Council, it was explained that the reason was the increased workload facing ministers, with demands from new congregations, the *Beth Din* and prayer book revision. Some compensation was found in the unofficial secondment to the YASGB of Rabbi Marim Charry, assistant minister at West London, who was a regular participant at leadership courses and study programmes. In fact, the YASGB became an important source of future ministers and an increasing number of rabbis were 'home-grown', having been brought up in the movement and progressed through the youth groups and then on to Leo Baeck College. In 1962 alone, it was reported that four former YASGB members had entered the college that year. The importance attached to the YASGB was shown not only in the funding the RSGB gave it, but by involving it in RSGB affairs, having an automatic place on Council and often being responsible for leading sessions at Conference, such as the *Oneg*. In turn the YASGB sometimes acted as the 'soul of the RSGB', protesting vehemently against the emigration of leading rabbis because of the poor reception afforded to them in Britain, as was discussed above.

The first of the famous YASGB summer camps took place at Carmel College for two weeks in August 1962, transferring the following year to Frensham Heights with which the camps became associated for many years. They provided a unique experience of fun, Jewish awareness and interaction that was to leave an indelible mark on a whole generation of participants. The first camp – organised by rabbis Marim Charry and Sonny Herman – consisted of 39 children (14–16 years) and ten managers. The numbers attending quickly multiplied, with youngsters also coming from Europe and Israel. The success of the holidays led to similar ventures for both older children ('Summer Worth') and younger children ('Spring Frensham'), as well as a winter holiday in England and tours of Israel. By 1972 the holidays had expanded into a major operation, with 280 youths participating in five separate ventures, all centrally organised. By 1979, there were 500 children on eight trips. Weekend programmes also continued throughout the year, acting both as a valuable link between the different synagogue groups, and an opportunity for those who were members of congregations without a viable youth club to meet other Jewish children.

Youth work was not necessarily the priority of all synagogue councils despite the many successful groups. At the 1960 conference Neville Sassienie, then chairman of the YASGB and described as 'the Angry Young Man of the movement', gave an impassioned speech, criticising the lack of interest displayed by some communities and the tendency to put 'more emphasis on new buildings rather than the quality of people who frequent those buildings'.[33] Following recommendations made by a special sub-committee investigating the YASGB, a Standing Youth Committee was established in 1964 to help the body. Its brief was to advise on its spiritual life, general planning and administration, as well as maintain a link between the YASGB and its parent body. It was a timely move as the YASGB had changed considerably since its formation, especially in the age range to which it appealed. Whereas its members were originally over 21 years, it now attracted much younger members. The format of the YASGB was changed, with junior groups catering for the 13–16 age-range, and senior groups for those aged 16 and over. Expanding numbers and groups meant a need for greater secretarial assistance. Whereas previous help had come from a part-time secretary of West London's Religion School, in 1965 the RSGB engaged a part-time secretary specifically for the YASGB.

The next three years proved a difficult time owing to lack of leadership and the collapse of some local groups. It was not just a YASGB phenomenon, but part of the changing youth culture in the 1960s generally. In the immediate post-war period the YASGB membership had been largely in the early to middle twenties age group. Young people had little money to spend and were attracted to the modest programmes and idea of renewal that the YASGB had to offer. By the 1960s those in that age-group were much more affluent – a fact recognised by the commercial world, which actively courted them – and they moved away from the YASGB into more sophisticated pursuits. Indeed, the Liberal youth organisation, the FLPJYG – with which the YASGB maintained intermittent contact and occasionally held a joint weekend together – disintegrated entirely at this time. A YASGB commission, chaired by Sassienie, was undertaken to look at the structure and direction of the movement. One result was the launch of a section for those aged 18 and over, Reform Jewish Action, which was involved primarily in social service work, particularly housing and community relations among the immigrant population of Paddington.

Another, more far-reaching outcome was the call at the 1968 conference for a professional youth organiser. The idea had actually been mooted much earlier, with a similar resolution being passed by the 1960 conference but lack of funds preventing any progress. In June 1969, however, John Kay was appointed the RSGB's first youth development officer. Not only was he a professional youth worker, previously serving as a warden of a youth and community centre in Berkshire, but he was immersed in the movement. His father, Sam Kay, had been chairman of the Settlement Synagogue, while he himself had been involved in the YASGB for several years and had been a Frensham leader. Grants from the Jewish Youth and Tercentenary Fund (JYTF) and the Association of Women's Guilds meant that the intended special 'youth levy' surcharge of ten per cent of annual assessments for one year could be reduced to five per cent. As with its general secretary, the RSGB's first youth officer turned out to be an inspired choice, channelling enormous energy and enthusiasm into both the youth groups and synagogue councils. Tangible evidence of the new confidence could be seen in the in-house magazines produced by both junior (*Info-Dig*) and senior (*Focus*) groups. The religious underpinning of the YASGB was also revived, with the introduction of the annual 'Ten Days of Penitence Scheme' and the publication of a YASGB prayer anthology, *Kol Chaverim*, edited by Michael Gluckman and Jonathan Romain. External recognition of the successful work being performed by the youth division came in a grant awarded by the government's Department of Education and Science in May 1970. Kay's appointment coincided with another influential development, the publication of the YASGB Commission's report, 'Towards The Seventies'. Amongst the many recommendations subsequently adopted was that the age of synagogue membership be lowered to 18 and be at a reduced rate to encourage young adults to join and feel part of the community. Synagogues were also encouraged to involve their young people by inviting them to serve on sub-committees. In addition, youth groups should be directly represented on synagogue councils and given full voting rights, both to maintain communication between them and to show the youth that their voice was valued.

The frequent YASGB residential weekends took place in a variety of conference centres throughout the country. Many felt that permanent premises owned by the YASGB and tailored to its needs would be more suitable. In 1972 the junior groups launched the 'Home of Our Own' campaign, seeking to raise £5,000 towards the purchase of a youth centre for weekends away. Urgency was unexpectedly added to the campaign when Davidson House in Skeet Hill, Kent became available the following year. 'Skeet', as it was called, was already known to hundreds of YASGB members for whom it had long been a popular venue for weekends and who had enjoyed a friendly relationship with the ghost that reputedly occupied the 250-year-old premises. Thanks to the support of Alan Summers of Edgware, the campaign became an RSGB project, changing its name to the 'Home in View Appeal' with the object of raising half the sum required. The RSGB agreed to purchase the lease of the house, jointly with Brady Settlement, from the freeholder, the JYTF, for the sum of £50,000. Although Manchester objected to the purchase because of the location of the house, the 1975 Conference voted in its favour and the purchase was made later that year.

After various structural improvements were completed, Skeet was officially opened on 5 September 1976. Indicative of the enthusiasm for the new home – and of future problems with it – was the fact that it was designed to sleep 42 people and the first YASGB booking contained 70. Martin Chaplin (West London) was elected chairman of the Skeet Management Committee and had the unenviable task of supervising its everyday running from afar and dealing with its financial implications. The main problem was that not enough bookings were being made by RSGB groups

– partly because of its small size and partly because of the advantages of having varied venues. Some adult groups also used it – such as the RSGB executive – but attempts to market Skeet more widely in the movement failed to produce sufficient interest. By September 1978 Chaplin was recommending to Council that the RSGB sell its half-share. He argued that not only would it release capital for other youth projects, save management problems, and pre-empt possibly large financial commitments for repairs in the future, but RSGB would still be able to use its facilities just as much – or, more pertinently, just as little. Council rejected this proposal as defeatist so soon after its acquisition, but the problems continued, exacerbated by the difficult economic situation in the country at large, with bookings falling and some of the original pledges for the 'Home in View Appeal' not being honoured. Eventually the cost of supporting Skeet became too much of a burden and in 1982 the RSGB surrendered its lease back to the owners of the freehold, the JYTF, which was then taken up by Brady. It was a sad episode, initiated for the very best of motives and with high hopes, but ultimately involving much needless energy and substantial costs. Although the YASGB still went there for splendid weekends, for many the once-magical name of Skeet had become tinged with regret as the home won and lost.

By this time other major changes had taken place within the field of youth. After four successful years in office John Kay resigned as youth development officer to move on to a new career in July 1973. His successor was Jenny Freedman (later Jenny Wiseman), who was previously a youth worker at Brady. Two years later she left to start a family of her own and was replaced by David Jacobs, a professional youth worker for Essex County Council who had grown up at Manchester Reform Synagogue and who, like his family, had been highly involved in the movement. In 1977 his work was augmented by the arrival of Chaim Lederman from Israel, as the first *shaliach* to the RSGB. Funded by the Jewish Agency, Lederman's work included adults but involved considerable attention to the youth groups, organising programmes, stimulating interest in Zionism and arranging individual and group trips to Israel. His arrival had been awaited with some trepidation by a movement once indifferent, if not hostile to, Zionism, but his warm personality and infectious enthusiasm made his two-year stay so successful that the Jewish

Agency, in an unusual reversal of its normal policy, extended the appointment for a third year. On his departure back to Israel it was clear that the experiment had proved highly beneficial and he was followed by a succession of *sh'lichim* on a two-year cycle.

A Standing Youth Conference had been proposed to Council in mid-1978 as a means of bringing together once or twice a year all those involved in youth work and to create a forum for exchange of views on present and future needs. Some doubted if it would serve any practical purpose, but a trial meeting was agreed. It did not take place for another year but by that time there was a major problem to discuss owing to the decline of senior groups, with widespread apathy and a shortage of leaders to run central events. The voluntary executive system – whereby the youth ran their own affairs with very little external help – which had worked so well was now in disarray. Another major issue was the decision of YASGB to change its name to Reform Synagogue Youth (RSY). The new name marked the new ideological direction of the youth groups and the Zionist bent that had been encouraged by Lederman. It also marked the transition from being a youth organisation that linked separate clubs to a youth movement that had a clearly defined and unifying identity. It was a dual identity – Reform and Zionist, committed to the religious life and Reform approach for which the RSGB stood, and committed to a strong relationship with the land of Israel and the people of Israel. One of the recommendations emanating from the Standing Youth Conference meeting in September 1979 was that the youth work should be linked with the proposed new Education Department, together forming the Department of Education and Youth. At the same time David Jacobs announced his resignation after four successful years in order to return to local authority youth work. He was not replaced immediately, partly because of financial constraints facing the RSGB but also because the changes within the YASGB and the new Education Department meant re-evaluating the nature of the position. Instead Ian Stern (Finchley) was appointed as the first RSY national organiser for an experimental period, and it was determined that the new appointee would be designated a youth field worker rather than youth development officer.

The falling age-range of the YASGB meant that there was an increasing problem of how to keep in touch with those over 18 years. For those at university, there was the Joint Chaplaincy

Commission with the ULPS which had a list of 450 Jewish students, with eight Reform and Liberal rabbis acting as spare-time Progressive chaplains to 12 universities. Nevertheless it was a very passive organisation and did not initiate any programmes, either centrally during the vacation or at individual campuses. Some funding was given to the appointment in 1969 of a full-time Orthodox Jewish chaplain to Oxford University who was committed to serving Progressive students too, but little developed from it. The need for a much more dynamic approach was not fulfilled until 1971 when the Progressive Jewish Students Commission was established under the leadership of Andrew Oppenheimer. It helped set up Progressive groups at seven universities to supplement the Jewish Societies, which tended to be either Orthodox-based or religiously indifferent. It also promoted study days and weekends during the vacations, and, utilising the talents of many student rabbis at Leo Baeck College, attracted a good number of religiously committed Progressive Jews. Some went on later to become involved in the World Union for Progressive Judaism Youth Section (WUPJYS). The latter had received a boost in 1964 when Lionel Blue had been appointed religious director of the European Board, with special responsibilities for the Youth Section. As well as establishing and supporting communities in Europe, he helped set up young adult groups in several countries – particularly the Netherlands, Belgium and Germany – and forged links between them through a series of joint conferences. He encouraged British young adults to participate too, involving the YASGB in a work camp in Paris in February 1966 and bringing over students from Leo Baeck College as guest lecturers. Although it was very hard to keep up the same momentum after Blue returned to Britain three years later, WUPJYS maintained its activities on a less ambitious scale through voluntary and part-time leaders. Indeed it not only proved a useful training ground for student rabbis to practise their sermons and study groups, but also became a pathway for many thinking of entering the rabbinate.

Relations between the two parent bodies, however, were less easy. As in the previous decade many in the RSGB felt hostile towards the World Union because they felt that its leadership was largely in the hands of the Liberals and because they feared that joint membership of WUPJ associated the two movements together. Some were concerned also about implied links with the

American Reform movement, whose radical policies were felt to be far removed from the RSGB's own religious stance. After a vigorous debate the 1959 conference voted by 32 to 19 to resign from the Union, although individual synagogues were still free to affiliate in their own right, as did Cardiff. Within a year the situation had changed, as the Liberal influence lessened when the World Union's headquarters were transferred from London, where it had been housed at the Liberal Jewish Synagogue, to New York. Moreover the European Section was formed, and many felt that the RSGB had a responsibility to help the several small European synagogues, most of which were as traditionally minded as the RSGB. Edgware proposed that the movement rejoin the Union, a motion which was carried at the 1960 conference by 45 to 11. A resolution the following year to disaffiliate again was substantially rejected and prompted the passing of a resolution that 'a decision by Conference to become affiliated to any organisation of synagogues shall be effective for a minimum of three years and shall not be the subject of any resolution during that period unless Council decides to the contrary'.

The holding of the Twelfth International WUPJ Conference in London in July 1961 brought Progressive delegates from 23 countries and helped involve the RSGB in its work again. Ties were further cemented through Lionel Blue's appointment as religious director of the European Board. In 1969 the European Board offices moved from The Red Lodge, home of Lily Montagu, to 34 Upper Berkeley Street, premises owned by West London, a development that also assuaged the remaining fears of some within the RSGB; Jeffrey Newman, then a student at Leo Baeck College, was appointed part-time youth director. The once ambivalent relationship had turned into a firm commitment. The wider outlook espoused by the RSGB was also responsible for the decision of the World Union in 1972 to affiliate to the World Jewish Congress, which worked on behalf of Jewish interests in all lands and was recognised by the United Nations as an advisory body. The increasing involvement of the WUPJ with Israel, which once would have led to more cries for resignation, was backed fully by the RSGB. In 1975 the Union joined the World Zionist Organisation and moved its headquarters to Jerusalem, both as an act of identification with Israel and to strengthen the voice of Progressive Judaism there. The following year many RSGB leaders were present in the Negev for the dedication of Yahel, the first Progressive *kibbutz* in Israel, which had been sponsored by the World Union.

The change in attitude to Zionism – from hostility to indifference in the 1940s and 1950s – turned into fervent support in the 1960s. It was epitomised by an article in the *Synagogue Review* by Robin Hyman urging the RSGB to 'show more recognition of the remarkable fact that out of all the Jews in the last two thousand years it is we who have lived in the age which has brought the re-establishment of the State of Israel'.[34] The first RSGB tour to Israel took place in March 1965, attracting 120 participants and proving a great success. Shortly afterwards the Friends of Progressive Judaism in Israel was established as a way of maintaining contact with sister congregations in Israel and assisting them in the struggle against the antagonism they faced from Orthodox groups. As a result of discrimination by various state institutions, the RSGB threw its weight behind the WUPJ's negotiations with the Israeli government to remove these restrictions. They were informed by the Prime Minister, Ben-Gurion, that this would happen 'as soon as an Israeli rabbi was rabbi of a Progressive congregation in Jerusalem'.[35] In the event, the latter occurred long before the former, and the political power of Orthodox factions in the Knesset enabled them to deny the religious rights of the Progressives for several decades. The RSGB also took action on behalf of Progressive immigrants to Israel, eliciting a letter from Moshe Sharett, then chairman of the Jewish Agency, promising equal assistance to all immigrants including those converted by Reform and Liberal rabbis.[36]

The danger posed to Israel's survival in 1967 not only electrified British Jewry but had a great impact on the Reform movement. The crisis coincided with that year's Conference, which took place in Blackpool from 2 to 4 June amid mounting tension in the Middle East. The resolution passed unanimously typified the reaction of British Jewry at large and ended any lingering speculation that might have existed about the RSGB's commitment to Israel:

> The RSGB deplores the aggression of Israel's neighbours, threatening the peace of Israel and of the World. We confirm our wholehearted and brotherly solidarity with the leaders and the people of the State of Israel. We reiterate our prayer for peace and we further pledge our moral, material and

> physical support for the defence of Israel's territorial sovereignty, international rights and all measures necessary to safeguard her inhabitants. We call upon each and every one of our fellow Jews in all our constituent synagogues to express this feeling of solidarity through devout prayer and personal support of all local and national efforts to guarantee the security of Israel and its right to continue to play its constructive role among the family of nations. We ask everyone to make immediate and urgently needed financial contributions in keeping with the need of the hour and in the finest tradition of Jewish generosity.

YASGB itself played a major part in setting up the Jewish Youth Organisation Emergency Committee for Israel. Following the euphoria generated by the Six Day War there were a variety of measures strengthening ties with Israel. An RSGB Israel Commission chaired by Rabbi Henry Brandt in 1968 urged the establishment of a Progressive Jewish settlement in Israel and recommended that Leo Baeck College students spend a year of their studies in Israel. In 1969 an exchange programme between Israeli and British youth was initiated, an RSGB Israel Committee was formed, as were several local ones by individual synagogues. One of the few departures from the enthusiasm for Israel was an article by Lionel Blue in *Living Judaism* pointing out the sufferings of the Arabs and the danger of nationalism leading Jews to become persecutors.[37] Although it aroused considerable controversy, it gave prophetic voice to a concern felt by some, later to be echoed by many others. It was also an early step in the path to Jewish–Muslim dialogue and led to a conference between Jews, Christian and Muslims initiated by Blue in Berlin the following year, which was to prove the first of many subsequent ones.

The RSGB's open support for Israel led to improved relations with Zionist bodies it had previously shunned. Members were encouraged to support the Joint Palestine Appeal, later known as the Joint Israel Appeal (JIA). In return the RSGB was assured that donations would not go to institutions inimical to Progressive interests, while the chairman of the Council of Reform and Liberal Rabbis (see below) became one of the honorary presidents of the Appeal in July 1968. However, it was decided not to support its *Kol Nidre* Appeal as the idea of linking one of the most spiritual occasions in the Jewish calendar to thoughts of money was not acceptable to most congregations. The first JIA Mission to Israel sponsored by RSGB and ULPS to involve participants in the work for Israel and to enthuse their communities on their return took place in 1974. Negotiations were also held with the Zionist Federation (ZF) but met with less success owing to the domination of the Orthodox viewpoint in the latter. When asked if Leo Baeck College graduates would be accepted as teachers in ZF schools, or if the curriculum would reflect the pluralist nature of contemporary Jewish life, it was unwilling to make any concessions. Moreover, the RSGB had reservations about the democratic basis of the ZF and worries over the political in-fighting between its different factions. After several years of fruitless discussion, Pro-Zion was established together with the Liberals in 1978 as the political voice of Progressive Judaism. Creating a separate but related body also solved the additional problem of a religious body joining a political organisation, a move which would have prejudiced its charitable status. In this respect, Pro-Zion mirrored the American Reform Zionist group, the Association of Reform Zionists of America (ARZA). The first chairman was Arthur Hill and although it failed to attract the 1,000 members for which it hoped, it did affiliate with the ZF and represented Progressive interests in its affairs. Two years later it joined the International Federation of Reform and Progressive Religious Zionists (ARZENU), the international body linking all Progressive groups, with members in Canada, South Africa, Australia, the Netherlands and the United States.

The 1973 Yom Kippur War prompted major fund-raising appeals amongst RSGB synagogues, while Raymond Goldman was in charge of the administration of one of London's two blood donation centres. Problems of a different kind surfaced in the renewed 'Who is a Jew?' debate in Israel the following year. Under Israel's Law of Return, Jewish status was awarded to anyone claiming to be born a Jew or converted to Judaism by a rabbi. The Orthodox parties, whose votes were need to form a coalition government, wished to change the law to Orthodox criteria: Jewish by birth proven through the matrilineal line, or through conversion by an Orthodox *Beth Din*. The RSGB chairman, Eva Mitchell, sent a strongly worded letter to Prime Minister Yitzhak Rabin pointing out that it was not only an issue of accepting the validity of Reform conversions but had much wider implications of the Israeli government conferring second-class status on the rabbis and members of non-Orthodox synagogues throughout the world: 'No one can or would question the right of the Knesset to legislate for Jews in Israel, but [recent proposals] imply a ruling by the Israeli government against the authenticity of a form of Judaism sacred to millions of Jews... Israel NEEDS and Israel HAS the united support of Diaspora Jewry. We trust that Israel will do nothing to damage or divide that support.'[38] In the event the status quo remained unchanged, although further attempts to amend the Law of Return and redefine Jewish status were mooted when Menachem Begin was elected to office in 1977, and a similar protest was made.

Criticism of some aspects of Israeli policy did not imply any less support for Israel as a whole. This was manifest in November 1975 in the wake of the infamous United Nations resolution equating Zionism with racism. The RSGB Council made plain its rejection of the move and its continued regard for Israel: 'We totally reject the attempt of Israel's enemies spuriously to differentiate between Jew and Zionist. Those who owe allegiance to Judaism and those who owe allegiance to Israel are one. We again pledge our every support in whatever way our energies or influence may be of service, in the face of this new attempt to isolate Israel from the World Community.'[39]

A dramatic example of that pledge came exactly a year later when several RSGB leaders went to the Negev to be present at the dedication of Kibbutz Yahel, the first Progressive settlement in Israel and sponsored by the World Union. The ceremony took the form of carrying a *Torah* – one of the Czech scrolls housed at Westminster Synagogue – under a *chuppah* to the ark in the *kibbutz*'s synagogue. Equally striking was the message sent by Prime Minister Rabin: 'With the establishment of this *kibbutz*, the pluralistic and spiritual life of Israel is enriched. It marks a new and perhaps historic threshold of Reform Judaism's involvement in the actual life of the Jewish State... I hope that Yahel will become a beacon of light for Reform youth everywhere.'[40] Another historic event had already occurred a few months earlier when, during a visit to England, Israel's President, Professor Ephraim Katzir, attended West London for a Friday night service. Speaking afterwards to the congregation, he declared:[41]

> I have come here in order not only to express my thanks to all of you, to the Jews in Great Britain, who expressed their

> solidarity with Israel, but also to indicate that we have to all be united in these difficult times. As President of Israel, just as I am supposed to represent every Jew in the State of Israel, I want our home in Jerusalem to be a home for every Jew in the Diaspora, for Orthodox Jews and for Reform Jews and for Liberal Jews.

A further milestone took place in February 1978 at the Twenty-ninth Zionist Congress in Jerusalem. The RSGB was represented by Bernard Davis, then a vice-president. For the first time in its 80-year existence, the Congress recognised the pluralism of Judaism, and a resolution was passed calling for equal treatment for every Jew regardless of his religious identification. It was not just the result of a sense of fair play but reflected the enormous contribution of Reform communities in Britain and elsewhere to Zionism, whether financially, politically, through immigration, or in other ways. It was also evidence of the effective political influence that Pro-Zion and other constituents of ARZENU were beginning to exert.

Two long-term related developments should be noted. In 1976 the Israel Action Group was founded under the chairmanship of Dow Marmur to stimulate consciousness of Israel among the congregations. It promoted a variety of activities and lectures, as well as sponsoring the Special Spinal Rehabilitation Unit at Tel Hashomer Hospital. Apart from being a worthy cause in itself, it was intended as a way of channelling funds to Israel from those who had reservations about sending money via the JIA and not knowing for what ventures it would be used, but who were willing to finance particular projects in Israel. It reflected the growing unease with the problems being experienced in the West Bank and Gaza, and doubts over contributing to government developments in those areas. A total of £26,000 was raised and used to purchase a special X-ray machine. The RSGB itself failed to raise the £100,000 target it set for assisting Kibbutz Yahel, but did raise sufficient money to provide the shelving, furniture and books for a library there. Some individual synagogues had their own campaigns, for instance West London, which equipped Yahel's dental clinic. The second development, mentioned earlier, was RSGB's agreement to have a *shaliach* seconded to the movement, funded by the Jewish Agency. His task was to heighten the awareness and involvement of the RSGB, organising programmes in England as well as leadership seminars and tours in Israel for adults, children and students. The arrival of Chaim Lederman in August 1977 for an experimental two years became a permanent arrangement with a succession of *sh'lichim* that is still continuing. Although the *sh'lichim* gave added impetus to the Israel activities of the RSGB, their presence was more a symptom than the cause of the movement's now strongly Zionist character.

Good relations with fellow Progressives in England were sometimes harder to maintain than with those in Israel. It has already been shown that there were many whose desire to distance themselves totally from the Liberals made them oppose any suggestion of co-operation in areas of mutual interest lest they be seen as associated together. Others wished to act jointly whenever possible, with the added hope that they might one day merge. In a seminal article on the two bodies Rabbi Charles Berg outlined both what they shared and where they differed. Although he criticised the excess of logic and reason the Liberals seemed to display at the cost of certain traditions, he concluded with a warning against Reform feelings of superiority or disdain: 'Let us not look at the Liberals as the Orthodox look at us.'[42] Many outside the RSGB and the ULPS were simply puzzled as to their separate existence. During his visit to Australia and South Africa, Leonard Mendel, then chairman of the RSGB, found that he was met everywhere by the question 'Why are there two bodies of Progressive Jews in Britain...and what is the difference between them?'[43]

The closeness of the two movements led to occasional discussions as to a possible union – such as calls for unification by the Liberal leadership in 1969 – though always without a positive conclusion. More fruitful were particular projects that it was decided to undertake together. Following a meeting of Reform and Liberal ministers on the theme of social issues, it was agreed in May 1962 that rather than form their own committee, the RSGB would join the ULPS Social Issues Committee and turn it into a joint venture. It was responsible for raising funds for the Algerian Relief Appeal and protesting about the Fascist menace in Britain. The Joint Chaplaincy Commission was established in 1962 to serve Progressive Jewish students at universities. The ULPS first sent an observer to the RSGB conference in 1963, after which exchange of observers became commonplace. The following year the honorary officers of both movements met and agreed a wide range of joint projects. The two publications committees should meet to exchange ideas, as should the respective expansion committees. The youth groups should not merge but should encourage joint activities. The Joint Ministers' Conference recommended a merger between the *Synagogue Review* and the *Liberal Jewish Monthly* but the RSGB executive rejected this because it felt it important to maintain separate magazines, even though they might choose to syndicate articles.

The close relations between the ministers was an inevitable result of their co-operation in many areas, such as chaplaincy, social issues and the World Union, but most of all because they were so often dealing with similar issues in the congregational work. This applied also to their relations with the wider Jewish community and to British society at large. The advantages of being able to speak with a combined voice on matters of mutual concern led to the establishment in April 1968 of the Council of Reform and Liberal Rabbis. The executive consisted of four members, two from each movement, with the position of chairman alternating between RSGB and ULPS ministers. The first chairman was Werner Van der Zyl (West London), with John Rayner (Liberal Jewish Synagogue) as vice-chairman. The Council had a consultative role rather than an executive one, and was limited to public comments only on matters in which there was unanimity between the two movements. It meant that the Council laboured under too many constrictions to take the forceful role in British Jewry to which it might have aspired. However, it was a clear signal of co-operation, while it also provided a useful figurehead for any Jewish organisations that wished to include a representative of non-Orthodox Jewry alongside the Chief Rabbi as one of its patrons.

The most important link between the Liberal and Reform ministers was that after 1964 they trained side by side for the rabbinate at Leo Baeck College. Talks between the honorary officers of the ULPS and the RSGB in 1958 led to a motion at Conference two years later endorsing the plans for joint administration of the College. Despite objections from some quarters that 'it would lead eventually to fusion between the two movements', it was passed by a substantial majority. The change of heart was due to three factors. First, it was a matter of principle by those who wished to see as much co-operation in as many areas as possible. Second, there was a fear that if the College remained only RSGB-sponsored, it would not be able to survive. It would be impossible to attract sufficient students or a high calibre of teachers if there were two Progressive seminaries competing with each other. Third, by 1963 there was an acute financial crisis and extra funding was urgently needed. Although the College had become a company limited by guarantee in 1959 and was technically independent of the RSGB, the entire financial burden would have fallen on its shoulders. The annual contribution that the ULPS would make – £9,500 in 1964 – to match that given by the RSGB provided the vital injection of finance. The first Liberal student entered shortly after negotiations were completed, and from then on all students shared exactly the same course and received the same *semichah*. Representatives of the ULPS became part of the college administration and Liberal ministers joined the teaching staff. The financial arrangement was maintained until 1971 when the Liberals wished to reduce their input because of their smaller size compared to the RSGB. A new formula was devised of 'two to one' which was partially based on the per capita membership of the respective movements. Part of the five years' training involved taking services in small communities without a minister, and students were allocated to congregations from each movement so as to gain experience of both. Indeed the compatibility of approach that was engendered was shown in the fact that after graduation some students served synagogues different from the movement in which they themselves had grown up, while some rabbis switched between the two movements when taking new positions. Students also came from abroad, with some returning after ordination to serve Progressive communities in their homeland, and others remaining in Britain.

In 1966 Van der Zyl was appointed president of the College in recognition of his work in co-founding it and steering its affairs thereafter. When, three years later, the College celebrated its *bar-mitzvah* he was able to report that in its first 13 years it had produced 18 rabbis, of whom 11 were serving British congregations and the other seven were in Europe, South Africa and the United States. Evidence of the College's growing international reputation had already been seen the previous year when the renowned scholar Samuel Sandmel, Professor of Bible and Hellenistic Literature at the Hebrew Union College in New York, agreed to act as visiting principal of the College for a year.

Another landmark came in 1974 when Rabbi Dr Jonathan

Magonet was appointed full-time lecturer in Bible, becoming the first College graduate to join the teaching staff. At the time the College was under the leadership of Rabbi Dr Albert Friedlander. A further development that same year was the appointment of Hyam Maccoby as the College's first full-time librarian. It reflected not only the considerable library that was being built up, but the College's rapid development from very humble origins into a major institution of Jewish learning. Its success in producing rabbis who were able both to relate to the congregants they served and to enthuse them to become involved in communal life – not skills associated with all Anglo-Jewish ministers – was commented upon by those outside the movement: 'Anyone going about the community is bound to be struck by the impact made on their congregations by the young, lively and active Reform and Liberal ministers.'[44] By 1976 the College had produced its fiftieth rabbinic graduate, while its enormous influence on the movement was indicated by the fact that all but four ministers serving RSGB synagogues were from the College. Whereas almost 20 years earlier its future had seemed uncertain – the College 'is in being, but the plant is frail and could easily wither'[45] – both the ULPS and the RSGB now depended on its existence.

A significant aspect of the College was its decision to train women for the ministry. Female students wishing merely to attend lectures had been admitted since the College began, but in the mid-1960s a few women applied to study for the rabbinate. After numerous internal debates, the College declared that 'there was no objection in principle to train a woman rabbi, but the College would not be responsible for her placement in a rabbinic post after ordination'.[46] The decision had been preceded by a paper prepared by Rabbi Dorfler in which he had pointed out:[47]

> Progressive Judaism has failed pathetically in the last hundred years, both in having neglected the intensive education of women in Judaism... and in not having attracted them to the Ministry as a spearhead in the drive to invigorate Judaism within and without the Jewish home. Let us open the gates now, and after the destruction of our great, learned European Jewry, strengthen our ranks by recruiting gifted Jewish women to the Institutes of higher learning.

The initial female applicants did not complete the rabbinic course for personal reasons, but in 1975 Jacqueline Tabick became the first woman rabbi to graduate and then served as associate rabbi at West London. The College's fear that congregations might be less welcoming to women rabbis and that they might not be able to find jobs did apply in some cases. Women graduates usually only gained placements after male colleagues had acquired positions, while some communities stated openly that they would not consider a woman applicant. The struggle for their full acceptance turned out to be more a case of educating congregations than of educating women ministers. The situation improved, gradually but not totally, as more women became ordained and proved their worth both intellectually and pastorally. It reflected the difficulties women experienced in many other areas of professional life in Britain, and was to have parallels with the calls for and against women priests in the Church of England 20 years later. Meanwhile the College was continuing its other main function of training teachers for religion schools and awarding certificates in religious education. The College also began to receive applications from those who wished to pursue Jewish studies without entering the rabbinate. In response a three-year diploma course was developed in 1977. By 1979 the student body had grown to 23, making the premises – three of West London's Religion School classrooms, an office and a library – totally inadequate. The possibility of a new home had been aired some years earlier but was abandoned because of lack of funds; now the search was begun in earnest.

The growing co-operation between the RSGB and the ULPS during this period in the College and other areas was in marked contrast to the increasing gulf between Reform and Orthodoxy, primarily due to the hostility of the latter. The attitude was typified by the keynote lecture delivered by Rabbi Dr Wolf Gottlieb of Glasgow to the 1956 Conference of Anglo-Jewish Preachers, the professional body for Orthodox ministers. He described the Reform movement as 'A meeting place for assimilationists and mixed marriages, nourished by the urge for self-justification... They have launched a campaign of "soul-snatching", using the very "unorthodox" means of bribe, deception, and pretence in order to confuse the mind of the uninformed.'[48] The obvious growth of Reform communities caused considerable concern among Orthodox rabbis. It manifested itself particularly in attacks on Reform's status policy regarding conversion and divorce: 'It is unbelievable to contemplate that the Reform authorities are so savage in their intolerance of Jewish Law as to be blind to the heartaches caused by their attitude.'[49] The result was many instances in the next decade of petty discrimination against Reform synagogues and their rabbis. A lecture on apartheid due to be given to the Hasmonean School was cancelled because the speaker, Rabbi Ungar, was a Reform minister; the United Synagogue issued a directive to all its congregations not to let halls for wedding receptions to couples married in a non-Orthodox synagogue; the Chief Rabbi's Court vetoed a proposal for Bournemouth (Orthodox) Hebrew Congregation to share a chapel at a communal cemetery with Bournemouth Reform – there would have to be two chapels; in Cardiff the Reform synagogue found that local *kosher* caterers were being discouraged from dealing with it; in Edgware the Orthodox rabbis refused to co-operate within the confines of the Council of Christians and Jews; in Newcastle the Orthodox synagogues prevented the Reform community from being admitted to the Newcastle Representative Council.

Such incidents were unpleasant and divisive, but even more serious was the self-styled 'important announcement addressed to all rabbis and religious institutions throughout the Diaspora' by Chief Rabbi Brodie. It was an open attack on the Reform *Beth Din*: 'All their actions are in sharp contradiction to the laws and principles of the *Torah*, causing havoc in the personal and family life of our brethren in the Diaspora. Of course, their actions have no validity and are completely worthless, while their documents are mere scraps of paper.'[50] Although directed officially at rabbis abroad, its main intention was to frighten off nominally Orthodox Jews who might be tempted to turn to the Reform for matters of status because of its more flexible and sympathetic approach. It was the start of a co-ordinated campaign against the Reform movement by the Chief Rabbinate. Whereas previously the policy had largely been to ignore the existence of the RSGB and to treat it as irrelevant to Jewish life, it was now seen as posing too great a challenge to be denied. As Brodie told the Conference of European Orthodox Rabbis that same week, 'The time has come to go over to the offensive. We have been on the defensive for too long and too much. We have got to assert ourselves.'[51] Despite some calls for a forceful counter-blast, the RSGB reaction was 'to take all this calmly, though with great regret, as a counsel of spiritual despair on their part, not a sign of strength'.[52] The chairman of the Assembly of Ministers, Charles Berg, advocated patience as little would be achieved by rancour: 'We cannot convince them and they cannot convince us.'[53]

The struggle intensified with the publication of a pamphlet on Jewish marriage and divorce published by the Chief Rabbi's Court in March 1962 and written by *Dayan* Morris Swift. Labelling Reform as 'the subversive element in our midst', he declared that Reform divorces and conversion had no validity in Jewish law.[54] This second attack provoked considerable anger. The Assembly of Ministers issued an immediate public refutation defending the sacred character of its marriages and upholding the decisions of the Reform *Beth Din*. Lay members of the RSGB threatened legal action for libel against the Chief Rabbi's Court, and there was a private meeting between Van der Zyl and Brodie. The Chief Rabbi said that copies of the pamphlet had been exhausted and would not be reissued. He also acknowledged the high level of instruction of Reform proselytes and hinted that if *tevilah* was observed recognition might be granted, although no explicit statement was made or personal commitment given. He suggested that all cases of divorce be referred to his own Court.[55] In reality, nothing changed as a result of the meeting, and friction continued in other areas, such as the United Synagogue's refusal to allow a Reform rabbi to participate in what was intended as a 'representative service' for British Jewry on Israel Independence Day. It was during this time that the 'Jacobs Affair' became so acrimonious. The ostracism of one of the most gifted United Synagogue rabbis, Louis Jacobs, because he espoused the findings of Biblical criticism while still maintaining a traditional outlook and practice, was typical of the approach dominating the United Synagogue. The once 'broad church' not only had narrowed its parameters to the exclusion of many, but was also engaged in combating its own internal heresy.

It was hoped that a more harmonious atmosphere would prevail with the appointment of Immanuel Jakobovits as Chief Rabbi in 1967. Whilst severely disagreeing with the Reform approach ('an extreme tragedy because it is organising a defection from Jewish Law'), he admitted that many Jews would have been lost to the community but for Reform, and that 'the Reform Movement has helped to stem the drift from Judaism'.[56] He also hoped that its constructive features could trigger an outpouring of creative thinking in the traditionalist camp, in the same way that the Karaite heresy – a movement that arose in the eighth century and challenged the rabbinic interpretation of Judaism – had led to the writings in reply of Sa'adia Gaon and Ibn Ezra. In private meetings with Reform leaders before his installation he indicated that although there would be differences on matters of religious interpretation and that no joint services would be possible, there would be wide areas in which Reform and Orthodox could work together. He saw no reason why platforms could not be shared at meetings by Reform and Orthodox rabbis, and that he himself would go anywhere to teach and would consider it a privilege to lecture at Leo Baeck College. In this respect he was no doubt influenced by his previous ministry in New York, where Orthodox–Reform relations were much more cordial, if only because of the numerical superiority of the latter. However, his stated good intentions tended to dissipate once he became more re-acclimatised to British Jewry, where Orthodoxy still dominated synagogue membership and he felt obliged not to antagonise his own constituency.

In some areas there was a closer rapport. The Chief Rabbi gave a lecture at Leo Baeck College in 1968, and consulted the Assembly on the issue of organ removals with regard to legislation being introduced to Parliament. His office also tacitly accepted the *de facto* validity of most Reform marriages when it confirmed that the children of marriages 'which could have just as well taken place in an Orthodox synagogue...could become members and indeed be married in an Orthodox synagogue'.[57] Although this dismissed unions in which a Reform divorce, adoption or conversion was involved, it also contradicted deliberately misleading reports that a Reform marriage *per se* endangered the Jewish status of subsequent children. However, the RSGB was disappointed with the lack of real progress in communal unity, and the high expectations felt initially were increasingly dampened. When Jakobovits refused to read a psalm alongside Rabbi Hugo Gryn at a memorial meeting for the Munich Olympics' victims organised by the Board of Deputies, it provoked a stinging rebuke:[58]

> 'To build bridges of understanding across factional differences, to leave no stone unturned...in efforts at communal reconstruction' were the avowed objectives of

> Rabbi Dr Jakobovits before taking office. Five years later, as Harold Langdon has said, 'the builder of bridges has proved to be a demolition expert'... Perhaps we should take heart that the leaders of Orthodox Jewry are convinced that its whole edifice in this country might collapse if Reform and Orthodox rabbis recited psalms together. In fact we would rather see a strong Orthodox Judaism sufficiently confident in itself to be tolerant, sufficiently creative to enter into dialogue... Like a man in a boat boring a hole under his own seat, Rabbi Jakobovits seems unable to recognise that in today's world, whether he likes it or not, religious Jews are all together in the same boat fighting against indifference and secularism... Surely it is time for the Chief Rabbi to start translating earlier words into present deeds – to show some of the courage in leadership he once promised the Anglo-Jewish community.

The response sought by the RSGB was not forthcoming. The description of Reform as 'self-liquidating. It will not prevail' by the Chief Rabbi in a later interview with the *Jewish Chronicle* showed both a continued antipathy to and profound misunderstanding of the changing nature of British Jewry.[59]

Despite the public bitterness, there were some positive moves 'behind the scenes'. The Teff Committee – chaired by Solomon Teff, then president of the Board of Deputies – had brought all sides of the community together in friendly discussion in the mid-1960s. Representatives of the Chief Rabbi, the RSGB, the ULPS and the Spanish and Portuguese in the mid-1960s met intermittently. On taking office, Jakobovits agreed to continuation of the Committee, provided that complete secrecy was maintained. A vehicle of Reform–Liberal communication was a committee led by Judge M.A.B. King-Hamilton formed in 1966 in the period between Brodie's retirement and Jakobovits' appointment. It comprised RSGB and ULPS members and was intended to formulate a strategy for asserting the independence of the Progressives from Chief Rabbinate. It was known as the Joint Standing committee on Anglo-Jewish Relations and was particularly active during the Clause 43 debate, which will be discussed below. Orthodox–Progressive relationships also became tense in 1973 when efforts were made to have the chairman of the Council of Reform and Liberal Rabbis appointed as the second

Jewish president of the Council of Christians and Jews (CCJ). It was a repetition of earlier attempts in 1965, 1968 and 1971, and reflected the growing stature of the RSGB in general and its heavy involvement in the work of the CCJ in particular. On each occasion the matter had been abandoned because of the 'far from cordial' reaction of the Chief Rabbi at the time and the lack of support from Jewish members of the CCJ executive. This time, too, the proposal was vetoed, although by way of compromise a Consultative Committee on Jewish–Christian Relations was established to discuss all matters addressed by the CCJ as well as other areas. Its convener was to be the immediate past chairman of the Council of Reform and Liberal Rabbis (at that time Gryn) and it would meet at the home of the Chief Rabbi. Other participants were the *Haham*, the presidents of the Board of Deputies, the Anglo-Jewish Association and the United Synagogue, as well as the chairmen and the general secretaries from the RSGB and ULPS. It was envisaged that the committee would run for two years and then be reassessed, but its proven value as a forum for direct exchange of views in which all participants met on equal terms meant that it became a permanent institution. Although it meant yet another defeat for a CCJ Progressive president, the outcome was perhaps of more value in terms of communal co-operation than the original proposal.

The right of the Reform voice to be heard and listened to was also becoming apparent at the Board of Deputies. By 1968, 17 of the 24 RSGB synagogues sent representatives to the Board, and were active in all aspects of its work. That same year, the Board's constitution was changed to make the chairman of the RSGB, rather than the president of West London, the certifying authority through which Reform synagogues obtained membership of the Board. In 1971, 23 out of 118 committee places were filled by Reform deputies. Yet there was also concern at the second-class treatment accorded to Reform and Liberal members. In 1969, for instance, there was a series of perceived snubs: at a special session of the Board on education at which the Chief Rabbi spoke, no Progressive minister was allowed on the platform; no Progressive deputy was included in the Board's delegation to the Prime Minister's Conference in Israel; there was no unified service at the Board's vigil outside the Iraqi Embassy; and the Board's campaign defending *shechitah*, which had been supported fully by the RSGB, culminated in a pamphlet citing the Chief Rabbi and the

Haham as the 'Jewish Ecclesiastical Authorities of Great Britain'. As Sigmund Schwab commented in his report to Conference that year: 'Although we became numerically stronger, we cannot yet see real evidence that the Board is the truly representative body of Anglo-Jewry that it claims to be. Time and again the Movement is snubbed (or at best smoothed over with honeyed words) in matters concerning us.' He was adamant, however, that the RSGB should remain part of the Board and work for change from within.

The attempt to bring change came in a resolution to amend Clause 43 of the Board's constitution. It stated that in all religious matters the Board should be guided by its Ecclesiastical Authorities, which were the Chief Rabbi and the *Haham*. Congregations which did not accept their jurisdiction would not be affected by this guidance. A suggestion in 1966 that the Assembly of Ministers be included as an Ecclesiastical Authority had been rejected by the honorary officers of the Board as unlikely to receive sufficient support. Three years later, and with the Council of Reform and Liberal Rabbis now established, it was requested that the Board consult with the Council as well as its existing Ecclesiastical Authorities. When the Board offered to do so but only in matters 'specifically' affecting the Progressives, this was rejected as applying to so few instances that it would nullify the amendment. A long series of meetings ensued in which attempts were made to try to find a compromise formula acceptable not only to the Progressives but also to Orthodox delegates who wished to resist any wording that would imply recognition of the religious authenticity of the Progressives or place their rabbis on equal status with Orthodox ones. A variety of wordings were employed that were regularly rejected by the Board. The mounting crisis led to an emergency meeting of the RSGB Council together with all RSGB deputies. Whereas some urged patience and continued negotiation, others demanded forthright action if the amendment was blocked, including withdrawal from the Board. The general view was that the president of the Board, Alderman Michael Fidler, was being over-cautious and that great pressure against change was being exerted by the Chief Rabbi.[60] Ironically, the more Orthodox elements felt that the Chief Rabbi was not being forceful enough and accused him of 'erratic conduct' and 'indecisiveness'.[61]

On 26 July 1970 an amendment to Clause 43 was put forward

concerning those not under the jurisdiction of the Board's Ecclesiastical Authorities, stating that 'the Board shall consult with such groups of Congregations or their respective Religious Authorities on religious matters concerning them'. The idea that Progressive 'Religious Authorities' had consultative status was still unacceptable to many Orthodox deputies. The amendment was passed by 129 votes to 70, but failed by four votes to achieve the two-thirds majority necessary to change the constitution. According to West London deputy, Felix Mitchell, the vote showed that the dispute was not between the Progressives and the main body of the community, but between 'the right-wing Orthodox and the rest of the community'. According to the Board's constitution, the amendment could be accepted if it was proposed again at another meeting by its Law and Parliamentary Committee and passed by a simple majority. After further pressure the president, who had supported the original amendment, withdrew his backing and declared that it would not be reintroduced. A joint emergency meeting of the RSGB and the ULPS Council agreed to withdraw from the Board by 31 October 1971 if one of their amendments had not been accepted. The Progressive deputies demonstrated the seriousness of their threat by holding a rival meeting to the Board's monthly meeting in July 1971. Following more negotiations the honorary officers of the Board introduced a slightly altered version of the amendment to Clause 43, stating that 'the Board shall consult with those designated by such groups of Congregations as their respective religious leaders on religious matters in any matter whatsoever concerning them'. The new wording sought to allay Orthodox fears that the position of the Chief Rabbi was being undermined, but acknowledged the Progressives' own religious rights. At the meeting on 24 October 1971, the amendment was passed by 228 to seven and the constitution was duly changed. Attempts by the Chief Rabbi to reopen the debate and change the wording failed. Some 80 deputies from the Federation of Synagogues and the Union of Orthodox Hebrew Congregations resigned in protest, although most rejoined in 1973 following assurances that the guidance of the (Orthodox) Ecclesiastical Authorities before the amendment had not been impaired.[62]

Once the controversy had subsided RSGB deputies continued their active participation in the Board's affairs. In 1975 Lord Fisher, then president of the Board, attended the RSGB

Conference. Closer co-operation was shown by the Board's insistence that the community must take united action when fighting discrimination against Jewish students, and refused to give way to those Orthodox groups who wanted the names of Progressive Jews or Progressive organisations deleted from the Board's publicity. In 1977 the chairman of the Council of Reform and Liberal Rabbis was included in the deputation from the Board which presented a Loyal Address to the Queen on her Silver Jubilee. In 1979, for the first time, a Progressive candidate, Harold Langdon (deputy for the RSGB) stood for the position of vice-president; although he was not elected the number of votes cast in his favour was well above the total Progressive voting strength and indicated the cross-denominational support he received. The same elections saw three Progressive Jews elected as committee chairman when previously there were none: Aubrey Rose (Defence), Philip Mishcon (Information) and Harold Langdon (Public Relations). The RSGB was playing the full role in the Board of Deputies that befitted its growing role in British Jewry at large.

That role was manifest in other communal spheres too. In 1968 five of the honorary officers of the Jewish Welfare Board were members of Reform synagogues, while most of the past presidents were from either the RSGB or the ULPS. A similarly high involvement, although not to the same degree, could be cited in other welfare organisations, as well as cultural bodies such as the Jewish Historical Society of England, the Jewish Museum and the Council of Christians and Jews. The same applied to groups such as the Association of Jewish Ex-Servicemen (AJEX), B'nai Brith and the Anglo-Jewish Association. The lack of participation in Zionist circles was now a relic of the past, and the leadership lists of the Joint Israel Appeal or Magen David Adom showed a strong Reform representation. 'We can state quite simply', said Harold Langdon, 'that our contribution to the leadership of Jewish communal life has been much greater than our membership would suggest.'[63] The RSGB Council had specifically encouraged this by forming the Anglo-Jewish Relationship Study Group in 1965 to report on ways of enhancing the RSGB's public profile and influence. It had issued a series of recommendations: all synagogues should be fully represented at the Board of Deputies and co-ordinate with each other on matters of common interest; the RSGB should inform government departments, ecclesiastical authorities and other bodies of the RSGB's existence; AJEX should be urged to invite a Reform minister to attend all official functions. Van der Zyl added that the RSGB should request all national Jewish organisations which automatically included the Chief Rabbi and *Haham* as patrons to give similar recognition to the Reform rabbinate. It was important not only for Reform members to contribute to the wider community, but for the wider community to appreciate the Reform contribution being made.

NOTES

1. See Appendix 1.
2. *Synagogue Review*, Aug. 1958, p. 310.
3. RSGB Conference, 1964, Minutes; at Reform Synagogues of Great Britain Archive, the Sternberg Centre for Judaism, London.
4. *Synagogue Review*, Nov. 1964, p. 54.
5. Idem.
6. Quoted the *Synagogue Review*, Sept. 1961, p. 21.
7. RSGB Council, Minutes, 28 Nov. 1971; at Reform Synagogues of Great Britain Archive, the Sternberg Centre for Judaism, London.
8. *Prayers for the Pilgrim Festivals* (1965), p. 1.
9. *Living Judaism*, Winter 1969, p. 104.
10. *Forms of Prayer* (1977), Vol. 1, p. 292.
11. *Forms of Prayer* (1977), Vol. 1, p. 296.
12. *Forms of Prayer* (1977), Vol. 1, p. ix.
13. *Forms of Prayer* (1977), Vol. 1, p. 256.
14. *Forms of Prayer* (1977), Vol. 1, p. 260.
15. *Forms of Prayer* (1977), Vol. 1, p. 161.
16. *Forms of Prayer* (1977), Vol. 1, p. 65.
17. Jonathan Magonet, *The New Reform Prayer Book* (1988), p. 5.
18. The *Jewish Chronicle*, 4 Nov. 1977.
19. The *Jewish Gazette,* 7 Oct. 1977.
20. Michael Curtis, 'The Beth Din of the Reform Synagogues of Great Britain', in D. Marmur (ed.), *Reform Judaism* (1973), p. 130.
21. Idem.
22. For more detailed information see Jonathan Romain, *The Reform Beth Din: its influence on the growth of the Reform Movement and its significance for Anglo-Jewry* (1992).
23. Norman Cohen, 'Trends in Anglo-Jewish Religious Life', in J. Gould and S. Esh (eds), *Jewish Life in Modern Britain* (1964), p. 46.
24. RSGB Council, Minutes, loc. cit., 11 March 1979.
25. See Appendix 2 for a complete list of RSGB congregations and their dates.
26. RSGB Council, Minutes, loc. cit., 3 Oct. 1965.
27. RSGB Council, Minutes, loc. cit., 20 Feb. 1966.
28. RSGB Conference, Minutes, loc. cit., 22 May 1960.
29. RSGB Council, Minutes, loc. cit., 8 April 1973.
30. RSGB Council, Minutes, loc. cit., 11 May 1980.
31. RSGB Conference, Minutes, loc. cit., 3 June 1961.
32. RSGB Council, Minutes, loc. cit., 3 April 1966.
33. Quoted the *Synagogue Review*, July 1960, p. 291.
34. *Synagogue Review*, Nov. 1962, p. 58.

35. RSGB Council, Minutes, loc. cit., 25 May 1963.
36. RSGB Executive, Minutes, 12 Dec. 1964; at the Sternberg Centre for Judaism, London.
37. *Living Judaism*, Winter 1968/69, p. 21.
38. Quoted *Inform*, Dec. 1974.
39. RSGB Council, Minutes, loc. cit., 23 Nov. 1975.
40. Quoted *Inform*, Feb. 1977.
41. 18 June 1976, quoted *Inform*, Oct. 1976.
42. *Synagogue Review*, Sept. 1958, p. 23.
43. *Synagogue Review*, April 1959, p. 208.
44. Editorial in the *Jewish Chronicle*, 7 Feb. 1975.
45. *Synagogue Review*, Nov. 1957, p. 53.
46. Minutes, Leo Baeck College Academic Committee; quoted in Jacqueline Tabick, 'I Never Really Wanted To Be First', in Sybil Sheridan (ed.), *Hear Our Voice* (1994), p. 18.
47. *Living Judaism*, Spring 1967, p. 81.
48. Quoted in the *Synagogue Review*, Oct. 1959, p. 29.
49. Revd Leslie Hardman in the *Jewish Review*, 20 Dec. 1959.
50. *Jewish Chronicle*, 25 March 1960.
51. Quoted in the *Jewish Chronicle*, 1 April 1960.
52. *Synagogue Review*, May 1960, p. 217.
53. RSGB Conference, Minutes, loc. cit., 22 May 1960.
54. Morris Swift, *Jewish Marriage and Divorce* (1962), p. 12.
55. West London Synagogue Council, Minutes, 18 Oct. 1962, Archive of West London Synagogue of British Jews; Assembly of Ministers, Minutes, 31 Oct. 1962; at Reform Synagogues of Great Britain Archive, Sternberg Centre for Judaism, London.
56. *Living Judaism*, Summer 1967, p. 116.
57. Office of the Chief Rabbi to Rabbi Sidney Brichto, 28 Nov. 1967; at Union of Liberal and Progressive Synagogue Archives.
58. *Living Judaism*, Nov. 1972.
59. *Jewish Chronicle*, Jan. 1978.
60. RSGB Council, Minutes, loc. cit., 7 June 1970.
61. A. Bornstein and B. Homa, *Tell It In Gath – British Jewry and Clause 43: The Inside Story* (1972), pp. 52–3.
62. For a more detailed examination of the Clause 43 controversy see Bornstein and Homa, op. cit., and H. Langdon, 'The Place of Reform in Anglo-Jewry Today', in D. Marmur (ed.), *A Genuine Search* (1979), pp. 244–52.
63. H. Langdon, op. cit., p. 244.

8 The Movement, 1980–1995

The 1980s witnessed the momentous changes that transformed the RSGB from a loose federation of synagogues located in a room on the second floor of West London Synagogue, into a dynamic movement whose spacious new headquarters formed the largest Jewish centre in Europe. It was a remarkable expansion – both in its extent and in the short space of time in which it occurred. As it moved increasingly onto the centre-stage of British Jewry, the Movement took a lead in formulating responses to a host of contemporary issues such as abortion, mixed-faith marriage, and women at worship. Equally challenging were the dramatic outbreaks of both war and peace in Israel, as well as the collapse of Communism in the Soviet Union. The question of merger with Liberal synagogues proved a contentious and exhausting issue that was eventually dropped, but may yet return. By the end of the period the RSGB had changed beyond recognition and was having a major impact on British Jewry.

The catalyst for the journey from Upper Berkeley Street via Swiss Cottage to the Sternberg Centre in North London was the RSGB's decision to establish an Education Department. West London was unable to offer the extra space this would require and it was clear that the RSGB would have to find alternative accommodation. The move would have considerable ramifications: it would mean a major change in the relationship with the synagogue that had been responsible for founding, supporting and housing the RSGB; it would also mean going out into the commercial world and paying a much more competitive rent; more positively, it would signify the RSGB's independence from the benign patrimony of West London and increase its stature as a religious organisation in its own right; it would give the RSGB the physical space not only to create an Education Department but to have the freedom to develop even more projects; perhaps most important of all for the future was the confidence in its own existence and purpose that it would indicate.

When premises became available at College House, New College Parade, at the Swiss Cottage end of Finchley Road, an Extraordinary General Meeting was held on 13 January 1980 to consider the move. Some delegates were worried by the financial liabilities involved and the effect this might have on individual synagogues. The chairman, Alf Strudwick, urged a positive response, pointing out that the RSGB was 'at a turning-point and was about to take its place as a leading body in Anglo-Jewry'. Biblical support was provided by Hugo Gryn who reminded the council of Jeremiah's purchase of a field in Anatoth as an act of faith in the future despite the uncertainties of the time. The motion to acquire the lease was passed by a substantial majority; contracts and alterations were completed in time for the May council meeting to be held at the RSGB's new home, College House. In the address Strudwick prepared for Conference that year – which was read in his absence as he suffered a collapse before being able to deliver it – he wrote of the momentous changes heralded by the move and informed delegates:

> I must tell you that there are waverers who believe that the Reform Movement should stand still. They see no role for the Movement other than to be a loose association of like-minded synagogues. They complain of our activities...they do not appreciate why we have moved from being the small association of six synagogues in 1942 which could only exchange ideas to being a major force in British Jewry. Fortunately they are few and they must be swept up and swept forward by our zeal and enthusiasm.

However, enthusiasm alone could not pay bills. A year earlier the RSGB had launched the Reform Foundation with the aim of raising £1 million to provide proper funding for the movement and to enable it to develop beyond the constraints of relying only on income from synagogue assessments. However, the response so far had been fairly slack and the RSGB's cash-flow system was so precarious that in September it was only able to meet its commitments thanks to South West Essex volunteering to pay £15,000 of its assessment in advance. Several congregations warned the RSGB of not committing itself to expenditure it could not meet. It is somewhat ironic that within a few weeks the then main concern – a possible budget deficit of £10,000 for 1981 – was to be dwarfed by the intense efforts to find the £2,000,000 necessary to purchase and refurbish the Finchley Manor House.

The site had been found by members of the New Highgate and North London Synagogue (Masorti), which soon afterwards changed its name to New North London Synagogue. It was an associate congregation of Rabbi Louis Jacobs' New London Synagogue, and was then looking for premises in the area. The site was far too large for them alone, but they made contact with Dow Marmur, for whom the Manor House presented a practical way of realising his dream of establishing a Reform Jewish day school. It was a Grade II listed building of Georgian architecture that had been built as a private residence in 1723 and then turned into a convent in 1919. With 33,000 square feet of accommodation – including a school, chapel and dormitory block – set in seven and a half acres of ground, it would be the perfect home for a synagogue and school if others could be brought in to share both the space and the cost. Peter Levy, a property developer and member of North Western, quickly became involved in the project; the RSGB was approached, and also Leo Baeck College which was searching for premises of its own outside the West London Synagogue. The Westlon Housing Association was invited to participate with a view to building sheltered housing for the elderly in the grounds. The Manor House site offered an unparalleled chance to establish a Reform centre that could combine many different facets of the Reform Movement, linking administrative headquarters, primary school, rabbinic college, education department, youth activities, facilities for the elderly. It could also include other non-Orthodox groupings, especially if the Liberals relocated there, either wholly or partially. Moreover, unlike Skeet, which failed partly for geographical reasons, Finchley was in the very heartland of London Jewry, as well as being 'the right side of London' for access by the majority of provincial communities.

Indeed, others had realised the Manor House's potential. The original price quoted to Leo Baeck College, which was acting on behalf of the RSGB and other parties, was £750,000. A counter-bid of £800,000 was made by Sir Isaac Wolfson, President of the United Synagogue, who was determined both to deny the site to the Reform and to acquire it for the United Synagogue – both objects being equally important in his eyes. The College made a final offer of £850,000 and hurried to conclude the deal, signing the lease on 23 December 1980. Although it meant that an extra £100,000 had been spent needlessly, the result was that the United Synagogue remained in totally inadequate premises for the next decade and a half, while the Reform Movement was catapulted into possession of a vast Jewish complex. Moreover, the real value of the site may be gauged from the fact that the College was advised to insure it for £2.5 million. Whilst many people had been involved in the project, it would simply not have been possible without Peter Levy, who was instrumental both in negotiating the purchase and in providing the financial guarantees. But for him it could not have been seriously contemplated. The award of an OBE in 1991 for his efforts on behalf of cystic fibrosis sufferers indicated the wide range of his many charitable activities.

A speedy decision by the RSGB was necessary as to whether it wished to become a partner in the venture. Peter Levy told a special meeting of Council on 22 February 1981 that the Manor House offered a unique opportunity to create a centre for Judaism such as could not be found anywhere outside the United States. Yet delegates were also warned that it would need the active involvement of every congregation, and the appeals committee chairman, Stephen Barclay, sombrely pointed out that if the finances could not be raised and the site had to be sold it could spell the end of RSGB as a movement. 'The decision', he said, 'needed to be about money not emotion.' In fact it was a combination of both and, despite the repeated emphasis on the enormous financial responsibilities that would be entailed, the council members were more influenced by the vision that lay before them. They voted by an overwhelming majority to join the Manor House and to commit current and future funds from the Reform Foundation Appeal to the newly created Manor House Trust. The appeal target itself was doubled from one million to two million pounds.

The purchase of the site was completed on 31 March 1981 and shortly afterwards Messrs Hildebrand and Glicker were appointed architects for the redevelopment. There followed a frantic period of fund-raising and building work, in which the achievements of the latter were often overshadowed by the problems surrounding the former. Despite a highly organised appeals campaign taken to each congregation and targeting different income-levels, there was a poor response. This was particularly true of provincial communities, some of which questioned whether they would benefit from a London-based centre. At the January 1982 council meeting Peter Levy spoke of the critical cash-flow situation and warned that having to sell the site was a real possibility. The RSGB was given three months in which to back the project or jettison it. Redoubled efforts improved the situation, although much depended on the major contributions of a few individual donors, including an anonymous donation of £230,000. However, many of the pledges were over a seven-year period, creating an immediate shortfall, while the building costs proved to be more expensive than originally estimated. The continuing financial problems over the next two years meant that the offer of a gift of £300,000 from the Sternberg Charitable Foundation was most welcome even though the condition attached – that the Manor House be renamed the Sternberg Centre for Judaism – aroused some controversy.[1]

Despite the financial traumas, the tangible benefits of the centre were equally dramatic. By September 1981 the primary school had opened with its first entry form of 12 pupils and Michael Barnett as head teacher. It was known as Akiva School, named after the second-century rabbi renowned for his Jewish learning and personal heroism. Its historic position as the first Reform Jewish day school was accompanied by a fine academic reputation, which continued to develop when Judith Roback succeeded Barnett in 1987. Its intake grew year by year until by 1992 it had reached the full complement of 140 pupils originally envisaged. Akiva's success led to calls for similar schools elsewhere in London and at the time of writing there are proposals for further schools in Hertsmere and Redbridge.

The Westlon Housing Association decided not to proceed with its plans for sheltered accommodation on the site and withdrew from further involvement. The ULPS also opted not to participate, partly because of commitments to the property in Whitfield Street which served both as its headquarters and as the home of the West Central Synagogue. The ULPS also had concerns over losing its distinctive identity if it was to share the same premises as the much larger RSGB. However, New North London Synagogue did move to the Manor House and expanded rapidly. Tenancies were granted at various stages to the Manor House Bookshop, the Museum of the Jewish East End (later renamed the London Museum of Jewish Life), the Michael Goulston Educational

Foundation and the Heimler Foundation. A cafeteria was established that not only provided refreshments for staff and visitors, but also work experience for handicapped or disabled young people from the Ravenswood Foundation in a mutually beneficial arrangement. Perhaps the most significant development was the appointment of Rabbi Tony Bayfield as director of the centre in January 1983. He had acquired a fine reputation as the first minister of North West Surrey Synagogue and had also become very involved in the RSGB through the Assembly of Rabbis, including a highly successful period as chairman, during which time his contribution extended far beyond purely rabbinic matters. Under his leadership the Sternberg Centre became a hive of activity that exceeded the most optimistic hopes. The existing organisations were encouraged to interact and cross-fertilise; thus student rabbis at Leo Baeck College both received training from the Education and Youth Department and helped lead some of its projects.

A series of cultural ventures was launched. One was the quarterly journal, *MANNA*, which attained a high level of contributions on a wide range of Jewish topics. It also included as a permanent feature a centre-fold 'Theological Supplement', sponsored by the RSGB, which gave rise to major articles by leading contemporary thinkers on topics important to Reform Judaism. Unfortunately, like so many other Anglo-Jewish journals, *MANNA* never attained the subscription level it hoped for, hovering around the 1,000 mark and well below the number of Reform households. Another venture was the Manor House Society, which offered a series of seminars, talks, concerts and exhibitions of art, photography and sculpture. Its aim was to provide a level of Jewish cultural activity to which individual synagogues could not aspire, and which would also appeal to unaffiliated Jews who identified with Judaism not through religious services but through ideas and culture. There was also a specific programme of outreach, particularly to those outside the stereotype 'normal happy family'. Seminars and counselling were held for, among others, the divorced, singles, and sexual minorities. SATMAH (Students At The Manor House) catered for the needs of Jewish students, supplementing the work of Progressive Jewish Students (PJS) by offering activities during the vacations as well as a book club and a counselling service. Another task was providing a religious policy for the site itself, with the centre being akin to a *moshav* of 60 Progressive Jews working together. Provision for daily prayers, communal observances on working festivals such as *Yom Ha'atzma'ut*, collections for charity, common policy on non-smoking, *kashrut*, paper recycling and environmental concerns were all part of creating an atmosphere which helped further the sense of camaraderie among the disparate groups.

The formal opening ceremony of the centre was performed by the then Prime Minister, the Rt. Hon. Margaret Thatcher, who was also the local Member of Parliament. Originally scheduled for June 1983, when the major refurbishments were complete, it had to be delayed till the following June because of the intervention of the general election and other commitments. When she returned five years later in July 1989 for the unveiling of the Founders Column the centre had become a byword for creativity and energy, not just within the Reform Movement but in British Jewry at large. Among the many projects associated with it by then were seminars on caring in the community, major art exhibitions, a Jewish book fair, the erection of a Holocaust memorial, choir festivals, a Biblical garden and a major programme of outreach for mixed-faith couples. New institutions connected with the site included the Association of Reform and Liberal *Mohalim*, the Ha'Makom group for those in their twenties and early thirties, the first Reform *mikveh*, and Manor House Media which promoted Jewish audio and video media. Other developments that followed were the Manor House Centre for Psychodynamic Counselling, the Medical Ethics Group, the Plus U Network for singles and the Manor House Dialogue Group. The latter brought together leading Jewish and Christian theologians, and was to culminate in the publication of a book of essays by the participants, *Dialogue with a Difference* (1992). The group developed later into a trialogue, regrouping to include Muslim leaders and becoming an important forum at a time of much higher Muslim profile in Britain at large. The establishment of the Leopold Muller Interfaith Centre made RSGB the first Jewish organisation to have a specific space for inter-faith work, a field in which it had become 'a market leader'.

Almost every year saw new developments in response to new issues, be it the Singles Commission or the Manor House Business Ethics Group. The latter was in reaction to major scandals in the financial world, some of which had included Jews, and was designed to research how best to apply Jewish ethical teachings in the context of modern business practices. Major rebuilding in the early 1990s saw the new youth and education block, and a greatly expanded London Museum of Jewish Life. The Museum's stature had grown to such an extent over the decade that in 1995 it amalgamated with the long-established Jewish Museum. It brought together the outstanding collection of the latter and the innovative programme of exhibitions and community outreach of the former, under common management but retaining the two sites. At the same time Sir Sigmund Sternberg's role as British Jewry's voluntary 'foreign secretary' led him to involve the Centre in his diplomatic work, and brought visits from a variety of ambassadors, high-ranking civil servants, religious leaders and political figures. His contribution to the amicable settlement of the controversy over a Carmelite convent established at Auschwitz, along with his position as chairman of the International Council of Christians and Jews further enhanced the name of the Centre. The combination of his contacts, Peter Levy's generosity and Rabbi Bayfield's creativity produced a wealth of Jewish culture in a remarkably short time. The fears of some that the benefits of the Centre would only be felt by surrounding congregations were proved wrong in that it had become a focal point for the movement as a whole, while many of the resources – particularly in the fields of education and youth – radiated out to the most distant communities, as will be seen below. The only significant logistical problem was the lack of access for disabled people to all floors. A lift system had been part of the original plan, but it had to be abandoned because of the very high cost and the extreme shortage of finances at the time.

The nascent Education Department that had spurred such massive changes was to prove well worth the upheaval. It had three main areas of activity: the first was formal education in religion schools. This involved training teachers, providing resources, developing curricula and researching the objectives and methods of Hebrew teaching. The second area was adult education, with the aim that all adults should learn to read Hebrew and deepen their level of Jewish learning. The third area was informal education by promoting youth clubs, holidays, weekends and summer courses. The youth work was done in conjunction with Reform Synagogue Youth (RSY) but extending the depth and range of its activities considerably. From the very beginning Asher Amir put into practice the principle that the Department should revolve round the needs of the congregations rather than act independently of them. This influenced not only the way in which the Department developed but also the fact that he and other staff frequently visited the different communities and organised local workshops and seminars for them.

At the end of the first year, Jeffery Rose, the first chairman of the Council of Education and Youth, could report to the 1981 conference: 'There can be little doubt now that it was right to establish the Department. There can be even less doubt that the right man was appointed.' However, the remarkable progress was interrupted by Amir's own family situation, which forced him to return to Israel in July of that year. Despite his short stay he had made a decisive contribution in establishing the Department and then demonstrating its value. It was to prove the bedrock of all subsequent developments, while Amir himself was to maintain contact with the RSGB by acting as a permanent visiting consultant. Rabbi Michael Heilbron – previously director of education at the North Western – was appointed his successor. The Department continued to grow both in its activities and its staff. A children's festival attracted 350 participants, the learning centre expanded greatly, a group for head-teachers was formed, the Northern Learning Centre was established at Manchester Reform Synagogue, the use of computers in Jewish education was investigated, a programme for the *barmitvah* or *batmitzvah* year was produced, a course was organised for kindergarten teachers, and material was published on the festivals and Hebrew reading. Department staff were sent on courses to Israel and the United States to bring back new skills and programmes. By 1985 the original staff of four people had grown to ten, while the Northern Learning Centre had also increased its facilities and staff.

The services offered by the Department would have been even greater had it not been for the continuous financial constraints under which it operated. At the time of its founding it had been agreed that the Department would not be funded from synagogue assessments. In its initial years it was supported by grants from the Reform Foundation, the Jewish Educational Development Trust and the World Zionist Organisation via the Pincus Foundation, which was to prove remarkably generous, giving $300,000 over the next five years. It was a measure of the high reputation the Department enjoyed that the Pincus Foundation helped support it for so long and for up to 50 per cent of its budget, usually preferring to give seed money for a much shorter period. It was clear, however, that the RSGB had to make provision for the time when such external funding would not be available. It was also a matter of the movement taking financial responsibility for its own educational programmes. In May 1986 Peter Levy once again played a critical role by proposing the creation of an institute for the advancement of Jewish education, backed by the resources of the Manor House Trust, of which he was chairman. The institute would comprise of the RSGB Education Department, along with the Extra-Mural Department and Education Department of Leo Baeck College, with the possibility of the ULPS Education Department joining too. It would also serve to bring together and rationalise the differing educational groups under Progressive auspices and weld them into a more effective partnership. Youth work would no longer be part of its brief, thus splitting the existing Department of Education and Youth into two separate bodies, with each having its own structure and management team. A funding body would be created – the Advancement of Jewish Education Trust (AJET) – under the control of the Manor House Trust, and an associate director of the Manor House Trust who would have responsibility for fund-raising would be appointed. The proposals were welcomed by Council and confirmed by Conference the following month. The Liberals agreed to join the project and the new body became known as the Centre for Jewish Education (CJE). Stephen Horne was made associate-director, although when he left a year later to work for another Jewish charity, the position was retitled 'Appeals Organiser' and Francis Isaacs appointed to the post.

The new arrangements called for some painful reorganisation. Youth work and education had been brought together by the RSGB into one combined department in 1979 – the Department of Education and Youth – which now had to be dismantled and new structures created. A professional management study was undertaken with the help of West Central Counselling and Community Research. The use of outside consultants was, in itself, a new and important development, signalling a willingness to expose the RSGB to rigorous market-place evaluation. It constituted a radical departure from the traditional Anglo-Jewish tendency to hallow its institutional structures and let those in office continue unchallenged until their retirement. Monitoring the effectiveness of those institutions and insisting on the accountability of office-holders was a measure of the new approach emanating from the Sternberg Centre. The report offered both praise of the existing education work and criticism of certain aspects of it. Building on the past formula, it laid down three tasks for the CJE. First, Jewish education was best done in the communities themselves, and so it was vital to identify their needs and then work with the communities directly. Second, the CJE should educate the educators – through initial teacher training courses and in-service reinforcement. Third, resources should be developed through the resources centre and then be brought to the notice of congregations. It emphasised that the role of the CJE was to be a consultancy organisation, rather than being there to do the teaching itself.

It was during this transition period that Rabbi Heilbron decided to retire after five years at the helm. His successor was Natalie (Lali) Ray, who arrived in September 1987 from New York where she had been a senior staff member of the New York Board of Jewish Education. She was accompanied by her husband, Eric Ray, a noted scribe who was to be of great service to RSGB communities, checking and repairing their scrolls, as well as writing *gittin* for the Reform *Beth Din*. Lali's own talents quickly became apparent, while the CJE staff was further strengthened a year later by the addition of a deputy director, Michael Shire, a former member of Birmingham Progressive Synagogue who had trained and worked in Jewish education in the United States for many years. The CJE became widely recognised as an innovative and dynamic agency that served some 5,000 children in the 70 congregations belonging to the two Progressive movements (3,500 children coming from the RSGB). It was among the first Jewish educational organisations in Britain to promote the need for a much wider definition of Jewish education. It developed early childhood learning programmes through kindergarten and other courses, recognising the value of 'under-five' education. The CJE also emphasised 'family education', encouraging congregations to organise events for both parents and children to learn together and to boost the level of Jewish home life, without which much of the formal religion school education was wasted. Another innovation was the production of a comprehensive Hebrew Reading Programme – known as *Ha'Sefer Sheli*. It was designed to offer a co-ordinated course of Hebrew learning throughout a child's stay at religion school – rather than the usual haphazard succession of different books using different systems. Its widespread adoption throughout the movement also facilitated the integration of children transferring from one religion school to another. In this respect it echoed – albeit independently – the moves towards a national syllabus in British education in general.

The success of the CJE was indicated by its award of the prestigious Shazar Prize in 1992 by the Government of Israel for its pioneering work in Jewish education. The citation mentioned particularly its Israel programming, which included organising teachers' seminars in Israel, as well as its Hebrew curriculum development. By this time Michael Shire was director, having succeeded Lali Ray in a pre-planned transition two years earlier. Another major initiative he helped develop was the establishment in September 1992 of a two-year part-time Masters degree in Jewish Education in conjunction with London University's Institute of Education. The ability to gain such external validation from the non-Jewish academic world reflected the esteem in which the CJE was held outside the RSGB, while the leap in its budget – from £25,000 in 1980 to £300,000 at the end of the decade – indicated the enormous financial commitment that the RSGB, along with the ULPS, was investing in it.

The move to the Sternberg Centre also had an effect on the youth wing of the original Department of Education and Youth. With a new venue for residential weekends now available, there was even less need for the home at Skeet, the lease of which was released in March 1982, as was noted above. Even more important than the physical move was the appointment as youth director in 1981 of Ian Wainer, who had been a senior officer in Habonim and then spent three years in Israel. Building on the changes already set in motion, he gave RSY the structure of a classical Zionist youth movement, with a clear ideology and a coherent management framework and guided by a strong central policy. It was based firmly on three 'pillars': Reform Judaism, Reform Zionism and *Tikkun Olam* ('repairing the world'). The movement was divided into three groups: *Garinim* ('seeds') for the 9 to 13 year age-group, *Shtilim* ('saplings') for the 13 to 16 year age-group, and *Ilanot* ('trees') for the 16 to 18 year age-group, each governed by its own *mazkirut* (youth workers' committee). Great emphasis was laid on *hadracha* – training and leadership – in terms of both Jewish commitment and responsibility for wider social concerns. The intense identification with Israel was evident in the content of its programmes, the encouragement of members to visit and study in Israel, and the extensive use of Hebrew terminology. In many respects RSY became much more Zionist-oriented than RSGB at large, and many within the parent body expressed doubt about the extent of the changes taking place. The bewilderment often caused by the frequent Hebrew phrases in RSY reports to Council was only partially rectified by the inclusion of a vocabulary sheet.

At its 1982 annual general meeting RSY decided to expand its name by adding Netzer to it – standing for *Noar Tzioni Reformi* ('Reform Zionist Youth'). It was an act of identification with other Reform youth movements around the world, which carried the same title (for example, Netzer Australia), and emphasised the links with Netzer Olami, the world Jewish youth movement established by WUPJ. The name-change marked the final transition from the loose federation of youth clubs known as YASGB to the ideologically based youth movement, RSY-Netzer. In turn it reflected the changing role of Jewish youth clubs generally: no longer designed to Anglicise the children of immigrants, but to Judaise third- and fourth-generation British Jews. Their mastery of English culture was complete, now it was time to reinforce the Jewish identity that had often been neglected in the process.

Despite the obvious success in the running of RSY-Netzer groups, a major problem raised at the 1982 conference was that it only reached 800 participants every week out of 12,000 young people in the RSGB. One way of appealing to those not involved was through the extensive holidays in England, Israel and on the Continent that were developed. By 1985 they had become so large that a full-time camps' organiser – Andrew Leigh – was needed. The 90 participants at the 1982 Shemesh camp jumped to 224 by 1987, and increased to 310 in 1994. The one Israel tour in 1982 had expanded into four separate simultaneous tours in 1991, while the original 50 participants grew to 158, the largest number sent by any British youth organisation. Another development was the appointment of Ruth Godfrey as the first Northern Youth Worker in 1985 to strengthen youth work in the northern communities. It was no accident that both she and Leigh were themselves graduates of RSY-Netzer, reflecting the active policy of training Movement members for future management positions and ensuring the continued supply of leaders. By 1986 the weekly attendance figure had grown to 1,300 – still only ten per cent of its full potential, but making it one of the largest Jewish youth movements in Britain, second only to Bnei Akiva. When Wainer left his position that year, it was clear that his five years' tenure had not only effected a radical transformation of RSY-Netzer, but had also turned it into one of the major Jewish youth movements in the country. Under his leadership RSY-Netzer also influenced the rest of the RSGB in integrating the idea of active Zionist commitment into the life of the movement. Furthermore, the new RSY-Netzer was a force for change in the wider context of the youth and Zionist worlds – fighting for the right of Reform for an equal role and for recognition of its position within the community. In both circles it led to a profound change in the general perception of Reform and appreciation of its contribution. The value of its role was evident from generous grants from the Jewish Agency, while even wider recognition of the importance of its youth programme came from regular grants awarded by the government's Department of Education and Science.

The most dramatic expression of RSY-Netzer's commitment to Israel came in the form of *Misgeret Kerem* – a framework for emigration to Israel which was set up by the *shaliach* Itzik Aharoni in 1984. Its object was to encourage and train those who were considering making *aliyah* by a series of seminars in England and tours to Israel. Not all those who participated in *Misgeret Kerem* activities settled in Israel, but over the next decade it was to be responsible for two or three a year doing so, and influencing others to make that decision at a later stage. Highly committed to active Reform Zionism they gave added impetus to the Reform movement in Israel. Many of them were involved in Progressive projects such as the *kibbutzim* Yahel and Lotan and the observation post (*mitzpeh*) *Har Halutz* or helped start a Reform settlement in the Galilee in 1989, known as *Gan Ner*, whose name meant Garden of Light but was also an allusion to Lord Barnett Janner in whose memory it was founded. Nevertheless, their small number compared to mass emigrations from elsewhere prevented them having any major impact on Israeli society. Two years later came another project which was to prove highly successful – *Shnat Netzer* – by which RSY-Netzer members spent a year in Israel both learning about the country and gaining leadership training. These skills were put to the benefit of the movement on their return and also helped provide it with a large number of senior trained graduates, assuring RSY-Netzer of continuous development. In all these initiatives the role of the *sh'lichim* was crucial in galvanising Israel-consciousness, while both RSY-Netzer and the RSGB at large benefited enormously from the Israelis who each made a distinctive contribution during their two-year stay. Perhaps the secret of the series of successful relationships lay in the sensitivity with which the appointments were made: choosing those who understood the religious principles of the RSGB and who could relate to its aims.

If the RSGB was transformed by the move to the Manor House, the same applied to Leo Baeck College. The extra space, along with the burst of confidence at having a home of its own, led to a large growth in its activities beyond its rabbinic programme. The Extra-Mural Department provided a range of day-time and evening courses that attracted large numbers from the general Jewish public, while annual courses for Christian theological students not only proved very popular but were to have an important influence on a whole new generation of Christian religious leaders. Another milestone came in 1989 when the Council for National Academic Awards (CNAA) gave the College the right to confer degrees, including BAs, MAs and PhDs. It was the smallest academic establishment in the country to be entrusted with this right. The decision had followed an exhaustive examination of the College's academic standards and was a tribute to its reputation in scholastic circles. When the CNAA was disbanded by the government three years later the College received similar certification from the Open University. The availability of degree courses served to attract new students as well as enhance the opportunities for rabbinic candidates and graduates. Much of the credit for these developments lay with Professor Ben Segal who was appointed principal of the College in 1982. He had recently retired as Professor of Semitic Languages at the School of Oriental and African Studies, London University, and his three years as principal significantly tightened the College's academic disciplines and organisational structure. In 1985 he was succeeded by Rabbi Dr Jonathan Magonet, himself a graduate of the College and head of its Bible Department. His prolific lectures and writings in other theatres helped give the College a high profile in both Jewish and non-Jewish circles, as well as in the religious and scholarly worlds.

Another similarity with the RSGB, albeit less welcome, was the financial difficulties the College faced, particularly after putting most of its capital into the Manor House, with the result that no investment income was produced to meet day-to-day running costs. To prevent the real danger of the College collapsing in 1984, the RSGB Council agreed to add £5 to the per capita sum due from each constituent synagogue for one year only. However, it was recognised that this was merely a short-term solution and that the root of the problem stemmed from serious under-funding by the RSGB and the ULPS over many years. A Sponsoring Movements Committee was established under the chairmanship of Marcus Bower to examine the issue. It proposed that the contribution of both movements be radically increased and in a manner proportionate to their respective size so that, in the case of the RSGB, the then two per cent of assessment that was given to the College should be enlarged to five per cent within two years. At the same time the report demanded tighter controls on College spending and reforms to its decision-making procedure. It also clarified the College's objectives: training congregational rabbis rather than producing scholars, although not excluding other forms of rabbinic service.

The new financial and structural plan proved highly beneficial, providing a secure future for the College and allowing it to concentrate on its core work of producing rabbis. By 1994 it had 113 rabbinic graduates, including 19 women rabbis, providing the vast majority of all Reform and Liberal ministers in Britain and supplying the rabbinic needs of most European Progressive communities. It had also begun training rabbinic students from eastern Europe following the collapse of the Soviet Union. A month-long intensive seminar in Jewish studies took place in 1989 for ten students from Hungary, while the arrival in 1991 of the first of several students from Russia and the former Soviet Union to train for the rabbinate symbolised both the massive changes in Jewish life in eastern Europe and the pioneering role the College was playing. Its world-wide influence was second only to the rabbinic seminaries in the United States. The 73 students enrolled at the College in 1994 included those from the Czech Republic, France, Germany, the Netherlands, India, Israel, Russia, South Africa, Ukraine and the United States, providing a rich mix of cultures and different Jewish expressions. Its range of influence in England itself was extended that year when a duplicate of its MA course in Jewish Studies was established at Manchester Reform Synagogue, so as to be available to northern communities. Meanwhile, an important adjunct of the College, its library, had expanded enormously under the guidance of Hyam Maccoby, and it currently has a collection of 30,000 books. Amongst the many valuable bequests were books from the former Hochshule Library in Berlin, destroyed by the Nazis, given in recognition of the role of the College in continuing its tradition of liberal scholarship and effectively being its direct descendant. A Room of Prayer designed by Roman Halter and a sculpture by Naomi Blake in the forecourt dedicated to the memory of one of the College's great supporters, Hyman Arbeid, added to its physical presence at the Centre.

For some of the graduates of the College the 1980s proved a difficult time and there was often reference to 'a malaise within the rabbinate' both by the rabbis themselves and by others. Part of the problem lay in the increasing demands made by congregations on the rabbis, with long hours of work, unrealistic expectations, pressure on the rabbi's family life, and lack of time for personal study or refreshment. It was compounded by the fact that the comparatively young age of the rabbinate – in many respects a great credit to the movement and highly beneficial – also meant that there was little mobility in terms of congregational placements and little scope for promotion. The sense of there being a lack of avenues for development was heightened by the departure abroad of two leading figures – Dow Marmur to Canada and Michael Boyden (at the time chairman of the Assembly of Rabbis) to Israel. A Rabbinic Manpower Working Party was established to consider the problem and examine all aspects of the role of the rabbi. Chaired by Jerome Karet, it consisted of representatives of both the rabbinate and laity, while the ULPS were invited to send a member as the issues concerned them equally. Reporting in 1986, it clarified what could be reasonably expected of a rabbi, and what was unreasonable in terms of workload. It suggested possible structural changes: a team rabbinate in which several colleagues worked together in a certain location, each concentrating on particular skills (such as education, pastoral care or counselling). Another option was part-time positions, in which a rabbi worked part-time with a congregation and part-time in other fields; the development of full-time educational or administrative posts was also put forward.

For those rabbis – always assumed to be the majority – who

would still be in full-time congregational posts, a 'Rabbinic/ Congregational Charter' was drawn up. Amongst many recommendations it emphasised the importance of a healthy relationship between the rabbi and the lay leadership, suggested regular meetings between the rabbi and synagogue chairman, and urged that the rabbi be provided with adequate administrative and secretarial support. The report commended the provision of in-service training for rabbis – both in working techniques and personal development; it also stressed the importance of reasonable financial remuneration so as to attract new rabbis and retain existing ones. The latter was effectively resolved through the revised scale of the Rabbinic Salaries Working Party, a body established in the early 1970s which laid down national guidelines for rabbinic remuneration and took the pressure off individual congregations and ministers having to face potentially difficult annual negotiations. The salary scale was based on the number of years of service since each rabbi's ordination and also included a 'London weighting' to provide for the vastly differing costs of accommodation for those in the metropolis.

The report helped restore the sense of self-confidence amongst the Assembly, and three subsequent groups continued the work of monitoring the professional health of the rabbinate: the Rabbinic Development Committee was an Assembly body chaired by Rabbi Henry Goldstein in 1990 which sought to promote the intellectual and spiritual dimension of rabbis. In the same year, the joint Assembly–RSGB Rabbinic Recruitment Working Party – chaired by Jeffery Rose – recommended a series of measures to combat the shortage of rabbis caused by the growth of the two Progressive movements and an insufficient number of new ordinands. They included rabbis encouraging potential candidates within their communities to consider the rabbinate, publicising Leo Baeck College, and appointing a Progressive chaplain whose function, *inter alia*, would be to promote the rabbinate as an attractive career amongst students. The Rabbinic Careers Structure was a joint RSGB–ULPS body led by Alan Magnus in 1992 that re-examined the nature of rabbis' contracts, along with their role in relationship to both their congregations and the movements at large.

Despite its internal concerns, the Assembly still managed to initiate a variety of religious developments. The curiously named *Shabbat* Working Party chaired by Rabbi Michael Leigh tackled the difficult issue of how Reform observed the Sabbath, and what activities were permitted or forbidden. It was a critical debate for 'Reform *halachah*', one of the first attempts to give detailed guidance without being authoritarian, and to harmonise the right of free choice by individuals with the need for standard procedure by congregations. The booklet that resulted in 1983 – *Remember the Sabbath Day* – managed to straddle the prescriptive and liberal approaches within the Assembly. Among its many practical recommendations were two important principles that characterised the distinctive and innovative thinking of Reform in general. One was that the concept of 'work' had to be redefined from the traditional understanding: what constituted laborious activity in talmudic times (for example, travel) was not necessarily the case nowadays. Moreover, there could be individual variations in the definition of work, whereby one person's chore was another person's relaxation, for instance in the case of gardening. Thus the question of what was appropriate for the Sabbath would in part depend on subjective criteria – although within the context of certain objective standards, such as that the activities were not at the expense of time with other members of the family, or clashing with synagogue services. Another Reform principle in evidence, first spelt out in Rabbi Tony Bayfield's pamphlet, *God's Demands and Israel's Needs* (1981), was the 'hierarchical approach', by which the importance of one observance may override another of less significance. Thus the value of keeping in touch with family can justify the use of the telephone on the Sabbath, even though its use for work purposes should be avoided.

Other publications included new and greatly expanded editions of the triennial *Calendar of Torah and Haftarah Readings* (1984 and later), edited by Rabbi Dr Jonathan Romain (Maidenhead). He also wrote a monthly syndicated 'Ask the Rabbi' column for the newsletters of those congregations without a minister so as to provide regular rabbinic input to communities that would otherwise lack it. His pamphlet, *How To Grow* (1993), was accompanied by a video of the same name produced by Manor House Media and was the first use of video by the RSGB as a teaching tool for synagogue councils. A short series of fact sheets was produced by Assembly members in the early 1980s entitled 'Reform Fact and Fiction'. They sought to answer pressing issues such as 'Are Reform Conversions "*Kosher*"?' in response to the questions of RSGB members and against a background of the misinformed attacks from the Orthodox sector. The publication of a large-print version of the Daily and Sabbath Prayer Book in 1981 – coinciding with the United Nations' 'Year of the Disabled' – was welcomed by the *Jewish Chronicle* as an important innovation for British Jewry and serving the needs of a significant but neglected sector of the community. The Social Action Group was set up under the aegis of the Assembly and, under the dynamic leadership of Rabbi Barbara Borts, was responsible for some pioneering work in confronting contemporary issues that was to have a great influence on the RSGB as a whole. As well as producing seminars and position papers, the group was responsible for two publications: *Abortion – A Jewish Response* (1984) gave a cogent summary of the issues involved, traditional viewpoints and a Reform standpoint. Four years later *Women and Tallit* gave voice to the small but growing number of women wearing a *tallit* and *kippah* for worship, as well as dealing with the wider issues of women and the *mitzvot*. Amongst the many positive developments it recorded, it also demonstrated the discrepancy between the theoretical equality of women in Reform Judaism and the practical instances where this was not the case, sometimes because of male resistance and sometimes because women themselves did not take up their rights to full participation. Dow Marmur's booklet *The Jewish Family Today and Tomorrow* (1983) was the culmination of a commission on the changing pattern of Jewish family life. It recognised the need for the community to cater for those who did not conform to the assumed norm of 'happily-married couples', such as single parents, widows, divorcees, mixed-faith couples and those living together unmarried.

In the 1990s a new series of pamphlets by rabbis were issued on conversion, women, cremation, *mikveh* and mixed-faith marriages. Although these addressed particular issues, usually ones of practical concern, a much more ambitious attempt to present a coherent Reform theology was made by Tony Bayfield. In an article that appeared in the Spring 1990 edition of *MANNA* entitled 'Progressive Judaism – A Collective Theological Essay' (also known as the 'Manna Platform'), he tackled the substantial issues of God, life and suffering. This was followed by a series of responses from leading theologians world-wide. Another landmark came in 1992 with Jonathan Romain's book, *Faith and*

Practice, published as part of the Jubilee celebrations of the RSGB. It was a comprehensive guide to all aspects of Reform beliefs and observances and a response to the long-standing demand for a clear presentation of what Reform Judaism stands for. The book reflected the endemic dichotomy of the RSGB, which combined central initiatives with local autonomy, by being a guide rather than a rule book, incorporating the varying traditions amongst RSGB congregations, and presenting the different options open to each individual.

There was a deeper significance to the book. For a long time, Reform Judaism had failed to define itself in anything other than negative terms, having no clear statement of its own religious position and accepting the label of 'non-Orthodox' Judaism. This was partly due to a lack of articulate writers, and partly due to a fear of laying down a definitive standpoint that would become a new orthodoxy and stultify any further development. *Faith and Practice*, along with Bayfield's essay, a monograph, *Halakhah – Orthodoxy and Reform* (1994) by Dr Moshe Ish-Horowicz, and the RSGB's *Statement of Religious Ethos* issued in 1992, were both a radical departure and a sign of maturity, indicating that the RSGB was breaking out of this mould and daring to define itself positively.

The reputation of the Assembly, and that of the RSGB, was furthered by books published independently by its members. These included Marmur's *Beyond Survival* (1982), Howard Cooper's *Soul-Searching: Studies in Judaism and Psycho-Therapy* (1988), Romain's *The Jews of England* (1988), and *The Gospels and Rabbinic Judaism* (1988) by Michael Hilton and Fr. Gordian Marshall, as well as the prolific publications of Lionel Blue, often in conjunction with Jonathan Magonet. In addition, several rabbis achieved national prominence through their involvement in religious broadcasting on radio and television. Most notable were Lionel Blue, whose 'Thought for the Day' helped wake up listeners to Radio 4 and start their morning with a smile, while Hugo Gryn's wit and wisdom illuminated contemporary issues in 'The Moral Maze'. In addition, there were a number of full-length television programmes which centred on them. At a time when the religious leadership of the Church of England was criticised by some as lacklustre, Blue and Gryn became among the best-known religious names in Britain. The award of a CBE to Gryn in 1992 and an OBE to Blue in 1994 were not only a recognition of their own talent but a reflection of the religious impact of the exponents of Reform Judaism on the country at large.

It is noticeable that the initiative for many of these instances came from individual rabbis rather than from the Assembly of Rabbis as a body. With some exceptions the Assembly did not, as might have been expected, act as the generating arm of the RSGB in terms of new religious and ethical developments. Instead, it largely confined itself with rabbinic concerns and served as a trade union for its members. One reason was that it was not always possible to obtain unanimity on major questions, with liberal and conservative wings existing within it. In addition, its cumbersome structure militated against speedy responses to current issues. Occasionally, however, it did promulgate public statements. During the national debate on AIDS, it opposed the view put forward by some Jewish and Christian leaders that it was divine punishment against promiscuity and homosexuality. The Assembly asserted that 'AIDS is a viral disease and we wholly reject the suggestion that it be understood as the wrath of God visited upon a particular group of sinners'. It called for a sympathetic response to AIDS sufferers and their families: 'The pain of this disease is compounded by the ignorance and prejudice surrounding its origin and transmission... Compassion in the face of human suffering is needed here as in all cases of disease.'[2]

Perhaps the most tangible religious development was the production of the new High Holy Day Prayer Book in 1985, *Forms of Prayer*, Vol. II, supervised by the Assembly but primarily the work of its editors, Lionel Blue and Jonathan Magonet. It followed the style they pioneered in the Daily and Sabbath liturgy, combining traditional texts with modern material, and using an English translation that was meaningful and flowed well. It was characterised by an honesty about the problems facing contemporary Jews and a willingness to accept religious insights from a variety of Jewish sources. As the Introduction declared: 'In the confusion of our times, the word of God has come to us (as perhaps it always has) in unexpected ways and through unexpected people... We find our spirituality in the diaries of an adolescent girl, in the records of ghetto doctors, and in the honesty of modern Jewish writers.'

A special feature of the *machzor* is its recognition that many Jews come to the High Holy Days unprepared and then find it very hard to summon up the concentration and spiritual energy that they demand. The *machzor* therefore had a Calendar of Repentance containing short readings for each day of Elul, the month preceding *Rosh Hashannah*, designed to help one's personal preparation. They culminated in a *Selichot* service – previously omitted in the Reform liturgy, but now one of many traditions that was restored, albeit with the addition of some modern compositions. With a similar preparatory intent, each section of the High Holy Day services had an introduction and series of meditations that express its special themes. Some were written specifically for the *machzor*, such as that before the Yom Kippur afternoon service:[3]

> As this quiet time ends, I look back on the year and recall as well the good things it gave me:
>
> I remember the friends I made and the jokes I heard and told.
>
> I remember the times I was able to put up with fools, and people who were irritating and ungrateful.
>
> I remember the times when they were able to put up with me.
>
> I remember the occasions when the strength of my own courage and generosity surprised others as well as myself.
>
> I remember the times when I dared to think for myself, and found I could be alone.
>
> I remember all that was spontaneous and uncalculating in me, when I seemed to recover the innocence of childhood.
>
> I remember the illnesses from which I was spared, the disasters which never occurred, and my worries about things that never happened.
>
> I remember the moments when I knew I had a soul.

As with the Daily and Sabbath edition, the *machzor* also contained a substantial study anthology, with commentaries on the *Torah* and *Haftarah* readings, as well as readings on High Holy Day themes. Line drawings and other illustrations were another repeated feature, chosen not so much to illustrate the book but to enhance the mood of the different sections of the service. Among the passages restored from the past was the large section detailing the rituals of the High Priest in temple times, although with interpretations that reflected on the sacrifices involved in modern times and the perplexing questions they raise. At the same time, prayers and study passages referred to contemporary issues such as refugees, the Holocaust, ecology and the misuse of sex.[4] The new liturgy received an enthusiastic welcome – despite having been expected several years earlier and delayed because of production difficulties. In fact, several congregations reported that they maintained a higher level of attendance throughout Yom Kippur that year because congregants, who might have left synagogue earlier in the day, found their attention held by the drama unfolding through the pages of the prayer book.

The one major drawback with the new book was that it was issued shortly before a key change in the perception of the language of prayer took place both in the Jewish and the Christian world: recognition of how male-oriented was the liturgy, both in its reference to worshippers and to God. In the past, male terminology was seen as neutral and all-encompassing but was now increasingly perceived as excluding women and therefore inappropriate. New forms of reference were being developed but the *machzor* did not incorporate such changes, as it was published just before the time when 'inclusive language' became commonplace. It was an unfortunate omission that was quickly appreciated, and the Assembly agreed that the third and final part of the liturgy to be revised – the Festival Prayer Book – should contain inclusive language. Initially this decision faced some opposition among the congregations: some were hesitant at changing familiar formats, in the same way that the departure from 'thee's' and 'thou's' had once been resisted; others feared that it signalled the ascendancy of a feminist minority in the movement; others took fright at some of the more ungainly attempts at creating inclusive liturgy. However, the use of an experimental format for *Shavuot* which demonstrated how gender-free language could be both inoffensive and elegant helped assuage most people's fears. A similar development was taking place at the same time amongst the Liberals, whose new draft edition of their Daily and Sabbath Prayer Book used inclusive language and encountered both praise and hostility for doing so.

When the RSGB's Festival Prayer Book was published in 1995 it continued the pioneering role of previous Reform liturgies, being one of the first British prayer books to employ neutral terminology. Thus instead of the opening paragraph of the *Amidah* speaking of 'our God and God of our fathers' it refers to 'our God and God of our ancestors'. It also included the names of the matriarchs alongside those of the patriarchs. Whereas earlier translations of the second paragraph of the *Alenu* stated 'all mankind shall speak out in Your name', it now had 'all humanity'. Instances of 'every man' were replaced by 'every person'. The principle of avoiding specifically male terminology was also applied to descriptions of God. The once familiar term 'king of the universe' was translated as the less limiting 'sovereign of the universe', while 'master' became 'ruler'. In all such cases the essential meaning of the word was retained but the gender problem was removed. Not only did the innovation prove to be in keeping ideologically with the new attitude to language in society at large, but it became clear that the longer the new phrases were in use, the more they became familiar and were taken for granted.

The very existence of a new liturgy designed only for Reform congregations might not have occurred had there been a different outcome to one of the most controversial debates during the early 1980s: merger with the Liberals. Attempts at closer union between the two Progressive movements had been made intermittently over several decades, but received a new impetus when Jerome Karet became chairman of the RSGB in 1981. His call to build bridges between RSGB and ULPS was echoed by the Liberal chairman, Clive Winston, who was a guest at the 1981 conference and told the Reform delegates: 'Your determination and decisiveness has left us behind you and quite breathless. We are alive to the importance of the Manor House and to the opportunities it affords us both... We must be there, and we must be involved with you.' An obvious factor behind this mutual enthusiasm was that the acquisition of the Manor House meant that instead of the theoretical discussions of co-operation in the past, there was now immediate physical space available for joint activity. Another factor was that the conditions of the grants awarded by the Pincus Foundation had involved the education departments of the two movements working more closely, creating yet another area of co-operation and begging the question as to whether it was time for a more fundamental restructuring of the two organisations. There was also the conviction that it was an anomaly that Britain should be the only country in the world to have two separate Progressive movements. In addition it was felt that while RSGB and ULPS had only limited influence by themselves – consisting of 15 per cent and seven per cent respectively of synagogue-affiliated British Jewry – together they would be a much stronger force in the community.

However, there were also voices against either union or more contact with the Liberals. When a working party under the chairmanship of Don Glazer was formed by the RSGB in November 1982 to establish 'the extent of the common ground' that existed between the movements, its terms of reference were amended to include the words 'and the differences'. Those objecting to the moves feared that the RSGB's *halachic* standards would be compromised, that any possible *rapprochement* with the Orthodox would be jeopardised, and that closer links might lead to large-scale resignations from their members. The working party's report six months later gave such a balanced summary of the points of similarity and difference that both proponents and opponents of merger found their positions confirmed. It referred to the historical differences between the two movements but claimed that there was now considerable identity of thought, with both movements undergoing a period of change and containing a wide spectrum of views which often reflected each other. The crucial point of departure lay not in theology or observances but in status matters, with three particular distinctions: the Reform required male converts to be circumcised and all converts to undergo immersion, while the Liberals did not insist upon them; the Reform required a *get* before a remarriage could take place, whereas the Liberals did not; the Reform accepted the matrilineal line, whereby Jewish status was handed down through the mother, whereas the Liberals accepted as Jewish a child with one Jewish parent and who was brought up with a Jewish education, irrespective of the gender of that parent. For some, these differences meant that the two movements were incompatible and there was no point in pursuing the matter any further; for others, it showed how close they were in all but a few respects and how discussion could lead to a viable merging.

A lengthy and occasionally stormy debate on the report took place at the Council meeting on 11 September 1983, with the two camps rehearsing by now familiar arguments and the rabbis being as divided as the laity. Rabbi Gryn stated that both movements shared a modern approach and lacked any ideological conflict. At a time when polarisation was on the increase and when British Jewry was diminishing in size it was 'all the more important to swim against the tide and demonstrate a commitment to greater unity'. He was supported by Rabbi Boyden (Menorah) who pointed out that membership of either movement was often 'no more than an accident of geography', with people joining whichever synagogue was nearest. Rabbi Leigh (Edgware), by contrast, claimed that merger would lead to greater polarisation by taking away the middle ground. Citing massive discontent, Bournemouth Synagogue claimed that it might lose a third of its members if talks proceeded. Opposition also came from the RSY-Netzer representative who declared that the two youth movements did not share the same views. At the end of the session a resolution was presented by West London instructing the executive body to institute discussions with the ULPS on 'the desirability and feasibility of a single synagogue organisation embracing the RSGB and ULPS'. It was passed by 43 votes to 18. A report was to be made within 12 months, and if any change in the RSGB's format was recommended it would have to come before a general meeting and be approved by a 75 per cent majority.

The RSGB discussion team consisted of three rabbis, four lay people, the executive director and an RSY-Netzer representative. In turn they set up smaller groups on the six areas of potential difficulty: *halachic* issues, *kashrut* and observance, youth and education, prayer book and services, Israel and the Jewish people, administration and finance. The tensions between the pro- and anti-merger camps within the RSGB led Raymond Goldman to issue a call for mutual trust and understanding at the 1984 Conference. It was accompanied by a warning that 'any proposal which may eventually emerge will only be worth pursuing if it is capable of being incorporated without completely disturbing the equilibrium...between the more radical and the more conservative elements in RSGB'. For their part the Liberals had followed a similar course, with their own working party and internal discussions. They, too, had developed diametrically opposed groups: one certain that merger would be highly beneficial, the other adamant that merger would betray the principles of Liberal Judaism, and also fearing that 'merger' might turn into 'take-over', with the smaller ULPS losing its identity. Nevertheless, the ULPS decided to co-operate fully in the joint feasibility study.

When the study was presented to the RSGB council on 3 March 1985 it presented compromise proposals which, in the event of merger, could resolve the areas of difference. Thus each synagogue would be free to adopt whichever prayer book it pleased, while status issues would be decided by a joint assembly of Reform and Liberal rabbis after a five-year period. Individual congregations would, as before, be responsible for their own policy on *kashrut* and *Shabbat*. The existing co-operation on education ensured that few difficulties arose, but the strong Zionist orientation of RSY-Netzer meant a considerable gulf existed between it and the Liberal youth movement, ULPSNYC, and it was envisaged that the two would remain separate. It was recognised that a series of administrative reforms would be necessary if the merger went ahead, but that the result would be the more cost-effective use of resources. Perhaps most significantly of all, the study noted that much of the difference lay in ethos rather than strict practice. The key question was whether there was a sufficient degree of tolerance among members of each movement to accept the right of members of the other movement to differ over what was considered important or irrelevant.

However, the report had fulfilled only half its brief, making recommendations as to the feasibility of merger, but refraining from commenting on its desirability. This, it was felt, lay in the hands of the two movements themselves. In fact, the matter was never properly discussed by the two councils, for the two executives drew their own conclusion and presented a joint statement that effectively ended the merger talks:[5]

> In the view of the Officers of both RSGB and ULPS the report demonstrates substantial areas of common ground and they urge that these be actively explored with a view to developing closer co-operation. Education, Soviet Jewry, Social Issues and Community Relations, as well as their existing joint involvement with the Leo Baeck College, are the fields in which the potential for working more closely together should be examined.
>
> At the same time they take the view, and they so recommend to their respective Councils, that the creation of a single synagogual organisation, embracing both groupings, is not practicable in the current situation. To contain the existing diversity of attitudes and practice within the parameters of one synagogual organisation would require too broad a stance, making it difficult to generate policy and to provide any clear direction.

The decision was taken for two main reasons: first, a concern that certain differences were unbridgeable and that no amount of negotiation could successfully overcome them. This particularly affected status issues but was also based on the chasm between the youth movements. Second, there was a fear that those opposed to a merger would not stay within the RSGB but might break away, including the second-largest congregation, Edgware; if that happened the emotional and financial cost of merger would be too high. The officers, already shaken by the rancour and threats unleashed by the merger talks, were seeking to pre-empt that situation. With hindsight, it is clear that compromise was possible; what was lacking was the will to implement it. Moreover, it was ironic that the youth, who might have been expected to be the most open to change and to radical developments, should have proved more conservative than the adults.

The RSGB council met on 12 May and expressed considerable disquiet that the issue had been decided in advance of any discussion by them. A motion noting the executive's recommendation was passed by 33 votes to 24, the narrow margin representing both the dismay of those favouring merger and those upset that such a lengthy debate had come to such an abrupt halt. Council then passed a motion urging that 'both Movements continue their discussions leading towards closer association'. It expressed a desire to capitalise on the many areas of similarity and to ensure they were maintained and increased even without merger. An even more urgent task was a process of internal healing. At the Conference a few weeks later, Maurice Michaels declared in his Chairman's Report that 'It would be foolish to belittle the degree of heat and antagonism engendered by this issue... [and] some of the deepest internal divisions in RSGB's history'. It was a tribute to the maturity of the movement as a whole that his call for unity and common purpose was taken up so unanimously. Just as remarkable as the friction caused by the merger talks was the speed with which those tensions disappeared. By the following Conference, Michaels was able to report that the tensions had virtually disappeared and that the RSGB had recovered its sense of purpose and identity. However, the desire to put the merger issue firmly in the past meant that little energy was invested in the Joint Standing Committee formed with ULPS representatives to investigate areas of co-operation. Moreover the committee suffered from the lack of any way of implementing what it discussed and in March 1987 it was disbanded and replaced by bi-annual meetings of the RSGB and ULPS officers.

The emphasis quickly turned from union at the centre to co-operation at local level. A model for such links had been created in the midst of the merger talks by the establishment of the Eastern Counties Association of Progressive Synagogues (ECAPS). It encompassed eight synagogues: Barkingside Progressive, Buckhurst Hill Reform, Cambridge Reform, Harlow Reform, Settlement, Southend Reform, South West Essex Reform and Woodford Liberal. ECAPS had arisen from a joint Israel Independence Day service in 1984 and led to co-operation in education for children, Israel and Soviet Jewry activities, and fund-raising for Leo Baeck College. Most notably it was responsible for an adult education institute that served the needs of all the synagogues in the area, which none would have been able to achieve by themselves. By pooling resources, avoiding duplication and facilitating contact and good relations between ordinary members, ECAPS became an example for other congregations. Similar, albeit less extensive, links were forged between West London and St Johns Wood Liberal, while in 1987 INTERSYN was formed bringing closer co-operation between six Reform and Liberal congregations in north-west London: Finchley Reform, Finchley Progressive, Hendon Reform, North Western Reform, Southgate Progressive and Southgate Reform.

In the eyes of some, the merger talks had been a complete waste of time and highly divisive. For others, they were another halting step in the union that they believed would eventually happen and that it was just a matter of the right moment. There is no doubt that the issue will resurface again at some future point, although the outcome cannot be predicted. It is equally clear that certain advances came from the talks, such as closer partnership in areas of obvious common ground, which in turn led to institutional changes: the Sponsoring Movements Committee which reformed the finances of Leo Baeck College, the merging of the two education departments into the Centre for Jewish Education, the creation of an umbrella organisation for Israel-related activities (Progressive Jews for Israel), and the decision of the two rabbinic bodies to have two joint meetings a year and co-operate more fully. These developments may mean that a merger is more likely next time the matter is debated. By then the decision of the Assembly of Rabbis to award Jewish status to children of Jewish fathers and non-Jewish mothers in certain situations will have softened (although not solved) one of the main points of distinction between the movements. In addition the more Zionist orientation of the ULPS youth movement will also have breached a previous chasm. Nevertheless, the endemic tendency of British Jewry – to avoid rationalisation and to maintain fiercely independent organisations that largely duplicate each other – may prove more resilient than the forces for change.

The failure of merger talks with the Liberals should not be allowed to hide the fact that the RSGB was continuing to expand through its own growth. The 1980s and early 1990s witnessed the addition of another nine congregations: Beth Shalom (Cambridge), Brighton (which rejoined after 12 years as an independent Reform synagogue), Buckhurst Hill (originally known as Epping Forest), Hull, Kol Chai (Hatch End), Mill Hill (which later merged with the Wembley community), Milton Keynes, Thanet and South Hampshire. They brought the total number of constituent synagogues to 37. The fact that only three of the nine were in the Greater London area confirmed the RSGB's ability to maintain its role as a national movement rather than, as with several other synagogual organisations, a London-based one. The return of Brighton in 1984 had been the result of the personal initiative of Jerome Karet, who had made it one of his aims on becoming chairman of the RSGB. It was coupled with the realisation by Brighton that isolation brought many disadvantages, especially the inability to find a successor to its rabbi, Erwin Rosenblum, who was about to retire. There was still the issue of the unpaid subscriptions which had been the original cause of the dispute, but the RSGB council felt it would be unfair to burden the current Brighton membership with the debts of a previous generation, which by now had long been written off RSGB accounts. Brighton's commitment to contribute towards the Reform Foundation was seen as a compromise solution and they were welcomed back into the fold. Hopes of achieving a similar *rapprochement* with the only other independent Reform synagogue, Westminster, did not materialise, largely because of its history as being founded as a breakaway community from West London and its desire to continue that principle. Nevertheless, it continued to pay a token amount to the RSGB for the use of some of its facilities, particularly its rabbinic court. A similar arrangement applied to the Belsize Square Synagogue, which had left the ULPS in 1989 to become an independent congregation but which also contributed to the RSGB so as to take advantage of the Reform *Beth Din*.

Small groups of Reform-minded individuals arose in disparate parts of the country, but were often not large enough to become viable congregations. Occasional meetings took place in Barnet, East Grinstead, Edinburgh, Maidstone and Walthamstow, but all failed to develop further. Some collapsed because of lack of numbers, others from proximity to existing congregations, others from internal problems. Even those ventures that were successful were still unable to reach a size capable of supporting a rabbi, a problem that applied also to some existing constituents. In 1984 Conference sought to remedy this by the creation of a foster rabbi scheme to provide rabbinic support to communities without a minister. The intention was that the rabbis involved in the scheme would spend 100 hours a year with their foster congregation, comprising four annual visits, and concentrate on giving religious and educational guidance rather than service-taking. However, the scheme proved unwanted in its proposed format as congregations largely required rabbis to take services. The fact that the ULPS managed to operate a similar rabbinic foster scheme more successfully, as well as to provide lay service-takers via its *Ba'al Tefillah* scheme, highlighted the lack of time and resources given to congregational development by the RSGB at that point. It was largely seen as a matter for local initiative, with only a small and hopelessly overworked congregational development committee giving any back-up from the centre. The gap between what could be done and what was done was appreciated, but lack of finances and preoccupation with other issues prevented any progress.

It took a further seven years before the long-suggested appointment was made of a part-time congregational development co-ordinator. Donald Black's role was to provide both physical support and general encouragement, as well as simply 'being in touch'. The mere fact of having an RSGB appointee who visited 21 congregations in his first year was central to the growing awareness that progress in a whole variety of areas could best be made through strong central input at a local level. A structural device to assist that process had been introduced at the 1992 conference when the RSGB constitution was changed to create a new category of membership alongside the existing Constituent Synagogues – that of Associate Congregation. It allowed developing communities to have a formal status within the RSGB, permitted them to send observers to Council meetings, and had the intention of facilitating their progress into fully-fledged constituents. By 1994 there were five Associate Congregations: Beit Klal Yisrael (North Kensington), Coventry, Sheffield, Darlington and Swindon. The latter two congregations were of particular note as they had been long-standing Orthodox communities which transferred their allegiance to Reform. In both cases they were isolated from other Jewish life and were finding it extremely difficult to maintain the requirements of an Orthodox synagogue. Moreover, the lifestyle and attitude of their membership was more akin to the Reform. The fact that the rabbis of neighbouring Reform synagogues – Newcastle and Maidenhead respectively – offered tangible support and took an interest in their affairs persuaded them that they would be best served by affiliating to the RSGB. Theoretically it is a pattern that many other nominally Orthodox congregations in the provinces could follow, and thereby greatly add to the size of the RSGB. However, the need to gain the near-unanimous approval of members, the ability to maintain burial rights and funeral expense schemes, and the limitations attached to the deeds of some synagogue buildings make this a complex path to pursue and mean that a mass transfer of congregations is unlikely. The impasse underlies the common adage that most of British Jewry 'belongs to the Orthodox but thinks Reform'. It is symptomatic of a problem that has constantly bedevilled the Reform Movement, failing to turn popular sympathy into actual membership. Another strategy that arose was the decision taken in 1991 to examine the potential of 'in-fill' congregations: areas of high Jewish density such as north-west London where there might be room for a new Reform congregation on the model of Kol Chai in Hatch End. Attempts thus far have not been productive and have shown how difficult it is to induce artificially the establishment of a congregation unless there is a spontaneous local initiative, as was the case with Kol Chai.

Despite the occasional set-backs, the steady expansion is even more of an achievement when measured against the decline in the size of British Jewry. This growth applies not only to the number of congregations but also to the RSGB's overall membership. Throughout the 1980s and early 1990s its net total increased by an average of two per cent a year. Bearing in mind that a six per cent increase had to be recruited simply to replace losses through deaths and resignations, it means that an even larger growth occurred to achieve the net gain. The 8,000 Reform members that were among the 450,000 British Jews in 1942 has grown to 42,000 out of a general community of 300,000 in 1994. With an estimated 240,000 Jews being members of synagogues, it meant that the RSGB accounted for one in six of all synagogue-affiliated Jews. From a small minority, the RSGB has become the second-largest synagogue grouping in the United Kingdom. The following figures collated by the Board of Deputies' Community Research Unit illustrate the comparative membership of religious groupings by percentages, and also trace changing trends in recent years. The statistics relate to the Greater London area, and apply largely but not exactly to the rest of the country:[6]

	1970	*1977*	*1983*	*1990*
Right Wing Orthodox	2.6	4.2	5.3	8.8
Central Orthodox	72.3	69.7	66.0	58.2
Sephardi	4.5	3.3	3.3	3.7
Reform	11.9	13.7	16.5	18.0
Liberal	8.7	9.1	8.9	11.3
Total	100.00	100.00	100.00	100.00

Many factors can be cited as responsible for the expansion: the confidence and energy unleashed by the Manor House; the impact of a young and dynamic rabbinate; the leadership shown by a succession of forward-thinking chairmen; the dedicated guidance of the RSGB's professional staff; the early awareness of the importance of the young generation and the resources given to education and youth; the appeal of the RSGB's religious message to a Jewry who found it related to their needs; the equal rights given to women in all aspects of synagogue life. All have played an important role, but perhaps the most crucial is the commitment of countless lay men and women who have given unstinted time at local and national level to slowly building up both the congregations and the central structure. It is essentially a movement that has revolved around neither buildings nor rabbis, but around the religious drive of lay people. In this respect it remains true to its origins and the formula that led to a quarrelsome schism has eventually resulted in a formidable institution.

Another major factor for growth was the refusal of the lay leadership to rest on its laurels but to push ahead and engage in a rigorous process of self-appraisal and forward planning. This was assisted by the application of modern management techniques with which many honorary officers were familiar in their business life. The process had begun in September 1980 through an administrative working party under the chairmanship of Jeffery Rose. It was established in order to counteract the 'disabling parochialism' of synagogues: 'RSGB is now 40 years old and yet has still in many instances to sell itself to its own constituents.'[7] After 18 months of deliberation it produced 30 recommendations regarding communications, decision-making, office management and leadership structure. The executive was strengthened through each officer having a job specification, while the ability of the Council to act as a more effective body was boosted by the stipulation that at least one of the representatives of each synagogue was to be the chairman. Perhaps most important of all it called for the RSGB to formulate a six-year plan so as to create an order of priorities and have a definite sense of direction. Until then the RSGB had often relied on *ad hoc* initiatives by leading personalities; now it was urged to be pro-active in its policy-making and to draw up a considered strategy based on wide consultation.

The idea of a long-term strategy was welcomed and was started at the annual residential weekend of the executive body in January 1983. A core group of Don Glazer, Raymond Goldman, Julian Levy and Maurice Michaels continued the work, producing a draft document which was presented to the Council in March 1984, debated and refined. The final version of the 'Six Year Plan' was a comprehensive survey of all RSGB activities and a major landmark in its development. It affirmed the objectives of the movement laid down in the constitution as still applicable, but made three additions: exploring other forms of Jewish religious community, participating in the work of the wider Jewish community, and fostering greater understanding among Jews. The first was a recognition of the growing need for alternative structures to congregations, such as informal *chavurot* groups; the last two were a reflection of the increased importance of the

RSGB within British Jewry and the responsibilities that now accompanied it. The plan laid down nine goals:

1. To continue to explore the religious direction and development of the movement.

2. To maintain and improve the effectiveness of the RSGB and its existing constituents.

3. By the end of the six year period every constituent should have, as a minimum, the part-time services of a rabbi and other communities under the RSGB's aegis should have access to rabbinic guidance through the association.

4. To achieve an improved level of Jewish knowledge and understanding throughout the RSGB and its associated bodies.

5. To establish the importance of *Eretz Yisrael* within the theology and teaching of Judaism.

6. To establish and support new communities and expand membership of the Reform Movement.

7. To expand the provisions of chaplaincy for students and add each year to the number of places of further education where this is available.

8. To examine the practicability of a national burial scheme.

9. To achieve a secure financial base for the continuation and furtherance of RSGB's work.

Each goal was accompanied by a series of strategies by which it might be achieved. Thus the first goal was to be accomplished by promoting the examination of tradition; researching religious aspects of problems confronting contemporary society; exploring the role of service and sacrifice in the religious life of individuals and of the community; encouraging individuals to be innovative in areas of service, structure and activity.

An important aspect of the Six Year Plan was that it should be monitored after three years so as to assess what progress had occurred. Some of the goals remained unfulfilled hopes, such as the national burial scheme, which seemed impossible to organise despite the many calls for it. Other goals were ongoing projects that needed decades of constant reinforcement, such as increasing the level of adult learning, although small improvements were being made all the time. More tangible steps could be seen in other areas, such as current religious issues, in the seminars on ecology, the position of women, medical ethics and the family. Most noticeable of all was the acceptance that leadership of both congregations and the RSGB could not simply be a matter of personal energy or religious commitment, but had to include management skills that needed to be acquired through nurture and training. The Six Year Plan itself was not to be regarded as a final goal but was to be subject to constant review and updating.

Other reports were commissioned in areas that needed greater attention. Thus the family working party was re-established in 1987 under the chairmanship of Wendy Greengross and pioneered a whole new field of care for the many individuals who had to face bereavement, single parenthood, early retirement and other problems. It also recognised and sought to alleviate the burden falling on many individuals who acted as carers and often felt very pressurised and isolated. A 'caring community group' was formed that both assisted local synagogue care schemes and was responsible for central seminars on specific issues such as divorce, mental illness, elderly parents and unemployment. Its work reflected in part the change in government policy which sought to lessen state institutional care and increase the responsibility of families and local communities. Another major report emerged from the congregational development strategy group in 1989. It pointed out that the Greater London area contained 75 per cent of British Jewry and so the RSGB should study areas of potential growth there, either through 'in-filling' or through more aggressive expansion in areas where there was an Orthodox synagogue but little Orthodoxy.

Several groups had already been in evidence before the Six Year Plan but they certainly benefited from its impetus. The publications committee added the word 'communications' to its name and took responsibility both for increasing communication between the RSGB and its members and for raising the profile of the RSGB in the wider community. The appointment of Viv Bellos as part-time music consultant in 1986 did much to revive the musical aspects of worship. She produced a music handbook, published settings for Sabbath and festive services, organised seminars and choir festivals, and established a choirs consultancy group that visited congregations and helped train their choirs. The success of the Northern Regional Committee in linking local congregations and initiating joint activities resulted in a similar move for those in the south. The Southern Regional Committee was formed in 1985 under the leadership of Eve Cowan and brought together Bournemouth, Brighton, Bromley, Cardiff, Maidenhead, North West Surrey, South Hampshire and Wimbledon. Apart from an annual residential weekend, it sponsored occasional youth events, while several of the rabbis met together on a regular basis.

The Association of Women's Guilds continued its welfare, educational and fund-raising activities but changed its name in 1986 to Reform Synagogue Guilds. The intention was partly to broaden the scope of its membership by allowing men to join. In this respect it followed the example of various individual guilds which had already dropped the word 'women' from their title. The change was also designed to identify the particular ideology of the movement, for the Association played a quiet but pervasive role in representing the RSGB in a variety of public areas and making the Reform voice heard where it might otherwise not have been, such as in the Association of Jewish Women's Organisations, the National Council of Women, the International Council of Jewish Women, the United Nations Association, League of Jewish Women, the Organisation for Educational Training and Technological Resources (ORT) and the Women's International Zionist Organisation (WIZO). Another group to change its name and reinvigorate itself was the Progressive Jewish Students Commission, which shortened itself to Progressive Jewish Students (PJS). Its activities were assisted through the creation of the position of students' activities co-ordinator, an annual appointment of a graduate to help individual groups, liaise with SATMAH and develop relations with RSY-Netzer, a source of future membership. The first co-ordinator was David Van Gelder in 1986. Several rabbis volunteered to serve as part-time chaplains to the major universities, but with a few exceptions their role was largely to respond to personal crises rather than spend much time on campus. It was a constant lament at Council meetings that there was no full-time Progressive chaplain anywhere in the country, especially at a time when Jewish students suffered both from the conversionist activities of Christian missionaries and the attacks of Islamic groups. Instead they either were left with no rabbinic support or had to turn to the increasing number of chaplains sponsored by the Lubavitch movement. Lack of funds rather than lack of will was the cause, but within the RSGB it was seen as a serious indictment that the movement was unable to provide for one of its most precious and also most vulnerable assets.

A much more comprehensive change occurred in the Soviet Jewry Group, the previous successes of which were developed even further under the dynamic chairmanship of Linda Isaacs and Alan Myers during the mid-1980s. A change of name to the more evocative 'Exodus' was typical of the many high profile and emotive campaigns it undertook. It had the highest number of visitors going from Britain to the Soviet Union, while it co-ordinated with the Assembly of Rabbis to organise a rota of rabbis who provided a succession of lectures on Jewish learning in Moscow, Leningrad and other major centres. Exodus also pioneered the idea of twinning those having a *bar/batmitzvah* in RSGB congregations with 13-year-olds unable to do so in Russia. Empty chairs in synagogue, invitations to the service in both children's names, exchange of letters and projects in religion school became commonplace and were emulated by other sections of the Jewish community. Various 'stunts' achieved national headlines, such as delivering a petition to the Soviet Embassy calling for the release of the Keis family – honorary members of Middlesex New Synagogue – signed by 43 councillors from the London Borough of Harrow. Exodus also encouraged sponsoring communities to maintain links with 'their refuseniks' once they had settled in Israel and itself intervened with members of the Israeli Government on behalf of individuals who were experiencing social and economic problems there. When Elena Dubianskaya and Eric Khassin, two refuseniks sponsored by Exodus, were released in June 1988 they were flown to England as dramatic guests of honour at that year's Conference. That same year the National Council for Soviet Jewry reformed its constitution and recognised Exodus's enormous contribution by increasing its representatives from one to five, making it the largest group alongside 'The 35s'. When the Communist system collapsed and Jewish emigration was virtually unhindered, Exodus appreciated that its work was done. In 1992 it disbanded and reconstituted itself as Exodus 2000 under the leadership of Rabbi Bob Shafritz and Linda Kahn. Its new brief was to support the Jewish identity of those choosing to remain in the former Soviet

Union and particularly to nurture the development of Progressive communities. Twinning was resuscitated, but this time it was between RSGB synagogues and emerging east European ones, with the former carrying news of the latter in their magazines, fund-raising for them and sending groups over to establish personal relationships between the members. Several rabbis made visits, while Rabbi Fred Morgan (North West Surrey) spent three months in Budapest serving the burgeoning Reform community there.

The plight of Syrian Jews also exercised world Jewry. The first committee to be established in Britain in their support had been set up at Sinai Synagogue by Rabbi Charles Emanuel and its efforts led to a resolution at the 1987 conference calling on the government to persuade Syria to allow Jews the right to emigrate. However, the Foreign Office in Israel advised that the different circumstance of Syrian Jewry to that of Soviet Jewry meant that more active efforts might be counter-productive and the RSGB duly refrained from launching a national campaign.

An entirely different story occurred in the area of social issues, a field in which the RSGB had not been greatly involved before but now took an active lead, both within and without the Jewish community. The impetus had initially come from a sub-committee of the Assembly of Rabbis, the social action group. The prophetic stance of righteousness and justice had always been a strong tenet of Reform Judaism, but there had been no organised vehicle for practical expression. In 1984 the group expanded into a full committee of the RSGB, known as the Social Issues Group, although continuing to be chaired by its founder, Rabbi Barbara Borts. Thenceforth it was responsible for a series of pamphlets, briefing papers, seminars and events that forced the RSGB to confront a variety of political and social issues. Apartheid was condemned, a boycott of South African goods and investments was called for, and a freedom *seder* was held outside South Africa House; the government was urged to improve its efforts for famine relief and a gathering of other British Jewish welfare agencies (such as the Jewish Welfare Board and the Central British Fund) was co-ordinated at the Sternberg Centre to meet with Frank Judd, the director of Oxfam. Conference became used to annual resolutions on subjects far beyond the confines of synagogue life and not even limited to British shores. They called for an end to the international arms trade with oppressive regimes, urged fulfilment of the United Nations' Declaration of Human Rights, objected to aspects of racism in the criminal justice system, expressed concern at world hunger and poverty. Their forthright nature alarmed some delegates, who felt that a religious organisation should not be so active politically. However, as the executive director pointed out in defence of the resolutions, a religious body could not ignore the issues of the day; moreover, there was a difference between politics and party politics: 'The prophets had taken moral and ethical stances and RSGB must be in that prophetic tradition... There would be times when our ethical and moral concerns would coincide with those of one or other political party but that did not entitle RSGB to shy away, nor should we.'[8]

The appointment of Vicky Joseph as part-time co-ordinator of the Social Issues Group in 1987 was both a reflection of the esteem in which its work was held and a spur to further activity. Many projects were conducted in conjunction with a parallel group from within the ULPS, the two maintaining their separate identity but known jointly as the Social Action Forum. A booklet entitled *Do Not Destroy My World* (1989) presented a Jewish perspective on ecology, along with information and suggestions. Apart from the individuals it influenced, it also had a significant impact on policy in synagogues and at the Sternberg Centre itself, with a shift to recycled paper, avoidance of non-biodegradable disposable cups, use of non-toxic cleaning materials. A 'Green Fair' at the Sternberg Centre the following year brought together 30 ecologically oriented organisations and attracted 1,500 people. A strategy developed whereby the Social Issues Group targeted a particular issue, brought it to public attention, left a core group to continue it and then turned its energy to a different topic. This happened with the theme of homelessness and the enormously successful *Bayit* (home) campaign launched in 1991. Just as the ecology issue had been built around the 'green' festival of *Tu Bi'Shevat, Bayit* was rooted in *sukkot* and its potent image of temporary housing. Apart from launching a series of 'sleep-overs' in the synagogue *sukkot* as a means of raising awareness and as fund-raising exercises, it prompted a long-term collection of second-hand furniture for the Kings Cross Homelessness Project. It also initiated political pressure to change the root cause of homelessness and to amend current housing legislation. The campaign led to local developments, too, most notably with

Finchley Reform Synagogue being the first to establish its own lunch and hospitality scheme for homeless people who needed a warm meal, washing facilities and the warmth of human contact.

Two years later, the *Matir Assurim* (Free those who are bound) campaign was begun. It focused on the rights of two separate groups, refugees and the disabled, and was centred on the festival of *Chanukah* and its theme of freedom from oppression. Once again, it was accompanied by a potent mixture of learning packs and action plans, and linked in with similar efforts being made by other groups in society. Indeed, in many ways, the Social Issues Group had carried the name of the RSGB into many parts of the public arena for the first time. RSGB's concern and actions were reported in newsletters of such diverse organisations as Shelter, the World Wildlife Fund and Friends of the Earth. The group also helped establish the Faith Alliance, an informal organisation of leaders of different faiths concerned with combating racism. Several Jewish single-issue groups were established directly or indirectly because of the Social Issues Group, including Jews Against Apartheid, Jewish Support for the Homeless, JONAH (Jews Organised for a Nuclear Arms Halt) and Tzedek (Jewish Action for a Just World). The group's activities permeated all aspects of the RSGB – public seminars, local synagogue initiatives, Assembly of Rabbis briefings, RSY-Netzer programmes, religion school projects, adult education study groups and conference presentations. Without doubt it was one of the most powerful and pervasive innovations of the 1980s and 1990s, and its impact was epitomised by a resolution passed at the 1994 conference through which the RSGB recognised 'that Judaism is concerned with how people organise themselves in society, and it is not only acceptable but also incumbent upon Reform Jews to speak out and involve themselves wherever social justice is absent'.

The higher profile RSGB was attaining in the non-Jewish world was more than matched by its increased publicity within the Jewish community. The main organ of British Jewry was the *Jewish Chronicle* and under the editorship of Geoffrey Paul (1977–90) was often felt to have a less than favourable attitude towards the Progressive movements. This was not necessarily because of any deep-rooted opposition to non-Orthodoxy but as a reaction to the way in which the paper had antagonised the Orthodox establishment by its support for Rabbi Dr Louis Jacobs under the previous editor and Paul's attempt to mollify the Chief

Rabbinate. Nevertheless, the growth of Reform could not be ignored and from the mid-1980s there was a gradual increase in the space given to news about individual Reform synagogues, while Reform rabbis were invited to contribute articles on Judaism and join the panel of commentators on the weekly *Torah* portion. Greater attention was given to the RSGB itself following the decision to invite *Jewish Chronicle* reporters to attend its council meetings. In this respect the *Jewish Chronicle* played an important communal role, acting as a unifying factor among the different groupings in British Jewry, by keeping their membership in touch with each other's developments, however dissimilar their practices and views. Despite the polarisation that was occurring within the community, the fact that a high percentage still subscribed to the same weekly journal, rather than reading their own splinter paper, was a harmonising factor in itself. A similar mellowing occurred with the Manchester papers, the *Jewish Gazette* and the *Jewish Telegraph*, which gradually acknowledged the existence of Reform congregations and rabbis in their columns.

On a purely internal level, many of the administrative improvements called for in the Six Year Plan were implemented. A database of resources and personnel was slowly built up; RSGB office equipment was upgraded and sophisticated technology was employed to handle more efficiently the ever-increasing administrative tasks and give better control of financial information. The oft-made call for an office manager to relieve the executive director of more mundane responsibilities was long unanswered because of financial constraints, but eventually resulted in the position of director of administration being created in 1990. The first appointment was not successful, but the arrival of Nicki Landau the following year provided the day-to-day office management of what had by then become the equivalent of a substantial business corporation, although sometimes still run as if it were a small society operating from a room in West London. One of the last links with that earlier era came with the retirement in 1992 of Ena Black who, along with her husband Donald, was an early graduate of the YASGB. She had worked for the RSGB's administration for nearly 17 years as assistant to Raymond Goldman, and like him had served in a voluntary capacity far beyond her duties as a paid employee. The need to provide future leadership had been a key provision of the Six Year Plan and it found fulfilment in a leadership training steering group (later to be known as the Leadership Training Task Group) chaired by Maurice Michaels in 1987. It brought together a team of professional trainers acting in a voluntary capacity who developed a number of courses for skills that were most needed by congregations. These included effective meetings, communications, inter-personal skills, attracting volunteers and nurturing new leaders. The plan's emphasis on training and exchange of information also led to regular seminars being organised by the RSGB for disparate groups such as synagogue treasurers, newsletter editors, computer users and administrators. The latter two proved so successful that they culminated in two new groups being formed: the Computer Advisory Group, co-ordinated by David Ruback, and the Association of Reform Community Management Personnel, chaired by Lynette Chazen. The latter – formed in 1993 – reflected not only the growing number of synagogues which employed administrators but the radical change in organising synagogue affairs, with a shift from voluntary to professional management.

The call in the Six Year Plan to promote the Land of Israel was made at a time when the virtually unanimous enthusiasm for Israel amongst Reform members seemed to be endangered by the anti-Reform stance of the *Likud* government under Menachem Begin. There was disquiet at the bias towards Orthodox establishments when funding education in the Diaspora and the lack of any recognition of Reform communities in Israel itself. Among the many obstacles faced were the difficulty of Reform synagogues and schools in obtaining planning permission, their inability to gain grants, the ban on Reform rabbis performing weddings, and the refusal to allocate land for Reform cemeteries. This was largely due to the political power wielded by Orthodox religious parties upon whose support every government since 1948 had been force to rely in order to maintain a coalition. Abba Eban expressed the frustration of many when he told a Pro-Zion meeting at the North Western Reform Synagogue: 'I believe in equality and I believe that Jews in Israel should at least be as equal as non-Jews. The Christians are not told which church they can marry in, nor the Moslems which mosque. The Bahais are not ordered to choose one temple instead of another – only Jews are given these regulations.'[9]

The threat of amending the Law of Return and disqualifying

Jews converted by non-Orthodox authorities, experienced already in 1974 and 1977, once again arose as a result of the inconclusive general election of 1984. A deputation from the RSGB, along with ULPS delegates, called on the Israeli ambassador to present their concerns, while the Assembly of Rabbis boycotted the new Prime Minister, Yitzhak Shamir, on his visit to Britain the following year because of his vote in favour of changing the status quo. The 1985 Conference passed a resolution noting with satisfaction that the vote had failed and calling on all Israeli politicians to recognise 'that the status of Jews the world over is affected by the Law of Return and that the cynical treatment of this matter for party political or coalition convenience can only damage the relationship between Israel and major sectors of Diaspora Jewry'. Similar protests were made against backdoor attempts by the Ministry of the Interior to refuse citizenship to non-Orthodox converts or put special marks on their identity papers. Nevertheless, problems recurred after a stalemate in the 1988 elections and the danger loomed of changes to the Law of Return being bargained for coalition votes. Israeli politicians were warned not to alienate Diaspora Jewry, Israel's 'one constant and reliable ally'.[10] The intensity of protests from both Progressive and Zionist groups around the world took Israeli political circles by surprise. It caused a backlash amongst the general population against the efforts of small Orthodox parties to exert power and was a factor in a Government of National Unity being formed instead. Although the Law of Return remained unchanged, the continued problems experienced by Progressive Jews in Israel led the 1994 Conference to urge 'the Government of Israel to correct the injustice and irony whereby Israel is the one democracy in which not all Jews enjoy complete religious freedom'.

Despite these concerns the RSGB made it clear that displeasure at policies pursued by particular governments would not undermine its support for Israel at large. Some council members suggested that Reform synagogues should stop their contributions to the Joint Israel Appeal (JIA), the main arm of Zionist fund-raising in Britain, which assisted certain groups inimical to Reform Judaism, and that they should instead give to specific Progressive charities in Israel. This debate was also fuelled by fears that some funds given to the JIA might be used for projects in the West Bank and Gaza, then under Israeli control but outside the 1967 borders. These worries were allayed by assurances by the JIA that donated money was only used for projects within the pre-1967 borders, and that they were taking a stand against providing financial support to Orthodox institutions which did not support the State of Israel. Whilst some individual synagogues decided to concentrate on raising funds directly for Israeli Progressive institutions, the RSGB's general policy was that it should not distance itself from major communal efforts and that constituents should continue to support the JIA even if they had additional campaigns for other charities. Moreover it was felt that the best way of achieving changes was by working within the Zionist system. Pro-Zion gradually built up its membership and played an increasingly important role in the Zionist Federation. This process was accelerated in 1983 after *Herut* and the General Zionists left the Federation to form a splinter group, thus creating a vacuum that Pro-Zion helped fill, with two of its members filling the positions of honorary secretary and treasurer of the Federation.

At the time of the 1987 allocation of delegates to the Zionist Congress in Jerusalem, Pro-Zion was instrumental in pressing for properly scrutinised elections rather than basing delegates on unverified membership lists that bore little if any relationship to the true situation. Such elections were held in all other countries and, despite the cost a postal ballot would involve, the stand was fully supported by the RSGB. In the event, elections proved impossible, but not only was Pro-Zion allocated three of the 27 mandates given to Britain (at the previous Congress four years earlier it received none), but its stance had attracted the attention of the Zionist world. The episode put Pro-Zion firmly on the political map, establishing its credentials as a group of integrity and in the forefront of rectifying the sometimes sullied image of back-room deals that characterised Zionist politics. Similarly energetic campaigns by Progressive Zionist movements in other countries resulted in sweeping gains by ARZENU, the world-wide Progressive organisation, including the election of Dick Hirsch, a former American Reform rabbi and now executive director of the World Union for Progressive Judaism, as chairman of the *Va'ad ha'Poel*, the Zionist General Council which governed the World Zionist Organisation between congresses. At the same time his colleague Rabbi Hank Skirball was made chairman of the Department of Education and Culture in the Diaspora, which put him in a position to control the distribution of major funding. A jubilant Bernard Davis, chairman of Pro-Zion, told the RSGB council: we 'truly came of age in 1987; it marked the start of a new era of successful involvement of Progressive Zionism in Zionist politics both in Britain and on the world scene'.[11] Anyone who doubted his words would have been persuaded the following year when Pro-Zion members were elected to a quarter of the places on the Council of the Zionist Federation of Great Britain. Another consequence of this active participation was greater understanding and support for the rights of Progressive Jews in Israel by members of other Zionist groups. Thus the Zionist Federation passed a motion of its own urging the Israeli Government not to alter the Law of Return during the 1985 crisis, while an even greater breakthrough was achieved in 1988 when the World Zionist Congress passed a resolution in the name of 'the Jewish people as a whole' calling the Knesset to grant 'complete equality of rights to all streams of Jewish religion, and giving their rabbis the legal right to perform all life-cycle events and other rabbinic functions'. There were material benefits, too, with finance now being available to the Progressive movement in Israel as well as to the RSGB through grants to its Israel Action Committee and to RSY-Netzer.

There were, however, other political developments in Israel that caused much heartache and soul-searching. The 1982 Lebanon Campaign, with its heavy number of civilian Arab casualties, large loss of Israeli life and military action far beyond Israel's borders, had alarmed many Jews, both inside and outside Israel. Many British Jews, including members of Reform synagogues, felt that for the first time they could not justify a war which Israel was fighting. Although the RSGB co-ordinated collections of funds, clothes and medical supplies for those in need, the eventual withdrawal of Israel from Lebanon was largely greeted with great relief. The tensions generated by the war were heightened in 1988 when the civil rebellion of the *Intifada* broke out. Many RSGB members felt deeply ambivalent about how to react: appalled at the hostile media treatment Israel was receiving and concerned at the physical threat Israelis faced from the rioters, yet also horrified at the role of occupiers that Israelis now held and worried about its brutalising affect on the national consciousness. There was also a reticence at publicly condemning Israel at a time when she was being pilloried in so many other quarters and most needed support. The dilemma was expressed succinctly by Rabbi Hugo Gryn who told the council: 'We protested about Soweto and other injustices but didn't want to add to Israel's difficulties; yet if we did not protest, Israel might feel that we condoned violence.'[12] It was resolved to issue a statement that expressed criticism but as a caring member of the family, stating that the RSGB 'expresses its solidarity with the citizens of Israel at this difficult time... shares the anxieties [at the] hurt and injury suffered by human beings... deplores the obstructionism of the Arab nations when, in the past Israel has moved unilaterally to alleviate the plight of the inhabitants of Gaza's refugee camps... calls upon Israel to break out of its current political deadlock'. The Israel resolution at that year's conference deplored the extreme provocation Israel faced but added: 'This in no way diminishes the ultimate responsibility for upholding Jewish teaching relating to times when war has to be waged and the treatment of prisoners, and which requires recognition at all times of the Divine Image in every human being, Jew and non-Jew alike.' While many other Jewish organisations in Britain agonised over the *Intifada* but kept silent in public, the RSGB was one of the few that was not afraid to criticise Israel when it felt it appropriate, pointing out that it was being a truer friend of Israel by doing so. Nevertheless, it was not a comfortable position, and Reform spokesmen often justified it by adding that the most strident criticisms were made by Israelis themselves and that the RSGB was merely reflecting the deep divisions within Israeli society.

Expressing reservations about certain policies did not lessen RSGB support for Israel as a whole. In the aftermath of the Lebanon Campaign the Assembly of Rabbis organised its first group trip to Israel. It was so well subscribed that concern was expressed at the RSGB council that the future of the movement would have been seriously jeopardised if their plane had crashed. It was suggested that in future rabbinic missions should take the precaution of travelling in two or more planes! Israel Action continued to disseminate information about Israel, organise tours and promote fund-raising initiatives. Many congregations conducted their own Israel activities, among the most notable being the Rami Keich campaign conducted by Menorah, spearheaded by Anita Boyden, to assist disabled soldiers through horse-riding. Support for the rights of Progressive Jews in Israel was stepped up through the Friends of Progressive Judaism in Israel. In 1994 they launched the *Shabbat Shekalim* campaign as a means of using the relatively obscure Sabbath shortly before *Purim* – in Biblical times when a half-shekel was collected from every adult for the upkeep of the Sanctuary – as an opportunity to raise awareness and funds.

The proliferation of Israel-oriented groups within the RSGB and the ULPS and the duplication this involved led to the establishment in 1987 of Progressive Jews for Israel. It was an umbrella organisation that linked together and co-ordinated Friends of Progressive Judaism in Israel, Israel Action, Pro-Zion, RSY-Netzer and the ULPS JIA Committee. The scope of its work was boosted when an Israel Desk was established at the Sternberg Centre two years later, with a co-ordinator funded by the JIA, Marilyn Redstone. The Israel Desk proved of great value, and took on an important role in providing synagogues with help and information as they worked to support Israel during the 1991 Gulf War. Even more crucial was the continuing succession of *sh'lichim*. Although their work was primarily with the youth – their time being officially allocated as 80 per cent with RSY-Netzer and 20 per cent with the RSGB – their influence extended throughout the movement. Hopes for a second *shaliach* to work with northern congregations were eventually realised in 1990. The fact that the post was largely funded by the Jewish Agency at a time when it was cutting back on its expenditure was an indication of the value attached to the work being done with RSY-Netzer in the Zionist world. In turn the increased involvement of Reform congregations in Zionist forums in Manchester – the Zionist Central Council and the Zionist Youth Council – served to give the RSGB a much higher profile locally. Reform synagogues had always found it more difficult to gain acceptance in the provinces where their own numbers were smaller and where a more close-knit Jewish social and cultural life allowed Orthodox rabbis to isolate Reform communities. Now the active participation in northern Zionism resulted in Reform being recognised as an equal partner that was entitled to full consultation in the decisions being made. Fund-raising efforts were strengthened even further in 1995 with the launch of the JIA–Progressive Partnership, which was designed to increase contributions to the JIA from RSGB and ULPS members. It was accompanied by a mutually beneficial agreement by which ten per cent of the first £500,000 raised would go to Progressive projects in Israel, and higher percentages of sums above that. The existence of such an arrangement – unthinkable a few years earlier – was indicative both of the JIA's awareness of the RSGB's financial importance and the willingness to take into account its ideological interests.

The RSGB had never made any attempt to identify with a particular political faction in Israel, both because it was primarily a religious organisation concerned with British Jewry and because the Reform membership encompassed a great variety of political opinion. However, a view common to many members was that the area of Gaza and the West Bank need not be retained by Israel for religious reasons in the belief that it was divinely sanctioned as Jewish territory. They may have favoured maintaining the areas for security reasons, but this would be subject to change should peace negotiations with the Arabs render this less necessary. There was general welcome, therefore, at the peace agreement between Israel and the Palestine Liberation Organisation (PLO) in 1993, and both parties were warmly congratulated: the council expressed 'admiration for the bravery and vision of Prime Minister Rabin' and saluted PLO chairman Yasser Arafat for 'matching the boldness of Israel's leadership with his own courageous response'.[13] The enthusiasm displayed by the RSGB contrasted with the reticence of many other Jewish organisations. When Arafat visited London a few months later, several of them urged that he be boycotted but the RSGB gave public support to the decision of Judge Israel Finestein, president of the Board of Deputies, to meet him. The RSGB also stood out when it was the only group to hold a memorial service for the Arab victims of the Hebron massacre early the following year. Held at West London and with Muslims participating, its object, said the RSGB chairman, David Walsh, was 'an expression of the Jewish community's sympathy and abhorrence of fanaticism and a need to do everything possible by rational people to ensure that the peace negotiations continue'.[14]

Behind the dramatic ups and downs often caused by political events there was also a quiet realisation in RSGB circles of the changing relationship between Israel and the Diaspora. The previous scenario of an economically weak and politically isolated Israel dependent on a prosperous and influential Diaspora was changing to one of a secure and developing Israel being a source of inspiration to a Diaspora that was declining in numbers and confidence. At the 1993 Conference the new situation was noted, along with the need to enhance the involvement of RSGB congregations in Israel education programmes in a way that would both be supportive of Israel and strengthen Jewish life in Britain.

The 1980s also witnessed some gradual changes in the religious direction of the RSGB. There were simultaneous moves to restore certain traditions – such as the reintroduction of Second Day *Rosh Hashannah* services by many congregations, and to adopt radical innovations – such as the liturgical changes already mentioned. The role of women in services became much more active. Although, in theory, equality of the sexes had long been accepted and mixed seating was universal, there were still a few synagogues that banned certain acts, such as women carrying scrolls on *Simchat Torah*, or that did not encourage girls to have a *bat-mitzvah* in the same way that boys were expected to have a *bar-mitzvah*. Now the full participation of women became much more common, while specific ceremonies for female life-cycle events were developed, such as prayers after birth, on miscarriage and naming ceremonies for girls at home. *Rosh Chodesh* study groups for women began to spread and special liturgies for *Rosh Chodesh* were created. There was still opposition among some communities to employing a female rabbi, although it was based on habit rather than ideology, and none of those who appointed women rabbis found that the fears of communal splits or loss of membership materialised. The publication in 1994 of *Hear Our Voice*, a collection of essays by women rabbis on Jewish feminist themes, gave expression to the growing impact of women rabbis and helped mark their transformation from novelties on the Jewish scene to part of Jewish institutional life. The equal status afforded to women, including the right to ordination, not only brought many benefits to RSGB congregations in terms of their contribution and insights, but was a major factor in keeping women involved in Jewish life and appealing to non-members. When the review 'Women in the Community' was published in 1994 by the new Chief Rabbi, Jonathan Sacks, it revealed widespread disillusion and alienation of many women affiliated to Orthodox synagogues, and demonstrated that women who were members of Progressive synagogues felt much more religiously fulfilled.

Another issue that affected the whole of British Jewry was that of mixed-faith marriages, with an estimated minimum of one in three Jews from all sections of the community marrying out of the faith. The standard response of the Jewish establishment was largely to deny that the problem existed or to ostracise those who did marry non-Jews. In 1988 a public seminar for those who had non-Jewish partners was held at the Sternberg Centre in an attempt to come to terms with the phenomenon, help couples in that situation explore the options available to them and encourage them to maintain links with the Jewish community. Spearheaded by Rabbis Tony Bayfield and Jonathan Romain it attracted 250 participants and became a major annual event as well as prompting similar seminars throughout the country. Moreover, it pioneered a more welcoming approach in the community at large to those in mixed-faith relationships and led to a significant shift in attitude and approach. As a result, many who might otherwise have been lost to Judaism, not to mention their offspring, were kept within the fold. Nevertheless, this course of action did not imply any lessening of the RSGB's commitment to Jewish–Jewish unions. Indeed, officiating at a mixed-faith marriage was one of the misdemeanours that entailed expulsion from the Assembly of Rabbis.

One consequence of the high rate of mixed-faith marriage was the large number of children born to Jewish fathers and non-Jewish mothers and who thus did not have Jewish status. It was a situation that most of the parents accepted, although in a minority of cases the conversion of the mother to Judaism meant that the children became Jewish too. However, during the 1980s a growing number of instances arose in which the mother did not wish to convert – because it would cause pain to her parents or because she had her own religious allegiance or because she did not feel inherently religious – yet was willing for the children to be brought up as Jewish and to assist her husband in doing so. The Assembly of Rabbis would have preferred the mother to convert and the whole family to be Jewish, but felt it had to consider the needs of the children and respond constructively to the new situation. The result was a radical innovation in status issues, which became official policy in 1992 after many years of debate. If certain conditions were fulfilled – the mother attending a course on Judaism similar to that required for conversion to Judaism, home ceremonies being practised, both parents giving a written undertaking to bring the children up as Jewish – the child of a non-Jewish mother could appear before the Reform *Beth Din* and gain Jewish status in his/her own right. It differed from the position of the ULPS, which accepted any child as Jewish who had one Jewish parent and a Jewish education. The RSGB still adhered to the matrilineal line of descent, and only acknowledged children of Jewish fathers and non-Jewish mothers if the special procedure was carried out and if the status change was ratified by a *Beth Din*.

The Reform *Beth Din* itself underwent a change of identity when Rabbi Lionel Blue retired in 1988 after 18 years as its convener. Under his guidance the court had become renowned for providing a sympathetic and efficient service, with the hearings conducted with warmth, dignity and rigorous fairness. These were not necessarily compliments that could be applied so generously to the courts of other Jewish organisations, and, as the RSGB chairman, Marcus Bower, pointed out: 'No part of RSGB's functions has won more respect than the *Beth Din*.'[15] Perhaps most notable of all was the way in which Blue had succeeded in giving the *Beth Din* of a non-*halachic* movement an authority and stature far beyond its own circle. As in the previous period, the Reform *Beth Din* continued to serve the needs of British Jewry as much as those of the RSGB, with only a minority of the cases that came before it being from those who were originally members of Reform synagogues. Rabbi Rodney Mariner was appointed as the new convener and quickly won acclaim for maintaining both the high standards and the sympathetic approach of his predecessor. Despite the popularity of the court, it was noticeable that the number of conversions rose only marginally between the 1960s and the 1990s, from approximately 100 per year to 120. This was especially surprising considering both the sharp growth of the RSGB and the steep increase in mixed-faith marriages. It gave the lie to the accusation made by some detractors that Reform conversions were attractive because they were easy and undemanding. It also reflected a reduction in the social pressures that previously existed in the Jewish community for non-Jewish partners to convert and 'at least unify the family'. Another implication was that not all Reform rabbis welcomed proselytes and that many potential candidates were discouraged from proceeding. Rabbis Michael Boyden and Hugo Gryn had both issued calls for a significant outreach programme to encourage the non-Jewish partners of members to consider conversion, but few rabbis felt sufficiently motivated to do so. Provincial congregations were especially wary of attracting large numbers and exacerbating Orthodox claims that nobody joined Reform synagogues because they wanted to, but only because they had to do so for status reasons. At the same time the number of divorce cases appearing before the Reform *Beth Din* remained static, even though the divorce rate among Jews was increasing rapidly, in line with that in society at large. However, this reflected the corresponding drop in marriages between Jews, which required a *get* to be fully dissolved in Jewish law, and the rise in mixed-faith marriages, which did not require one. It also mirrored an increasing trend for second marriages, which were often the motivation for obtaining a *get*, either to be mixed-faith marriages or to be between two Jews but in a registry office. In this respect, the Reform *Beth Din* acted as a barometer of the changing religious patterns within British Jewry.

The collapse of the Soviet Union had been accompanied by a renaissance of Jewish life in eastern Europe. It had also led to the need for a Progressive *Beth Din* to serve the many status issues arising. There were cases requiring attention in disparate parts of western Europe too, where there were either no Progressive congregations, as in Spain, or an insufficient number of Progressive rabbis to deal with them, as in Germany. Rabbi Mariner and the chairman of the Assembly of Rabbis, David Soetendorp (Bournemouth), were among those instrumental in establishing a unique trans-continental *Beth Din* in 1994 to meet the new situation. Carrying the title Rabbinic Court for the Progressive Communities of Central and Eastern Europe, it differed from normal rabbinic courts that usually held local, or at most, national jurisdiction. Its ambit stretched to wherever there was a need. It was supported by all constituents of the World Union for Progressive Judaism including the ULPS, and was the first time that rabbis from both the Reform and Liberal movements operated under the aegis of the same *Beth Din*.

Those women who did convert through the Reform *Beth Din* sometimes found that Orthodox *mohalim* were unwilling to circumcise any sons they had, whilst many born Jews felt that the form of service offered by members of the Initiation Society was not appropriate. A course had been established by Rabbi Hugo Gryn and Dr David Levi in the early 1970s to train doctors to become *mohalim* and serve Progressive congregations. Another such venture took place in 1988 at the Sternberg Centre under the aegis of Rabbi Tony Bayfield and Dr John Cohen. Shortly afterwards the Association of Reform and Liberal *Mohalim* was established, which was a further step in making the Progressive community self-supporting in its religious needs.

Another aspect of Jewish life which the Orthodox refused to countenance was that of homosexuality. The more tolerant atmosphere in British society which allowed homosexual men and women to be open about their identity and form support groups permeated the Jewish community too. For Orthodoxy, homosexuality was an anathema, directly contravening Biblical commands; for Reform it was a reality affecting perhaps ten per cent of British Jewry, and for whom it was a natural and God-given condition. A booklet by Wendy Greengross entitled *Jewish and Homosexual* was published by the RSGB in 1982 which acknowledged the difficulties faced by Jewish homosexuals and their families, and urged that their sexuality should not lessen the welcome given to them or bar them from any aspect of communal life. Not everyone felt comfortable with this approach, and Leo Baeck College experienced some controversy when two lesbian women were admitted as students and later ordained as rabbis. The fact that such a widely respected figure as Rabbi Lionel Blue stated publicly that he was homosexual helped calm the debate and demonstrated that a person's sexual inclination need have no bearing on their professional life. When criticism was expressed over an article by Rabbi Rodney Mariner favouring lowering the age of consent for homosexuals, he was stoutly defended by Rabbi Bayfield who declared that the RSGB should 'take every opportunity to articulate a liberal, pluralist, socially conscious view of Judaism, a perspective that is sadly lacking in the religious news media in this country. We may not always get it right, but if we are silent we do not exist.'[16]

Bayfield's remark highlighted the general lack of forthright statements emanating from the RSGB, as well as the loose and *ad hoc* nature of religious decision-making. The absence of a Reform Chief Rabbi meant that there was no religious hierarchy responsible for initiating, or impeding, new developments, while individual rabbis were not subject to any central vetting as to their theology or practices. The chairman of the Assembly of Rabbis changed every two years – in 1993 it became a three-year post – which meant that the office-holder could have little long-term effect on the RSGB. Instead, religious issues rested in the more democratic hands of the Assembly as a whole, and new directions were often introduced because of the personal initiative of individual members. The process usually entailed lengthy debates and cumbersome procedures, but resulted in the decisions that emerged being based on a high degree of consensus, which was vital in view of the autonomous character of the individual synagogues. When occasional comments were made that it might be an idea to have a Reform Chief Rabbi – usually by a lay member keen to have a publicly recognised equivalent of the United Synagogue's Chief Rabbi – the suggestion was invariably drowned in a chorus of disapproval by rabbis and laity alike, both groups equally keen to preserve autonomy and avoid any religious regimentation.

The religious changes in Reform Judaism that have arisen over the years are differences in nuance rather than character. Even the reintroduction of traditional practices were often accompanied by new interpretations. Thus in some synagogues Second Day *Rosh Hashannah* services are more experimental in nature; regulations concerning witnesses of *tevilah* have been amended; the refusal of one partner to award a *get* to the other can be overridden by the Reform *Beth Din* if it considers the grounds to be spurious. It has attempted to uphold traditions it respects yet has been unafraid to find ways of making them more responsive to the needs of modern Jews: refusing to officiate at mixed-faith marriages, but reaching out to those in that situation; adhering to the matrilineal line, yet seeking to include children excluded by it. It would be wrong to measure whether British Reform has become more 'right-wing' or more 'left-wing'. Instead, the best analysis is that it has grown much more confident, willing both to readopt traditions rejected by earlier generations and venture into areas from which they would have shied away.

The religious confidence exuded by the RSGB, along with its increased physical impact in north-west London, only served to exacerbate the hostility previously displayed by the Orthodox establishment. Verbal attacks by Orthodox rabbis continued – which was regrettable but not surprising. More disturbing were incidents that affected non-religious inter-communal activities in which the Chief Rabbi had intimated that British Jewry should work together in harmony. When the National Council for Soviet Jewry organised a major Soviet Jewry youth event at the Sternberg Centre in March 1982 several Orthodox youth organisations refused to attend because of the location. That same year *Dayan* Ehrentreu refused to meet the Pope on his visit to Manchester because Rabbi Reuven Silverman was part of the inter-faith delegation. At a time when Jewish students were facing serious problems because of anti-Zionist groups, Progressive Jewish Students was prevented from affiliating to the Union of Jewish Students – although this particular issue was resolved a few years later and relations between the two became harmonious. On a local level, Reform synagogues in the provinces usually experienced greater difficulties than did their London counterparts, as in Leeds where there were attempts to prevent Rabbi Walter Rothschild from taking assemblies at state schools, becoming a hospital or prison chaplain, being a governor of a Zionist Federation day school, or to prevent meetings of the Council of Christians and Jews from taking place at the Reform synagogue.

Commenting on the strained Orthodox–Progressive relations, the then RSGB chairman, Maurice Michaels, told the 1985 Conference: 'The variety of the confrontations suggested a co-ordinated approach by the Orthodox...we must be aware that these attacks emanate from our success.' He warned that continued RSGB growth would attract further disparagement and pointed out the fallacy behind them: 'The problem is that the Orthodox are labouring under a misapprehension. They believe themselves to have something which we seek – namely their seal of approval.' In the past that view may have been true, and even today many Reform Jews wish the Chief Rabbi would endorse the fact that they belong to an equally authentic form of Judaism; but it is obvious that such a move is unthinkable and the situation will only change if, as in the United States, the non-Orthodox are in the majority and the Orthodox have to come to terms with sociological realities. Despite some calls for the RSGB to retaliate in kind, the dominant mood was that it was incumbent on the RSGB to minimise confrontation and work towards creating an atmosphere of mutual respect. This policy was reinforced by a resolution at the 1987 Conference urging all sections of British Jewry to strive for communal harmony and pledging the RSGB's full co-operation.

There was one particular problem that the RSGB felt unable to ignore: the refusal of Orthodox day schools to admit children whose mothers had converted under Reform auspices. The ban arose in the mid-1980s in 'mainstream' schools such as the Jews Free School, London and the King David School in Manchester. It reversed previous policy, and sometimes led to children being denied entry to schools which already contained older siblings. The King David School in Birmingham opted to segregate the children already enrolled and only teach religious education to those whom it deemed *halachically* Jewish. It was a sign of the changing religious climate that those outside Progressive circles joined in the protest, with the *Jewish Chronicle* labelling it 'Apartheid in the classroom'.[17] Appeals to the school in conjunction with the ULPS failed, so complaints were made to the local authority which ruled the move to be illegal. When in 1991 the Manchester King David School refused admission to children of Reform-converted mothers, the RSGB felt it had to act to defend the validity of its *Beth Din*. After it proved impossible to reach agreement with the governors, the matter was referred to the Secretary of State for Education. The solution he recommended, that, like Catholic schools, King David was obliged to take a percentage of 'other children' (i.e. non-Catholics) carried the unacceptable implication that Reform children were non-Jews. Eventually a compromise was reached whereby five per cent of the annual intake was available for 'others professing allegiance to Judaism'. Although the percentage was less than hoped for, it did ensure for the first time that children of Reform proselytes could enter the school as of right.

It would be wrong to characterise Reform–Orthodox relations as purely a matter of antagonism, for there were also positive developments, albeit a lesser number. These were instances of co-operation on a local level, such as the communal day centre that was based at Bournemouth Reform Synagogue, or the decision by Reading Orthodox, Maidenhead Reform and Thames Valley Liberal synagogues to form an association, hold joint meetings for members and co-operate in areas such as Soviet Jewry, AJEX and a Mothers and Toddlers group. More centralised attempts at unity came through the establishment of Forum/*Bamah* in 1987 which held a series of public meetings between leaders of Orthodox and Progressive Jewry. Behind the scenes a small group from the leadership of the different sections of British Jewry met as a 'fire-fighting' body to defuse communal controversies. After many years of secrecy, this 'Liaison Group' made its existence public in 1993 in order to let it be known that, despite the many divisions, there were also channels for civilised exchange of views and co-operation. The decision also indicated the improved atmosphere that was gradually emerging, without which such a revelation might have meant that the group would have had to be disbanded.

A factor in the new climate was the advent of a new Chief Rabbi two years earlier. Before his election Rabbi Dr Jonathan Sacks had been one of the few Orthodox ministers willing occasionally to speak at the same communal events with Reform rabbis or support communal ventures involving the RSGB. The hope felt by many in both Orthodox and Reform circles that Sacks would bring a greater sense of unity to British Jewry has only been partially realised. Whilst he unequivocally condemned derogatory comments and acknowledged both the impact and the contribution of Reform Judaism, he also denied that it was a valid form of Judaism and urged Reform Jews to return to the 'true, revealed and binding' tradition.[18] For many RSGB members it was highly puzzling that a person with such a distinguished academic background in philosophy, and who could accept the pluralism of different faiths, could not accept that same pluralism within Judaism. It was also a source of frustration and disquiet that in the country at large the Chief Rabbi was often perceived as representing British Jewry as a whole, whereas he only spoke for the Orthodox community, and in fact only part of that. It meant that Reform Jews felt they were sometimes associated with views they did not hold, while it also inferred a lack of public awareness as to the RSGB's separate identity. Nevertheless, there was constant private dialogue at the highest level between rabbinic and lay leaders from the Orthodox and Progressive camps, and different viewpoints did not prevent close personal relationships among them.

During the 1980s, British Jewry saw the birth of the Masorti movement, which largely followed the approach adopted by Rabbi Dr Louis Jacobs in the 1960s and was allied to the Conservative movement in the United States. The new grouping attracted members of the United Synagogue who were dissatisfied with what they considered the increasingly right-wing direction of its rabbinate. It also appealed to some Reform members who preferred the more traditional format of its services. However, the fact that it arose during this period indicated that Reform synagogues were not necessarily the automatic home of those dissatisfied with Orthodoxy. The rise of Masorti presented a challenge to the RSGB's claim to be the movement most able to answer the needs of modern Jews. It remains to be seen whether the existence of Masorti will limit the growth of the RSGB or whether its lack of cohesion (as in the great variations between its synagogues over women's participation in services) will prevent it becoming a major rival.

Religious controversy once again arose with the Board of Deputies concerning the nature of guidance on religious matters. The long and acrimonious battle over Clause 43 at the end of the 1960s had resulted in the Board's being obliged to consult all religious authorities. However, on certain occasions this requirement rendered the president of the Board unable to give a unanimous opinion in response to government questions because of the conflicting advice he received and stymied any effective action, as happened with the 1984 Matrimonial and Family Proceedings Bill. The United Synagogue therefore proposed an amendment to the clause (now known as Clause 74) to the effect that the Board should forward any opinion received from its Ecclesiastical Authorities (the Chief Rabbi and the *Haham*) as the opinion of the Board. The proposal was seen by the RSGB as an attempt – unwitting or otherwise – to reverse the rights the Progressives had won previously and ignore their religious perspective. After a series of determined representations by the RSGB and the ULPS a compromise was reached which would enable the Board to issue statements yet safeguard the Progressive position: the clause was not altered but guidelines were introduced obliging the president to attempt to reconcile differences of opinion where they occur; if differences remained, any submission by the Board had to indicate that the Board was submitting advice on the guidance of its Ecclesiastical Authorities only and thus acknowledging the right of the Progressives to submit their independent view. In practice it was unlikely that legislation would be considered by the government on behalf of the Jewish community if there were differing Jewish views.

Apart from this incident, relations between the RSGB and the Board remained free of conflict and highly constructive. Concern at the RSGB's active involvement and the number of its members holding committee posts prompted the United Synagogue to urge its constituents to take up all their seats at the 1985 triennial elections and increase its voting power. Nevertheless, many Board members were unwilling to vote along religious lines and in the contest for senior vice-president, Eric Moonman of the ULPS beat the United Synagogue president, Victor Lucas.

Four years later, the Board decided to enlarge its executive committee by co-opting the chairman of the RSGB, then Marcus Bower, and all subsequent chairmen in order to increase the effectiveness of its work. Similar recognition of the RSGB's growing importance came in 1990 when, for the first time, the two candidates for the office of president the following year, Israel Finestein and Eric Moonman, both attended the conference to canvass support.

The RSGB's own representation among the honorary officers increased at that election, with Aubrey Rose (North Western) becoming the senior vice-president and Ron Shelley (Edgware) the treasurer. Bearing in mind the comparatively low voting strength of RSGB synagogues, the comment of Ruth Cohen, then chairman of RSGB, was well-founded: 'People were looking for the best leaders in the community without prejudice.'[19] Both men were reappointed in the 1994 elections, while Andrew Gilbert (Finchley) was elected as chairman of the Board's Education and Youth Committee.

The RSGB played an active role in most other areas of the Jewish community, supporting all major communal endeavour. It welcomed new initiatives that arose in the 1990s, such as the expanded role of the Central Council for Jewish Community Services, and co-operated fully with the Chief Rabbi's Jewish Continuity project. In one instance its backing even proved counter-productive: the strong involvement of the RSGB in the Jewish Social Responsibility Council led to it being so identified with the Reform that some other sectors of the Jewish community shied away from it. Countless individual RSGB members made distinctive personal contributions in the wider Jewish community. They also provided the leadership of various Jewish institutions during the 1980s and early 1990s, such as Melvyn Carlowe (executive director of Jewish Care), Sir Trevor Chinn (president of the Joint Israel Appeal) and Eva Mitchell (executive director of the Central British Fund). The RSGB's role in British society at large has been seen already in its contribution to the debates over issues such as nuclear arms, racism, asylum rights and homelessness. In addition to its full participation in Jewish–Christian dialogue, it also helped pioneer better Jewish–Muslim relations, as well as inter-faith work in general following the lead of Rabbi Hugo Gryn. The RSGB was also among the first religious organisations in Britain to produce a coherent response and action plan for its members during the Bosnian crisis in 1993. An eight-page document entitled 'A Statement on the Former Yugoslavia' spelt out a clear moral position and suggested methods of help to all RSGB synagogues.

The RSGB continued to be active also in the World Union for Progressive Judaism, in which it was becoming an ever more important component. One problem, however, was that only a small number of rabbis and lay leaders had been drawn into its affairs. The image of the WUPJ amongst most ordinary Reform congregants was that of a set of initials they could not decipher but representing a distant cause they knew to be worthy. This began to change in 1990 with the holding of its Twenty-eighth Biennial International in London, hosted jointly by the RSGB and the ULPS. The gathering of delegates from 20 countries representing one and a half million Progressive members had a significant impact in reminding RSGB members that they were part of a massive world-wide movement. The conference planning committee was led by Rabbi Tony Bayfield and proved a triumph for his attempt to give it religious and philosophical content rather than the heavily political overtones that characterised many WUPJ conferences. It also demonstrated how the Sternberg Centre had become the showplace for Progressive Judaism in Europe and a fine manifestation of the RSGB's creative vitality.

It was in 1990 also that the RSGB revived the position of president. The only two previous incumbents had been Leonard Montefiore (1946–51) and Rabbi Leo Baeck (1951–56) and thereafter the position had been allowed to lie vacant. Rabbi Werner Van der Zyl had been honorary life president (1973–84) in a special *ad personam* appointment. It was now felt that the RSGB had reached a stage where its standing in the community would justify its having a person of recognised calibre as an active figurehead. It was unanimously agreed that Rabbi Hugo Gryn's contribution to the RSGB, the respect in which he was held in the wider Jewish community and his renown amongst the wider public for his inter-faith and media activities made him the obvious candidate. By happy chance, the appointment coincided with the 150th anniversary of West London (1840–1990) and was a fitting reminder of both the debt owed to it by RSGB and the synagogue's continuing influence. In 1993 Gryn was re-elected to the three-year post, with tributes being paid to the way in which he was an ambassador for Jewry in general and Reform Judaism in particular in the country at large. At the same time, the clause in the constitution limiting a president to a maximum of two three-year terms was deleted, thus allowing for an indefinite presidency should that be desired.

Meanwhile the RSGB had celebrated its own achievement on reaching its golden jubilee in 1992 and had organised a series of national and local events throughout the year to highlight its fiftieth anniversary. The most moving of these was a service of thanksgiving at West London, which included seven past chairmen each bearing a scroll in front of the Ark, along with a procession of 42 children each carrying a banner with the name of one of the congregations. An ethos statement summarising Reform beliefs was issued during the year. It concluded with the words: 'The Reform Movement is committed to maintain a living Judaism that enables the Jew to be both faithful to Judaism and fully involved in the modern world through a constantly evolving religious understanding, which is informed by more than three thousand years of Jewish piety, wisdom and experience.'[20] An inaugural Jubilee lecture by Rabbi Dow Marmur – by then senior minister of Holy Blossom Temple, Toronto – set the pattern for what was to become a prestigious annual event. Almost a thousand people attended 'Jubilation' – a fun-day for all the family – at the Sternberg Centre in July, which also served to honour Peter Levy and saw him open the new Youth and Education Block on the site. The Jubilee also witnessed the return of David Jacobs – a former youth development officer – to the RSGB staff to help organise the year's events, and thereafter to work with both new and existing communities following Donald Black's retirement as congregational development co-ordinator.

The many advances made by the RSGB were dependent not only on the enormous amount of time and effort devoted by members, but also on having the funds to finance the many new developments it undertook. The budget was a constant problem, with treasurers having to worry not only about the balancing the books but about the interventions of constituents. During the worry over funding the purchase of the Manor House, Wimbledon demanded that all intended appointments be frozen, while North Western voiced serious objections. In the event it was necessary for the Council to agree to a 65p surcharge for all full members in 1981 to avoid a deficit. It was clear that new financial controls were necessary and that same year, the Conference agreed to change the rate of assessment from a per capita rate to a percentage charge of synagogue subscription income, with the amount being fixed at 12 per cent for a three-year trial period. The new system allowed synagogue treasurers to budget ahead without waiting for the RSGB to calculate its demands, and also removed the unfairness of synagogues paying out a capitation fee that might be higher than the actual amount they received from a member who was paying a reduced subscription. Despite the success of the change, which became a permanent method, the RSGB still suffered from cash-flow problems because it did not receive expected income on time from some individual synagogues which lacked sufficient control of their own finances and themselves experienced cash-flow problems. The idea of the RSGB charging interest to late payers was mooted, but rejected on the grounds that it would merely add to the difficulties.

The commitments made in 1985 by the RSGB to provide a higher level of funding for Leo Baeck College meant an increase in its own assessments, rising by 1987 to 15 per cent. While this meant that the congregations funded the College commitment directly themselves, the RSGB still faced the problem that many of them had not fulfilled their original fund-raising targets for the Manor House. This resulted in the RSGB paying substantial amounts of interest on its loans from the bank – £6,000 a month in 1985 – which was not even matched by cash-flow from donations. The RSGB was caught in a depressing cycle of servicing the interest charge but not paying off the loan, and with no prospect of reducing the burden. The ending of the massive support given by the Pincus Fund for the CJE the following year put further strains on finances. One obvious solution was to cut back on major items of expenditure such as education, but the Conference condemned it as morally unacceptable and instructed the RSGB to explore ways of making good the anticipated deficit. The efforts of Peter Levy and the creation of AJET as the fund-raising arm of the CJE could not offset the crisis caused by the severe increase in interest rates in the late 1980s. A special council meeting on 17 September 1989 was confronted with the challenge of taking responsibility for its own future. Congregations were told that they had often talked about exciting new projects but had failed to find the funds to make them happen. Treasurer David Walsh reminded them that they were the second-largest synagogue grouping in Britain, and needed to come to terms with being a national movement with national responsibilities. The largest group – the United Synagogue – set an assessment rate of 34 per cent from its constituents, more than double that of the RSGB. Another defect that needed to be remedied was that despite the substantial growth of the RSGB there had been no major additions to its staff, with Raymond Goldman being the only senior management officer.

The council responded positively by agreeing to an annual increase of three per cent per year for the next three years, producing a 24 per cent rate by 1992. The decision – confirmed by an extraordinary general meeting in December – was much more than a rescue package, but marked a crucial stage in the development of the RSGB, both in practical terms and in philosophical approach. It recognised the work for students, outreach, community care, social action, education, youth and rabbinic training as having an importance over and beyond the needs of each individual congregation. Indeed, the latter three accounted for over half of the RSGB's expenditure in 1991, with approximately 16 per cent of its budget being spent on the CJE, 15 per cent on the Youth Department and 27 per cent on Leo Baeck College. As the then chairman, Marcus Bower, told the conference: 'We are moving from an RSGB view to a Reform Movement view.'

Unfortunately the high hopes of at last establishing a secure financial footing were to be dashed by the recession that followed soon afterwards. Many synagogues found that their own income was reduced because members who were unemployed could not pay full subscriptions, and fund-raising activities were considerably impaired. Meeting the new levels of RSGB assessments was simply beyond many of them. Further debates at Council resolved that the 1992 level would be limited to 20 per cent, with the deficit in income resulting in some cut-backs to the RSGB's auxiliary staff and intended projects being deferred. Council also made it clear that the 20 per cent assessment should be considered a maximum level for future years too, lest it over-burden congregations and endanger their own viability. The extra money required by the RSGB would have to come from fund-raising activities spearheaded by the Reform Foundation.

The new situation produced more than just monetary guidelines. The need to reorganise the finances of the RSGB coincided with a new vision of its role and also with the forthcoming retirement of the executive director. Raymond Goldman had been the one constant pivotal person in the development of RSGB for the past 27 years. It was recognised not only that the RSGB owed him an enormous debt of gratitude, but also that the role he had occupied so successfully could no longer be carried out by one person. As Bower had rightly pointed out, the RSGB was changing from an association into a movement, and a complete overhaul of its ethos and structure was necessary to accompany the transformation and to enable its ambitious plans to be implemented. A working party had been established in November 1990 to formulate a 'Strategy for the Reform Movement' and it was assisted by management consultants to enable it to make the leap from 'what had always been' to 'what could be'. The strategy was adopted by the 1992 Conference which acknowledged and affirmed the process of change that was under way. Among the initial recommendations to the council in December 1992 were integrating the work of the RSGB and the Manor House, and the appointment of Rabbi Tony Bayfield as chief executive designate. He would work alongside Goldman during the transition and come into his new post in January 1994. Bayfield's appointment was widely welcomed in recognition of the way he had built up the Sternberg Centre and within a few years had turned an empty property in Finchley into the heartbeat of Reform Judaism nationally and a major institution in British Jewry. It was notable, too, that a rabbi was chosen as chief executive. Recommending his appointment, the RSGB chairman, Ruth Cohen, told the council: 'As a religious organisation we had to be guided in spiritual terms and needed a Reform rabbi to lead us. In Rabbi Bayfield we had an outstanding leader.'[21]

A transitional management team was formed to develop the new structure, with a key element being close consultation with the congregations on their needs and their wishes for the movement. The final document that emerged, 'Blueprint for the Reform Movement', was most notable for the greater professionalism that was envisaged, with the work of the RSGB channelled through four divisions, each headed by a professional divisional director and each managing its own budget. However, the voluntary character of the movement would be maintained by the work of each division being conducted under the auspices of a divisional management team chaired by and predominantly consisting of lay members of the RSGB. The four divisions were:

Programmes (a host of religious, social and cultural activities articulating Jewish values), Synagogue Partnership (a range of programmes to assist the congregations with their needs), Education and Training, and Youth and Students. The increasing burden of work falling on the RSGB chairman, which was in danger of limiting future incumbents to those not working or retired, was alleviated by splitting the role in two: the Chairman of the Movement would be at its helm and would represent it to the outside world, as well as chairing council meetings and the conference. The Chairman of the Board would be responsible for the more day-to-day management of the movement, which was supervised by the Board, a more streamlined body replacing the former executive. The crucial role of the rabbinate in the movement's development was given more prominence by having a member of the Assembly on each divisional management team, and both the Assembly chairman and the principal of Leo Baeck College sitting on the Board.

The new structure also intended to dismantle the old image that sometimes arose of the RSGB being the centre of the organisation and synagogues at the periphery. Henceforth the movement and the synagogues were to be inseparable, and this would be achieved in two ways. First, the synagogues would be given a greater feeling of 'ownership' of the movement, both through real empowerment via democratic structures and through better communication with the mass membership. Second, considerable emphasis would be placed on getting staff and programmes out into the congregations and servicing the needs of constituents locally and 'at the coal face' itself. Underlying the new operational structure was a vision of a more effective movement, growing significantly, whose members had a greater sense of belonging and a deeper commitment to Reform Judaism. The new logo of the movement reinforced its 'corporate image' and summed up its religious ethos with the slogan 'Rooted in tradition, responding to change'.

The 'Blueprint' and the new concept it put forward was debated at length and in minute detail by the congregations and welcomed with only a few minor alterations made. The readiness of the RSGB as a whole to institute such a wide-ranging change indicated not only the timely nature of the proposals, but also the forward thinking of the general membership. It was also a noticeable contrast to the resistance of the Board of Deputies to adopt suggestions for its modernisation, which were being made at the same time. The notorious unwillingness of Anglo-Jewish organisations to reform themselves at the right time was avoided by the RSGB. The only real point of dissension was whether to maintain its existing name or to signal the change by adopting a new title. After some inconclusive votes, it was decided to keep the existing name but to review the matter at a later date. The 'Blueprint' was unanimously accepted at the council meeting of 6 March 1994 and the following month saw the induction of Rabbi Bayfield as chief executive of the Movement. That year's conference saw the election of David Walsh as first Chairman of the Movement, with David Liebling as first Chairman of the Board. Soon afterwards the professional directors of the four new divisions were in place: Rabbi Elizabeth Sarah (Programmes), David Jacobs (Synagogue Partnership), Michael Shire (Education and Training) and Sara Leviten (Youth and Students). The conference theme that year was fittingly entitled 'Continuity and Change', highlighting the two key principles of Reform Judaism, with the attempt to maintain those two opposites in equilibrium being at its heart. Raymond Goldman was the keynote lecturer for the first time since he had started working professionally for the RSGB out of one sub-divided room in a remote corner of West London Synagogue. As he had told an earlier gathering, 'I rub my eyes when I look back to what was then [when first starting his voluntary involvement with RSGB as chairman of YASGB in 1950], and see what is now and the breadth of achievement'.[22] The standing ovation he received was as much related to his life-time's service as to the content of his forceful lecture.

Despite the euphoria at the genesis of the Reform Movement, there still remained the familiar problem of finances and the possible restrictions on new developments this might entail. A key element in overcoming this was the role of a finance advisory group to set a realistic budget commensurate with the anticipated income from assessments and to ensure strict monitoring of expenditure. Another important component was the new Reform Foundation Trust (successor to the Reform Foundation), led by Ruth Cohen. Its purpose was to supplement the movement's income through an active and entrepreneurial fund-raising campaign. It also had the task of contributing to the growth of the Reform Movement by raising its profile. One of its first acts was to establish a marketing and public relations think-thank consisting of professionals within the movement. It also sponsored the creation of the Jewish Information and Media Service, using the expertise of Assembly members, which raised the profile of the RSGB by presenting a Reform perspective on social and ethical issues in the Jewish and national media. It was a sign of the increased confidence of the RSGB – unafraid to promote its position independently of other sectors of the Jewish community. The project was one that had long been planned, but for which there had never been the resources previously. Another goal that had also been desired for many years and that was at last realised in 1994 was the appointment of a chaplain for students in the north of England, the first incumbent being Rabbi Warren Elf who also served Sha'arei Shalom. A major step in catering for the needs of young adults in general, not just students, had been started the previous year with a working party on 'The Missing Generation', 18–35 year-olds who were not involved in the RSGB. Chaired by Adrian Sieff, its brief was to evaluate the reasons for the disinclination towards synagogue involvement among young people and propose steps to kindle their interest.

All these initiatives were indicative of the new sense of purpose permeating the Movement and its determination to be pro-active to the needs of synagogues and Reform Jews. Almost 30 years earlier Bernard Davis had complained: 'We were not a Movement and we were unlikely to become a Movement if recommendations and resolutions were only put into action by our synagogues if they suited their parochial view.'[23] The Reform Movement had now come into being, partly due to the vision of those at the centre of the RSGB, but also because synagogues had begun to understand the advantages of a Movement with interests larger than themselves and were willing to back it with proper resources. At the time of writing the name 'RSGB' is still in operation, but it seems likely that at some point it will be changed to wording that incorporates 'the Reform Movement'. As with previous changes of titles – from ABS to ASGB to RSGB – it will once again reflect an important new development, although this time the most profound of all. It denotes a crucial difference from previous milestones: the first Reform synagogue, West London, was founded reluctantly by its members, while the first Reform organisation, the ABS, came into being almost by accident. Unlike them, the Reform Movement has been carefully pre-planned and is the result of an ideology and vision once lacking but now very much in evidence.

NOTES

1. RSGB Council, Minutes, 2 Dec. 1984; at Reform Synagogues of Great Britain Archive, the Sternberg Centre for Judaism, London.
2. Assembly of Rabbis, Minutes, 16 Dec. 1986; at Reform Synagogues of Great Britain Archive, loc. cit.
3. L. Blue and J. Magonet (eds), *Forms of Prayer* (1995), Vol. III, p. 534.
4. L. Blue and J. Magonet, op. cit., pp. 583, 588, 574 and 569.
5. RSGB Council, Minutes, loc. cit., 5 March 1985.
6. M. Schmool and F. Cohen, *British Synagogue Membership in 1990* (1991), p. 25.
7. Jerome Karet, Chairman's Address, RSGB Conference, June 1982; at Reform Synagogues of Great Britain Archive, loc. cit.
8. Raymond Goldman, speaking at RSGB Council: Minutes, loc. cit., 6 Dec. 1987.
9. 31 Jan. 1982, quoted *Inform*, March 1982.
10. Marcus Bower, speaking at RSGB Council: Minutes, loc. cit., 27 Nov. 1988.
11. RSGB Council, Minutes, loc. cit., 8 May 1988.
12. RSGB Council, Minutes, loc. cit., 28 Feb. 1988.
13. RSGB Council, Minutes, loc. cit., 5 Sept. 1993.
14. RSGB Council, Minutes, loc. cit., 6 March 1994.
15. RSGB Council, Minutes, loc. cit., 27 Nov. 1988.
16. RSGB Council, Minutes, loc. cit., 6 March 1994.
17. Quoted RSGB Council, 6 Sept. 1987, Minutes, loc. cit.
18. Jonathan Sacks, *One People?* (1993), p. 224.
19. RSGB Council, Minutes, loc. cit., 15 Sept. 1991.
20. *A Statement of the Religious Ethos of the Reform Synagogues of Great Britain* (1992); a full examination of the tenets and observances of Reform Judaism can be found in Jonathan Romain, *Faith and Practice: A Guide to Reform Judaism Today* (1991).
21. RSGB Council, Minutes, loc. cit., 6 Dec. 1992.
22. RSGB Conference 1992, Annual Report, loc. cit.
23. RSGB Council, Minutes, loc. cit., 3 April 1966.

Appendices

Appendix 1

Aims and Objects of the Associated British Synagogues

The following was drawn up and agreed at Conference on 23rd July 1946

Intention

A body known as 'Associated British Synagogues' was formally established on 4th January 1942 by certain congregations generally known as 'Reform' whose common Aims in this Association are: Mutually to strengthen each other and, by common endeavour and collective action, more effectively to serve the Jewish cause. Thereby this association intends to promote and foster a robust and virile Judaism which will contribute to the life of the entire Jewish Community, and which will play its part, together with other religions, in the spiritual and physical betterment of mankind.

Method

To further these Aims, the 'Associated British Synagogues' shall, by their common action:

1. Define and renew Jewish teaching and practice, in their relation to contemporary life; periodically revise and publish Prayer Books; and prepare and publish other liturgical writings.
2. Promote and assist the establishment of new congregations wherever the need is apparent.

3. Admit to membership in the Association other like-minded congregations.
4. Seek means of training Rabbis and teachers.
5. Promote and co-ordinate the religious instruction of Jewish Youth by issuing their own publications and by distributing those of other appropriate bodies, by the establishment of classes, and by the preparation of syllabi.
6. Promote adult education and Jewish learning.
7. Encourage and co-ordinate their Youth Organizations.
8. Publish a journal and occasional pamphlets on Jewish subjects.
9. Establish a central library of Jewish writings and Jewish music.
10. Invite the co-operation of other bodies, which share a progressive religious outlook, and specifically the co-operation of the 'Union of Liberal and Progressive Synagogues'.
11. Maintain membership of the World Union for Progressive Judaism.
12. Wherever opportunity arises, co-operate with fellow Jews, in whatever congregations or association they may be, to promote and assist the religious, physical and educational betterment of the Jewish People.
13. Hold an annual conference and such other conferences as may from time to time seem desirable.
14. Sponsor a Rabbinical Court and Rabbinical Conferences

Appendix 2

The Expansion of the Reform Movement

Synagogues

West London Synagogue of British Jews (1840)
Manchester Reform Synagogue (1856)
Bradford Synagogue (1873)
*Settlement Synagogue** (1919)
North Western Reform Synagogue (1933)
Glasgow New Synagogue (1933)
Edgware and District Reform Synagogue (1935)

1942 – Associated British Synagogues formed

Sinai Synagogue, Leeds (1944)
Bournemouth Reform Synagogue (1947)
Cardiff New Synagogue (1949)
Southport New Synagogue (1949)
Hendon Reform Synagogue (1950)
Wimbledon and District Synagogue (1950)
Maidenhead Synagogue (1954)
Brighton and Hove New Synagogue (1955)
South West Essex Reform Synagogue (1957)
Harlow Jewish Community (1960)
Middlesex New Synagogue (1960)
Blackpool Reform Jewish Congregation (1961)
Finchley Reform Synagogue (1962)
Southgate and District Reform Synagogue (1962)
Menorah Synagogue, Cheshire Reform Congregation (1964)
Bromley and District Reform Synagogue (1965)
Newcastle Reform Synagogue (1966)
North West Surrey Synagogue (1969)
Southend and District Reform Synagogue (1971)
Radlett and Bushey Reform Synagogue (1973)
Hampstead Reform Jewish Community (1978)
Sha'arei Shalom Synagogue, North Manchester Reform Congregation (1979)
Hull Reform Synagogue (1981)
Buckhurst Hill Reform Synagogue (1982)

*Mill Hill, Kingsbury and District Reform Synagogue*** (1985)
Beth Shalom Reform Synagogue, Cambridge (1986)
Milton Keynes and District Reform Synagogue (1990)
Thanet and District Reform Synagogue (1990)
Kol Chai, Hatch End Jewish Community (1991)
South Hampshire Reform Jewish Community (1995)

Total: 37

ASSOCIATE CONGREGATIONS
(Reform congregations not yet full members of the RSGB)

Beit Klal Yisrael, North Kensington Reform Synagogue
Coventry Reform Jewish Community
Darlington Hebrew Congregation
Sheffield and District Reform Jewish Congregation
Swindon Jewish Community

Total: 5

Notes

Synagogues which are in italics are in the Greater London area.

The dates in parenthesis before 1942 indicate when the congregation was formed.

The dates in parenthesis after 1942 indicate when the synagogue formally joined the movement (although many were founded some years earlier).

* Formerly known as St George's Settlement Synagogue, it is jointly affiliated to the Union of Liberal and Progressive Synagogues.

** Wembley Reform Jewish Community was admitted as a member in 1976 but subsequently merged with Mill Hill, Kingsbury & District Reform Synagogue.

Appendix 3
Chronology of Important Dates

1840 19 Sephardim break away from Bevis Marks with five Ashkenazim to form their own congregation

1841 *Forms of Prayer: Daily and Sabbath* edited by David Woolf Marks

1842 West London Synagogue of British Jews consecrated in Burton Street (moves to Margaret Street in 1849 and to Upper Berkeley Street in 1870)

1856 Manchester Reform Congregation established

1881 Bradford Synagogue of British and Foreign Jews consecrated

1931 New edition of *Forms of Prayer: Daily and Sabbath* edited under Morris Joseph and Harold Reinhart

1942 Associated British Synagogues established, consisting of six Reform synagogues

1945 ABS joins the World Union for Progressive Judaism

1946 ABS becomes the Association of Synagogues in Great Britain

Youth Association of Synagogues in Great Britain established (becomes Reform Synagogue Youth in 1979 and RSY-Netzer in 1982)

1947 Assembly of Ministers established (becomes Assembly of Rabbis in 1976)

1948 Reform *Beth Din* established

1956 Leo Baeck College established by ASGB (the Union of

Liberal and Progressive Synagogues becomes a co-sponsor in 1964)

1958 ASGB becomes Reform Synagogues of Great Britain (consisting of 18 synagogues)

1962 Association of Women's Guilds formed (becomes Reform Synagogue Guilds in 1986)

1966 Raymond Goldman appointed General Secretary (becomes Executive Director in 1979)

1968 Council of Reform and Liberal Rabbis established

1969 Appointment of first Youth Development Officer (John Kay)

1975 First woman rabbi ordained (Jacqueline Tabick)

1977 New edition of *Forms of Prayer: Daily and Sabbath* edited by Lionel Blue and Jonathan Magonet

First *shaliach* appointed (Chaim Lederman)

1980 RSGB moves from West London to Swiss Cottage

Department of Education and Youth established (becomes Centre for Jewish Education in 1986)

1981 RSGB moves to the Manor House (becomes the Sternberg Centre for Judaism in 1984)

Akiva School (first Reform Jewish day school) established

1994 Launch of the Reform Movement, consisting of 37 constituent synagogues, five associated congregations and 42,000 members (one in six of all synagogue-affiliated Jews in Britain). Rabbi Tony Bayfield appointed Chief Executive.

Appendix 4

Officers of the Reform Movement

Chairmen

1942 Harry Marks (West London)
1945 Robert Henriques (West London)
1951 Edward Mocatta (West London)
1955 Alexander Levy (Manchester)
1957 Leonard Mendel (North Western)
1959 Richard Norton (West London)
1964 Sigmund Schwab (West London)
1967 Harold Langdon (North Western)
1970 Bernard Davis (South West Essex)
1973 Eva Mitchell (West London)
1976 Jeffery Rose (North Western)
1979 Alf Strudwick (Settlement)
1981 Jerome Karet (North Western)
1984 Maurice Michaels (South West Essex)
1987 Marcus Bower (Wimbledon)
1990 Ruth Cohen (North Western)
1993 David Walsh (West London)

Presidents

1946–1951 Leonard Montefiore
1951–1956 Rabbi Dr Leo Baeck
(position left vacant)
1973–1984 Rabbi Dr Werner Van der Zyl
(position left vacant)
1990– Rabbi Hugo Gryn

Glossary

Alenu	Prayer concerning the duties of Israel which occurs towards the end of all services
Aliyah	The honour of being called to recite the blessings over the *Torah* during a service; it can also mean emigration to Israel
Amidah	Central prayer in all services consisting of several different paragraphs; it is also known as the *Shmoneh Esreh* (the eighteen benedictions) and the *Tefillah* (the prayer)
Ascamot	Regulations governing the Spanish and Portuguese Jews
Ashkenazi	Jews originating from central and eastern Europe
Aufruf	The honour of reciting the blessings over the *Torah* given to a couple before their wedding
Ba'al koreh	Person who reads from the scroll during services
Ba'al tefillah	Person who leads public prayers
Barmitzvah/ Batmitzvah	Ceremony for boys and girls aged 13 in which they are called to read from the *Torah* to mark the beginnings of Jewish adulthood
Beth Din	Rabbinic court, dealing primarily with status matters, such as conversion, adoption and divorce
Bimah	Platform upon which the reading desk is situated in synagogue
Chalitzah	Ceremony in which a man signals his refusal to marry his late brother's childless widow, based on Deuteronomy 25: 9
Chanukah	Festival of Dedication, celebrating the re-dedication of the Temple in Jerusalem by the Maccabees and the survival of the Jewish faith despite attempts to destroy it
Chasidim (adj. *chasidic*)	Jewish sect founded in eastern Europe in the late eighteenth century as a revivalist

movement, now part of the ultra-Orthodox establishment

Chavurot Small groups of individuals who meet together for prayer, study and Jewish celebrations

Chazan Trained singer who leads the congregational prayers

Cheder 'Room' – a term often used colloquially for a religion school

Cherem Social excommunication that was used as a sanction to impose discipline within the Jewish community

Chevrah Self-help association to assist with illness, unemployment or burial

Chuppah Canopy under which a bride and groom stand during the wedding ceremony

Davar Torah Short homily expounding Jewish teaching

Dayan (pl. *dayanim*) Judge who sits on a rabbinic court and administers Jewish law

Eretz Yisrael The Land of Israel

Get (pl. *gittin*) Document through which a couple obtain a religious divorce

Haftarah Reading from the Prophets during Sabbath and festival services

Haggadah Book read at the Passover meal that recounts the Exodus from Egypt

Haham Religious leader of the Spanish and Portuguese Jews

Halachah (adj. *halachic*) Jewish law and practice

Haskalah Enlightenment movement in Jewish society that began at the end of the eighteenth century

Havdalah Ceremony that concludes Sabbaths and festivals

Hesped Funeral eulogy

Kaddish Prayer in praise of God which has come to be regarded as a memorial prayer, with the names of the deceased often mentioned beforehand

Kashrut The dietary laws concerning permitted and forbidden food and rules of preparation

Kibbutz (pl. *kibbutzim*) Communally-owned settlement in Israel

Kiddush Blessings over bread and wine made before Sabbath and festive meals

Kippah (pl. *kippot*) Head-covering worn during prayer

Kol Nidre Evening service for the Day of Atonement, which takes its name from the opening prayer of the service

Kosher Food that is permissible for Jews to eat according to the dietary laws

Machzor Prayer book for festivals

Midrash Homiletical literature of the rabbis commenting on the Bible

Mikveh (pl. *mikvaot*) Ritual pool for immersion used by those converting to Judaism, or by women following their menstrual period

Minchah The afternoon service

Minhag Custom

Minyan Quorum of ten adults which is required in order for certain prayers to be said publicly

Misheberach Blessing in honour of an individual or institution

Mishnah Rabbinic commentary on the Bible completed at the end of the second century

Mitzpeh Observation post, situated at a strategic point in Israel

Mitzvah (pl. *mitzvot*) One of the 613 commandments; also refers to an honour given in a synagogue service

Mohel (pl. *mohalim*) Person who is trained to perform circumcision

Moshav Israeli settlement that is owned part-communally and part-privately

Musaf The additional service which concludes morning prayers on Sabbaths and festivals

Oneg Communal activity on the Sabbath involving study or songs

Pesach Festival of Passover celebrating the Exodus from Egypt

Piyutim Liturgical poems used to embellish the service

Purim Festival of Lots, celebrating the deliverance of the Jews of Persia from attempts to kill them

Rosh Chodesh The first day of a new Hebrew month, marked by the appearance of the new moon

Rosh Hashannah The Jewish New Year and a time of renewal

Seder Service surrounding the Passover meal

Sefer Torah Scroll of the *Torah*

Selichot Penitential prayers recited during the month

preceding the New Year

Semichah Ordination ceremony for rabbis

Sephardi Jews originating from the Spanish Peninsula and the Mediterranean countries

Shabbat The Sabbath – a time of rest, lasting from sunset on Friday evening until after dark on Saturday

Shaliach (pl. *sh'lichim*) Emissary from Israel to educate Jews in the Diaspora about Israel

Shavuot Festival of Weeks, celebrating the revelation at Mount Sinai

Shechitah Jewish method of killing animals for food

Shema Verses from Deuteronomy 6: 4–9; 11: 13–21 and Numbers 15: 37–41 recited at morning and evening services

Shemini Atzeret An additional eighth day of *Sukkot* in the Orthodox calendar, but combined with *Simchat Torah* by the Reform

Shochet Person trained to perform the killing of animals intended for consumption

Shofar The horn of a *kosher* animal, often a ram, blown at the New Year and Day of Atonement

Shulchan Aruch Summary of the main practices of Jewish law, written in the sixteenth century by Joseph Caro

Siddur Daily and Sabbath prayer book

Simchat Torah Festival of the Rejoicing of the Law, celebrating a new cycle of public readings in synagogue from the Pentateuch

Sukkot Festival of Tabernacles celebrating the wanderings of the Israelites in the wilderness; also refers to the booths erected during the festival

Tallit Prayer shawl worn at morning services

Tefillin Prayer boxes worn at weekday morning services

Tevilah Immersion in a *mikveh* or river, generally by a proselyte for conversion or by a woman at the end of her menstrual period

Torah The five books of Moses; also used to refer to the entirety of Jewish teaching

Tu Bi'Shevat The New Year for Trees, originally a time of tithing; nowadays when saplings are planted

Yehidim Members of the Sephardi congregation

Yeshivah Religious seminary

Yigdal Song at the end of Sabbath and festival evening services, summarising Maimonides' Thirteen Principles of Faith

Yizkor Memorial service for those who have died, held on the Day of Atonement and at other times

Yom Ha'atzma'ut Israel Independence Day

Yom Kippur The Day of Atonement, spent in prayer, repentance and fasting

Bibliography

Primary Sources

Anglo-Jewish Archives, Parkes Library, Southampton University:
Bruno Italiener Papers
Harold Reinhart Papers
West London Synagogue of British Jews:
Letter Boxes
Copy Letter Books
Membership Books
Minute Books
West London Synagogue Association Annual Reports
Board of Deputies of British Jews Minute Books, 1841–1883
Great Synagogue Minute Books, 1825–1850
Reform Synagogues of Great Britain Archives, The Sternberg Centre for Judaism, London:
Beth Din Archive
Minute Books of Assembly of Rabbis
Minute Books of Executive and Council
Minute Books of Associated British Synagogues
Minute Books of Association of Synagogues of Great Britain

Unpublished Sources

Lectures

Cassell, C., 'The First Nine Years of the West London Synagogue of British Jews' (undated).
— 'The Founders of Reform Judaism and the Oral Law', Harold Reinhart Memorial Lecture (1980).
— 'Continental Jews and Early Anglo-Jewish Reform', Salzberger Memorial Lecture (1982).

Theses

Kramer-Mannion, M., 'The Growth and Development of Reform Judaism in Manchester 1940–1985', University of Manchester, 1989.

Romain, J.A., 'The Reform Beth Din: The Formation and Development of the Rabbinical Court of the Reform Synagogues of Great Britain 1935–1965', University of Leicester, 1990.

Newspapers and Journals

(place of publication London unless otherwise stated)

Bradford Chronicle (Bradford)
European Judaism
Inform
Jewish Chronicle
Jewish Echo (Glasgow)
Jewish Gazette (Manchester)
Jewish Review
Jewish Telegraph (Manchester)
Jewish World (Leeds)
Living Judaism
MANNA
Morning Advertiser
Morning Chronicle
New Ideas
Synagogue Review
The Times
Voice of Jacob
West London Synagogue Magazine
West London Synagogue Association Magazine

Secondary Sources

Articles

Bayfield, T., 'Progressive Judaism – A Collective Theological Essay', *MANNA* (London, Spring 1990).

Bayme, S., 'Claude Montefiore, Lily Montagu and the Origins of

JRU', *Transactions of the Jewish Historical Society of England*, Vol. XXVII (London, 1979).
Cohen, N., 'Trends in Anglo-Jewish Religious Life', in Gould, J., and Esh, S. (eds), *Jewish Life in Modern Britain* (London, 1964).
Cohen, S., 'First World War Anglo-Jewish Opposition to Zionism', *Transactions of the Jewish Historical Society of England*, Vol. XXX (London, 1987–88).
Cohn, H.J., 'Progressive Jews and Zionism', in Marmur, D. (ed.), *A Genuine Search* (London, 1979).
Curtis, M., 'The Beth Din of Reform Synagogues of Great Britain', in Marmur, D. (ed.), *Reform Judaism* (London, 1973).
Finestein, I., 'Jewish Marriages and the English Law', *Jewish Journal of Sociology*, Vol. VII (June 1965).
— 'An Aspect of the Jews and English Marriage Law during the Emancipation', *Transactions of The Jewish Historical Society of England*, Vol. III (London, 1965).
— 'The Anglo-Jewish Revolt of 1853', *Jewish Quarterly* (Winter 1978).
Goulston, M., 'The Theology of Reform Judaism in Great Britain', in Marmur, D. (ed.), *Reform Judaism* (London, 1973).
Henriques, U., 'Lyon versus Thomas: The Jewish Abduction Case', *Transactions of the Jewish Historical Society of England*, Vol. XXIX (London, 1982–86).
Langdon, H., 'The Place of Reform in Anglo-Jewry Today', in Marmur, D. (ed.), *A Genuine Search* (London, 1979).
Liberles, R., 'The Origins of the Jewish Reform Movement in England', *Association of Jewish Studies Review* (1976).
Lipman, V.D., 'The Development of London Jewry', in Levin, S.S. (ed.), *A Century of Anglo-Jewish Life 1870–1970* (London, 1970).
— 'The Rise of Jewish Suburbia', *Transactions of the Jewish Historical Society of England*, Vol. XXI (London, 1968).
Littmann, E., 'The First Ten Years of the Leo Baeck College', in Marmur, D. (ed.), *Reform Judaism* (London, 1973).
Shane, A.L., 'Isaac d'Israeli's Quarrel with the Synagogue', *Transactions of the Jewish Historical Society*, Vol. XXIX (London, 1988).
Singer, S., 'Orthodox Thought in Early Victorian London', *Association of Jewish Studies Review*, Vol. X, No. 2 (1985).
Spector, D., 'Brighton Jewry Reconsidered', *Transactions of the*

Jewish Historical Society of England, Vol. XXX (1987–88).
Tabick, J., 'I Never Really Wanted To Be First', in Sheridan, S. (ed.), *Hear Our Voice* (London, 1994).

Pamphlets

A Statement of the Religious Ethos of the Reform Synagogues of Great Britain (RSGB, 1992).
Bayfield, A., *God's Demands and Israel's Needs* (RSGB, 1981).
Bornstein, A., and Homa, B., *Tell It In Gath – British Jewry and Clause 43: The Inside Story* (London, 1972).
Borts, B., *Abortion – A Jewish Response* (RSGB, 1984).
— *Women and Tallit* (RSGB, 1988).
— Chiat, S., and Joseph, V., *Do Not Destroy My World* (RSGB, 1989).
Greengross, W., *Jewish and Homosexual* (RSGB, 1982).
Ish-Horowicz, M., *Halakhah – Orthodoxy and Reform* (RSGB, 1994).
Leigh, M., *Remember the Sabbath Day* (RSGB, 1983).
Magonet, J., *The New Reform Prayer Book* (RSGB, 1988).
Marmur, D., *The Jewish Family Today and Tomorrow* (London, 1983).
Romain, J.A., *Calendar of Torah and Haftarah Readings* (RSGB, 1984).
— *How to Grow* (RSGB, 1985).
— *I'm Jewish My Partner Isn't* (RSGB, 1993).
— *The Reform Beth Din: Its influence on the growth of the Reform Movement and its significance for Anglo-Jewry* (RSGB, 1992).
Schmool, M., and Cohen, F., *British Synagogue Membership in 1990* (London, 1991).
Simmons, V.G., *Reform In Judaism* (London, 1942).
Swift, M., *Jewish Marriage and Divorce* (London, 1962).

Books

Alderman, G., *The Federation of Synagogues* (London, 1987).
— *Modern British Jewry* (Oxford, 1992).
— and Holmes, C. (eds), *Outsiders and Outcasts* (London, 1993).

Barnett, A., *The Western Synagogue Through Two Centuries* (London, 1961).
Bayfield, A., *Prejudice* (London, 1977).
— and Braybrooke, M. (eds), *Dialogue With A Difference* (London, 1992).
Bermant, C., *The Cousinhood* (London, 1971).
Birmingham Jewish Research Group, *Birmingham Jewry 1749–1914*, Vol. 1 (Birmingham, 1980).
Blue, L., *To Heaven with Scribes and Pharisees* (London, 1975).
—*Backdoor to Heaven* (London,1979).
—and Magonet, J. (eds), *Forms of Prayer*, Vol. I (London, 1977), Vol.II (London, 1985). Vol. III (London, 1995).
Briggs, A., *Victorian Cities* (London, 1980 edition).
Brook, S., *The Club* (London, 1989).
Borowitz, E.B., *Reform Judaism Today* (New York, 1977).
Cesarani, D. (ed.), *The Making of Modern Anglo-Jewry* (Oxford, 1990).
— *The Jewish Chronicle and Anglo-Jewry 1841–1991* (Cambridge, 1994).
Clark, G. Kitson, *The Making of Victorian England* (London, 1962).
Chadwick, D., *The Victorian Church*, Vols. I and II (London, 1966).
Cohen, S., *English Zionists and British Jews* (Princeton, 1982).
Cooper, H., *Soul-Searching: Studies in Judaism and Psycho-Therapy* (London, 1988).
Dash Moor, D., *At Home In America* (New York, 1981).
Encyclopaedia Judaica (Jerusalem, 1971).
Endelman, T., *The Jews of Georgian England 1714–1830* (Philadelphia, 1979).
— *Radical Assimilation in Anglo-Jewish History* (Indiana, 1990).
Feldman, D., *Englishmen and Jews* (Yale, 1994).
Friedlander, A.H., *Leo Baeck: Teacher of Theresienstadt* (New York, 1968).
Goldberg, P., *The Manchester Congregation of British Jews 1857–1957* (Manchester, 1957).
Golden, L., and Golden, J., *Harold Reinhart* (London, 1980).
Goldsmith, S.J., *Twentieth Century Jews* (New York, 1962).
Goldstein, A., *Mishnah Kadimah* (London, 1985).
Gottheil, R., *The Life of Gustav Gottheil* (New York, 1936).
Gould, J., and Shaul, E. (eds), *Jewish Life in Modern Britain*

(London, 1964).
Grizzard, N., *Follow the Bradford Jewish Heritage* (Bradford, 1984).
Henriques, H., *Jewish Marriage and the English Law* (Oxford, 1909).
Hilton, M., and Marshall, G., *The Gospels and Rabbinic Judaism* (London, 1988).
Holmes, C., *Anti-Semitism in British Society 1876–1939* (London, 1979).
Hyamson, A., *The Sephardim of England* (London, 1951).
Joseph, M., *The Ideal in Judaism* (London, 1893).
— *The Spirit of Judaism* (London, 1930).
— *Judaism as Creed and Life* (London, 1958, 4th edition).
— and Reinhart, H., *Forms of Prayer, Daily and Sabbath* (London, 1931).
Kadish, S., *Bolsheviks and British Jews* (London, 1992).
Kershen, A.J., *150 Years of Progressive Judaism* (London, 1990).
—*Uniting the Tailors* (London, 1995).
Leigh, M., *Jewish Observance in the Home* (London, 1966).
Levin, S.S. (ed.), *A Century of Anglo-Jewish Life 1870–1970* (London, 1970).
Levy, A., *History of the Sunderland Jewish Community 1755–1955* (London, 1956).
Lipman, V.D., *Social History of the Jews in England 1850–1950* (London, 1950).
— *A History of the Jews in Britain Since 1858* (London, 1990).
Loewe, L. (ed.), *Diaries of Sir Moses and Lady Montefiore* (London, 1983).
Magonet, J., *Returning* (London, 1975).
Marks, D.W., *Sermons* (London, 1851).
— *Forms of Prayer: Daily and Sabbath* (London, 1841).
Marmur, D. *Beyond Survival* (London, 1982).
— (ed.), *A Genuine Search* (London, 1979).
— (ed.), *Reform Judaism* (London, 1973).
Maybaum, I., *Creation and Guilt* (London, 1969).
— *Happiness Outside the State* (London, 1980).
— *Jewish Existence* (London, 1960).
— *The Faith of the Jewish Diaspora* (London, 1962).
— *The Face of God After Auschwitz* (London, 1965).
— *Trialogue Between Jew, Christian and Muslim* (London, 1973).
Meyer, M., *Response to Modernity* (New York, 1988).

Newman, A., *The United Synagogue 1870–1970* (London, 1977).
Norman, E.R., *Church and Society in England 1770–1970* (London, 1970).
Philipson, D., *The Reform Movement in Judaism* (New York, 1931).
Picciotto, J., *Sketches of Anglo-Jewry* (London, 1956 edition).
Plaut, W.G., *The Rise of Reform Judaism* (New York, 1963).
Prayers for the Pilgrim Festivals (London, 1965).
Romain, J.A., *The Jews of England* (London, 1988).
—*Faith and Practice: A Guide to Reform Judaism Today* (London, 1991).
Roth, C., *A History of Jews in England* (Oxford, 1978 edition).
Sacher, H., *The Course of Modern Jewish History* (New York, 1982 edition).
Sacks, J., *One People?* (London, 1993).
Salbstein, M.C., *The Emancipation of the Jews in Britain* (London, 1982).
Sharot, S., *Judaism – A Sociology* (London, 1976).
Sheridan, S. (ed.), *Hear Our Voice* (London, 1994).
Simons, H., *Forty Years A Chief Rabbi* (London, 1980).
Sklare, M., *Conservative Judaism* (New York, 1972).
Stroud, O., *The Story of the Stroud Family* (Bradford, 1974).
Theodores, T., *The Rabbinical Law of Excommunication* (1854).
Tropp, A., *Jews in the Professions 1881–1991* (London, 1991).
Umansky, E., *Lily Montagu and the Advancement of Liberal Judaism* (New York, 1988).
Williams, B., *The Making of Manchester Jewry* (Manchester, 1985).
Wolfe, H., *Now A Stranger* (London, 1933).
Wolff, W. (ed.), *Werner van der Zyl: Master Builder* (London, 1994).
Wright, D., and Jowitt, T. (eds), *Victorian Bradford* (Bradford, 1981).

Synagogue Histories

Blackpool: 'Portrait of a Community', *Synagogue Review*, (Dec. 1961).
Bradford: *Bradford Synagogue Centenary Brochure*

1873–1973 (1973).
Bradford Synagogue Foundation Centenary Dinner Booklet (1980).
Bromley: *Voices 1964–1990* (1990).
Cardiff: Liss, A.S., *A Short History of Reform Judaism in South Wales* (1970).
Edgware: Budd, Sidney, *Towards the Golden Year: The First Half Century of Edgware and District Reform Synagogue 1935–1985* (1985).
Finchley: *Tree of Life Silver Jubilee Issue: Finchley Reform Synagogue 1960–1985* (1985).
Glasgow: Anson, Martin, 'Glasgow New Synagogue – Long Ago', *Kol* (Sept. 1987).
Hendon: Bronkhorst, Susan, and Rais, Guy, *Hendon Reform Synagogue: 40th Anniversary 1949–1989* (1989).
Maidenhead: 30th Anniversary Issue, *Hadashot* (1983).
Manchester: Goldberg, P. Selvin, *The Manchester Congregation of British Jews 1857–1957* (1957).
Menorah: *25 Anniversary Brochure* (1988).
Newcastle: 'A Short History of Newcastle Reform Synagogue', *Focus* (May/June, 1989).
North Western: Rose, June, *50 Years of Alyth: A Short History of North Western Reform Synagogue* (1983).
Settlement: *St George's Jewish Settlement: 50th Anniversary Review 1914–1964* (1964).
Sinai, Leeds: Sterne, Ernest, *The Early History of Sinai Synagogue, Leeds 1944–1970* (1985).
Southgate: *Southgate and District Reform Synagogue Silver Jubilee Brochure 1961–1986* (1986).
Southport: *Southport New Synagogue 40th Anniversary Brochure: 1948–1988* (1988).
West London: Diamond, A.S., *The Building of a Synagogue: A Brief History* (1970).
Celebrating 150 Years 1840–1990 (1990).
Wimbledon: Bower, Marcus, *Wimbledon and District Synagogue – A Historical Review 1949–1984* (1984).

Index